Data Structures and Algorithms for Game Programming in C++

Write high-performance code and solve game development challenges with expert-led C++ solutions

Zhenyu George Li
Charles Shih-I Yeh

<packt>

Data Structures and Algorithms for Game Programming in C++

Portfolio Director: Rohit Rajkumar
Relationship Lead: Neha Pande
Project Manager: Sandip Tadge
Content Engineer: Shreya Sarkar
Technical Editor: Kushal Sharma
Copy Editor: Safis Editing
Indexer: Pratik Shirodkar
Proofreader: Shreya Sarkar
Production Designer: Vijay Kamble
Growth Lead: Namita Velgekar

First published: June 2025
Production reference: 4080626

Published by Packt Publishing Ltd.
Grosvenor House
11 St Paul's Square
Birmingham
B3 1RB, UK.

ISBN 978-1-83588-986-2
`www.packtpub.com`

Foreword

I have known and worked with George Li in various capacities for more than 20 years.

We first met as colleagues at a private college of interactive arts in downtown Vancouver, Canada. I was a full professor of linguistics at a university in the area, with extensive experience in developing a cognitive science program at the university. Establishing a curriculum for such a program involved familiarizing myself with areas well beyond the area of my specific academic position and collaborating closely with colleagues – particularly in computing science (cognitive), psychology, and philosophy (particularly concerning socio-epistemological issues such as AI).

It was in this spirit that I was happy to associate myself with a private college, focusing on language study and teaching, together with preparing students to handle 3D computer applications (e.g., 3ds Max, 3D GameStudio, and Unreal) and showing them how to generate animation materials for film, TV, and games.

George Li was in charge of all the technical requirements of the college. I very quickly realized that he was not only extremely competent and forthcoming (he had already occupied high-level computing-teaching/-application positions, software engineering for instance, in China prior to emigrating to Canada) but also computationally competent and brilliantly innovative. He also had a particular interest in the development of game engines and was already collaborating with his colleague, Charles Yeh, on a practical reference book, *XNA PC and Xbox360 C# Game Programming*, with proprietary-produced text and games to his credit.

As colleagues in the college, George and I found common, mutually-strengthening interests. Eventually, he and I found ourselves in charge of creating a two-year interactive arts program curriculum for the college.

My whole career (at universities in the UK and Canada, and as a member of the editorial boards of a major academic journal and a very influential series) has closely involved the evaluation of the intellectual quality of people's capabilities and work, and in my opinion, George Li's innate talents shine out clearly throughout his work and will continue to do so in the future. His ability to express his knowledge of the subject at hand is outstandingly demonstrated in all his work, performance, expressions, and character.

This book, co-authored with Charles Yeh, is designed for independent developers, company training, and post-secondary reference use. The knowledge presented herein is most intelligently, clearly, and effectively presented so as to be as efficiently applicable and pedagogically effective as possible on any device or platform, producing high-quality games, accessories, and edits.

This volume will certainly stand the test of time and fulfill the majority of the needs of those working in the field of gaming. However, I am certain that George and Charles, working together, will make further, very crucial contributions to this topic.

Until then, this volume will serve you excellently, helping you enjoy and prosper with your future activities and products.

Dr. E. Wyn Roberts (M.A. Ph.D (Cantab.))

Emeritus Professor of Linguistics, Simon Fraser University, Burnaby, Canada

Contributors

About the authors

Zhenyu George Li is a passionate video game developer with over 20 years of experience in the field. As a seasoned software engineer, George has contributed significantly to the development of numerous games throughout his career and currently serves as a senior development engineer at Unity.

George's fascination with video games was sparked during his college studies, igniting a passion that would shape his professional journey. During the early stages of his game development endeavors, George immersed himself in technologies such as Visual Basic, C/C++, DirectX, OpenGL, Windows GUI, SQL, and so on. These foundational experiences laid the groundwork for his subsequent success in the industry.

Throughout his career, George has made substantial contributions to various commercial games. Notable titles on his portfolio include Unity demo and starter kit games, *Sandbox, Halo Infinite, Magic Arena, Stela, Dead Rising 2, The Bigs 2*, and others. His involvement in these projects has allowed him to gain extensive knowledge and practical experience in a wide range of domains, including programming, game engines, gameplay and AI, graphics, animation, multiplayer, game physics, frontend, and multiplatform. In practical applications, George has used Unreal, Unity, and some propriety game engines in the development of real game projects.

In addition to his achievements as a game developer, George has also honed his teaching abilities during his eight years of college-level instruction. He has shared his knowledge and expertise with aspiring developers, serving as a lecturer at the Vancouver Film School, College of Interactive Arts, and Hefei Union University. While teaching at Vancouver Film School, George guided students through the intricacies of Unreal Engine, helping them build a strong foundation in professional game development.

I express my gratitude to my wife, Alison Guo, for her support in handling family responsibilities and for enabling me to dedicate time to completing this book. I also extend my thanks to Mike Oakes and my other colleagues for their encouragement and support throughout the writing process.

Charles Shih-I Yeh pursued his computer science studies at the University of Southern California before embarking on a career in the video game industry in the early 2000s. He has held various pivotal roles in game programming, including building proprietary game engines, crafting **Digital Content Creation** (**DCC**) tools to streamline production pipelines, and designing engaging gameplay mechanics alongside robust multiplayer and MMORPG tournament services.

Charles is also passionate and committed to sharing expertise and insights by delivering lectures on game programming at several esteemed universities. He is also the author of two game design books as well as the official translator of several famous game programming books, such as *Game Programming Gems 4*, into his native language, Mandarin.

I would like to express my heartfelt gratitude to my wife, Min-hwa Lee, for her unwavering support, and to my son, Phillip Yeh, whose encouragement means everything to me. My sincere thanks also go to my colleague, Mike Oakes, for his tireless dedication, as well as to all the technical reviewers and editors whose valuable feedback and commitment have been indispensable throughout this journey.

About the reviewers

Michael Oakes is a software development manager for Unity who has worked in the games industry for 9 years, and in the IT industry for 27 years. Originating from Grimsby in the UK, he now lives in Calgary, Canada, and holds a Master's degree in computer science and is a Certified Project Management Professional. He has worked with real-time 3D and games for over 9 years, specializing in mixed reality design and development, shader programming, and AI and multiplayer systems. Michael has worked as a technical consultant on several other titles, including *Unity ML-Agents – Fundamentals of Unity Machine Learning*, *Practical AI on the Google Cloud Platform*, and *Unreal Engine 5 Game Development with C++ Scripting: Become a professional game developer and create fully functional, high-quality games.*

First of all, I would like to thank my wife Camie for her support and patience for the time I spent locked away in my office conducting this book review, and also my late mother Sally, for her unconditional love and support in all my endeavors—my sister and I miss you dearly. Finally, I would like to thank Packt for providing the opportunity, support, and their trust.

Akhilesh Tiwari is director of production engineering at InvestCloud and has over two decades of software development experience. He obtained his MTech from BITS Pilani, India. Akhilesh has developed software solutions for the world's leading organizations such as Merck, Novartis, BNY Mellon, Fujitsu, Cognizant, and Persistent Systems, to name a few. Akhilesh is a passionate software engineer. Even in his free time, he is hacking Raspberry Pi with his kids. Akhilesh now resides in New Jersey, USA, where he enjoys a fulfilling family life.

First of all, I would like to thank the Supreme Personality of Godhead, Krishna, for everything. I would like to thank my loving parents for their unconditional love and support. I would not have been able to do this book review without the support of my loving wife, Sanchita, and my two young ones, Osh and Radha. Last but not least, I would like to thank Packt for this opportunity and their trust.

Table of Contents

Chapter 6: 3D Graphics Rendering 169

Part 3: Breathing Life into Your Games 251

Chapter 8: Animating Your Characters 253

Chapter 9: Building AI Opponents 283

Chapter 10: Machine Learning Algorithms for Game AI 319

Preface

Game development is a unique and fascinating field where creativity meets technical expertise. At its core, every game is built upon a foundation of efficient data structures and algorithms, enabling seamless gameplay, intelligent AI, and immersive worlds. Whether you're designing smooth character movement, optimizing rendering performance, or implementing complex game AI, a strong understanding of these fundamental concepts is essential.

This book, *Data Structures and Algorithms for Game Programming in C++*, is designed to bridge the gap between theoretical knowledge and practical game programming. While many books cover data structures and algorithms from a general perspective, this book focuses specifically on their applications in game development, providing real-world examples and C++ implementations tailored for interactive experiences.

This book is structured around practical applications rather than strict learning methodologies, making it both an effective guide for learning and a valuable reference for game developers. To reinforce key concepts, it provides sample projects that demonstrate the natural, real-world usage of the introduced algorithms. These projects are built using **raylib**, a free and lightweight graphics library, with a simple engine layer, **Knight**, designed on top of it to facilitate hands-on learning.

Data Structures and Algorithms for Game Programming in C++ focuses on C++ programming, utilizing basic C and C++ syntax while intentionally avoiding complex data types and advanced modern C++ features. This approach ensures that readers can concentrate on understanding game algorithms without being overwhelmed by intricate language details, making the content accessible to both beginners and novice developers.

Reading this book offers several key benefits that will support your learning journey. First, it is designed to streamline the learning process, making it easier to grasp complex concepts efficiently. The structured organization of topics eliminates the need for scattered searches, allowing you to focus on relevant information without wasting time on unrelated materials. Additionally, this book serves as a reliable reference guide, providing a comprehensive resource that you can revisit for deeper study and practical application.

As you start this journey, I encourage you to stay curious, take your time, and enjoy the process of learning by doing. Game development can feel complex at times, but every step you take builds your skills and brings you closer to creating something truly your own.

This book is meant to be a helpful shortcut—a clear and practical path that can guide you toward a more professional and advanced game development career. Whether you're just starting out or already have some experience, I hope this book gives you the tools and confidence to keep growing and building. Let's dive in and make something great!

Who this book is for

This book is intended for junior game developers, hobbyists, junior technical artists, and computer science students who want to sharpen their skills through practical, real-world C++ solutions. A foundational understanding of C++, data structures, and core game development concepts is recommended. Whether you're aiming to deepen your knowledge or looking for a trusted reference, this book will be your companion in building better games.

Novice game programmers

If you have some experience with C++ or have used it in academic or personal projects, this book will help you strengthen your knowledge of the essential algorithms and data structures used in game systems. The examples and techniques presented will support better code structure, optimization, and problem-solving in real development scenarios.

Junior technical artists and tool developers

For those aspiring to get into the technical side of game production—such as game design, content creation, or pipelines—this book offers insight into how core algorithms and structures are applied in gameplay mechanics, rendering, and animation systems. It provides the technical grounding to bridge creative tools with efficient implementation.

Junior game developers

If you're already familiar with the basics of game development and want to reinforce your skills, this book offers a structured path toward practical performance-focused programming. You'll gain a deeper understanding of how to apply C++ techniques to real-time systems and gameplay challenges.

Educators and students (with prior experience)

This book can be a valuable resource for students and instructors in advanced game programming courses. Those with prior knowledge of C++, object-oriented programming, and basic game development principles will find the examples clear and applicable for hands-on learning and classroom use.

Understanding the code samples in this book

The sample code snippets provided throughout this book are closely related to the code in the **Knight** demo game projects available in the book's GitHub repository, though there may be slight variations in structure or implementation. These differences arise because the actual implementation code must account for several key factors:

- **Supporting features**: The demo game code is designed to accommodate multiple examples and use cases.
- **Compatibility**: The implementation considers various scenarios and requirements to ensure flexibility.
- **Error handling**: Additional conditional checks are included to prevent errors and ensure stability.

In contrast, the code snippets within the book focus primarily on explaining the *core algorithms and methodologies* relevant to each topic. To enhance clarity, these examples are presented in a simplified form, minimizing dependencies on unrelated code. This approach ensures that readers can grasp the key concepts without unnecessary distractions, allowing for a deeper understanding of the introduced techniques.

Using a conservative subset of C++ in this book

While modern C++ standards introduce many powerful features—such as smart pointers, lambdas, ranges, and concurrency tools—this book intentionally avoids relying heavily on them. Our goal is to present algorithms and data structures as clearly and accessibly as possible. By using a simpler legacy subset of C++, the focus remains squarely on the logic of the algorithms themselves, without the added complexity of advanced language constructs that could distract or confuse readers.

Another important consideration is compatibility. By avoiding modern or compiler-specific features, the code examples in this book can be easily compiled and run across different platforms and with a wide range of compilers, making it straightforward for readers to practice and experiment in their own environments.

Finally, many game engines and libraries still rely on legacy subsets of C++ for stability, integration, and performance reasons. Following this industry practice, the book emphasizes practical, foundational programming techniques.

By limiting the use of modern C++ features, the sample projects provide readers with portable, easy-to-follow examples that highlight the essentials of implementing data structures and algorithms in game development.

What this book covers

This book provides a comprehensive guide to practical game development with C++, focusing on the data structures and algorithms that power modern games. It begins by setting up the C++ development environment and introducing fundamental data structures for efficient game functionality. Readers will explore essential game algorithms, including randomization, sorting, procedural generation, and object pooling, followed by techniques for 2D and 3D rendering, camera controls, and character animation.

The book delves into AI programming, covering Finite State Machines (FSMs), behavior trees, steering behaviors, and A* pathfinding, and introduces modern AI techniques like neural networks and deep learning. Each chapter combines theoretical insights with practical C++ implementations, providing hands-on experience in building efficient, scalable, and intelligent game systems.

Below is a list of chapters with brief descriptions to give you a quick overview of the book's structure and the key topics covered:

Chapter 1, Gearing Up: C++ for Game Development, introduces the book's practical approach to learning game development algorithms with C++. It covers the importance of algorithms in creating efficient games, explains why C++ is the preferred language, and guides you through setting up your development environment. You'll also get familiar with raylib and the Knight demo project, which will serve as a learning tool throughout the book.

Chapter 2, Data Structures in Action: Building Game Functionality, explores fundamental data structures like arrays, linked lists, stacks, and queues, demonstrating how they manage game data efficiently. You'll learn how proper data organization affects game mechanics and performance. The chapter also explains how game screenshots are captured and processed to enhance visual output.

Chapter 3, Algorithms Commonly Utilized in Game Development, introduces essential algorithms, including randomization, selection, sorting, and procedural generation, and how they apply to real-world game mechanics. The chapter introduces object pooling for memory optimization and demonstrates how these algorithms improve task scheduling, animation processing, and performance.

Chapter 4, 2D Rendering and Effects, covers 2D rendering techniques that enhance both 2D and 3D games, including animations, color blending, and parallax scrolling. You'll learn how to use N-patch textures for UI design and implement isometric map rendering to create visually engaging games.

Chapter 5, The Camera and Camera Controls, guides you to explore how camera systems shape player perception in 3D games, from first-person and third-person views to chase and rail cameras. The chapter also covers object culling for performance optimization and techniques for managing multiple split-screen cameras.

Chapter 6, 3D Graphics Rendering, dives into GPU programming and the graphics pipeline, covering vertex transformations, shading, and rasterization. You'll learn about lighting models, point light attenuation, and normal mapping, which are essential for creating realistic 3D environments.

Chapter 7, Rendering a 3D Game World, introduces techniques for rendering large, immersive 3D worlds by combining billboard rendering, particle systems, and multi-pass rendering. The chapter also covers lighting, shadows, and environmental design to enhance the visual appeal of your game world.

Chapter 8, Animating Your Characters, explores keyframe animation, skeletal animation, and Inverse Kinematics (IK) to create smooth, natural character movements. You'll learn how to animate characters dynamically using hierarchical bone structures and real-time joint calculations.

Chapter 9, Building AI Opponents, discovers AI techniques used to create intelligent game opponents, starting with FSMs for simple decision-making. The chapter introduces behavior trees for complex logic, steering algorithms for realistic movement, and A* pathfinding for strategic navigation.

Chapter 10, Machine Learning Algorithms for Game AI, introduces neural networks, deep learning, and reinforcement learning in game AI. You'll gain hands-on experience by building a neural network-controlled turret defense system, showcasing the power of adaptive AI in games.

Chapter 11, Continuing Your Learning Journey, reflects on the key C++ game development concepts, data structures, algorithms, graphics, animation, and AI covered in the book. It emphasizes the importance of continuous learning and experimentation while offering guidance on what lies ahead in your game development journey.

To get the most out of this book

To get the most out of this book, you should have a solid foundation in C++ programming, including an understanding of Object-Oriented Programming (OOP) and data structures. Familiarity with game-related concepts and knowledge, such as rendering, animation, physics, and frame rate management, will also be beneficial in understanding the practical applications of the algorithms introduced. While this book avoids overly complex modern C++ features, a basic grasp of C++ syntax and programming logic is essential for following along with the examples.

The following table outlines the software and hardware requirements for this book:

Software/hardware covered in the book	Operating system requirements
Microsoft Visual Studio 2002 with the C++ compiler	Microsoft Windows 10 and up

If you run the samples on systems other than Windows, such as macOS, you will need to manually set up the project and copy the source code into the project.

If you are using the digital version of this book, we advise you to type the code yourself or access the code from the book's GitHub repository (a link is available in the next section). Doing so will help you avoid any potential errors related to the copying and pasting of code.

Note that the authors acknowledge the use of cutting-edge AI, such as ChatGPT, with the sole aim of enhancing the language and clarity within the book, thereby ensuring a smooth reading experience for readers. It's important to note that the content itself has been crafted by the authors and edited by a professional publishing team.

Download the example code files

The code bundle for the book is hosted on GitHub at `https://github.com/PacktPublishing/Data-Structures-and-Algorithms-for-Game-Programming-in-CPP`. Since it's not possible to cover every data structure and algorithm use case in a single book on game programming, be sure to check the GitHub repository for additional demo projects and the latest updates. We also have other code bundles from our rich catalog of books and videos available at `https://github.com/PacktPublishing`. Check them out!

Download the color images

We also provide a PDF file that has color images of the screenshots/diagrams used in this book. You can download it here: `https://packt.link/gbp/9781835889862`.

Conventions used

There are a number of text conventions used throughout this book.

`CodeInText`: Indicates code words in text, database table names, folder names, filenames, file extensions, pathnames, dummy URLs, user input, and Twitter handles. For example: " However, when we assign `CameraMode` as `CAMERA_FIRST_PERSON` and add it to the scene, Knight will activate first-person mode and enable input control for first-person mode."

A block of code is set as follows:

```
OrthogonalCamera* OrthCam = NULL;
OrthCam = _Scene->CreateSceneObject<OrthogonalCamera>("Orthogonal
Camera");
OrthCam->SetUp(Vector3{ 0.0f, 15.0f, 15.0f }, Vector3{ 0.0f, 0.0f, 0.0f },
20.0f);
```

When we wish to draw your attention to a particular part of a code block, the relevant lines or items are set in bold:

```
//Push the sample data into the dataset
sampleData.clear();
sampleData.push_back(inputs[0]);
sampleData.push_back(inputs[1]);
sampleData.push_back(targets[0]);
sampleData.push_back(targets[1]);
dataset.push_back(sampleData);
```

Bold: Indicates a new term, an important word, or words that you see on the screen. For instance, words in menus or dialog boxes appear in the text like this. For example: " When installing VS2022, make sure to enable the **Desktop development with C++** module to install the C++ compiler together with the IDE."

Warnings or important notes appear like this.

Tips and tricks appear like this.

Further, to maintain consistency and minimize confusion, the C++ sample code in this book primarily follows the **Visual Studio C++ coding preferences**. For detailed guidelines, you can refer to the official documentation at `https://learn.microsoft.com/en-us/cpp/ide/how-to-set-preferences?view=msvc-170`.

Additionally, some special coding conventions used in the sample code are inspired by **OpenStack's C++ Coding Standards**. You can find more details in their documentation at `https://wiki.openstack.org/wiki/CppCodingStandards#:~:text=Private%20member%20data%20variables%20should,all%20lowercase%20with%20underscore%20separation`.

In certain cases, exceptions may be made for compact expressions that enhance readability and fit within the page layout constraints, ensuring clarity without compromising comprehension.

Acknowledgment of art and content contributions

We would like to extend our heartfelt appreciation to those who generously contributed artwork and content used in the examples throughout this book. Their creative support has added clarity, style, and character to the projects and helped bring our demonstrations to life.

Special thanks to:

- Yi-Hong Chou of Play5 Studios
- Cheng-Yen Chou of Play5 Studios
- Cheng-Hsun Chou of Play5 Studios
- Cheng-Jung Chou of Play5 Studios
- I-Hong Chen of Agileen Inc.

Your contributions have greatly enhanced the visual quality and overall experience of this book. We are sincerely grateful for your support.

Get in touch

Feedback from our readers is always welcome.

General feedback: If you have questions about any aspect of this book or have any general feedback, please email us at `customercare@packt.com` and mention the book's title in the subject of your message.

Errata: Although we have taken every care to ensure the accuracy of our content, mistakes do happen. If you have found a mistake in this book, we would be grateful if you reported this to us. Please visit `http://www.packt.com/submit-errata`, click **Submit Errata**, and fill in the form.

Piracy: If you come across any illegal copies of our works in any form on the internet, we would be grateful if you would provide us with the location address or website name. Please contact us at `copyright@packt.com` with a link to the material.

If you are interested in becoming an author: If there is a topic that you have expertise in and you are interested in either writing or contributing to a book, please visit `http://authors.packt.com/`.

Subscribe to Game Dev Assembly Newsletter!

We are excited to introduce Game Dev Assembly, our brand-new newsletter dedicated to everything game development. Whether you're a programmer, designer, artist, animator, or studio lead, you'll get exclusive insights, industry trends, and expert tips to help you build better games and grow your skills. Sign up today and become part of a growing community of creators, innovators, and game changers.

`https://packt.link/gamedev-newsletter`

Scan the QR code to join instantly!

Free Benefits with Your Book

This book comes with free benefits to support your learning. Activate them now for instant access (see the "*How to Unlock*" section for instructions).

Here's a quick overview of what you can instantly unlock with your purchase:

PDF and ePub Copies

- Access a DRM-free PDF copy of this book to read anywhere, on any device.
- Use a DRM-free ePub version with your favorite e-reader.

Next-Gen Web-Based Reader

- **Multi-device progress sync**: Pick up where you left off, on any device.
- **Highlighting and notetaking**: Capture ideas and turn reading into lasting knowledge.
- **Bookmarking**: Save and revisit key sections whenever you need them.
- **Dark mode**: Reduce eye strain by switching to dark or sepia themes.

How to Unlock

UNLOCK NOW

Scan the QR code (or go to `packtpub.com/unlock`). Search for this book by name, confirm the edition, and then follow the steps on the page.

***Note:** Keep your invoice handy. Purchases made directly from Packt don't require one.*

Share your thoughts

Once you've read *Data Structures and Algorithms for Game Programming in C++*, we'd love to hear your thoughts! Scan the QR code below to go straight to the Amazon review page for this book and share your feedback.

`https://packt.link/r/1835889875`

Your review is important to us and the tech community and will help us make sure we're delivering excellent quality content.

Part 1

Data Structure and Algorithm Fundamentals

In this part, the primary focus is on building a strong foundation in data structures and algorithms specifically tailored for game development. While many traditional algorithm books emphasize theory through pseudo-code, this part bridges the gap between theory and practice by offering real-world C++ examples that demonstrate how these core concepts are applied in actual game scenarios.

You'll begin by exploring the essential role of algorithms in game design, and how they contribute to creating adaptive, high-performance, and engaging gameplay. From there, you'll learn how data structures organize and manage game data efficiently, and how algorithms manipulate that data to drive meaningful in-game behavior.

Finally, you'll dive into a curated set of practical algorithms—ranging from randomization and shuffling to procedural generation and object pooling—that are commonly used in game development projects.

This part includes the following chapters:

1

Gearing Up: C++ for Game Development

Game algorithms are essential for creating high-performance, adaptive, and engaging games. While many algorithm books focus on theory and concepts using pseudo-code, they often lack practical examples relevant to game development. This book bridges this gap by offering real-world game development examples that not only explain algorithms but also demonstrate how to apply them effectively. This approach enables you to grasp both the theory and practical implementation of algorithms within the context of game development, fostering a deeper understanding and facilitating their application in creating compelling games.

This chapter serves as the introduction to the book, outlining its purpose, organizational structure, and the tools used to illustrate algorithms in practical game development scenarios. Key topics covered in this chapter include:

- Why learn algorithms for game development?
- Why is C++ used in this book?
- Understanding the structure for introducing algorithms in this book
- Setting up your development environment
- Utilizing the raylib graphics library
- Introducing Knight
- Investigating `Demo1.cpp`

Free Benefits with Your Book

Your purchase includes a free PDF copy of this book along with other exclusive benefits. Check the *Free Benefits with Your Book* section in the Preface to unlock them instantly and maximize your learning experience.

Technical requirements

As a reader of this book, you are expected to have basic computer operational skills. You should also be capable of installing the required applications and setting up your programming environment.

To follow this chapter, you are required to install **MS Visual Studio 2022** or a later version along with the **C++ compiler**. Additionally, download the sample code from this book's GitHub repository.

Here is the link to the GitHub repository:

`https://github.com/PacktPublishing/Data-Structures-and-Algorithms-for-Game-Programming-in-CPP`

Additionally, you can access the `Demo1` project here: `https://github.com/PacktPublishing/Data-Structures-and-Algorithms-for-Game-Programming-in-CPP/tree/main/Knight`

The recommended minimum development environment for running the sample projects is as follows:

- Operating System (OS): Windows 10
- Central Processing Unit (CPU): Intel 7th generation or equivalent
- Graphics Processing Unit (GPU): GTX1080 (or AMD equivalent)
- Random-Access Memory (RAM): 8GB
- Hard Drive Storage: 20GB of available space
- OpenGL API: 3.3

To check the OpenGL version supported by your system, you can download and install the free app, **GPU-Z**, from the following link: `https://www.techpowerup.com/download/techpowerup-gpu-z/`.

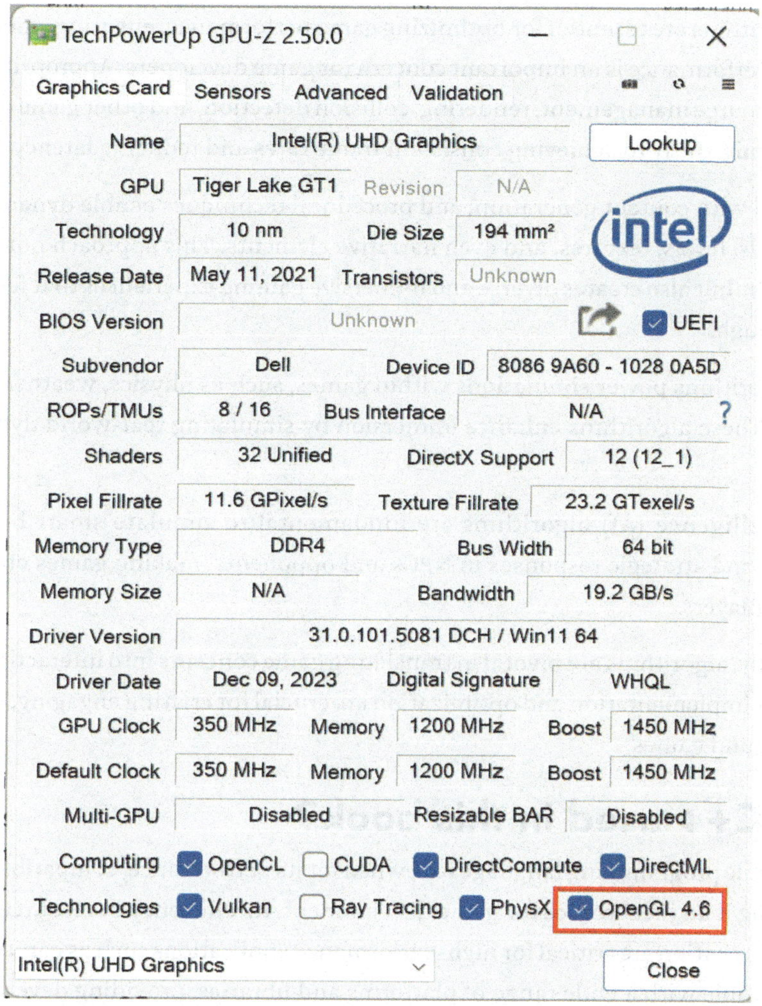

Figure 1.1 – Using GPU-Z to check the OpenGL version on your system

Why learn algorithms for game development?

Algorithms play a crucial role in game development, serving as the backbone for many core functionalities and features. Here are several key points highlighting their importance.

Algorithms can be used to define how game mechanics operate and even provide solutions for solving problems in effective and performative ways, including player interactions, artificial intelligence behavior, physics simulations, and so on. For example, pathfinding algorithms determine how Non-Player Characters (NPCs) navigate through environments, enhancing realism and player engagement.

Efficient algorithms are essential for optimizing game performance, ensuring smooth gameplay experiences. Performance is an important concern for game developers. Appropriate algorithms applied for resource management, rendering, collision detection, and other game operations can contribute significantly to achieving consistent frame rates and reducing latency.

They also deal with content generation, and procedural techniques enable dynamic generation of game worlds, levels, textures, and even narrative elements. This approach not only saves development time but also creates diverse and immersive gaming experiences that feel unique with each playthrough.

Advanced algorithms power simulations within games, such as physics, weather, and complex simulations. These algorithms enhance immersion by simulating real-world dynamics and interactions.

Artificial Intelligence (AI) algorithms are fundamental to simulate smart behaviors, decision-making, and strategic responses in NPCs and opponents, making games challenging and engaging for players.

Fundamentally, algorithms are pivotal in translating game concepts into interactive experiences. Their efficient implementation and optimization are crucial for crafting engaging, enjoyable, and technically sound games.

Why is C++ used in this book?

C++ is a versatile programming language renowned for its performance, compatibility, and adaptability, making it an ideal choice for game development. Its efficiency in resource management and speed of execution are critical for high-performance applications such as games. Additionally, C++ is compatible with a wide range of platforms and libraries, providing developers with the flexibility to create complex and interactive gaming experiences.

C++ is widely used in game development because of its performance, versatility, and precise control over system resources. It is supported by many leading game engines, such as Unreal Engine and Unity, as well as proprietary SDKs developed and used by game studios.

This book explains algorithms directly in C++ instead of using pseudo-code, offering fully functional and executable sample code. You can experiment with the code and observe the algorithms in action. Each sample project is based on the covered algorithms, demonstrating their real-world applications. This practical approach helps connect theoretical concepts with hands-on experience.

We've chosen to use traditional C++ programming syntax to ensure that the code is easy to read and understand. By using widely supported legacy C++ syntax, the code remains portable, re-usable, and easy to integrate across diverse platforms and compilers. The primary goal of the sample code is to simplify the learning process, allowing you to quickly grasp the essentials of implementing the introduced algorithms. Therefore, comprehensibility takes the highest priority, while performance and code structure rules are not strictly adhered to in the sample code (see Preface for more details).

The sample code provided in this book serves as a valuable resource for accelerating your game development process. By reusing these samples, you can quickly develop high-quality, professional solutions for your projects. These examples are designed to be practical references, easily integrated and adapted for real-world applications. Whether you are looking to understand the basics of an algorithm or seeking a foundation to build upon, the sample code offers a robust starting point.

Incorporating these code samples into your projects not only saves time but also ensures that you are building upon proven, functional algorithms. The code can be modified and expanded to suit the specific needs of your game, providing a flexible and reliable base for your development efforts. By leveraging the provided examples, you can focus on enhancing your game's features and performance and be confident in the quality and reliability of your underlying code.

Understanding the structure for introducing algorithms in this book

In this book, we will explore a wide range of algorithms that are essential for game development. Each chapter is structured to provide a comprehensive understanding of an algorithm through several key components. Each algorithm will be introduced and explained following this structure:

1. **Use case and requirement analysis**: Each algorithm will begin with some use case examples that address the challenges in game development.
2. **Algorithm explanation**: We will delve into the algorithm's logic and thought process. This section aims to break down the algorithm and introduce the idea and steps, which explain the underlying principles.

3. **C++ implementation**: Based on the algorithm's theory, the book presents key blocks of code of the C++ implementation to help you grasp the core idea of the algorithm. To better understand the source code, you can read into the demo projects' code, which contains helpful comments.
4. **Code explanation**: After presenting the C++ code, when needed, we will explain the important lines and blocks of code in detail.

Some chapters will include examples of the algorithm applied to real game scenarios, such as collision detection or AI behavior. When specific problems aren't relevant, generalized examples will showcase the algorithm's versatility. This approach ensures you gain both theoretical and practical insights, making the book a valuable resource for developers at any level.

Now, let's dive in and set up your work environment to start experimenting with the samples and code provided in this book.

Setting up your development environment

By now, you are aware that we are using C++ and Knight to demonstrate algorithms in this book. In the final section of this chapter, we will provide guidelines for setting up your work environment. This will enable you to explore the sample code and experiment with your own implementations.

Now it's time to get hands-on by following these steps to set up your working environment.

Install Visual Studio 2022

Microsoft Visual Studio (**MSVS**) is an **Integrated Development Environment** (**IDE**) that can be used to create, edit, debug, and compile your C++ code. You should have a Microsoft account before installation.

To install MSVS, you can visit the official website (`http://visualstudio.microsoft.com/vs/`) and download the Visual Studio 2022 (VS2022) Community version installation package. This is what the website should look like:

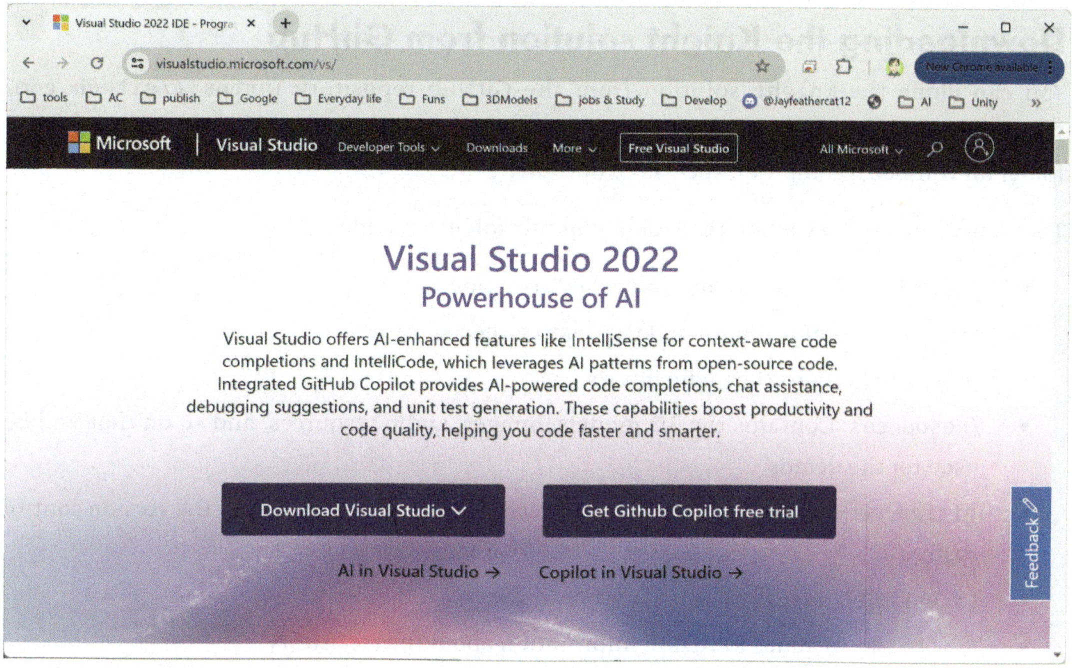

Figure 1.2 – Downloading VS2022 from Microsoft

When installing VS2022, make sure to enable the **Desktop development with C++** module to install the C++ compiler together with the IDE.

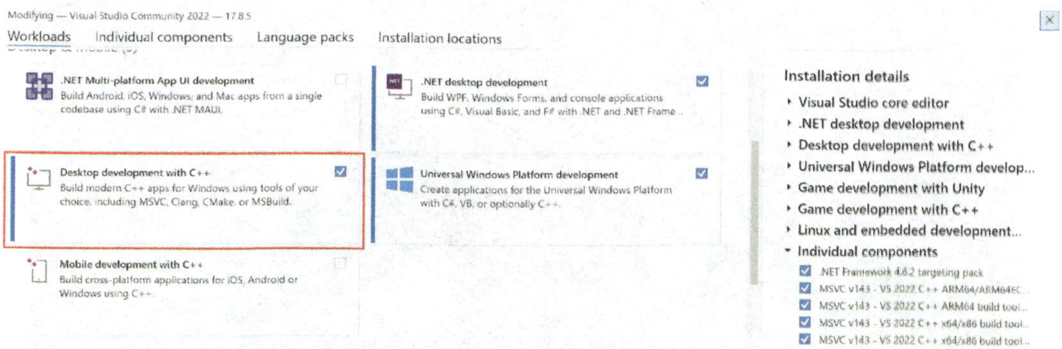

Figure 1.3 – Installing the VS2022 IDE with the C++ compiler

Next, let's download Knight from GitHub.

Downloading the Knight solution from GitHub

You can clone the `Knight` solution from the GitHub repository (`https://github.com/PacktPublishing/Data-Structures-and-Algorithms-for-Game-Programming-in-CPP`) into a folder on your local computer, such as `C:\Knight`.

The cloned root folder contains the following sub-folders and files:

- `/.git`: Contains Git version control information
- `/Knight`: Contains Knight and the demo projects
- `/raylib`: Contains the raylib library
- `/resources`: Contains the 3D models, images, audio resources, and so on that will be used for the demos
- `.gitignore`: Specifies which files and directories should be ignored by the version control system
- `License`: Includes the license information
- `README.md`: Includes README information about the repository

In Visual Studio, open `<Install Folder>/Knight/Knight.sln`, build the solution, and press the play button to run `Demo1`. It should open the game windows and show the game scene.

Figure 1.4 – Demo1 screenshot

Use the left and right mouse buttons to switch between the character's *Walk* and *Run* animations.

Next, we will delve into the graphics library and SDK used in this demo, along with its source code. Let's begin by explaining raylib, the graphics library utilized in this demo.

Utilizing the raylib graphics library

raylib is a straightforward and free-to-use open-source programming library written in C, primarily for video game development. It supports the creation of both 2D and 3D games and graphical applications, offering a wide range of functions and utilities for graphics handling, input management, audio integration, and physics simulations.

raylib is lightweight and cross-platform, compatible with Windows, macOS, Linux, and other operating systems. Its simplicity makes it accessible to developers of all levels, supported by clear API documentation and practical examples. While lacking fancy interfaces, visual helpers, and GUI tools, raylib compensates with robust code examples and comprehensive functionality.

The game engine, Knight, and the samples provided in this book are developed based on raylib. raylib is already integrated and well-configured with the downloaded package when you check out the sample projects from this book's GitHub repository.

Additional resource

If you want to explore raylib further, you can download it from its repository here: `https://github.com/raysan5/raylib`. The official raylib examples can also be accessed at `https://www.raylib.com/examples.html`.

The following screenshot shows raylib's homepage:

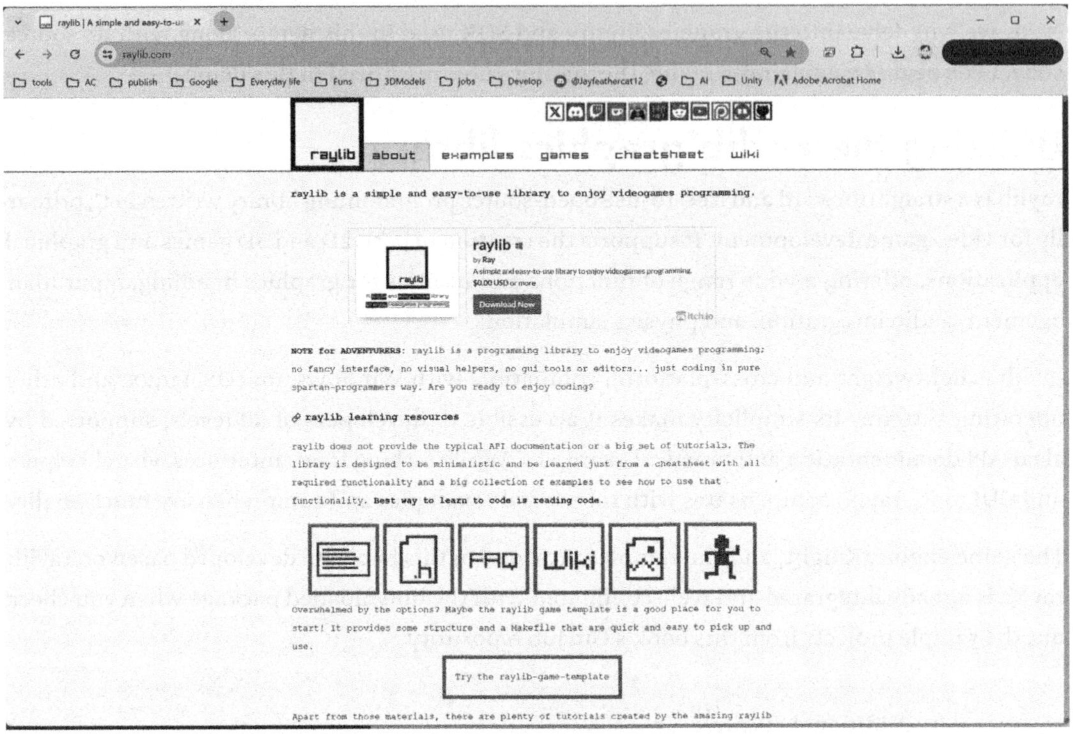

Figure 1.5 – Visiting the raylib.com homepage

With the understanding of raylib and its capabilities in graphics rendering, we are now poised to explore the custom graphics SDK, Knight, developed specifically for the samples of this book.

Introducing Knight

Knight is an object-oriented programming (OOP) wrapper written in C++ that builds upon raylib. Serving as a higher-level engine layer, Knight offers enhanced game development tools designed to simplify the process for you by abstracting away raylib-specific rendering details. Let's inspect the new features included in Knight.

What's new in Knight?

In addition to raylib's fundamental rendering and low-level operations, Knight introduces higher-level concepts and tools. These include a streamlined game-flow structure centered around `Start`, `Update`, `DrawFrame`, and `EndGame` functions. Knight also defines key concepts such as `Scene`, `SceneObject`, and `ObjectComponent` to facilitate the creation of hierarchical scenes.

Let's start understanding the game flow structure next.

Introducing the game flow structure

Knight is designed with a very straightforward structure that encompasses only the most basic game flow elements. Using Knight is simple: you just inherit from the `Knight` class and override its four member functions: `Start`, `Update`, `DrawFrame`, and `EndGame`. The following flow chart illustrates how these four strategies are interconnected within the game flow:

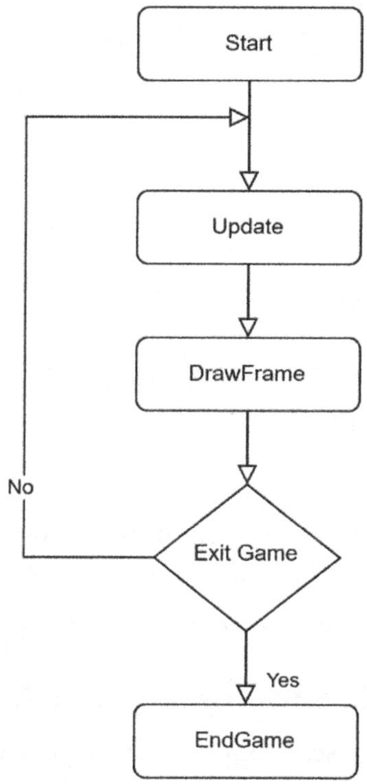

Figure 1.6 – Knight game flow structure

The nodes in the flow chart represent the member functions:

- The `Start` function is called to initialize the game, including spawning scene objects, setting up the scene camera, configuring lighting effects, and so on.
- The `Update` function takes care of game logic, such as processing player inputs, Non-player Character (NPC) behaviors, collision detections, interactions, networking communications, etc.

- The DrawFrame function draws all 2D images and 3D meshes to visualize the frame of the game based on the current scene state.
- The EndGame function is in charge of destructing scene objects, deallocating resources, releasing memory, and restoring game states before the game is shut down.

The following code snippet demonstrates how the Demo1 class extends the Knight class and overrides the four member functions:

```
#pragma once
#include "Knight.h"

class Demo1 : public Knight
{
public:
    void Start() override;
    void EndGame() override;
protected:
    void Update(float ElapsedSeconds) override;
    void DrawFrame() override;
};
```

Based on the declaration of the new class member functions, you can write code to implement these functions. The primary task of the implementations is to construct the game scene. The game scene is composed of scene objects arranged in a hierarchical tree structure.

Introducing Scene, SceneObject, and Components

Knight introduces the concept of a **scene**, representing a game world that contains various scene objects. These objects are organized in a hierarchical tree structure, where each object can have multiple child objects that move, scale, and rotate together with their parent object. This structure allows for efficient management and transformation of objects within the game world.

In a game scene, all objects must be added to the hierarchy, starting from a single root object that contains all other scene objects. This root object serves as the foundation, ensuring a clear and organized structure for the game scene.

A **scene actor** extends a **scene object** and includes transformation information that handles its scale, location, and rotation. Child actors calculate their relative transformations based on their parent object, providing consistent world transformation data.

Scene objects can also be enhanced with multiple components, such as cameras, models, primitive shapes, sprites, effects, and more. These components add functionality and visual elements to the scene objects, enabling the creation of complex and dynamic game scenes.

By using this hierarchical structure and component system, Knight offers a flexible and powerful framework for game development. Refer to *Figure 1.7* to see the scene structure of the `Demo1` project:

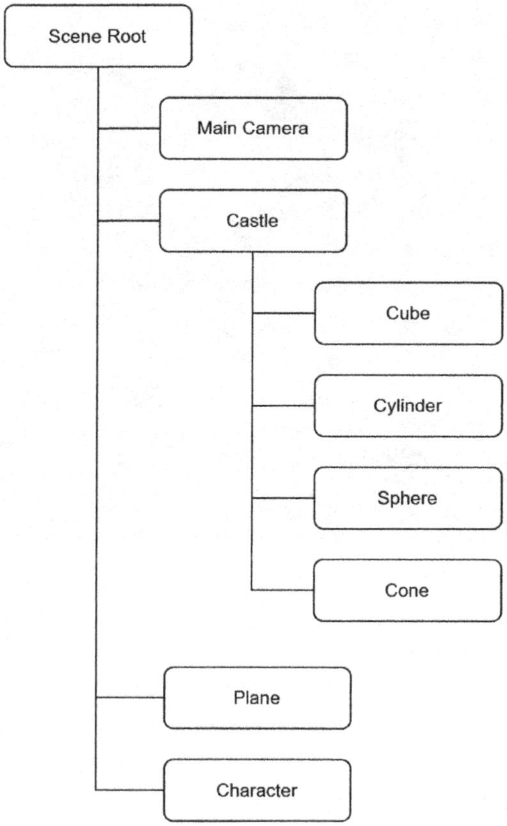

Figure 1.7 – Demo1 scene structure

After constructing the scene, the game appears as shown in the screenshot (see *Figure 1.4*). As the castle spins, together with it, the child objects—Cube, Cylinder, Sphere, and Cone—rotate around the castle.

Now that you have seen what `Demo1` looks like, let's uncover the details and delve into the source code of `Demo1`.

Investigating Demo1.cpp

`Demo1` is a project that demonstrates how to use the Knight engine to create a game scene and add scene objects. In this project, eight scene objects are created and added to the scene:

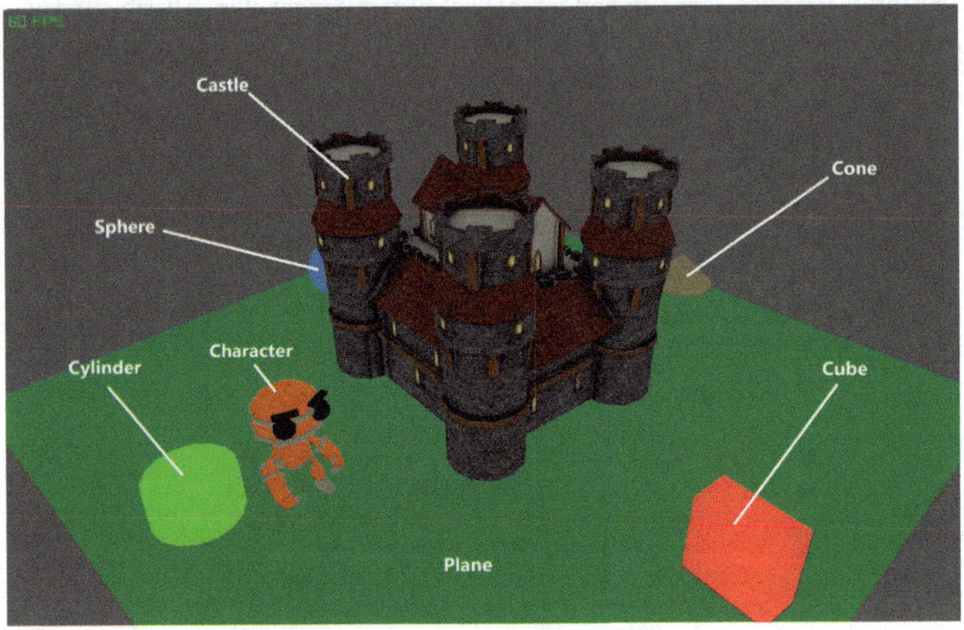

Figure 1.8 – Demo1 scene and the scene objects

1. **Main Camera** is a perspective camera positioned at coordinates (60, 60, 60) and aimed at the target coordinates (0, 10, 0). *Figure 1.8* is a screenshot captured from the camera's perspective, so the camera itself is not visible in the image.

> **Note**
>
> **Coordinates** represent positions in 3D space, and each component (X, Y, Z) represents a spatial axis. Here's a breakdown:
>
> - **X-coordinate** (60): Distance along the horizontal axis (left-right)
> - **Y-coordinate** (60): Distance along the vertical axis (up-down)
> - **Z-coordinate** (60): Distance along the depth axis (forward-backward)
>
> **Coordinate units** depend on the scene's scale, such as meters, centimeters, or pixels.

2. **Castle** is a scene actor with a model component that loads the castle model.
3. **Cube** is a scene actor with a cube component.
4. **Sphere** is a scene actor with a sphere component.
5. **Cylinder** is a scene actor with a cylinder component.
6. **Cone** is a scene actor with a cone component.
7. **Plane** is a scene actor with a plane component.
8. **Character** is a scene actor with a model component that loads the robot model and the character's animations.

Here, the `Cube`, `Sphere`, `Cylinder`, and `Cone` objects are children of the `Castle`, causing them to rotate around the castle as it spins.

While running the game, the player can use the mouse's left and right buttons to toggle between the character's Walk and Run animations. The castle's spinning speed adjusts to match the selected animation.

Implementing the main() function

As we know, the `main()` function is the entry point of a C++ program. To get started, we need to create an instance of the Demo1 class, named `KnightDemo1`. Then, we call the `Start()` and `GameLoop()` methods of `KnightDemo1`. Finally, upon exiting the game, we use the `delete` command to release the allocated memory for the KnightDemo1 instance.

The following code snippet shows how simple it is to write C++ game code based on the Knight engine:

```
int main(int argc, char* argv[])
{
    Demo1* KnightDemo1 = new Demo1();
    KnightDemo1->Start();
    KnightDemo1->GameLoop();
    delete KnightDemo1;
    return 0;
}
```

Next, let's examine the implementation of the `Knight::Start()` function.

Overriding the Knight::Start() function

The subclass `Demo1` of Knight should override the `Start()` function, and the primary task in `Start()` is to initialize the game. This involves creating all the scene objects and adding them to the scene.

Before adding scene objects, we want to introduce three useful engine variables:

- The `_Scene` variable represents the game's current scene, which is instantiated by default when Knight starts. You can create multiple scenes and designate any one of them as the current scene.
- The `ShowFPS` flag displays the game's frame rate in the top-left corner of the game screen (see *Figure 1.8*).

To create and add a new scene object to the scene, you can call the template function `CreateSceneObject` and specify the type of scene object you want to create. The following two lines of code create a perspective camera and a scene actor:

```
_Scene->CreateSceneObject<PerspectiveCamera>("Camera");
_Scene->CreateSceneObject<SceneActor>("Castle");
```

The only parameter of `CreateSceneObject` is the name of the new object.

We can create and attach components to scene objects. For example, adding a model component that loads the castle model will render the castle in the scene. Each scene object can contain multiple components, but each type of component is exclusive.

Calling the `SceneObject::CreateAndAddComponent()` template function can attach a component to a scene object. The following code snippet creates a `modelActor` object, and then creates a `modelComponent` and adds the component to the `modelActor` object:

```
modelActor =
_Scene->CreateSceneObject<SceneActor>("Castle");
ModelComponent* modelComponent =
    modelActor->CreateAndAddComponent<ModelComponent>();
modelComponent->Load3DModel(
    "../../resources/models/obj/castle.obj",
    "../../resources/models/obj/castle_diffuse.png");
```

Another option to add components to a scene object is by creating a component instance and then calling `SceneObject::AddComponent()`. The following code snippet demonstrates how to add a new `cubeComponent` to the `cubeActor`:

```
cubeActor = new SceneActor(Scene, "Cube");
CubeComponent* cubeComponent = new CubeComponent();
cubeActor->AddComponent(cubeComponent);
```

Note

Once a component is added to an object, it will be destroyed when the object is destroyed. A scene object is destroyed when the scene itself is destroyed.

Now it's time to override the functions that will be called within the game loop.

Overriding the Knight::Update() function

Game logic is managed within the `Update(float ElapsedSeconds)` function where the `ElapsedSeconds` parameter represents time in seconds elapsed between frames. In `Demo1`, it performs two tasks: setting character animations based on mouse button presses and incrementing the y angle to rotate the castle.

To get the pointer of the character's model component, you can call the `GetComponent` template function:

```
ModelComponent *characterModel =
    characterActor->GetComponent<ModelComponent>();
```

You can call the `GetAnimationIndex` and `SetAnimation` functions to get the current character animation index (an **animation index** is a numerical identifier that references a specific animation clip within a character's animation system) and set the current character animation.

The following code demonstrates how to switch between the character's Walk and Run animations, where the indices `6` and `10` represent the two animation states:

```
int animIndex = characterModel->GetAnimationIndex();
if (IsMouseButtonPressed(MOUSE_BUTTON_RIGHT) &&
    animIndex != 6)
{
    characterModel->SetAnimation(6);
    spinSpeed = 20.0f;
```

```
}
if (IsMouseButtonPressed(MOUSE_BUTTON_LEFT) &&
    animIndex != 10)
{
    characterModel->SetAnimation(10);
    spinSpeed = 10.0f;
}
```

Changing a scene actor's scale, position, or rotation values can resize, move, or rotate the scene object. For example, reducing the `modelActor`'s y-axis angle every frame results in the spinning of the model actor:

```
modelActor->Rotation.y -= ElapsedSeconds * spinSpeed;
```

Although `Demo1` overrides Knight's `DrawFrame` and `EndGame` functions, it doesn't perform any additional processes. Therefore, it's not necessary to override parent functions if you don't intend to add extra processes.

You can now review the complete `Demo1.cpp` code to understand how Knight can be used to develop further demos.

The full source code of `Demo1.cpp` code can be found here:

1. The main function instantiates the demo, calls the `Start` function and `GameLoop` function—which repeatedly invokes the demo's `Update` function—and, eventually, destroys the demo instance when the program ends:

   ```
   #include "Knight.h"
   #include "Demo1.h"
   PerspectiveCamera* camera;
   SceneActor*, cubeActor, sphereActor;
   SceneActor* cylinderActor, coneActor;
   SceneActor* modelActor, characterActor;
   float spinSpeed = 10.0f;
   int main(int argc, char* argv[])
   {
     Demo1* KnightDemo1= new Demo1();
     KnightDemo1->Start();
     KnightDemo1->GameLoop();
     delete KnightDemo1;
   ```

```
    return 0;
}
```

2. The Start function initializes the game by first adding the camera, the castle, and four shapes – a cube, sphere, cylinder, and cone:

```
void Demo1::Start()
{
    __super::Start();
    ShowFPS = true;
    camera = _Scene->CreateSceneObject<PerspectiveCamera>(
            "Camera");
    camera->Position = Vector3{ 60, 60, 60 };
    camera->CameraMode = CameraMode::CAMERA_FIRST_PERSON;
    camera->Target = Vector3{ 0, 10, 0 };
    modelActor = _Scene->CreateSceneObject<SceneActor>(
            "Castle");
    ModelComponent* modelComponent =
          modelActor->CreateAndAddComponent<ModelComponent>();
    modelComponent->Load3DModel(
            "../../resources/models/obj/castle.obj",
            "../../resources/models/obj/castle_diffuse.png");
    CubeComponent* cubeComponent = new CubeComponent();
    cubeComponent->SetColor(RED);
    cubeActor = new SceneActor(_Scene, "Cube");
    cubeActor->SetParent(modelActor);
    cubeActor->Position = Vector3{ 40, 0, 0 };
    cubeActor->AddComponent(cubeComponent);
    cubeComponent->Size = Vector3{ 10, 10, 5 };
    sphereActor = _Scene->CreateSceneObject<SceneActor>(
            "Sphere", modelActor);
    sphereActor->Position = Vector3{ -40, 0, 0 };
    SphereComponent* sphereComponent =
       sphereActor->CreateAndAddComponent<SphereComponent>();
    sphereComponent->SetColor(BLUE);
    sphereComponent->Radius = 5.0f;
    cylinderActor = _Scene->CreateSceneObject<SceneActor>(
            "Cylinder", modelActor);
```

```
    cylinderActor->Position = Vector3{ 0, 0, 40 };
    CylinderComponent* cylinderComponent =
cylinderActor->CreateAndAddComponent<CylinderComponent>();
    cylinderComponent->SetColor(GREEN);
    cylinderComponent->Radius = 5.0f;
    cylinderComponent->Height = 5.0f;
    coneActor = _Scene->CreateSceneObject<SceneActor>(
           "Cone", modelActor);
    coneActor->Position = Vector3{ 0, 0, -40 };
    ConeComponent* coneComponent =
         coneActor->CreateAndAddComponent<ConeComponent>();
    coneComponent->SetColor(BROWN);
    coneComponent->Radius = 5.0f;
    coneComponent->Height = 5.0f;
```

3. The second part of the `Start` function adds the ground plane and the character to the scene:

```
    SceneActor* plane =
           _Scene->CreateSceneObject<SceneActor>("Plane");
    plane->Position = Vector3{ 0, -5, 0 };
    plane->Scale = Vector3{ 100, 1, 100 };
    PlaneComponent* planeComponent =
       plane->CreateAndAddComponent<PlaneComponent>();
    planeComponent->SetColor(DARKGREEN);
    characterActor =
       _Scene->CreateSceneObject<SceneActor>("Character");
    characterActor->Scale = Vector3{ 3.0f, 3.0f, 3.0f };
    characterActor->Position.z = 30.0f;
    characterActor->Rotation.y = 90.0f;
    ModelComponent* animModelComponent =
characterActor->CreateAndAddComponent<ModelComponent>();
    animModelComponent->Load3DModel(
         "../../resources/models/gltf/robot.glb");
    animModelComponent->SetAnimation(10);
    characterActor->AddComponent(animModelComponent);
}
```

4. The `Update` function handles player inputs to change characters' animations.

```
void Demo1::Update(float ElapsedSeconds)
{
  ModelComponent *characterModel =
         characterActor->GetComponent<ModelComponent>();
  int animIndex = characterModel->GetAnimationIndex();
  if (IsMouseButtonPressed(MOUSE_BUTTON_RIGHT) &&
         animIndex != 6)
  {
    characterModel->SetAnimation(6);
    spinSpeed = 20.0f;
  }
  if (IsMouseButtonPressed(MOUSE_BUTTON_LEFT) &&
         animIndex != 10)
  {
    characterModel->SetAnimation(10);
    spinSpeed = 10.0f;
  }
  modelActor->Rotation.y -= ElapsedSeconds * spinSpeed;
  super::Update(ElapsedSeconds);
}
```

Now, you should be prepared to delve deeper into the algorithms introduced in this book through practical game development examples.

Summary

This first chapter of the book served as a foundational introduction, aimed at equipping you with the necessary prerequisites for delving into subsequent chapters and gaining proficiency in game development. It began by elucidating the book's objectives, outlining how it will empower you to advance as a proficient game developer. Emphasizing the use of C++, the chapter underscored its suitability for illustrating the concepts and implementations discussed throughout the book.

Central to this chapter was the introduction of the format used to present algorithms throughout the book. Following this, we introduced raylib, an open-source graphics library, and Knight, an easy-to-use OOP game engine developed by the author. We discussed the structure and fundamentals of Knight, emphasizing its role in streamlining game development through practical, hands-on examples. This included an in-depth exploration of Demo1, a demo project that showcases the engine's capabilities and serves as a concrete example of its application.

A comprehensive guide on setting up the development environment was the last section of this chapter, which ensured that you could seamlessly access and review the source code of demo projects, thereby enhancing your understanding of algorithms and their real-world applications in game development.

Overall, *Chapter 1* laid a robust foundation, preparing you to navigate subsequent chapters with confidence and clarity.

In the next chapter, you will get hands-on experience applying fundamental data structures and related algorithms to game development scenarios.

2

Data Structures in Action: Building Game Functionality

A **data structure** organizes data for efficient access and processing. By itself, data is just raw information; to solve problems or reach goals, you apply a step-by-step procedure called an **algorithm**.

Much like any other computer program, a video game is composed of a set of data structures and the algorithms that operate on them.

Imagine a typical video game battle scene where you control a player character fighting against a group of NPC monsters. These monsters are essentially just data with attributes such as **health points** (**HP**). However, it's the algorithm that drives the monsters to search for the nearest player-controlled hero and attack when they get close enough. In a video game, both data and algorithms must work together to create a fun experience. The way we arrange and store these data—through data structures—plays a crucial role in making algorithms work more efficiently.

This chapter will focus on the most common data structures needed to create a simple playable game (yes, you can complete a playable game as early as in this chapter).

In this chapter, we'll cover the following main topics:

- Data structures and algorithms in games
- Deciphering the secrets of game screenshots
- Evaluating data structure and algorithm

- Basic data structure for collections
- The order matters – LIFO and FIFO

By the end of this chapter, you will be able to implement a simple game with one-on-one fighting by using the data structures we have learned about.

Technical requirements

Before downloading/cloning the sample project, please refer to the technical requirements in *Chapter 1*.

All demos for data structures introduced in this chapter can be accessed in the GitHub project at `https://github.com/PacktPublishing/Data-Structures-and-Algorithms-for-Game-Programming-in-CPP/tree/main/Knight`, specifically under these project names:

Project Name	**Description**
`Demo2a`	This project implements several different `Entity` classes to represent the player, enemy, and terrain.
`Demo2b`	This project demonstrates how to prevent actual array insertion and deletion when adding/removing entities.
`Demo2c`	This project demonstrates how to use `std::vector` to implement an array.
`Demo2d`	This project implements enemies as a list instead of an array.
`Demo2e`	This project demonstrates how to implement a simple popup UI system with `std::stack`.
`Demo2f`	This project implements a simple fighting game with multiple data structures introduced in this chapter.

Table 2.1 – Projects used in this chapter

Data structures and algorithms in games

To learn how data structures are applied in game development and which ones are suitable for specific game development scenarios, one of the most intuitive approaches we found is to observe the game's *visuals*.

We want to approach our learning journey from a slightly different perspective. Instead of listing each popular data structure one by one, as most textbooks do, imagine the stunning screenshot of the game you want to create, or simply look at as many video game screenshots as possible. Based on what you observe in those screenshots, consider the following questions:

- What kind of data structures do you need to make that screenshot work like a real game?
- What kinds of algorithms are required to manipulate the data behind the screenshot?

Let's walk through the thought process of identifying the data structures needed for video game development.

Deciphering the secrets of game screenshots

By simply looking at the example car racing game screenshot in *Figure 2.1*, let's try to identify the key visual elements within the image.

Figure 2.1 – Screenshot of a typical car racing game

For those who play video games frequently, your brain will automatically start looking for things such as the main player character and other NPCs; or if you're familiar with digital painting programs, you can easily decompose any video game screenshot into various visual elements, as shown in *Figure 2.2*:

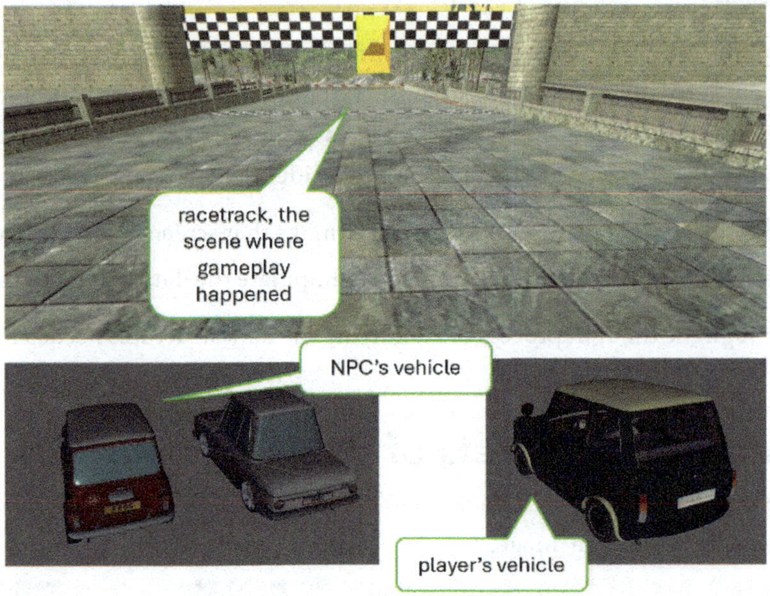

Figure 2.2 – Visual elements found in the screenshot

Now, how about another completely different 2D match-three hero card battle game?

Figure 2.3 – Visual elements found in the match-3 card battle puzzle game

There are many other visual elements, such as in-game items and visual effects. It's easy to reach this conclusion:

A video game image is created by rendering a series of visual elements to produce the final result.

In the previous chapter, you saw how Knight assembles the game visuals using `SceneActor`. A final screen image is composed by rendering a set of `SceneActor`. If we can identify and represent those elements with `SceneActor`, we can render them in Knight.

However, a game is not just about its visuals; it also needs to be playable. It must react to user input and respond to status changes from other visual elements. In game engine terminology, these visual elements are often referred to as **entities** (or **actors**) because we not only manage how to render them but also implement their behaviors designed for gameplay.

In conclusion, we organize entities into data structures and consider the algorithms needed to work with these entities to orchestrate the actual gameplay. Next, let's look at a screenshot from any game you've played and identify these entities!

Common entities found in video games

What kinds of entities can we identify across different video game screenshots?

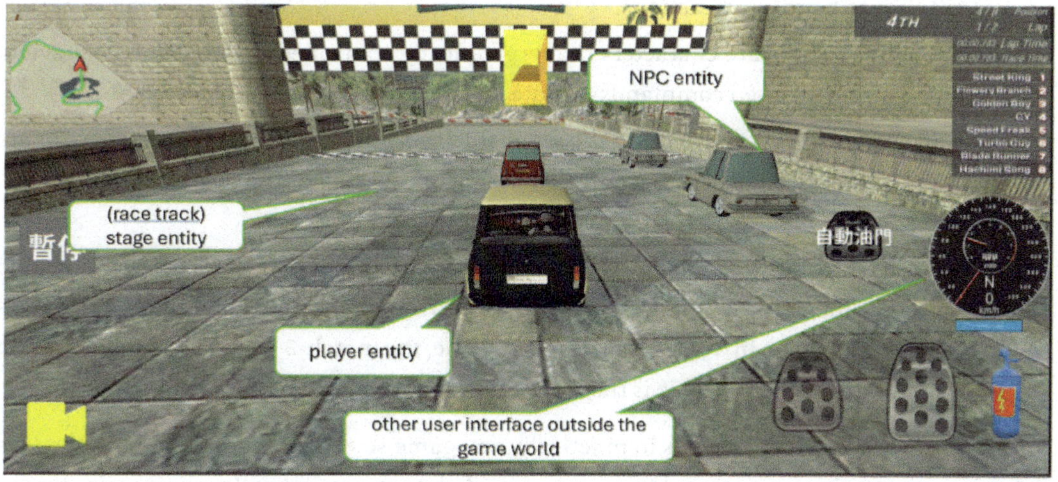

Figure 2.4 – Entities identified in a racing game screenshot

And how about an action role-playing MMO?

Figure 2.5 – Entities identified in a 3D MMORPG

Now, let's delve into these primary types of entities to understand them better:

- **Player entity**: This responds to the player's inputs. Some games, such as strategy or match-3 puzzle games, may not have a visible player entity. However, a player entity can still exist to handle interactions.
- **NPC entity**: These are characters that are typically controlled by predefined behaviors, ranging from scripted commands to state machines, or more sophisticated AI.
- **Prop entity**: These are objects in the scene that serve no major gameplay purpose or are simply decorative. If there is a crowd cheering on the side of the race track, those spectators are props entities.
- **Stage/terrain entity**: The **stage** is the physical environment that holds the player character, NPCs, and props. In many 3D action games, the **terrain** or indoor building structure serves as the stage. In a 2D match-3 puzzle game, the match-3 board acts as the stage. In a card battle game, the table is the stage that holds the player's and opponent's decks.

You can spot these types of entities in practically any game screenshot found online. When we develop our games in C++, we need to consider which data structures will make it easier for our program to handle them.

Defining the Entity C++ class

If we create a C++ class to implement an *entity*, the SceneActor of Knight will be part of this Entity class, and the rest of the Entity class will implement the gameplay logic for that entity.

For example, an NPC entity would have a SceneActor to render it visually on the screen, but it would also need to handle interactions, such as starting a dialog when the player clicks on the NPC to provide the next quest.

Let's start using C++ to represent the data structure of an Entity:

```
class Entity {
public:
  virtual void Create(Scene* pScene, Entity* pParent) = 0;
  virtual void Update(float elapsedTime);
  SceneActor* Actor;
};
```

In the preceding code, the basic base class for Entity contains an Actor, a SceneActor instance responsible for rendering its graphical representation (such as a 3D model or a 2D sprite). It also defines two key functions:

- Create(): An abstract virtual function that must be implemented by derived classes. This function is responsible for creating and initializing the entity. It should handle the creation/loading of the SceneActor and initialize data needed to perform the game logic of this entity.
- Update(elapsedTime): A virtual function that can be overridden to implement the entity's behavior logic. The elapsedTime parameter indicates the time difference since the last invocation of the Update() function. When overriding the default Update() method, it's important to call the base class version of Update() within your override to ensure correct functionality:

```
void MyEntity::Update(float diff) {
  __super:: Update(diff);
  //the rest of your customized logic
}
```

We can now extend the base Entity class to accommodate different needs of various types of entities:

```
class PlayerEntity : public Entity {
public:
  void Create(Scene* pScene, Entity* pParent) override;
};
// class EnemyEntity : public Entity ... (too)
// class TerrainEntity : public Entity ...
// class PropEntity : public Entity ...
```

In the Demo2a project, we've also moved the SceneActor creation code into the Entity class' Create() function. This allows each derived Entity class to perform its own specific initialization. Here is an example of entity initialization in Entities.cpp:

```
void PlayerEntity::Create(Scene * pScene, Entity* pParent){
  Actor = pScene->CreateSceneObject<SceneActor>("Player");
  Actor->Scale = Vector3{ 3.0f, 3.0f, 3.0f };
  Actor->Position.z = 30.0f;
  Actor->Rotation.y = 180.0f;
  //...
}
void TerrainEntity::Create(Scene* pScene, Entity* pParent)
{
  Actor = pScene->CreateSceneObject<SceneActor>("Terrain");
  //...
}
```

In the preceding code snippet, PlayerEntity and TerrainEntity both inherit from the base Entity class, but each has its own specialized Create() functions. The same approach is used for the EnemyEntity and PropEntity classes.

With all these entities defined, we can now refactor the example project from *Chapter 1* to start using entities. The new Demo2a app class contains four different Entity classes:

```
class Demo2a : public Knight
{ // ...
  PlayerEntity* player;
  EnemyEntity* enemy;
```

```
    TerrainEntity* terrain;
    PropEntity* prop;
    // ...
    void InitEntities();
```

The `InitEntity()` utility function is a private function called by the `Start()` function to create and initialize the preceding entities:

```
void Demo2a::InitEntities()
{
    terrain = new TerrainEntity();
    terrain->Create(_Scene, NULL);
    player = new PlayerEntity();
    player->Create(_Scene, terrain);
    // ... continue initialize other entities
}
```

After all the initialization is complete, during the application's runtime, we will call the `Update()` method of all entities from the `Update()` function of `Demo2a` app class. This allows each entity to process its own logic:

```
void Demo2a::Update(float ElapsedSeconds){
    player->Update(ElapsedSeconds);
    enemy->Update(ElapsedSeconds);
    prop->Update(ElapsedSeconds);
    terrain->Update(ElapsedSeconds);
    __super::Update(ElapsedSeconds);
}
```

Run the `Demo2a` project to see our player, terrain, enemy, and prop entities in action. In *Figure 2.6*, the player entity uses a robot model that continuously performs a running animation, the terrain is a simple platform, the prop entity on the terrain is the *well*, and the enemy entity is represented by a *green* ghost:

Figure 2.6 – Rendering PlayerEntity, PropEntity and EnemyEntity

Now, there's a problem in the code: games often have more than one NPC and more than one prop. In fact, some games feature complex scenes with hundreds of props and enemies. To manage this, we need a *collection* data structure to hold groups of entities. This is where different types of data structures come into play.

Evaluating data structure and algorithm

Now, we need to find a way to manage our **collections of entities**. With so many different data structures invented over the past decades, how do we evaluate whether a data structure is suitable for our needs?

Some basic data structures are designed for general-purpose use, while others are created to solve specific scenarios and perform better in those intended situations. As you might guess, there is no one-size-fits-all solution. The general rule of thumb is to choose the most *efficient* data structure for your specific use case.

Measuring the efficiency of data structures

Complexity and **scalability** are two major factors to consider when determining which data structure is most efficient for our use case.

Measuring of complexity

How do we measure the complexity of a given data structure? We often need to weigh the optimal balance between time, space, and implementation complexity:

- **Time complexity**: A good data structure should allow operations (such as insertion, deletion, and search) to be performed quickly. The time complexity of these operations should be suitable for the problem domain.
- **Space complexity**: The data structure should use memory or temporary storage efficiently. Minimizing space complexity is particularly important in environments with limited memory, such as phones or handheld gaming devices.
- **Implementation complexity**: The data structure should be easy to implement, understand, and use. While complex data structures may offer powerful features, they can also be difficult to maintain or debug.

Measuring scalability

In games such as massively multiplayer online games, scalability is a critical factor to consider:

- **Performance with scale**: A good data structure should maintain strong performance even as the size of the data grows. It should be capable of handling large datasets without significant degradation in performance.
- **Adaptability**: The data structure should be flexible enough to accommodate changes in the size or structure of the data. For example, a virtual world should be able to handle players frequently joining and leaving the game world.

Choosing the right data structure often involves balancing the factors mentioned above based on the specific needs of the use case and the characteristics of the data. The execution environment can also influence your final decision. For example:

- If the game is expected to run smoothly on a machine with a less powerful CPU, *time complexity* becomes a more decisive factor in selecting the data structure, as efficient processing is crucial.
- If the game is running on a device with lots of memory, *space complexity* may be less critical, allowing greater flexibility in other areas.

When designing data structures, there is no absolute *best* choice. All options are typically trade-offs based on factors such as the game's requirements, its execution environment, and the complexity of development.

Next, let's learn how to understand algorithm complexity from a mathematical perspective.

Big O: Measuring the efficiency of data structures and algorithms

Understanding the performance of algorithms is crucial for highly interactive, real-time applications such as video games, especially those that require scalability. What we care about here is how to categorize the performance of algorithms as they handle increasing amounts of data.

Big O notation is a mathematical concept used to describe the performance or complexity of an algorithm. It provides an upper bound on the time or space required by an algorithm as a function of the input size, typically denoted as `n`.

Big O notation helps us categorize the efficiency of different algorithms and understand how they scale with larger data inputs. There are several common Big O notations used to describe algorithmic efficiency:

- **Constant time – O(1)**: The algorithm takes the same amount of time to execute, regardless of the input size.
- **Logarithmic time O(log n)**: The time complexity grows logarithmically as the input size increases. Typically, this occurs in algorithms that repeatedly divide the problem in half using divide and conquer.
- **Leaner time O(n)**: The time complexity grows linearly with the size of the input. If the input size doubles, the time taken also doubles.
- **Linear logarithmic time O(n log n)**: The time complexity is a combination of linear and logarithmic growth. This is common in efficient sorting algorithms.
- **Quadratic time O(n^2)**: The time complexity grows quadratically with the size of the input. If the input size doubles, the time taken increases fourfold.
- **Exponential time O(2^n)**: The time complexity doubles with each additional element in the input. This is common in algorithms that explore all possible combinations.

Figure 2.7 shows an idea of the performance difference of each category of the Big O notation:

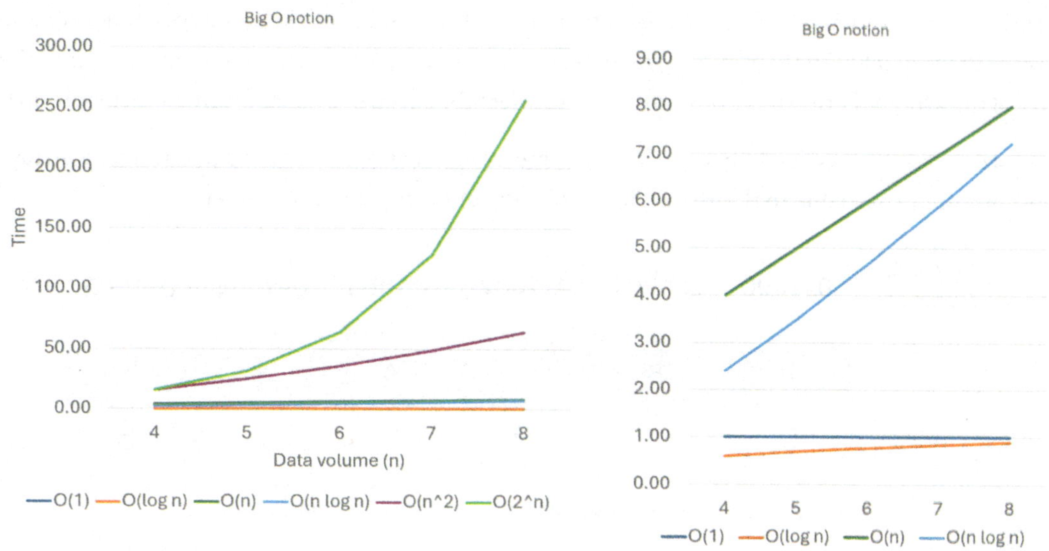

Figure 2.7 – Comparison of different Big O notations

The right chart doesn't include *O(n^2)* and *O(2^n)* for easier comparison of the rest performance categories. Later, when we begin introducing individual data structures, we will evaluate their speed efficiency using Big O notation.

In the next section, we will start with the very basic data structure for collections to some more advanced variations of them.

Basic data structure for collections

Continuing from our `Demo2a` app class in the previous section, we need some sort of data structure to store a bunch of enemies and props. There are two kinds of basic data structures that may be suitable for this purpose: array and list.

Array

An **array** is a linear data structure that holds a sequence of data elements arranged in adjacent memory space. Each data element in an array can be accessed directly using an **index**, which represents its position within the array.

Arrays are typically used when you need to store multiple items of the same type together and access them quickly by their index. The performance in Big O notation is *O(1)*, meaning that the size of the array, whether large or small, doesn't affect the speed of accessing any element within it.

The size of an array is fixed once it is created, meaning it cannot be resized dynamically. Arrays are commonly used due to their simplicity and efficiency in accessing elements.

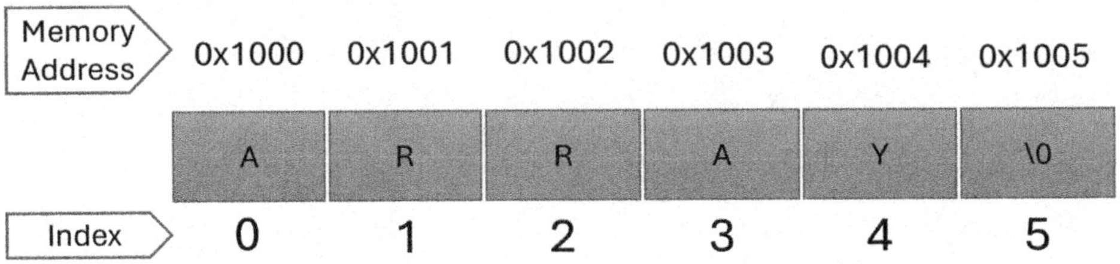

Figure 2.8 – Data in an array is stored in contiguous memory locations

Now, assume we will always have a maximum of five enemies in the scene. We can use an array for our enemy entities as follows:

```
#define MAX_NUM_ENEMIES 5
EnemyEntity enemies[MAX_NUM_ENEMIES];
```

After the declaration of the preceding data structure, the next step is learning how to use it.

Common operations on arrays

There are several common operations performed on arrays, including accessing particular data elements, enumerating elements, and inserting or deleting specific elements.

Access a specific element

In the match-three card battle game screenshot, the player can always put a maximum of five hero cards into the battle position at the bottom. It means the number and position of heroes will always be pre-determined when the battle starts.

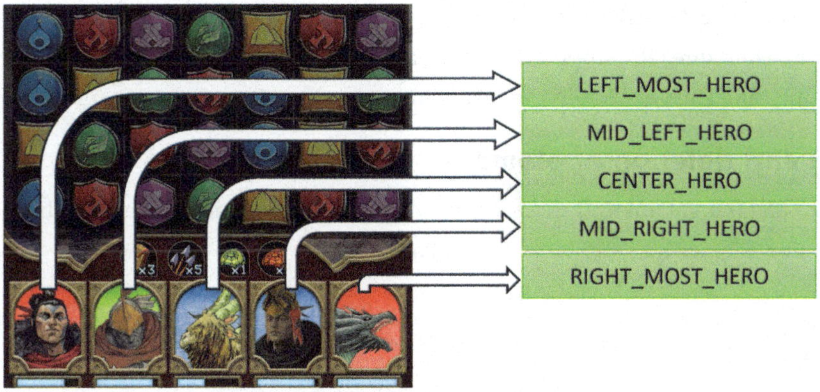

Figure 2.9 – Store hero team characters as an array

The following code snippet demonstrates a possible implementation using Knight:

```
PlayerEntity PlayerHeroes[MAX_NUM_CARDS];
EnemyEntity Enemies[MAX_NUM_ENEMIES];
```

Now we can assign each element of the `PlayerEntity` array to each player hero position:

```
#define LEFT_MOST_HERO 0
#define MID_LEFT_HERO 1
#define CENTER_HERO 2
#define MID_RIGHT_HERO 3
#define RIGHT_MOST_HERO 4
```

We can access the `PlayerEntity` in the center position by simply using the index:

```
PlayerHeroes[CENTER_HERO].Actor->Scale = Vector3{ 3.0f, 5.0f, 3.0f };
```

The array's rapid index-based access makes it ideal for applications requiring quick random data access.

Enumerating elements in the array

Since elements in the array can be easily accessed through an index, we just need to enumerate all indices with a loop to traverse the entire array in any direction we want. The following code snippet enumerates all `EnemyEntity` in the array:

```
for(int i=0;i< MAX_NUM_ENEMIES; i++)
  enemies[i].DoSomething();
```

The performance clearly scales along with the size of the array, so it's an $O(n)$ operation to traverse an array. The same $O(n)$ applies to search a particular element in the array – the worst case is that you only find the element in the last element in the array.

Insertion and deletion of element

If we want to insert an element into an array, all subsequent elements must be shifted to accommodate the new element, as shown in *Figure 2.10*:

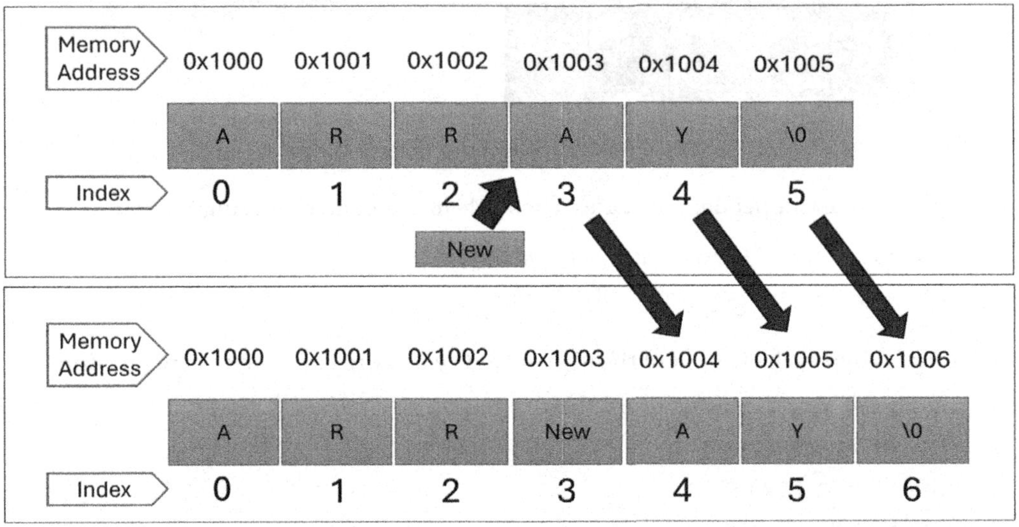

Figure 2.10 – Inserting a new element into an array

The same applies to deletion; all elements after the removed element need to be shifted to fill the gap.

If an array contains hundreds or thousands of elements, insertion and deletion operations require shifting many elements. This is a significant drawback of using arrays to store data that needs frequent insertion or deletion.

However, arrays still have advantages over many other, more complex, and so-called *more flexible* data structures:

- **Direct access**: You can directly access any element within the array.
- **Data locality**: Elements in an array are tightly packed in contiguous memory locations, which provides a hardware benefit called **data locality**. Modern CPUs use cache memory to speed up data access by loading a chunk of memory when you first access it. This makes access to nearby data much faster since it's probably already loaded into the cache.

Before we delve into other data structures, let's spend a bit more time with arrays and explore whether we can minimize the amount of data copying required during insertion and deletion operations.

Inserting/deleting versus enabling/disabling

The `Demo2b` project has a workaround to prevent array insertion and deletion. It contains a player hero intended to battle with a maximum of three enemies:

```
PlayerEntity* player;
EnemyEntity enemies[MAX_NUM_ENEMIES];
TerrainEntity* terrain;
```

However, the number of enemies can change during a battle session in the following ways:

- **Enemy defeated**: When a player defeats an enemy, the defeated enemy is removed from both the data structure and the screen.
- **Enemy respawn**: If the player cannot defeat all the enemies within a predetermined duration, the game may respawn new enemies to join the battle after a set period, we need to add a new `EnemyEntity` to the enemies' array.

To create a basic implementation of a battle session, we need to add an `HP` value to both `PlayerEntity` and `EnemyEntity`. We can add that in the base class and initialize with a default value of `100` for now:

```
class Entity { //...
  int HP;
   Entity();
};
Entity::Entity() {  //...
  HP = 100;
}
```

Any entity whose HP value drops to zero is considered *dead*. When the player defeats an enemy, we set the defeated enemy's `HP` to `0`. Additionally, we need to hide this defeated enemy, which can be accomplished using the Knight's API:

```
Actor->IsActive = false;
```

If a `SceneActor`'s `IsActive` is set to `false`, it will be *disabled* and ignored while rendering the frame.

Now, let's extend the EnemyEntity class to support the Die function:

```
void EnemyEntity::Die() {
    HP = 0;
    Actor->IsActive = false;
}
```

Now, we need a quick way to make an enemy die. For demo purposes, we just add hotkeys to pretend we have issued an attack. Pressing the number key *1* will make the first enemy die by calling the Die() function, while pressing key *2* will do the same for the second enemy. We'll add a CheckDefeatEnemy() function and call it every time the game's Update() function of the game is invoked:

```
void Demo2b::Update(float ElapsedSeconds) {
  CheckDefeatEnemy();
  player->Update(ElapsedSeconds);
  for(int i=0;i< MAX_NUM_ENEMIES; i++)
    enemies[i].Update(ElapsedSeconds);
  //… update terrain, etc.
}
bool Demo2b::CheckDefeatEnemy() {
  if (IsKeyPressed(KEY_ONE) && enemies[0].HP > 0)
    enemies[0].Die();
  else if (IsKeyPressed(KEY_TWO) && enemies[1].HP > 0)
    enemies[1].Die();
  else if (IsKeyPressed(KEY_THREE) && enemies[2].HP > 0)
    enemies[2].Die();
  else
    return false;
  return true;
}
```

The preceding code checks for key presses and calls the Die() function on any living enemies.

Since we only have three enemy entities in our case, this simple implementation is sufficient for testing. In a real game, enemies typically aren't defeated with a single blow; instead, you apply damage to their HP and check whether it has been reduced to zero.

Now, let's run `Demo2b` to see how it functions. In this implementation, we *disable* an enemy entity instead of deleting it, as shown in *Figure 2.11*:

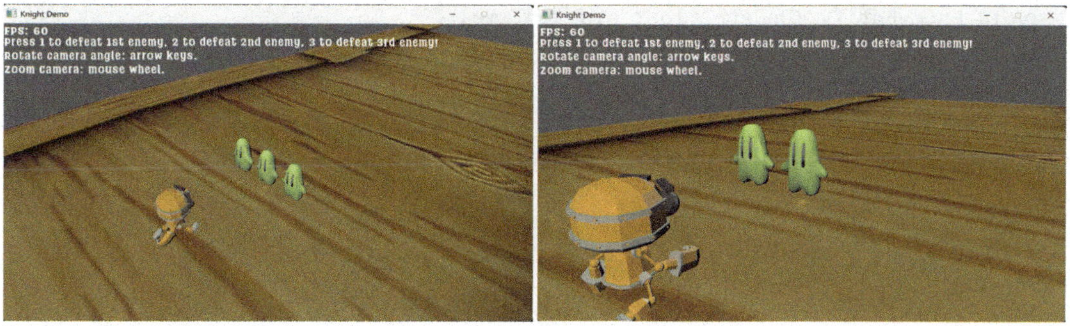

Figure 2.11 – The defeated enemy entity is disabled

This method is especially useful in scenarios with many enemy units, like in real-time strategy games, where copying many `EnemyEntities` in the `enemies` array for insertion or removal could be time-inefficient.

In many action games, if you don't defeat all the enemies in time, the defeated enemies might just reappear. For testing purposes, we can set a 5-second countdown after an enemy is defeated before it respawns (though in a real game, you wouldn't want to frustrate players by bringing enemies back too quickly!).

To implement this, we'll need to add a `Resurrect()` function and a `respawnInterval` variable for the countdown in the `EnemyEntity` class:

```
class EnemyEntity : public Entity {
public:
    void Resurrect();
private:
    float respawnInterval;
};
void EnemyEntity::Resurrect() {
    HP = 100;
    Actor->IsActive = true;  //enable the SceneActor
}
```

Since this countdown is calculated on a per-enemy basis, it needs to be implemented within `EnemyEntity`'s `Update()` function, not `Demo2b`'s `Update()` function:

```
void EnemyEntity::Update(float elapsedTime) {
  if (respawnInterval > 0.0f) {  // waiting respawn?
    respawnInterval -= elapsedTime;
    if (respawnInterval <= 0.0f) {  // countdown end!
      Resurrect();

    }
  }
}
```

Run the code and try pressing *1*, *2*, or *3*. After 5 seconds, you'll see the defeated enemies reappear. In this implementation, we reuse the element of the defeated enemy to spawn a new one, so there is no actual *insert* or *delete* operation performed.

However, it's not ideal to pre-create an array with a capacity for 5,000 props if only 80 to 120 props are used in a single game level. In such cases, there are better data structure solutions available. A dynamic array is one such solution.

Standard C++ implementation of dynamic array

The standard C++ library includes a robust dynamic array implementation that offers more features than a regular array. One of its most powerful features is dynamic sizing, allowing the array to grow and accommodate more elements as needed. This implementation is `std::vector`.

`Demo2c` project demonstrates how to use `std::vector` to implement an array for our previous sample `Demo2b`:

```
#include <vector>
class Demo2c : public Knight {
  vector<EnemyEntity> enemies;
};
```

Here, `vector` provides several key benefits over plain arrays: it's more flexible with dynamic resizing of the capacity, safer with array boundary checking, and easier to use.

Common operations on std::array

Let's look are some common operations when using `std::vector` instead of a plain array.

Accessing a specific element

The standard library's vector overloads the `[]` operator, allowing you to access elements in a vector just as you would with a regular array:

```
if (IsKeyPressed(KEY_ONE) && enemies[0].HP > 0) enemies[0].Die();
```

Enumerating elements

Starting from C++ 11, the standard library provides a convenient way to iterate through containers:

```
void Demo2c::Update(float ElapsedSeconds) {  //...
  for(EnemyEntity& enemy : enemies)
    enemy.Update(ElapsedSeconds);
}
```

One important detail is to use `EnemyEntity&` to retrieve the actual element instance inside the `enemies` vector.

Insertion and deletion

Even though we don't actually insert any elements in `Demo2c`, it's very easy to do with an `iterator`:

```
vector<EnemyEntity>::iterator it = enemies.begin();
enemies.insert(it+2, val);  //val is another EnemyEntity
```

In the preceding code, we first obtain an `iterator` for `vector<EnemyEntity>`. We then use `it+2` to insert the `val` (another `EnemyEntity` instance) as the third element.

Deletion of an element is trivial too:

```
vector<EnemyEntity>::iterator it =enemies.begin()+2;
enemies.erase(it);
```

In the preceding snippet, we use an `iterator` to remove the third element from the `enemies` collection.

Sort

The `vector` implementation also provides a handy `sort()` function to sort the `vector`:

```
std::vector<int> numbers = {5, 2, 9, 1, 5, 6};
std::sort(numbers.begin(), numbers.end());
```

This example will sort the `vector` into `{1 2 5 5 6 9}`.

List

For our `Demo2b` project, if we want the flexibility to easily remove a bunch of enemies and spawn several new ones, a linked list might be a better choice of data structure.

A **linked list** is a linear data structure in which elements are not stored in contiguous memory locations. Instead, the elements are connected using pointers shown in *Figure 2.12*:

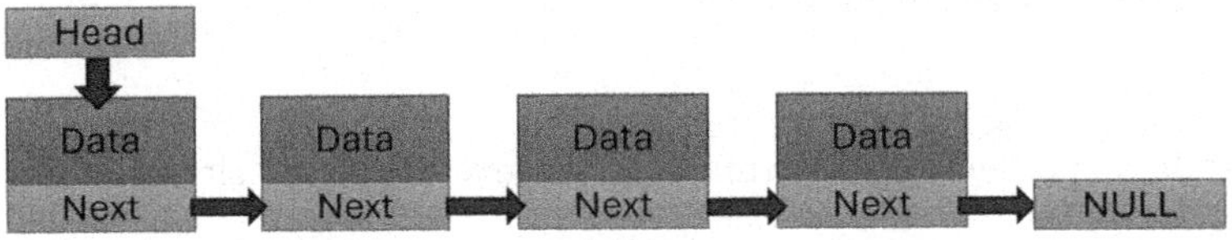

Figure 2.12 – Linked list uses the "Next" pointer to find the next element

A linked list can be initialized by creating a head element with a reference to the first element. Each subsequent element contains its data and a pointer to the next node. A simple linked list only has a pointer to the next element, and the last element's pointer is set to `NULL`.

There are also other variations of the linked list. A double-linked list features two pointers connecting the elements: one pointing to the next element, and another pointing to the previous element as shown in *Figure 2.13*. This allows fast traversal in either forward or backward order.

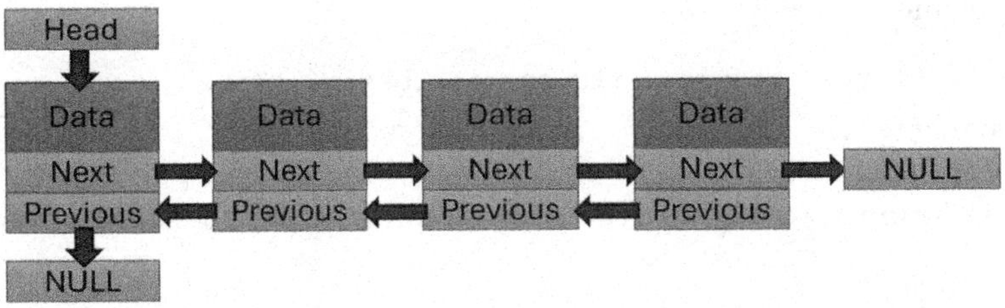

Figure 2.13 – Double linked list connect to both the previous and the next elements

In the standard C++ library, we can use the pre-defined `std::list` to implement our collection of enemies and props as a list. The `Demo2d` project shows how to implement enemies as a list instead of an array:

```
list<EnemyEntity> enemies;
```

Now that we store our enemy entities in a list, let's explore list operations.

Similar to vectors, common list operations include accessing individual data, inserting and deleting elements, and sorting.

Accessing a specific element

Since the only reference to an element in a linked list is the *Next* pointer from the previous element, random access to any element is not as straightforward as accessing an element in an array through an index.

The standard library uses an `iterator` to traverse elements in a linked list. While it does not inherently provide direct index-like access to a particular `N`-th element, you can use an `iterator` to reach the desired position by advancing it step by step:

```
int N = 4;
std::list<int> numbers = {10, 20, 30, 40, 50, 60, 70};
auto it = numbers.begin();
std::advance(it, N);     // Now *it contains value 50
```

As you can observe in this code, `std::list` doesn't have direct access to `Nth` elements like an array does.

Enumerating elements in the list

The elements in a linked list can be traversed by starting from the head element and following the references to the next element until the end of the list is reached. This is clearly an *O(n)* operation since the time it takes is directly related to the size of the list:

```
for (EnemyEntity& enemy : enemies)
  enemy.Update(ElapsedSeconds);
```

Inserting and deleting an element

Inserting and deleting elements in a linked list are generally fast operations. The process involves traversing to the desired position, which takes *O(n)*, and then the actual actions of insertion or deletion, which takes *O(1)*. This is because we only need to update the adjacent elements, without having to shift or move any other data following the inserted or removed element.

For instance, suppose we have a new `EnemyEntity` `em`. The following code snippet demonstrates how to access the data element inside the list:

```
enemies.push_front(em);  // push enemy at the beginning
enemies.push_back(em);  // add enemy at the end
auto it = enemies.begin();  // get an iterator at beginning
std::advance(it, 2); // Move iterator to the 3rd element
enemies.insert(it, em); // insert enemy as the 3rd element
enemies.erase(it);    // remove enemy
```

Sort

Sorting elements in a linked list is efficient because it only involves updating pointers, without needing to swap or move actual data. Since `std::list` is a doubly linked list, sorting is performed in *O(n log n)* time, which is still relatively fast:

```
Bool compare_hp(const EnemyEntity& first, const EnemyEntity & second) {
  return (first.HP > second.HP);
}
enemies.sort(compare_hp);  //sort enemies list by HP value
```

Compared to arrays, lists perform better in scenarios in which data elements need to be inserted and removed often.

The order matters – LIFO and FIFO

So far, both arrays and lists provide easy ways to traverse all elements. However, in some cases, we don't need to enumerate all elements or access them randomly; instead, we want to ensure that elements are processed in a specific order.

Two types of order are particularly important in game development: LIFO and FIFO.

- **Last In, First Out (LIFO)**: This principle is used in data structures where the last element added is the first one to be removed. It's analogous to a stack of plates: the last plate placed on top is the first one to be taken off.

- **First In, First Out (FIFO)**: This principle is used in data structures where the first element added is the first one to be removed. It's similar to a real-life queue, such as a line of people waiting to enter a concert hall.

While arrays and lists can be used for accessing data with specific order, there are other data structures specifically designed to work with specific access orders. Both stack and queue are most frequently used among these data structures.

Stack

A **stack** is a linear data structure that follows a specific order for operations: LIFO. Data can be added and retrieved from only one end of the stack. These operations are commonly referred to as **push** (for adding data) and **pop** (for retrieving data). *Figure 2.14* demonstrates how the stack works:

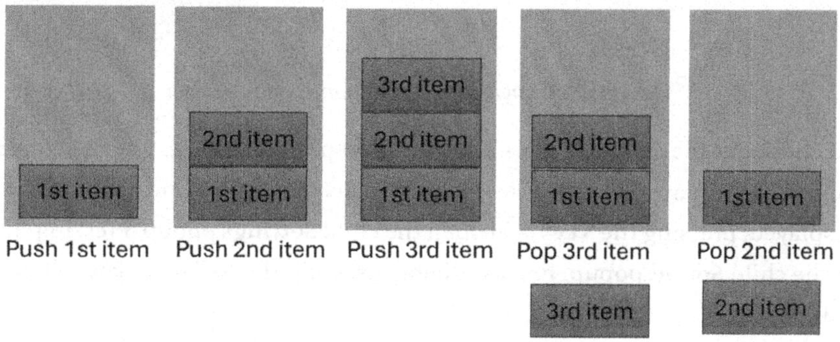

Figure 2.14 – Stack in action

A stack is typically implemented using an array or a linked list, and the standard C++ library provides an implementation through `std::stack`.

You've likely encountered stacks in action in almost every game you've played. Remember the in-game menu (which you can bring up during gameplay by pressing a hotkey to pause or change settings)? The user interface—especially those with popup dialog windows—is a perfect example of a stack in use.

For instance, imagine you want to access the settings to mute the game sound from the in-game menu. The UI navigation flow is a perfect fit for a stack: the first menu dialog opens the child settings dialog, and the **Settings** dialog opens the child **Sound** settings dialog. When you finish making changes and close the **Sound** settings dialog, it returns to the **Settings** dialog. Closing the **Settings** dialog then returns you to the **Main Menu** dialog. This behavior of common popup UIs can be implemented using a stack to keep track of which popup is currently active. *Figure 2.15* illustrates the UX flow:

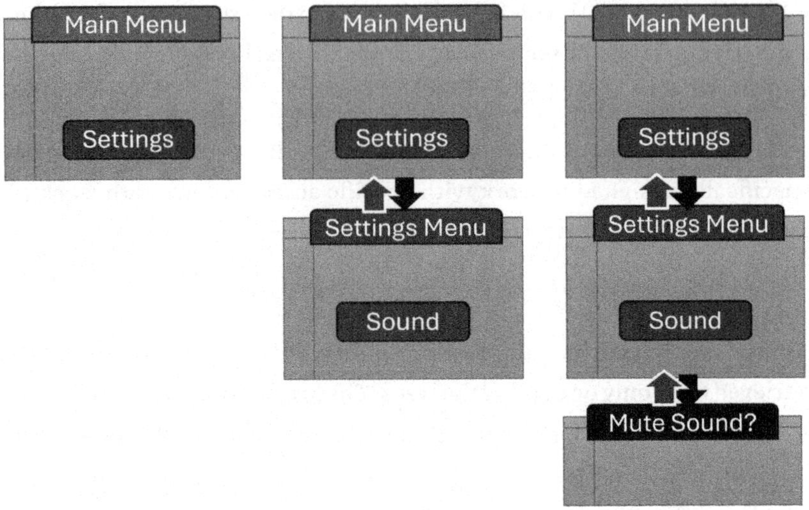

Figure 2.15 - Navigating the in-game menu system

It's time to check out the sample code – open and run project `Demo2e`. The in-game menu is by default hidden. If the player presses the *M* key, it opens the top-level in-game menu. Once this menu is displayed, pressing the *S* key will open the child **Settings** popup. Pressing the *V* key will then open the child **Sound** popup. In each dialog, pressing the *backspace* key will return you to the previous popup.

This code illustrates how to implement an in-game UI system like the one described previously using `std::stack`. In our demo project, the UI system behaves very similarly to the entities we've seen before: it consists of a collection of 2D graphic elements like window panels and buttons, along with the logic to handle user interactions. As a result, it bears a strong resemblance to the `Entity` class in the previous examples:

```
class UIPopupManager {  //...
    virtual void Create() = 0;
    virtual void Update(float interval);
    virtual void Draw();
    std::stack<UIPopup*> history;
};
```

We will continue to handle the creation of UI dialogs in the `Create()` function, manage the logic in the `Update()` function, and render the dialogs on the screen in the `Draw()` function:

```
void UIPopupManager::Draw() {
  if (history.size()) history.top()->Draw();
}
void UIPopupManager::Update(float interval) {
  if (history.size()) history.top()->Update(interval);
}
```

Only the topmost active `UIPopup` in the history stack will have its `Update()` and `Draw()` functions called. This means that when you open a child popup, the parent popup is effectively hidden. However, when you close the child popup, the parent popup is displayed again as it becomes the new topmost element in the stack.

We also define a class called `UIPopup` to represent all types of actual popup windows. This time, we use `std::stack` to store a `history` of which dialogs have been opened.

For each dialog popup window, even if they are different, they are still created, updated, and drawn in similar ways. So, we can define a parent class to represent the base version of all kinds of different UI popup windows:

```
class UIPopup {
public:
  virtual void Create(UIPopupManager *);
  virtual void Update(float interval) = 0;
  virtual void Draw() = 0;
protected:
  static UIPopupManager* ui_manager;
};
```

You might notice that we have a static member variable, `ui_manager`, to store the instance of `UIPopupManager`. This is because we need a convenient way to access the member functions of `UIPopupManager`, which creates these popup windows. Typically, a game has only one UI manager class to manage all UI-related behavior.

We will also need some UI-specific features other than the usual `Entity` class:

```
class UIPopupManager {
public: //...
  void Show(UIPopup *);
  void Show(const char *popupName);
  void Close();
  bool IsAnyPopupShown();
  virtual UIPopup* GetPopup(const char *name) = 0;
};
```

First, we want to be able to show or close any UI popup. We provide two implementations of the `Show()` function: one that takes a pointer to the `UIPopup` instance and another that retrieves it by its given name:

```
void UIPopupManager::Show(UIPopup* pp){
  history.push(pp);
}
void UIPopupManager::Show(const char* popupName) {
  UIPopup* uip = GetPopup(popupName);
  if (uip != NULL) Show(uip);
}
```

The `Show()` function basically just pushes the popup window into the `history` stack and makes it the top element inside the history stack. We will handle how to draw it in the inherited implementation of `UIPopupManager` class.

Since our implementation focuses on supporting popup window behavior, the `Close()` function always closes the most recently opened popup window by removing it from the `history` stack:

```
void UIPopupManager::Close(){
  if (history.size() > 0) history.pop();
}
```

We also have a handy function, `IsAnyPopupShown()`, which indicates whether a popup is currently being displayed on the screen:

```
bool UIPopupManager::IsAnyPopupShown() {
  return (history.size() > 0);
}
```

The `IsAnyPopupShown()` function simply checks whether there is a popup instance in the `history` stack.

Since `UIPopupManager` and `UIPopup` only define the basic behaviors of a popup window and its manager, we now need to create actual implementations that generate these popup dialogs and render them on the game screen. This is done in `Demo2eUI.cpp` and `Demo2eUI.h`:

```
void InGameDialogue::Draw() {
  Rectangle r;
  if (GuiWindowBox(CenterRectangle(r,800,600),"In Game Menu") == 1){
    mgr->Close();
    return;
  }
  if (GuiButton(CenterRectangle(r, 300, 60), "Settings"))
    mgr->Show(mgr->GetPopup("Settings"));
}
```

The preceding code uses `GuiWindowBox()` to draw a UI window panel and draw a **Settings** button with `GuiButton()` in the center of the window panel.

All three popup windows: `InGameDialogue`, `SettingsDialogue`, and `SoundDialogue` are implemented in a similar manner. Now, we can turn our attention to the UI manager class. We created a new class, `Demo2eUIManager`, which inherits from the base `UIPopupManager` class to implement our project-specific version of the popup UI manager.

The first thing is that we will have the above three popup windows in `Demo2eUIManager`:

```
class Demo2eUIManager : public UIPopupManager {
    InGameDialogue Menu;
    SettingsDialogue Settings;
    SoundDialogue Sound;
};
```

So, we can also provide our implementation of `GetPopup()` function to retrieve popup windows by their names:

```
UIPopup* Demo2eUIManager::GetPopup(const char* name){
  if (!_stricmp(name, "Menu")) return &Menu;
  else if (!_stricmp(name, "Settings")) return &Settings;
  else if (!_stricmp(name, "Volume"))return &Sound;
  return NULL;
}
```

Using a name to locate the object we want is a simple but not ideal approach; however, it will suffice for now.

Next, we need to render the topmost (currently active) popup window. This is where UI elements differ from the entities we've worked with before. In most video games, UI elements exist outside the *game world* and are always rendered on top of the game screen, after everything in the game world has been rendered:

```
void Demo2e::DrawGUI(){  Manager.Draw(); }
```

In the `Demo2e` project's `Update()` function, we will check whether the player has pressed the *M* key to open the first top-level menu, `InGameDialogue`. Once this menu is shown, its `Update()` method will be called every frame. If you press the *S* key, it will then open the `SettingsDialogue` child popup, and now, its `Update()` function is called every frame. If you press *V*, it will open the `SoundDialogue` child popup. In each dialog, if you hit the *backspace* key, it will return to the previous popup.

Common operations on the stack

Let's explore the following operations on the stack: accessing data and searching the entire stack, among others.

Accessing a specific element

Unlike an array or list, a stack has only one end access – pop data out from the top of the stack, and push data onto the top of the stack. This is a fast *O(1)* operation.

Enumerating elements in the stack

The elements in a stack can be retrieved by continuously popping the topmost element until the stack is empty. It's an *O(n)* operation, with respect to the depth of the stack.

Queue

A **queue** is a linear data structure that follows the FIFO principle. In a queue, data is entered from one end and retrieved from the other. An example of a queue is a line of consumers waiting for a resource, where the consumer who arrives first is served first. *Figure 2.16* demonstrates how a typical queue works:

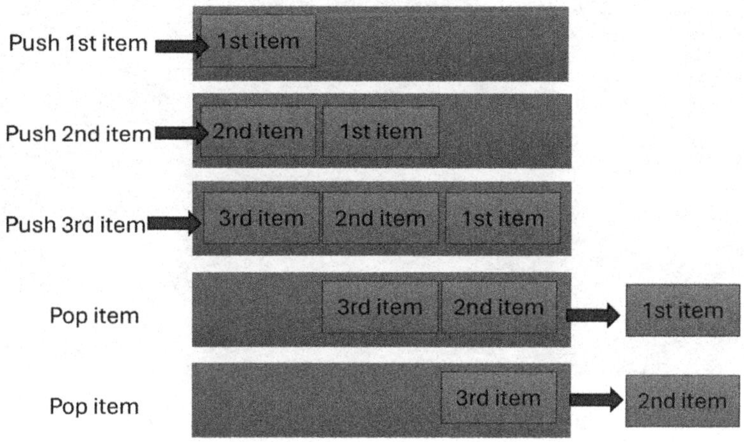

Figure 2.16 – Inserting and popping actions

In video games, player inputs (such as keystrokes or mouse clicks) and system events (such as collision detection or AI decisions) might be processed asynchronously. A queue can be used to store these events as they occur and process them in order during the game's update loop. This ensures all important events get processed according to the order they received.

The standard C++ library has a `std::queue` implementation.

The sample project

`Demo2f` uses a queue to implement an action-event system with the entities to simulate a one-on-one real-time battle system. This project is also the concluding sample project for this chapter. It uses more than one kind of data structure to implement a real playable real-time action game: a player character deathmatch with an enemy character. *Figure 2.17* shows how `Demo2f` looks like:

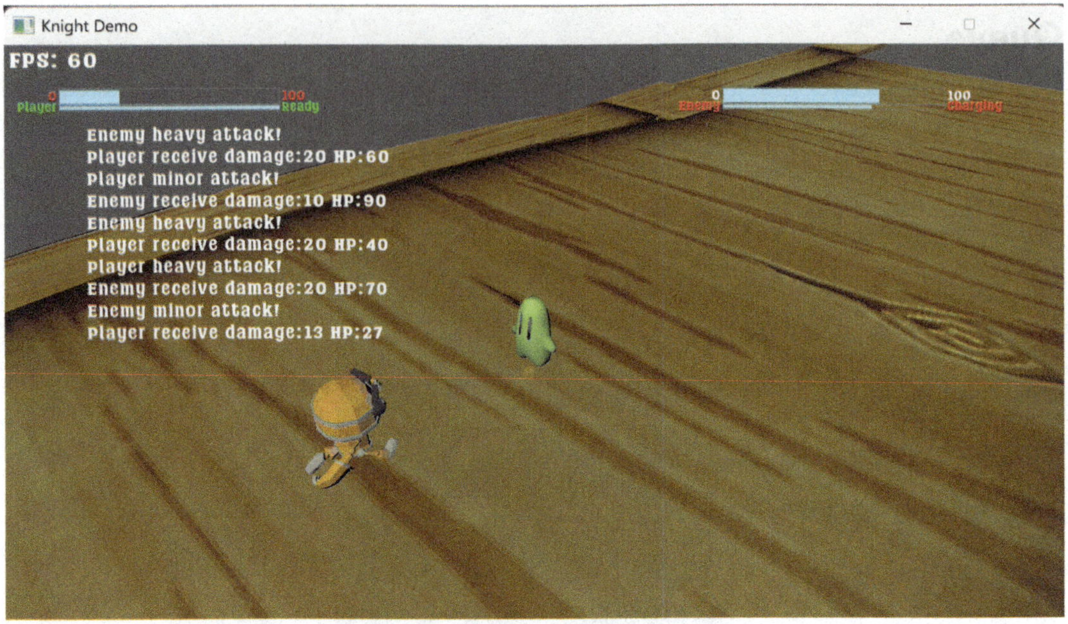

Figure 2.17 – Demonstrating a 1v1 battle session

The gameplay rules are simple: both the player and the enemy can attack each other in real time. However, there's a catch—after issuing an attack, there is a cooldown period (randomly between 1 to 3 seconds) before the next attack can be issued. Both the player and the enemy must wait for the cooldown to finish before launching another attack. Each attack deals 10 to 20 points of damage, so with an initial 100 HP, either side can be defeated in as few as five rounds of attacks.

Action event system implementation

Since attacks can occur at any time after cooling down, we will implement an event queue for both the player and enemy entities. Each entity will have an associated event queue to store action events, which will be processed during the entity's usual `Update()` function.

The event is defined as an `ActionEvent` class:

```
typedef enum {
    ApplyDamage = 1,
    LostLife
} ActionId;
struct ActionEvent{
```

```
    ActionId Id;
    int Value;
};
```

Each event contains a unique `Id` and a data value. You can extend the data carried by the event to accommodate future needs.

Since both the player and enemy require an event queue but `TerraEntity` does not, we will create a new class, `AliveEntity`, from which both `PlayerEntity` and `EnemyEntity` will inherit:

```
class AliveEntity : public Entity {
  int HP;
  queue<ActionEvent*> eventsQueue;
  AliveEntity* _target;
  void AddAction(ActionId id, int value);
};
```

In the preceding code, we move `HP` from the `Entity` class in the previous example to this one and define a new queue, `eventsQueue`, to hold a sequence of `ActionEvent` objects added to this entity. A new function, `AddAction`, is for the caller to add a new `ActionEvent` into this entity's `eventsQueue`. The queue is processed in the `Update()` function of this entity:

```
void AliveEntity::Update(float elapsedTime) {
  while (!eventsQueue.empty()) {
    ActionEvent* currentEvent = eventsQueue.front();
    eventsQueue.pop();
    switch (currentEvent->Id) {
      case ApplyDamage:
        DealDamage(currentEvent->Value); break;
      case LostLife:
        Die(); break;
    }
  }
  __super::Update(elapsedTime);
}
```

Next, let's move on to the aspects of handling damage and defeat.

Handling damage and defeat

When an ApplyDamage event is received, we call the entity's DealDamage() function to calculate the actual damage. If the damage causes the entity's HP to drop to zero, the entity will add a new LostLife event to its own queue and process it the next time Update() is called.

The following code snippet implements the DealDamage() function:

```
void AliveEntity::DealDamage(int originalValue){
    int dmgVal = originalValue;
    HP -= dmgVal;
    //...
    if (HP < 0)
        AddAction(ActionId::LostLife, 0);
}
```

You might wonder why we don't handle the entity's defeat immediately within the same Update() call, instead of sending an event to itself and processing it in the next Update().

True, there is virtually no difference in this demo if you choose to do so. However, in real video games, it's common practice to minimize the tasks performed in a single Update() call to prevent performance issues. Overloading an Update() function with too many tasks can delay rendering the next frame.

Defeating an entity in a real game typically involves much more than this simple project illustrates—it might include setting up new animations, triggering visual effects, playing sound effects, and more. Therefore, it's good practice to *do less* in a single Update() call and spread the workload across multiple updates.

The eventsQueue acts as a useful *to-do list*. Even if you don't process every ActionEvent in one Update() call, you can continue processing them in subsequent calls. If your event is processed in the next Update()—typically within 1/30 of a second, depending on your frame rate—it's perceived as occurring instantaneously by players.

Cooldown implementation

Now, let's explore another interesting feature: implementing the attack cooldown period. The Knight's Update() function includes an elapsedTime parameter, representing the time interval since the last call. We can use this feature to calculate the cooldown time. The first thing to do is to add the necessary variables:

```
class AliveEntity : public Entity { //...
    float attackCooldown;
```

```
    float rechargeTime;
};
```

Each time an attack is issued, the system randomly generates a cooldown time, assigns it to `attackCooldown`, and resets `rechargeTime` to zero. During each `Update()` call, we accumulate `rechargeTime` with the `elapsedTime` since the last `Update()` was called. Once `rechargeTime` is equal to or greater than `attackCooldown`:

- For `PlayerEntity`, we will check if the player presses the *space bar* to issue an attack.
- For `EnemyEntity`, the entity will automatically attack the player once the cooldown period is over.

The following code snippet implements the `Update()` function of the `PlayerEntity` and `EnemyEntity` classes:

```
void PlayerEntity::Update(float elapsedTime){
  if (rechargeTime >= attackCooldown) {
    if (IsKeyPressed(KEY_SPACE) && _target != NULL && _target->HP > 0)
      DoAttack();
  } else { //still in cool down period
    rechargeTime += elapsedTime;
  }
  __super::Update(elapsedTime);
}
void EnemyEntity::Update(float elapsedTime){
  //Still in gameplay?
  if (Demo2f::_gameOver == InProgress) {
    //Check if enemy can attack
    if (rechargeTime >= attackCooldown) {
      if (_target != NULL && _target->HP > 0) DoAttack();
    } else {
      rechargeTime += elapsedTime;
    }
  }
  __super::Update(elapsedTime); //process entity updates
}
```

If you try playing the demo, you'll find that it's very difficult to defeat the enemy. This is because our AI opponent is too perfect—it always attacks immediately after the cooldown period ends, with no delay. However, human players need time to think and react, so I'll leave it as an exercise for you to adjust the game balance.

The `EnemyEntity` class also needs to check whether the current gameplay status already reaches a victory or defeat in the `Update()` function. It will stop attacking the player if a victory is determined.

User interface and HUD updates

`Demo2f` also demonstrates how the entities update their user interface visuals. Both the player and the enemy have two progress bars: the *left bar* is for the player, and the *right bar* is for the enemy. The *top bar* represents HP, which decreases to zero when the entity is defeated. The *bottom bar* is the attack recharge bar, which resets to zero after each attack and fills up again so the entity can launch its next attack.

The `PlayerEntity` and `EnemyEntity` classes implement their own version of the `DrawGUI()` function and are invoked in the `DrawGUI()` function of the `Demo2f` game application class:

```
void Demo2f::DrawGUI(){
  player->DrawGUI();
  enemy->DrawGUI();
  switch (_gameOver) {
    case InProgress: {
      int line = 0;
        for (const auto& msg : messages) {
          DrawText(msg.c_str(), 150, 150 + 40 * line, 25, WHITE);
          ++line;
      }
      break;
    }
    //...
}
```

In this code, a new variable, `_gameOver`, is used to indicate that the game is still playing, or whether our player has won or lost.

Game over logic and debug output

The last point of interest in `Demo2f` is how we implement an in-game debug output. We use a list of strings to make a very simple version:

```
static std::list<std::string> messages;
```

The `Log()` function is declared as a static function in `Demo2f` so we can conveniently access it from anywhere in our code:

```
void Demo2f::Log(const std::string& message) {
  if (messages.size() >= 10)
    messages.pop_front();  // Remove the oldest message
  messages.push_back(message);  // Add the new message
}
```

The preceding code snippet ensures there is always only a maximum of the 10 latest messages in log data.

During a `DrawGUI()` call in the `Demo2f` class, we only keep and show the last 10 messages on the screen:

```
for (const auto& msg : messages) {
  DrawText(msg.c_str(), 150, 150 + 40 * line, 25, WHITE);
  ++line;
}
```

With these foundational techniques in place, you are now ready to explore algorithms commonly used in game development, which we'll explore in the next chapter.

Summary

In this chapter, we introduced four basic types of data structures—array, list, stack, and queue. With just these data structures, we can create a simple but playable game. We can always start with simple and straightforward solutions. Use basic data structures where possible. Even the basic data structures can handle many needs in game development.

Chapter 1 introduced the basic concepts of how the Knight works. In this chapter, we took a step further by utilizing the power of the Knight to create a playable game sample. In this simple game project, we've introduced how to use `Entity` and derived classes to encapsulate both gameplay logic and rendering the player and enemy. In the `PlayerEntity` class, we demonstrate how to handle user input, while in the `EnemyEntity` class, we need to handle combat logic and use `elapsedTime` in the `Update()` function for time-related features such as calculating attack cool-down.

We also leverage the UI functions provided by raylib to show health and timer bars, as well as a victory/defeat window. We also demonstrate how to use lists to handle console messages. The final example explained how minimal gameplay is achieved with multiple `Entity` classes.

In the next chapter, we will delve deeper into the algorithms that work with these data structures.

3

Algorithms Commonly Utilized in Game Development

Algorithms used in game development can range from simple to highly complex. However, effectively and seamlessly integrating these algorithms into real-world game projects can be challenging for developers. Some algorithms, while theoretically sound, may not be practical or feasible in certain situations. For example, the **quicksort** algorithm might not be the best choice for sorting a small dataset or one that is nearly sorted. Therefore, selecting and applying the right algorithms in actual game development is a crucial consideration for developers.

This chapter focuses on a selection of algorithms that are both widely adopted and frequently employed in game development. These algorithms are designed to address common challenges, enhance game performance, and improve code quality. By understanding these essential techniques, you'll be better equipped to tackle a variety of issues and optimize your projects. The topics covered in this chapter include:

- Exploring randomization
- Selection algorithms
- Shuffling for randomization
- Sorting algorithms
- Procedural generation
- Object pooling

Each section introduces one or more algorithms with illustrative examples. To cover more content while conserving space, we have not provided all the source code in the text. For a better understanding of the algorithms and their actual C++ implementations, please refer to the source code and comments provided in the demo projects (see the *Technical requirements* section). Engaging in your own exercises with the code will also be highly beneficial for reinforcing your learning.

Technical requirements

Download the `Knight` Visual Studio solution from GitHub. Here is the link to the repository:

`https://github.com/PacktPublishing/Data-Structures-and-Algorithms-for-Game-Programming-in-CPP`

The demo projects for this chapter are located within the `Knight` Visual Studio solution (`https://github.com/PacktPublishing/Data-Structures-and-Algorithms-for-Game-Programming-in-CPP/tree/main/Knight`), specifically under these project names:

Project Name	**Description**
`Demo3a`	Random and weighted-random selections
`Demo3b`	Exclusive random selection
`Demo3c`	Fisher-Yates shuffling cards
`Demo3d`	Sorting cards
`Demo3e`	Maze generation
`Demo3f`	Object pooling

Table 3.1 – Sample projects used in this chapter

These projects demonstrate the implementation of the concepts covered in this chapter and are integral to understanding the practical application of the discussed algorithms.

Exploring randomization

Randomization plays a crucial role in game development, significantly enhancing the player experience and ensuring the game's longevity. It is often used to create dynamic and replayable content, which keeps the game fresh and engaging each time it is played. By introducing elements of unpredictability, randomization enhances the challenge and excitement within a game, making it more thrilling and immersive. Additionally, it is used to simulate real-life systems and phenomena, adding a layer of realism and complexity that resonates with players. Overall, the effective use of randomization can transform a game, making it more enjoyable and captivating.

Generating a random number is the fundamental technique of randomization. Understanding how to generate a random number within a specific range is essential, as it forms the foundation for all other randomization algorithms in game development. This fundamental knowledge equips developers to effectively grasp and apply randomization techniques, enabling them to incorporate randomness into their games more effectively.

While essential, making your game both unpredictable and enjoyable for players is one of the biggest challenges in game development. In classic games like *Prince of Persia* (first released in 1989) and early "Space Arcade" games, such as *Space Invaders* (first released in 1978), the gameplay followed a pre-designed linear progression with a fixed storyboard. The number of enemies and their movements, paths, and speeds were all pre-planned and remained the same with each playthrough. This predictability allowed players to quickly learn the patterns, making it easier to beat the game, which often led to lower player retention.

A better approach would be to utilize randomized elements, such as the number of enemies, their movement speed, and their positions as they enter the scene. Introducing randomness in these aspects can help overcome predictability, enhancing the game experience and keeping players more engaged.

Let's begin by introducing the fundamental algorithm for generating a random number.

Understanding the algorithm

A common and easy-to-understand random number generation algorithm is the **Linear Congruential Generator** (**LCG**) method. It generates a sequence of pseudo-random numbers using the recurrence relation (an equation that finds the subsequent number dependent upon the previous number) based on the following formula:

$$R_{n+1} = (a * R_n + c)\ \%\ m$$

where:

- R_{n+1} is the generated random number.
- R_n is the previously generated random number.
- a, c, and m are constants.
- R_0 represents the initial number provided at the start.

The complexity of generating a random number is $O(1)$.

Implementing the code in C++

The following code snippet illustrates how to implement the Random class to help gain a deeper understanding of the process of generating random numbers. The first part defines variables that are used to generate random numbers:

```
#pragma once
#include <ctime>

class Random {
private:
  const unsigned long _a = 1664525;      //Multiplayer
  const unsigned long _c = 1013904223;  //Increment
  unsigned long long _m = 0xffffffff;
  unsigned long _seed;
public:
  Random(long Seed = -1) : _seed(Seed) {
    if (Seed < 0) {
      _seed = (unsigned long)std::time(0);
    }
    else {
      _seed = Seed;
    }
  }
```

The second part of the code implements a set of Next functions that generate long and int types of random numbers:

```
  /*Function: Next()
    Calculate the next random number within [0, m).
    Returns: The next random unsigned long number.
  */
  unsigned long Next() {
    _seed = (unsigned long)((_a * _seed + _c) % _m);
    return _seed;
  }
  /*Function: NextInt()
    Calculate the next random number within [Min, Max).
    Returns: The next random integer number.
```

```
    */
    unsigned int NextInt(unsigned int Min, unsigned int Max) {
      If(Min >= Max) {
        Return Min;
      }
      return Min + Next() % (Max - Min);
    }
```

The last part includes implementations of the overloaded functions that return float-type numbers:

```
    /*Function: NextFloat()
      Calculate the next random float-point number within [0.0f, 1.0f].
      Returns: The next random float-point number.
    */
    float NextFloat() {
      return static_cast<float>(Next()) / _m;
    }
    /*Function: NextFLoat()
      Calculate the next random float-point number within [Min, Max].
      Returns: The next random float-point number.
    */
    float NextFloat(float Min, float Max) {
      return Min + NextFloat() * (Max - Min);
    }
};
```

The key part of the above code snippet is the `Next()` function, which uses the value of `_Seed` and the formula to generate the next random number and store it back to `_Seed`.

The `Random` class contains three random number generation functions:

- `NextInt(Min, Max)` generates a random integer number within the specified range of `[Min, Max)`.
- `NextFloat()` generates a random float-point number within the range of `[0.0f, 1.0f]`.
- `NextFloat(Min, Max)` generates a random float-point number within the specified range of `[Min, Max]`.

> **Note**
>
> **Brackets, [or], are used to indicate an inclusive endpoint value.**
>
> **Parentheses, (or), are used to indicate an exclusive endpoint value.**

Now that you've learned how to generate random numbers, let's explore the first application of random number generation in the problem of selection.

Selection algorithms

Selection algorithms are used to optimize various in-game processes and enhance player experience. For instance, these algorithms can be applied to efficiently select the best moves or actions in strategy games, helping AI opponents to make decisions that simulate human-like behavior. In pathfinding and navigation, selection algorithms are also employed to determine the shortest or most efficient route for a character or object to follow. Additionally, they are used in procedural content generation, where elements such as terrain, dungeons, or loot are dynamically created, requiring efficient selection from a pool of possible configurations.

Three selection algorithms will be introduced in this section: simple random selection, weighted random selection, and the more advanced concept of reservoir sampling.

Random selection

Random selection enables the choice of one element from a list of candidates, adding unpredictability to the gameplay experience. One use case of random selection is spawning a character at a random location from several possible spawn points.

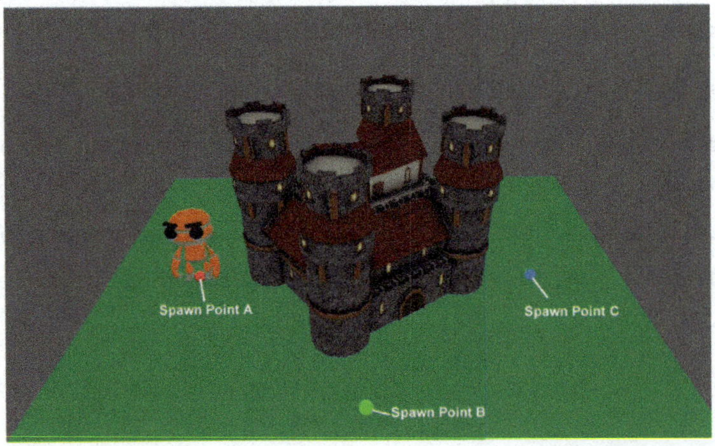

Figure 3.1 – Spawning the character at one of the spawn points with equal probabilities

The simple random selection algorithm selects a random element from an array by using a random index. Here's how it works:

1. **Generating a random index**: The algorithm uses a randomizer to generate a random integer within the range of valid indices, from `0` to the array's `size-1`. This random index represents the position of the element to be selected in the array.
2. **Returning the selected element**: The algorithm uses the random index to select and return the element from the array.

By using this approach, each element in the array has an equal probability of being selected, ensuring a fair and unbiased random choice.

The complexity of simple random selection is *O(1)*.

To implement random selection, we first create a class named `Selector`, which contains a private member, `_random`, of type `Random`, used for generating random numbers. The seed fed to the `_random` variable using the current time value increases the result of randomization:

```
class Selector
{
private:
  Random _random;
};
```

Additionally, we add a new `RandomSelect` member function to the `Selector` class that takes two parameters:

- `Options` — which is an array representing the available options for selection
- `ArraySize` — which indicates the length of the `Options` array

The `RandomSelect` function returns the selected item.

Here is the source code for the implementation of the `Selector` class and the simple `RandomSelect` function:

```
#pragma once
#include "Random.h"

class Selector
{
```

```
private:
  static Random _random;
public:
  /* Function: RandomSelect
    Parameters:
      Options: array which contains the optional items
      ArraySize: size of the Options array
    Returns the selected item.
  */
  template<typename T>
  static T RandomSelect(T Options[], int ArraySize)
  {
    int selectedIndex = _random.NextInt(0, ArraySize);
    return Options[selectedIndex];
  }
};

// create the random instance for generating random numbers
Random Selector::_random = (unsigned long)std::time(0);
```

The algorithm chooses an item from the options array with equal probability. However, in some situations, the options may need to have different weights, allowing certain options to have higher probabilities while others have lower probabilities. This need gives rise to the weighted random selection algorithm.

Weighted random selection

The **weighted random selection** algorithm selects an item from an array, where each item has a different probability (or weight) of being chosen. This allows some items to be more likely to be selected than others.

Let's introduce an additional condition for the spawn point selection example: **Spawn Point A** should have a **50%** probability of being selected, while **Spawn Point B** and **C** each have a **25%** chance of being chosen.

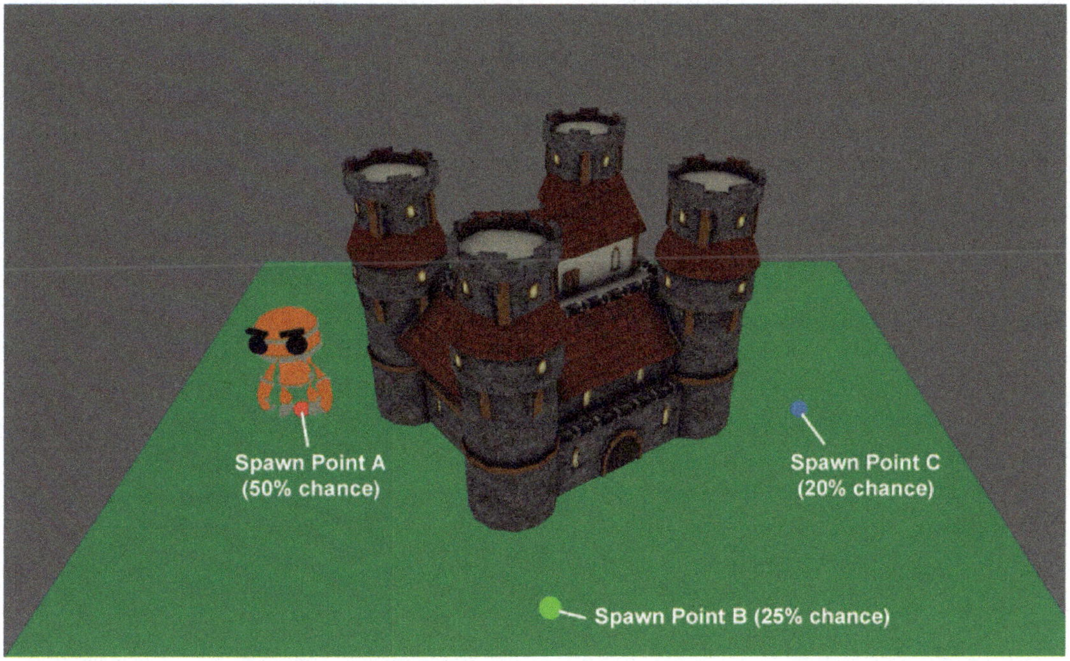

Figure 3.2 – Spawning the character at one of the spawn points with weighted probabilities

Here's how the weighted random selection algorithm works:

1. **Assigning weights to array items**: Each item in the list is assigned a weight, which represents its likelihood of being selected. Weights with higher values indicate a greater probability.
2. **Calculating the total weight**: The algorithm calculates the sum of all the weights. This total weight represents the probability range for selection.
3. **Generating a random number**: A random number is generated between 0 and the total weight. This number determines where within the probability range the selection will fall.
4. **Selecting the item**: The algorithm iterates through the list of items, accumulating their weights. When the cumulative weight exceeds or matches the randomly generated number, the corresponding item is selected.

The complexity of weighted random selection is $O(n)$.

The new `WeightedRandomSelect` function is introduced as a member function of the `Selector` class. The function takes three parameters:

- `Options`, which is an array representing the available options for selection
- `Weights`, which is an array representing the probabilities for each option
- `ArraySize`, which indicates the length of both `Options` and `Weights`

The `WeightedRandomSelect` function returns the selected item.

Here is the code implementation of the `WeightedRandomSelect` method in the `Selector` class:

```
#pragma once
#include "Random.h"
class Selector
{
private:
  static Random _random;
public:
  /* Function: WeightedRandomSelect
    Parameters:
      Options: array which contains the optional items
      Weights: array which contains weights for each item
      ArraySize: size of the Options array
    Returns the selected item.
  */
  template<typename T>
  static T WeightedRandomSelect(T Options[], float Weights[], int
ArraySize)
  {
    int i;
    float totalWeight = 0.0f;
    for (i = 0; i < ArraySize; ++i)
    {
      totalWeight += Weights[i];
    }
    float randomValue = _random.NextFloat() * totalWeight;
    for (i = 0; i < ArraySize - 1; ++i)
    {
      if (randomValue < Weights[i])
```

```
        {
          break;
        }
        randomValue -= Weights[i];
      }
      return Options[i];
    }
};
// create the random instance for generating random numbers
Random Selector::_random = (unsigned long)std::time(0);
```

Following the introduction of the random and selector algorithms, we will demonstrate their application using a real example project, `Demo3a`.

Demo3a: Random and weighted-random selections in action

Open and examine the source code of `Demo3a.cpp`. You will see how the `Random` and `Selector` classes are utilized and how the `WeightedRandomSelect` function randomly spawns the character at a selected spawn point (see *Figure 3.2*).

`Demo3a` uses the `SpawnPoints` array to store the potential candidates for spawn points A, B, and C. It then stores the selection probabilities for these three points in the `SpawnProbabilities` array, assigning a 50% chance for spawn point A to be selected, while spawn point B and spawn point C each have a 25% probability of being chosen:

```
Vector3 SpawnPoints[3] = {
  {0, 0, 30}, {30, 0, 0}, {0, 0, -30}
};
float SpawnProbabilities[3] = { 0.5f, 0.25f, 0.25f };
```

To determine the spawn point for the character, the `Selector::WeightedRandomSelect` function is called. This function returns a chosen spawn point position, which is then used to update the character's position:

```
Character->Position =
  Selector::WeightedRandomSelect<Vector3>(
      SpawnPoints, SpawnProbabilities, 3);
```

The Update function checks if the player has clicked the mouse's left button. If a click is detected, it selects a new spawn point and relocates the character accordingly:

```
void Demo3a::Update(float ElapsedSeconds)
{
  if (IsMouseButtonPressed(MOUSE_BUTTON_LEFT))
  {
Character->Position =
      Selector::WeightedRandomSelect<Vector3>(
        SpawnPoints, SpawnProbabilities, 3);
  }
  __super::Update(ElapsedSeconds);
}
```

We have already introduced the simple random selection and weighted random selection algorithms. These two algorithms are versatile and can satisfy most requirements and use cases in game development. However, both of them use a selection method with replacement, which means there is a possibility of selecting the same option multiple times.

For instance, if we need to spawn two characters, there is a chance that both could appear at the same location, causing them to overlap. This scenario highlights the need for a selection method without replacement, where once an option is chosen, it should not be available for the next selection.

Exclusive selection is the solution designed to solve this kind of problem.

Exclusive selection

Exclusive selection is an algorithm that chooses items from a collection where each selected item is removed from the pool of available options and won't be selected again for subsequent selections.

Use cases for exclusive selection in game development include choosing distinct spawn points for multiple game actors, assigning unique roles to players, and generating unique rewards from a loot table.

The exclusive selection algorithm includes four steps:

1. Randomly select one item from the collection:
   - If the collection size is n, the selected item's index is i, where $0 \leq i < n$.

2. Remove the selected item from the collection:
    - Swapping the selected item with the last item in the list, and then reducing the size of the list by one. This operation ensures the removal is done in *O(1)* time.
    - Alternatively, you can use a data structure, a linked list, for example, that supports efficient removals.
3. Select the second item from the modified collection (which now has the size `n-1`).

Repeat *steps 2* and *3* until the desired number of items has been selected.

The complexity of the weighted random selection algorithm is *O(n)*.

We introduce a new member function, `ExclusiveSelect`, to the `Selector` class. This function accepts four parameters:

- `Options`, which is an array representing the available options for selection.
- `ArraySize`, which indicates the length of both `Options`.
- `Selected`, which outputs an array. The selected items will be stored in this array once the selection operation is done.
- `SelectedCount`, which specifies the number of items the function should select. It also determines the length of the `Selected` array, which contains the selected items for output.

The `ExclusiveSelect` function returns true if it completes successfully; otherwise, it returns false.

The following code snippet, used in `Demo3b`, presents the C++ implementation of the `ExclusiveSelect` function in the `Selector` class:

```
#pragma once
#include "Random.h"

class Selector
{
  …
public:
  …
  /* Function: ExclusiveRandomSelect
     Parameters:
       Options: array which contains the optional items
       ArraySize: size of the Options array
       Selected: array which contains the selected items
```

```
        SelectedCount: size of the Selected array
      Returns true if succeeded or false if failed.
    */
    template<typename T>
    static bool ExclusiveSelect(T Options[], int ArraySize, T Selected[],
  int SelectedCount)
    {
      if (ArraySize <= 0 || SelectedCount > ArraySize)
      {
        return false;
  }
  //Clone the Options into a buffer
      T *optionsBuffer = new T[ArraySize];
      int size = sizeof(T) * ArraySize;
      memcpy_s(optionsBuffer, size, Options, size);
      //Loop to select the needed number of items
      for (int i = 0; i < SelectedCount; ++i)
      {
        int index = _random.NextInt(0, ArraySize);
        //Swap the selected item and the last item
  T temp = optionsBuffer[index];
        optionsBuffer[index] = optionsBuffer[ArraySize - 1];
        optionsBuffer[ArraySize - 1] = temp;
        Selected[i] = temp;
        //Decrement the array size
        ArraySize--;
      }
      //Free memory of the buffer
      delete[] optionsBuffer;
      return true;
    }
  };
```

Let's look at the next demo project, Demo3b, which uses the new ExclusiveSelect function to randomly select two spawn points out of three to spawn two characters.

Demo3b: Exclusive random selection

`Demo3b` illustrates how the `ExclusiveRandomSelect` function is used to place two characters at two distinct spawn points without overlapping. In other words, the `ExclusiveRandomSelect` function ensures that the characters do not spawn at the same location.

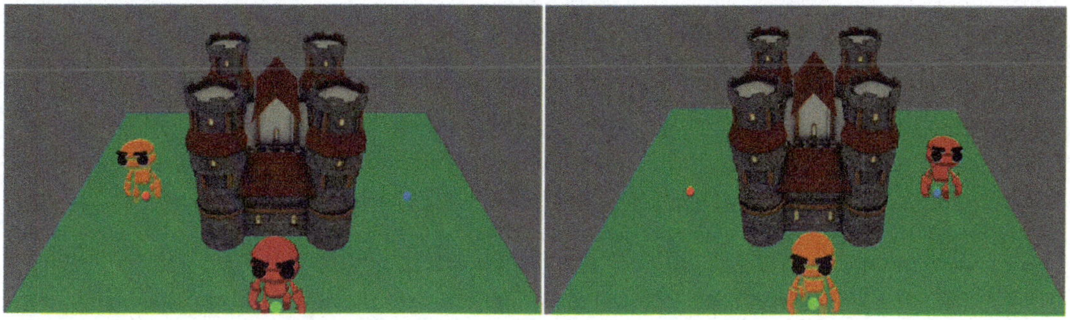

Figure 3.3 – Spawning two characters with the ExclusiveRandomSelect function

At the core of `Demo3b` is the `PlaceCharacter` function, which calls the static member function `ExclusiveRandomSelection` of the `Selector` class. Once the spawn point positions are successfully filled in the `SelectedPositions` array, they are assigned to the characters' `Position` field to relocate them.

Open the `Demo3b.cs` source code file and take a close look at the function's implementation in detail:

```
void Demo3b::PlaceCharacters()
{
  Vector3 selectedPositions[2];
  //Select two out of the three spawn points
  if(Selector::ExclusiveRandomSelect(SpawnPoints, 3, selectedPositions,
2))
  {
    //Relocate the two characters at positions of the two selected spawn
points
    Character1->Position = selectedPositions[0];
    Character2->Position = selectedPositions[1];
  }
}
```

By mastering the previously introduced randomization-related algorithms, you will be able to apply dynamic gameplay development skills and enhance your game's entertainment value for players. Let's now move on to the next exciting topic, shuffling, which still needs to utilize the function of random number generation.

Shuffling for randomization

Shuffling is the process of rearranging elements in a collection, an array, for example, in a random order. It must ensure that each possible ordering of the elements is equally likely. In game development, shuffling is often used to introduce unpredictability and variety, enhancing the gameplay experience. Here are a couple of use cases:

- **Card games**: In card games like Poker and Blackjack, shuffling is essential to randomize the order of cards in a deck. It ensures fairness and unpredictability, providing a new experience in each game session.
- **Randomized loot or item drops**: Many games, especially RPGs and action-adventure games, use shuffling to randomize loot or item drops. When a player defeats an enemy or opens a treasure chest, the game might shuffle a list of possible rewards to determine which item the player receives.
- **Randomized level design**: In procedurally generated games, such as *Hades* (2019), *Spelunky* (2008), or *Enter the Gungeon* (2016), shuffling is often used to randomize the order or placement of rooms, enemies, and obstacles within levels. The game may have a set of pre-designed rooms or sections that are shuffled to create a unique layout each time a player starts a new game or enters a new level.

We are going to introduce a simple shuffling algorithm, the **Fisher-Yates shuffle**, which can randomly and efficiently shuffle items of an array. The algorithm includes three main steps:

1. **Initializing**: Start with an array of `n` elements.
2. **Shuffling**:
    1. Iterate through the list from the last element to the first.
    2. For each item `i`, generate a random index `j` such that `0 ≤ j ≤ i`.
    3. Swap the items at indices `i` and `j`.
3. Output the first `k` items.

The complexity of the Fisher-Yates shuffle algorithm is *O(n)*.

We create a new class, `Shuffler`, which includes a static member function called `FisherYateShuffle`. This function takes four parameters:

- `Items`, which is an array representing the collection of items.
- `Size`, which indicates the length of the `Items` array.
- `SelectedItems`, which is an output array. The picked items will be filled in this array after shuffling.
- `SelectedSize`, which specifies the number of items the function should pick. It also determines the length of the Selected array, which contains the picked items for output.

The `FisherYateShuffle` function returns `true` if it completes successfully; otherwise, it returns `false`.

The following code snippet shows the C++ implementation of the `Shuffler` class and its member function `FisherYateShuffle`:

```
#pragma once
#include "Random.h"
class Shuffler
{
private:
  static Random _random;
public:
  /* Function: FisherYateShuffle
     Parameters:
     Items: array which contains the items to be shuffled
     ArraySize: size of the items array
     PickedItems: array which stores the picked items when completion
     PickedSize: size of the pickedItems array
     Returns: true-succeeded, false-failed
  */
  template<typename T>
  static bool FisherYateShuffle(T Items[], int Size, T PickedItems[], int
PickedSize)
```

```
    {
      if (Size <= 0 || PickedSize > Size)
      {
        return false;
      }
      //Shuffle the items
      for (int i = Size - 1; i >= 0; --i)
      {
        int j = _random.NextInt(0, i);
        T temp = Items[j];
        Items[j] = Items[i];
        Items[i] = temp;
      }
      //Fill up the output array with the selected number of items
      for (int k = 0; k < PickedSize; ++k)
      {
        PickedItems[k] = Items[k];
      }
      return true;
    }
  };
  // create the random instance for generating random numbers
  Random Shuffler::_random = (unsigned long)std::time(nullptr);
```

Now that we've introduced the Fisher-Yates shuffling algorithm and its implementation, let's see it in action. In the next section, we'll explore the `Demo3c` project, which applies this algorithm to shuffle cards efficiently.

Demo3c: Fisher-Yates shuffling

`Demo3c` illustrates the use of the Fisher-Yates shuffle algorithm to randomize a deck of poker cards and display the top 13 cards on the screen (see *Figure 3.4*). Clicking the *left mouse button* will reshuffle the deck.

Figure 3.4 – Shuffling a deck of cards and displaying the first 13 cards

To get `Demo3c` working, first, make `Demo3c` a subclass of `Knight`. Add the `Shuffle` member function to the `Demo3c` class, and override the `Start`, `Update`, `DrawGUI`, and `EndGame` functions. The code can be found in `Demo3c.h` here:

```
#pragma once
#include "Knight.h"
class Demo3c : public Knight
{
public:
    void Start() override;
protected:
    void Update(float ElapsedSeconds) override;
    void DrawGUI() override;
    void EndGame() override;
private:
    void Shuffle();
};
```

We override the `DrawGUI` function because this demo renders 2D images without using a 3D camera, making `DrawGUI` ideal for handling the drawing task.

Before we delve deeper into the code implementation in `Demo3c.cpp`, we need to define three arrays to store card information:

- `CardIDs`: Stores numbers from 0 to 51, representing the 52 cards
- `CardImages`: Holds the 52 loaded card images
- `PickedCardIDs`: Will contain the 13 picked cards' IDs after shuffling the deck

Here's the code:

```
#define IMAGE_FILENAME_BUFFER_SIZE 64
#define DECK_CARD_COUNT 52
#define PICK_CARDS_COUNT 13
int CardIDs[DECK_CARD_COUNT];
Texture2D CardImages[DECK_CARD_COUNT];
int PickedCardIDs[PICK_CARDS_COUNT];
```

In the `Start` function, the primary task is to initialize the card IDs and load the card images. The `CardIDs` array is initialized with sequential numbers representing card indices, which will later be shuffled. The card images are then loaded into the `CardImages` array in the correct order. The `LoadTexture` function loads card images from the provided path:

```
//Initialize card IDs and Load card images
for (int i = 0; i < DECK_CARD_COUNT; ++i)
{
  //Initialize the card ID
  CardIDs[i] = i;
  if (i < PICK_CARDS_COUNT)
  {
    PickedCardIDs[i] = i;
  }
  //Load card image
  sprintf_s(imageFile, IMAGE_FILENAME_BUFFER_SIZE, "../../resources/
textures/PokerDeckCards/%d.png", i);
  if (FileExists(imageFile))
  {
    CardImages[i] = LoadTexture(imageFile);
  }
}
```

At the end of the game, be sure to unload the card images. This can be done using the `UnloadTexture` function:

```
void Demo3c::EndGame()
{
  for (int i = 0; i < DECK_CARD_COUNT; ++i)
  {
    UnloadTexture(CardImages[i]);
  }
  __super::EndGame();
}
```

The `Shuffle` function consists of a single line of code that calls the `Shuffler` class's member function, `FisherYateShuffle`, to shuffle the `CardIDs` array and output the picked card IDs:

```
void Demo3c::Shuffle()
{
  Shuffler::FisherYateShuffle(CardIDs, DECK_CARD_COUNT,
      PickedCardIDs, PICK_CARDS_COUNT);
}
```

In the `DrawGUI` function, use a loop to call `DrawTexture` and display the picked cards on the screen:

```
int x = 15;
for (int i = 0; i < PICK_CARDS_COUNT; ++i)
{
  DrawTexture(CardImages[PickedCardIDs[i]], x, 180, WHITE);
  x += 120;
}
```

For full details of the source code, please refer to `Demo3c.cpp` in the GitHub repository.

With the shuffling process complete, the deck is now randomized and ready for use. Let's use a sorting method to arrange the cards in hand.

Sorting algorithms

In game development, **sorting algorithms** play a crucial role in optimizing performance and enhancing gameplay, whether managing lists of game objects, prioritizing tasks, or organizing level data. Efficient sorting is the basic required optimization, which helps streamline efficient and responsive responses, such as smoother game experiences, faster loading times, and more effective data handling operations.

A well-sorted collection of data significantly enhances efficiency by enabling rapid data retrieval. It contributes to user-friendly list views, allowing for easy navigation and management of information. Additionally, sorting helps in prioritizing tasks effectively, ensuring that critical operations are handled promptly and improving overall system performance and user experience.

Several major sorting algorithms are commonly used in game development to efficiently manage and organize data:

- **QuickSort** is favored for its speed and efficiency in handling large datasets. It is not suitable for almost sorted datasets. The algorithm's average complexity is $O(nlogn)$.
- **MergeSort** is known for its stability and predictable performance. The algorithm's average complexity is $O(nlogn)$.
- **HeapSort** is useful for scenarios where a priority queue is needed. The algorithm's average complexity is $O(nlogn)$.
- **InsertionSort** and **BubbleSort**, while less efficient for large datasets, can be handy for small or nearly sorted lists. The algorithm's average complexity is $O(n^2)$.

Sorting algorithms are widely covered in many courses and learning materials on data structures and algorithms, so we won't explain them in detail here. However, we still mention them in this book because they are essential and frequently used in game development.

The C and C++ **Standard Libraries (STLs)** provide built-in **Quicksort** functions that are ready for use, though they differ slightly in naming. In the C STL, the function is called `std::qsort`, while in the C++ STL, it is `std::sort`.

Demo3d: Sorting cards

Building on `Demo3c`, in `Demo3d`, we use the C STL function `std::qsort` to arrange the cards that were dealt in hand. It is easier for players to view their hands in an organized manner.

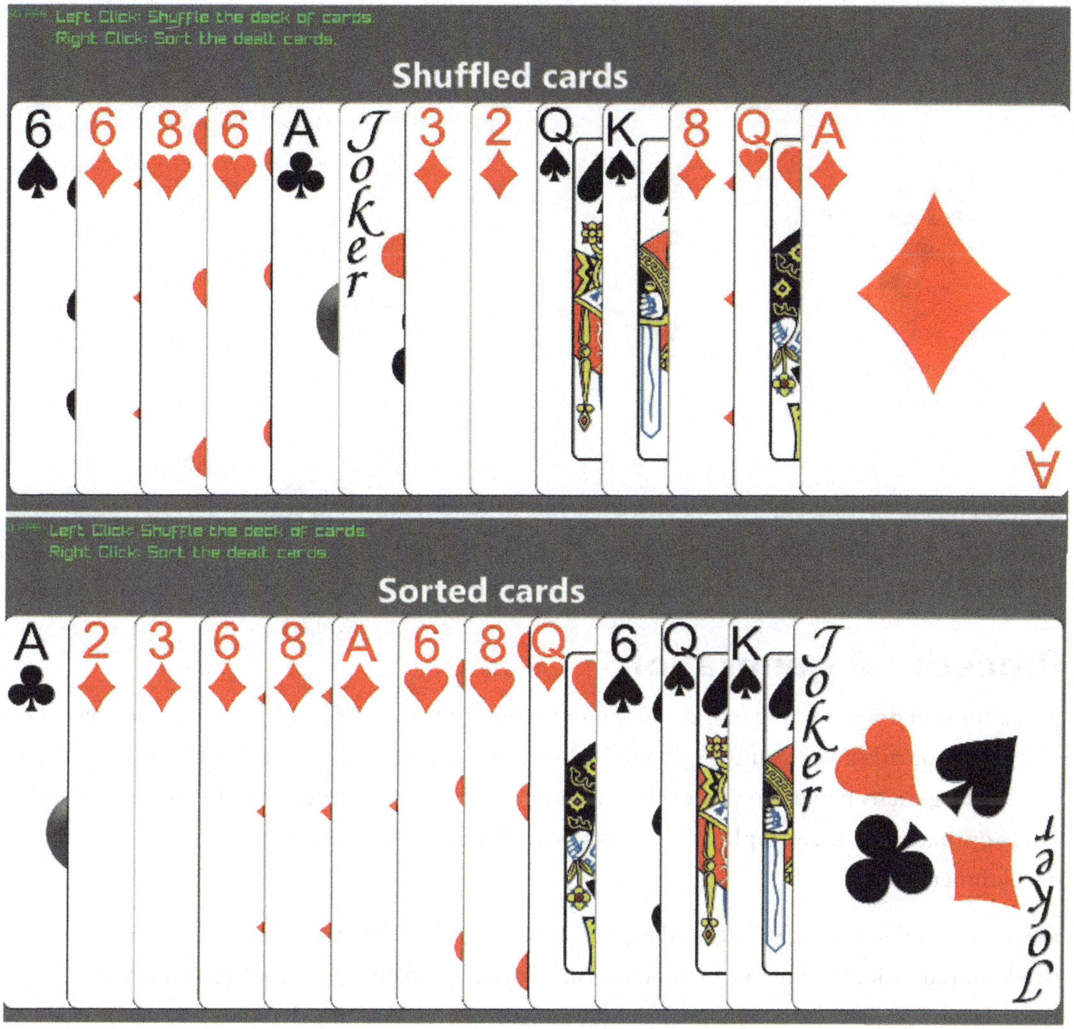

Figure 3.5 – Sorting to organize shuffled cards

The difference between `Demo3d` and `Demo3c` is the addition of the `SortDealtCards` function in the `Demo3d` class, which organizes the cards in hand:

```
void Demo3d::SortDealtCards()
{
  std::qsort(PickedCardIDs, PICK_CARDS_COUNT, sizeof(int), [](const void*
x, const void* y)
  {
    int arg1 = *static_cast<const int*>(x);
```

```
        int arg2 = *static_cast<const int*>(y);
        if (arg1 < arg2)
        {
          return -1;
        }
        if (arg1 > arg2)
        {
          return 1;
        }
        return 0;
      });
  }
```

After exploring sorting algorithms and their role in organizing data efficiently, let's move on to the next key concept: procedural generation. By leveraging procedural generation techniques, we can create dynamic game elements, enhancing the variety and complexity of the experience.

Procedural generation

Procedural generation in game development refers to the creation of game content based on algorithms or rules. For example, dynamically generating a game level in real time, rather than pre-crafting each element in the level, can bring variation and unpredictability to the gameplay. This approach enhances replayability and provides endless possibilities, as well as reducing development time.

Procedural generation may be based on a wide range of algorithms and rules tailored to specific needs and situations. Different methods are employed based on the desired outcome, whether it's creating randomized levels, generating unique characters, or building dynamic environments. The choice of algorithm can vary depending on factors like complexity, performance, or aesthetic goals.

In this section, we introduce the random acyclic maze generator algorithm as an example of procedural generation. It generates mazes through randomization, ensuring the generated maze is acyclic without loops while maintaining the connectivity and complexity of the maze.

The random acyclic maze generator algorithm accepts four parameters: the maze dimensions (rows and columns), along with the entry and exit points. It then uses the following steps to generate an acyclic maze:

1. Initialize the maze by blocking all grid cells with wall objects.
2. Set the entry and exit point cells based on the specified row and column numbers.

3. Starting from the entry point, use the **Depth-First Search** (**DFS**) method to find the next waypoint cell, marking it as visited (`FlagEmpty`).

> **Depth-first search**
>
> **DFS** is an algorithm that explores a graph by systematically visiting each vertex and its adjacent vertices, diving as deep as possible before backtracking. DSF is beyond the scope of this book. If you're not familiar with DFS, please consult online resources or other references for more information.
>
> Visit `https://www.geeksforgeeks.org/depth-first-search-or-dfs-for-a-graph/` for more information.

4. Recursively call the `DFS` function to locate the next waypoint based on the current visited cell. If a dead end is reached, backtrack to the previous cell.
5. Repeat *step 4* until the maze is fully generated, then return the completed maze.

The complexity of the random acyclic maze generator algorithm is `O(n * m)`, where `n` represents the number of rows and `m` represents the number of columns of the maze.

We develop a new class, `MazeGenerator`, which utilizes the DFS algorithm internally to help find a path from the entry cell to the exit cell, ensuring that there are no circular paths.

The definition of the `MazeGenerator` class can be found in the `Demo3e` project, which mainly provides two overloaded functions that can be called to generate the maze:

- `void GenerateMaze(int Entry[2], int Exit[2])`
- `void GenerateMaze()`

The former takes two parameters to generate the maze with the specified entry and exit points, while the latter uses the currently saved default entry and exit points to create a new maze.

The maze data is stored in a 2D array matrix that uses flags to indicate whether a cell is empty or blocked, as well as to mark the entry and exit points. When generating a new maze, the `Generate` function initializes all cells with the `FlagWall` flag at the start:

```
int** _maze;
...
//Initialize the maze with wall blocks
for (int row = 0; row < _rows; ++row)
{
```

```
    for (int col = 0; col < _cols; ++col)
    {
      _maze[row][col] = FlagWall;
    }
  }
```

Next, the cells for the entry and exit points are marked with the `FlagEntry` and `FlagExit` flags:

```
//Set maze entry and exit flags
_maze[_entry[1]][_entry[0]] = FlagEntry;
_maze[_exit[1]][_exit[0]] = FlagExit;
```

The `DFS` function is called to perform the recursive search for generating the maze:

```
//Find the path that starts at the entry point and leads to the exit.
DFS(_entry[0], _entry[1]);
```

The key to the maze generation process lies in the `DFS` function. This function first shuffles the four movement directions in the `directions` array, then iterates through these directions to examine the adjacent cells around the current cell. If a neighboring cell has already been visited or is out of bounds, it is ignored; otherwise, the neighboring cell is marked with the `FlagEmpty` flag.

For the newly marked neighbor cell, the `DFS` function is called recursively to find the next cell that could be used to continue the path:

```
/* Function: DFS
 *  Use Deep First Search method to visit the next cell
  *  Parameters:
  *     Rows: Count of rows of the maze
  *     Columns: Count of columns of the maze
  */
  void DFS(int row, int col)
  {
    int directions[] = { UP, DOWN, RIGHT, LEFT };
    Shuffler::FisherYateShuffle(directions, 4);
    for (int dir = 0; dir < 4; ++dir)
    {
      int direction = directions[dir];
      int newRow = row + 2 * dirRow[direction];
      int newCol = col + 2 * dirCol[direction];
      //Check if the new cell is valid
```

```
        if (newRow >= 0 && newRow < _rows &&
          newCol >= 0 && newCol < _cols &&
          _maze[newRow][newCol] == FlagWall)
          {
            //Cave the path by setting the cells connecting the two cells to
be empty
            _maze[row + dirRow[direction]][col + dirCol[direction]] =
FlagEmpty;
            _maze[newRow][newCol] = FlagEmpty;
            //Recursively find the next way point on the path to the exit
point
          DFS(newRow, newCol);
      }
    }
}
```

For a better understanding of the algorithm and its application in real maze generation scenarios, please examine the source code in the `Demo3e` project.

Demo3e: Maze generation

To demonstrate the use of the newly created `MazeGenerator` class in a real visual game, `Demo3D` generates mazes randomly and visualizes the results.

Figure 3.6 – A maze generated by the random acyclic maze generator algorithm

The Demo3e class instantiates the MazeGenerator when the Start function is called and destroys it in the EndGame function. You can then call the GenerateMaze function to create the maze:

```
void Demo3e::Start()
{
  ...
  _mazeGenerator = new MazeGenerator(MAZE_ROWS, MAZE_COLS);
  _mazeGenerator->GenerateMaze();
}
void Demo3d::EndGame()
{
  if (_mazeGenerator != nullptr)
  {
    delete _mazeGenerator;
    _mazeGenerator = nullptr;
  }
__super::EndGame();
```

Next, you can call the GetMaze method of the MazeGenerator class to retrieve the maze's data matrix. The Demo3e class uses this method before rendering the scene:

```
void Demo3e::DrawFrame()
{
  int** maze = _mazeGenerator->GetMaze();
  ...
}
```

The best way we suggest to gain a deeper understanding of the algorithm is by exploring the source code of the Demo3e project.

Having covered procedural maze generation, we will now turn to another essential optimization technique in game development: object pooling. In the next section, we'll dive into the pooling method and its benefits in game development.

Object pooling

The strategy of **object pooling** is to reuse objects rather than frequently creating and destroying them. Pooling helps reduce memory overhead and improve performance, especially in resource-intensive games.

In games, it's common to dynamically spawn and destroy objects. This is especially important when shooting bullets. Each time a bullet is fired, an object is created. When the bullet hits something or its lifespan ends, the object is destroyed. Over the course of a gameplay session, players may fire thousands of bullets, leading to thousands of memory allocations and deallocations. This can result in performance issues, memory fragmentation, overflow, and potentially even bugs.

Object pooling is an effective solution to avoid the issues mentioned above. An object pool contains a predefined number of pre-created bullets, each with an `IsActive` flag indicating whether the bullet is available or in use. When a new bullet needs to be spawned, the pool's `GetObject` function can be called to locate an inactive bullet in the pool, set its `IsActive` flag to `true`, and return the bullet object to simulate the spawning process. When the bullet's lifespan ends, it is returned to the pool, and the bullet's `IsActive` flag is reset to `false`.

Let's explore the pooling algorithm in detail to understand how game objects are managed inside the pool.

Outlining the pooling algorithm

The core of the `ObjectPool` class is the pool itself. To define the pool, we need three key elements:

- A base class, `PoolableObject`, which serves as a base for actual objects, such as `Bullet`.
- A template class, `ObjectPool`, which manages and contains the pool of objects.
- The `_pool` itself, represented as a pointer to allocated memory that holds a list of `PoolableObject` instances.

The `ObjectPool` class does the following four jobs:

- `GetObject`: Simulates object creation by retrieving an inactive object from the pool.
- `ExpandPool`: If no inactive objects are available, the pool size is increased using an **exponential growth strategy**—doubling the size and creating additional objects—and then an inactive object is returned.
- `ReturnObject`: Simulates object destruction by returning an object to the pool when it is no longer needed.
- `Update` and `Draw`: Manages the updating and rendering of active objects within the pool.

Let's examine the actual C++ class declarations to gain a better understanding of object pooling:

```
//The base class which serves as a base for actual poolable objects
class PoolableObject
{
protected:
  bool _isActive;
  float _lifespan;
public:
  void Activate() { isActive = true; }
  void Deactivate() { _isActive = false; }
  void SetLifespan(float Seconds) { _lifespan = Seconds; }
  float GetLifespan() { return _lifespan; }
  float DecreaseLifeSpan(float Seconds) {
    _lifespan -= Seconds;
  }
  bool IsActive() { return _isActive; }
  virtual void Update(float ElapsedSeconds) = 0;
  virtual void Draw() = 0;
}
```

Below is the code implementation for the `ObjectPool` template class. To provide a clear overview of its functionalities, we have listed only the method declarations here. For the complete implementation, please refer to the `ObjectPool.h` file:

```
//A template class which manages and contains the pool of objects
template<class T>
class ObjectPool
{
private:
      T** _pool;
  int _poolSize;
  int _activeCount;
  void ExpandPool();
  T* GetObject();
  void ReturnObject(T* objToReturn);
  void Update(float ElapsedSeconds);
  void Draw();
}
```

To learn more about detailed implementation and the practical application of `ObjectPool`, explore the source code in the `Demo3f` project.

Applying ObjectPool

In this demo, a character is present in the scene, and the player has a third-person view to observe it. Click the *left mouse button* to fire a bullet. Each bullet has a lifespan of 3 seconds and will be deactivated when this time expires.

Figure 3.7 – Firing pooled bullets

`Demo3f` defines a `Bullet` class that inherits from the `PoolableObject` class, allowing it to be managed by `_pool`, which is an instance of `ObjectPool`. Consequently, the `_bulletPool` variable is defined as a member of the `Demo3f` class in the `Demo3f.h` file:

```
ObjectPool<Bullet> _bulletPool;
```

Please refer to the following code implementation of the `Bullet` class for more details:

```
class Bullet : public PoolableObject
{
private:
  Vector3 _position;
  Vector3 _velocity;
  float _radius;
```

```
public:
  void SetPosition(Vector3 Position, Vector3 Velocity) {
    _position = Position;
    _veloicity = Velocity;
  }
  void Update() {
    if (_isActive) {
      _lifespan -= ElapsedSeconds;
      _position.x += _velocity.x * ElapsedSeconds;
      _position.y += _velocity.y * ElapsedSeconds;
      _position.z += _velocity.z * ElapsedSeconds;
    }
  }
  void Draw() override {
    if (_isActive) {
      DrawSphere(_position, _radius, RED);
    }
  }
  void Activate() override {
    __super::Activate();
    _lifespan = BULLET_LIFETIME;
  }
}
```

Congratulations on completing *Chapter 3*! You've now gained insights into some valuable algorithms and learned how to apply them in your game development practice. We hope you're excited to put these new techniques into action and that they add a new layer of creativity and efficiency to your work. Enjoy the journey and have fun as you bring your game development projects to life!

Summary

This chapter explored several key algorithms and techniques fundamental to game development, starting with randomization. It introduced the concept of generating random numbers in C++. Randomization forms the basis of many game mechanics, ensuring that experiences remain fresh and dynamic with each playthrough.

Building on this, the chapter moved on to selection algorithms. It covered random selection, which is useful for picking elements from a dataset. Weighted random selection was also discussed, allowing developers to assign different probabilities to various outcomes, which is ideal for games where certain items or events are rarer than others. Additionally, exclusive selection, which ensures no repetitions, was explored for spawning characters. These concepts were brought to life through C++ code examples in `Demo3a` and `Demo3b`, showcasing practical implementations.

Shuffling was introduced next, with a detailed explanation of the Fisher-Yates shuffle algorithm. This technique was demonstrated by shuffling a deck of cards. `Demo3c` showed the step-by-step process of how the Fisher-Yates algorithm is applied in C++ to randomize the order of cards in a deck.

Following shuffling, some C++ STL sorting functions were introduced. The `quicksort` function was used in `Demo3d`, demonstrating how to efficiently arrange cards in a hand, ensuring they are sorted in proper order.

The chapter then shifted focus to procedural generation, a powerful method for dynamically creating game content. In this section, the random acyclic maze generator algorithm was used to build a maze with one entrance and one exit, providing a hands-on example of procedural generation in action. `Demo3e` illustrated the step-by-step process of generating the maze.

Finally, the chapter concluded with a discussion on object pooling, a technique for managing memory efficiently by reusing a fixed pool of objects rather than creating and destroying them repeatedly. This section demonstrated how object pooling is applied to manage a limited number of bullets in a game. By employing an exponential growth strategy, the object pool expands as needed.

In the next chapter, the focus shifts to techniques for displaying 2D graphics and creating visual effects, setting the stage for the visual aspects of game development.

Part 2

Graphics Algorithms in Practice

In this part, the focus shifts to the visual foundation of game development: graphics rendering. Whether you're building a classic 2D side-scroller or a fully immersive 3D world, understanding how to render and control visual elements is essential to delivering a compelling gameplay experience.

You'll begin by exploring 2D graphics rendering, learning how to efficiently load and manipulate images, apply blending techniques, and create visual effects like parallax scrolling and isometric projection. From there, the journey continues into camera systems, which are critical to how players view and interact with the game world. You'll gain hands-on experience building a variety of camera types, including third-person, rail, and split-screen views.

Next, you'll dive into the world of modern 3D graphics, covering topics such as shader programming, lighting, and rendering pipelines from a GPU perspective. As you progress, you'll learn how to enhance the realism and performance of your scenes through advanced rendering strategies and custom shaders.

Finally, you'll bring all these elements together by constructing a complete 3D game world—featuring terrain, skyboxes, animated characters, particle effects, and more—rendered efficiently and convincingly.

This part includes the following chapters:

- *Chapter 4, 2D Rendering and Effects*
- *Chapter 5, The Camera and Camera Controls*
- *Chapter 6, 3D Graphics Rendering*
- *Chapter 7, Rendering a 3D Game World*

4

2D Rendering and Effects

In this chapter, we will delve into the core principles and practical techniques of 2D graphics rendering, gaining insights into how modern GPUs handle 2D operations. While often overshadowed by 3D engines, 2D visuals remain essential for many gaming scenarios—whether it's a standalone side-scroller or the user interface of a fully 3D title. You'll learn how to load and manage images efficiently, apply color and alpha blending for striking visual effects, and integrate practical features like N-patch textures to build flexible, resizable UI elements.

Moving beyond simple sprite drawing, the chapter also covers parallax scrolling, a popular method for creating depth in side-scrolling backgrounds, and isometric projections, which let you convey a pseudo-3D feel on a 2D grid. Through a dedicated sample project, you'll discover how to animate sprites, combine multiple layers for immersive scenes, and smoothly transition between images using additive or subtractive blending modes. In this chapter, you will learn about:

- Understanding 2D graphics operations behind the scenes
- Working with 2D texture rendering
- Using screen scrolling
- Rendering isometric maps

By the end of the chapter, you'll have a robust toolkit for 2D game development: from displaying sprites and orchestrating beautiful particle-like effects to creating entire isometric worlds and intuitive, high-quality user interfaces. This foundation will ensure your 2D or hybrid 2D/3D projects are both visually appealing and efficiently rendered.

Technical requirements

Download and open the project via the GitHub URL to open the example project demonstrated in this chapter: `https://github.com/PacktPublishing/Data-Structures-and-Algorithms-for-Game-Programming-in-CPP`

The following projects in the `Knight` Visual Studio solution (`https://github.com/PacktPublishing/Data-Structures-and-Algorithms-for-Game-Programming-in-CPP/tree/main/Knight`) are used as samples for this chapter:

Project Name	Description
`Demo4texops`	This project contains multiple demo code snippets for various texture drawing features in Knight. Use the *enter* key or *left mouse button* to go through them.
`Demo4ss`	This project demonstrates parallax side scrolling for a multi-layered background.
`Demo4iso`	This project demonstrates how to render an isometric map.

Table 4.1 – Sample 2D graphics projects for this chapter

Understanding 2D graphics operations behind the scenes

In this section, before we start writing a line of code to work with a 2D graphic image, let's first find out how the modern generation of GPU hardware and display drivers handle graphics images behind the scenes.

Loading and rendering a texture as an image

The GPU hardware renders and processes graphic image data in real time. Real-time rendering is now predominantly managed by the modern generation of GPUs. As a result, understanding key concepts related to graphics hardware is crucial for developing games with smooth visuals and good runtime performance.

Figure 4.1 shows the process of how a static image is rendered on the screen from a graphic file stored on a storage device.

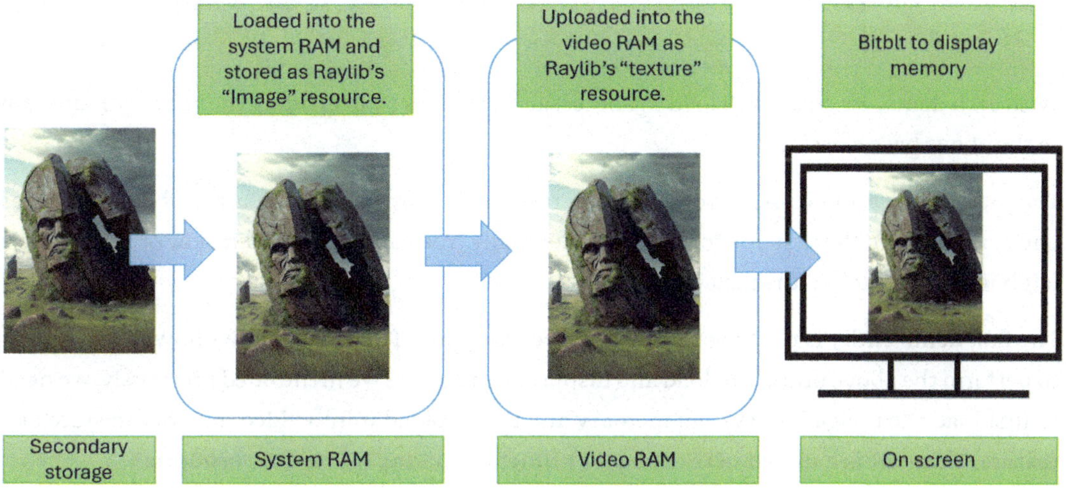

Figure 4.1 – The process behind displaying an image on the screen

In *Figure 4.1*, the image is first loaded from secondary storage (e.g., a hard drive or the cloud) into system memory by the CPU, then uploaded into the GPU's video memory (**VRAM**) as a texture.

VRAM is split into display memory, which drives what appears on the screen, and offscreen memory for textures and other rendering data. To show the image, the GPU copies its pixel data from the texture into display memory via a **Bitblt (bit-block transfer)**, a fundamental operation for moving pixel blocks between memory locations.

Consequently, rendering a 2D image relies on coordination between the CPU and GPU to move image data efficiently.

The `Demo4texops` project features a set of 2D graphics-related sample code, with each feature implemented and demonstrated in an inherited `Entity` class. The base class is relatively simple, as we saw in *Chapter 2*:

```
class Entity {
    public:
        virtual void Create() = 0;
        virtual void Update(float elapsedTime) {};
        virtual void Draw2D() = 0;
        virtual void Release() = 0;
        bool isReady;
```

```
        string title;
        string description;
        Entity();
};
```

With each demo, we create and load the necessary resources by overriding the `Create()` function in the above base class.

The main application class, `Demo4TexOps`, is responsible for creating an array of demo entities and running from the first one to the last sequentially. You can press the *enter* key or the mouse's left button to switch to the next demo.

The first demo entity is the `SimpleDrawTextureDemo` class. This demo shows how to use Knight to perform the above process to load and display an image. As we mentioned previously, we need to first load the image into system memory and then upload it into video memory to store as a texture. This part is handled in the `Create()` function in `SimpleDrawTextureDemo`:

```
void SimpleDrawTextureDemo::Create()
{
  Image art = LoadImage("resources/textures/demoart.png");
  texture = LoadTextureFromImage(art);
  UnloadImage(art);
  isReady = true;
}
```

In the above code, `Image` is a data structure provided by Knight to store graphic file data in the system memory. The next step is to use `LoadTextureFromImage()` to decode and upload the image data into VRAM as a `Texture2D` format resource.

You do not need to keep a copy of image data in system memory once you have a texture ready in VRAM. Unless you foresee any special need to re-upload the same image data into VRAM soon, it's good practice to call `UnloadImage()` to release the system memory no longer needed.

Before we leave the `Create()` function, we set the `isReady` variable to true. This lets the main application class know if it needs to call the `Create()` function to ensure the resources are all ready to run the demo class.

The counterpart of the `Create()` function is the `Release()` function. It ensures resources are properly released and the status is updated:

```
void SimpleDrawTextureDemo::Release()
{
  UnloadTexture(texture);
  isReady = false;
}
```

The actual action to draw the texture onscreen is executed in the `Draw2D()` function:

```
void SimpleDrawTextureDemo::Draw2D()
{
  Vector2 position = {(float)(SCREEN_WIDTH - texture.width) / 2.0f,
(float)(SCREEN_HEIGHT - texture.height) / 2.0f };
  DrawTextureV(texture, position, WHITE);
}
```

Here, we use raylib's texture drawing function, `DrawTextureV()`. It takes the texture that needs to be drawn, the screen coordinate position (the top-left side of the texture), and the color to blend with the texture to render the result on the screen.

Since `DrawTextureV()` uses the top-left corner of the texture as its drawing origin, we need to calculate the appropriate position if we want to center the image on the screen. In Knight, two constants, `SCREEN_WIDTH` and `SCREEN_HEIGHT`, define the dimensions of the application window. The `Texture2D` structure in raylib includes `width` and `height`, which represent the dimensions of the texture. To find the correct top-left position for centering the texture, we subtract the texture's `width` from `SCREEN_WIDTH` and divide by 2 to get the x-coordinate; the same calculation applies to the y-coordinate using `SCREEN_HEIGHT` and the texture's `height`.

The result is shown in *Figure 4.2*:

Figure 4.2 – Running SimpleDrawTextureDemo to draw a texture at the center of the screen

For optimal performance, pre-load as many required textures into GPU memory, minimizing the need for repeated uploads. However, because GPU memory is limited, overusing it prompts the driver to swap or discard textures, harming performance. Careful planning of memory usage—particularly texture sizes and formats—ensures your scene stays within typical GPU limits while still looking visually rich.

Choosing an appropriate texture format

When creating textures, we can specify their format. The format determines how individual pixels are stored and whether compression is used. We know that a screen is composed of pixels, and each pixel stores the values for the red, green, and blue channels, possibly including an additional transparency value. *Figure 4.3* shows the common pixel formats supported by Knight and the memory they consume.

The most common highest-quality format is the 32-bit full-color R8G8B8A8 format, but often, depending on the use case, we can use formats that are more memory-efficient.

Of course, this is entirely dependent on the source art. For cartoonish or anime/manga style drawing, it might use a smaller number of colors than a photo-realistic image.

For example, if an image is used as a graphics mask, each pixel might only need one bit to represent whether it should be drawn. For images with fewer or simpler colors, a format like R5G6B5 (five bits for red and blue/six bits for green) might be sufficient. It instantly reduces 50% of the texture memory.

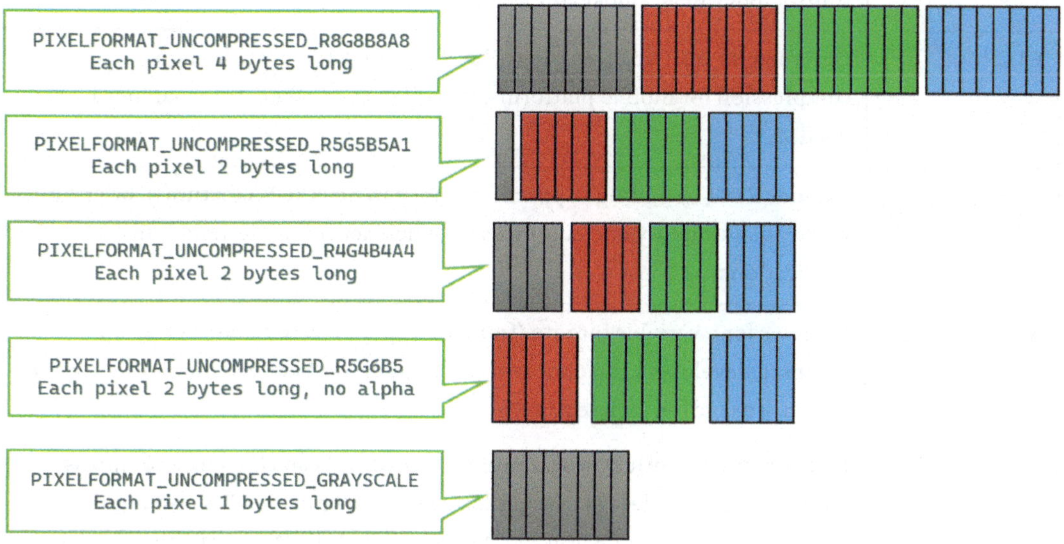

Figure 4.3 – Various uncompressed pixel formats

Modern GPUs also support various compressed texture formats to store more graphical data in video memory. These are called **lossy compression formats** because they reduce the memory required by sacrificing subtle details that are difficult for the human eye to perceive. In fast-paced games, losing some visual details often isn't a problem. Below are some common compressed texture formats:

Format	**Description**
DXT1 (`*.dds`)	Offers the highest compression ratio but does not support alpha channels (transparency), or it uses a 1-bit alpha (transparent or opaque). It compresses images in roughly a 6:1 ratio.
DXT3 (`*.dds`)	Supports explicit alpha, which means it stores transparency information without additional interpolation, giving better control over alpha blending. It's useful for textures where the alpha channel doesn't have smooth transitions.

Format	Description
DXT5 (`*.dds`)	Similar to DXT3 but with interpolated alpha, allowing for more flexible and nuanced transparency. This format is great for textures with gradients in transparency (e.g., smoke, fog).
ETC1	Designed for RGB textures (no alpha channel), ETC1 provides good compression for mobile platforms. It is often used where transparency isn't needed.
ETC2	Extends ETC1 by adding support for transparency (RGBA textures), offering better image quality and compression efficiency for modern mobile applications.
ASTC	It allows for a variable bit rate (from 4 bits per pixel to 12 bits per pixel), meaning developers can choose the best trade-off between image quality and memory usage for each texture. It also supports both RGB and RGBA textures and can efficiently compress textures with fine details or complex color gradients. ASTC is also highly scalable and can handle different levels of detail (LOD) in real-time rendering.
ATC_RGB ATC_RGBA	ATC is used on Qualcomm's Adreno GPUs, which are common in many Android devices. It supports both RGB and RGBA textures.
Crunch	Crunch is a format used in Unity and other game engines for compressing textures, especially for WebGL or mobile games. It allows for higher compression ratios while maintaining acceptable visual fidelity by combining DXT and ETC formats with additional compression.

Table 4.2 – List of compressed texture formats supported by different graphics APIs

Let's look at the second demo class, `CompressTextureDemo` (in `Demo4textOps.cpp`). This time, we loaded two textures. They are actually the same image, but one is in the original uncompressed format and the other is in compressed DXT3 format. The original one is 3.03 MB, and the compressed one is reduced to 896KB. In the `Create()` function, we load both textures:

```
void CompressTextureDemo::Create()
{
  Image art_org = LoadImage("../../resources/textures/demoart.png");
  original = LoadTextureFromImage(art_org);
  UnloadImage(art_org);
  Image art_cmp = LoadImage("../../resources/textures/demoart.dds");
  compressed = LoadTextureFromImage(art_cmp);
  UnloadImage(art_cmp);
  isReady = true;
}
```

In the above code snippet, Knight will determine the format of the file and create a texture according to the format of the source file. In this demo class, we render both the non-compressed texture and the compressed texture images side by side, so you can make a visual comparison in the following code:

```
void CompressTextureDemo::Draw2D()
{
  Vector2 position = { 0, (float)(SCREEN_HEIGHT - original.height/2) /
2.0f };
  DrawTextureEx(original, position, 0, 0.5f, WHITE);
  position.x += original.width / 2+100;
  DrawTextureEx(compressed, position, 0, 0.5f, WHITE);
}
```

As you can see in *Figure 4.4*, there is not much of a visual difference between these two textures:

Figure 4.4 – Side-by-side visual quality comparison of original and compressed texture format

Note

Keep in mind that some compressed formats of texture will have limitations for width and height of the power of two. For example, size 512x1024 or 2048x64.

Choosing the right compressed texture format depends on the specific needs of the game or application, including the platform, memory limitations, and the visual quality desired.

As for compression ratios, they can vary depending on the algorithm and the content of the original image, ranging from *1/6* to *1/2*. For very rough estimating purposes, we can assume an average compression ratio of *1/3*. This allows us to roughly estimate the amount of GPU memory needed.

Many visually stunning AAA games require far more graphic data than the memory available on a typical graphics card. However, they carefully manage the memory usage for each frame, ensuring that the amount of data used stays within the limits of the average gamer's hardware.

In addition to choosing compressed texture formats whenever appropriate, we can also reduce graphics memory usage by avoiding loading the same texture image multiple times. The next section will demonstrate the concept of the **cache** – a high-speed data storage layer that stores a subset of data, typically transient in nature, so that future requests for that data can be served faster than by accessing the data's primary storage location.

Using the cache to avoid loading the same texture repeatedly

A game screen often uses hundreds of textures, with many duplicates (like 50 identical trees in a forest). Without management, these textures might load multiple times unnecessarily. A **texture cache** is a data storage layer with the following rules enforced:

- Prevents duplicates by tracking loaded textures in VRAM
- Provides existing textures when requested again
- Loads new textures only when needed
- Manages capacity limits—either by the maximum number of textures allowed or by available VRAM size.

When the texture cache reaches capacity, it must evict existing texture(s) to make room for the new one. The most common eviction strategy is called **Least Recently Used** (**LRU**), which removes the texture that hasn't been accessed for the longest time.

Implementing an LRU texture cache

The next example project, `LRUTextureCacheDemo` (in `LRUTextureCacheDemo.cpp` of `Demo4TexOps`), demonstrates how to implement an LRU-texture cache. The following code defines the C++ class of `TextureCache` in `LRUTextureCacheDemo.h`:

```
class TextureCache {
private:
struct CacheEntry {
  Texture2D texture;  //the actual loaded texture object
  list<string>::iterator lru_it;  //the position iterator
};
```

The first part of the preceding code defines the data entry of the loaded texture in the CacheEntry struct. CacheEntry is stored in a new collection type, unordered_map:

```
unordered_map<string, CacheEntry> cache;
```

The unordered_map is a hash table-based associative container that stores key-value style data pairs with unique keys, providing fast retrieval of values based on their associated keys. Here, we use a **sting** – an image file name of texture – as a key to store the CacheEntry type data in cache.

The advantage of using unordered_map over an array or list is the performance. The time complexity of finding a particular element inside unordered_map is *O(1)*. This is better than *O(N)* for array and list when we have hundreds of textures stored in the cache.

We also need to define a list of texture image file names to represent a list of recently used textures in the variable lru_list. The front element of the list is the file name of the most recently used texture, and the back element is the least recently used texture file name:

```
list<string> lru_list; // Most recently used List
```

For simplicity, we will limit the maximum number of textures that can be stored in our TextureCache implementation. We need two variables to track the maximum number and the current number of loaded textures:

```
size_t max_size;  //maximum number of textures allowed
size_t current_size = 0; //current number of textures
```

The constructor function of the class sets the maximum number of textures that can be stored in this texture cache:

```
TextureCache(size_t size) : max_size(size) {}
```

The most important function is GetTexture(). This function implements the core logic of the cache mechanism:

```
Texture2D* GetTexture(const std::string& filePath)
{
```

This function first checks if the texture has been loaded and stored in the texture cache. If we find it, we also need to update lru_list to make this texture the most recently used texture (the front element of lru_list), and just return the previously loaded texture to the caller:

```
auto it = cache.find(filePath);
if (it != cache.end()) { //we find one!
```

```
    // Move to front of LRU list (most recently used)
    lru_list.erase(it->second.lru_it);
    lru_list.push_front(filePath);
    it->second.lru_it = lru_list.begin();
    NumHit++;
    return &it->second.texture;
  } else //nope, there is no such texture found
    NumMiss++;
```

The preceding code monitors cache performance through `NumHit` (cache successes – a texture is found and returned) and `NumMiss` (cache failures – no such texture exists) counters.

The rest of this function uses `LoadTexture()` to load the texture and check if we still have available room to store the texture. If we hit the maximum number of textures allowed, we just remove the last element of `lru_list` to make room for this newly loaded texture:

```
    Texture2D texture = LoadTexture(filePath.c_str());
    //…
    if (current_size >= max_size && !lru_list.empty()) {
      string lru_key = lru_list.back();//get the last element
      UnloadTexture(cache[lru_key].texture);//unload texture
      cache.erase(lru_key);  //remove data
      lru_list.pop_back();  //remove reference as well
      current_size--;  //update current size
  }
```

The final piece of the code is to add the newly added texture into `cache` and make it the most recently used texture (front of `lru_list`):

```
    lru_list.push_front(filePath);
    cache[filePath] = { texture, lru_list.begin() };
    current_size++;
    return &cache[filePath].texture;
  }
```

The demo usage of the `TextureCache()` class is implemented in `LRUTextureCacheDemo.cpp`. Just like other demos, it overrides the `Create()` and `Draw2D()` functions. Unlike other demo code, we do not pre-load the textures we need here:

```
void LRUTextureCacheDemo::Create()
{
    isReady = true;
}
```

Instead, all required textures are loaded only when they're needed. The `textureCache` will manage the loading of new textures and avoid loading already existing textures:

```
void LRUTextureCacheDemo::Draw2D()
{
  int index = ((int)GetTime()/2) % texturePaths.size();
```

The preceding code calculates the index of the required texture by the time since the game application started, passing the filename into the `GetTexture()` function of `textureCache`:

```
  Texture2D* texture=
    textureCache.GetTexture(texturePaths[index]);
```

Without caching, `Draw2D()` would reload the same textures every frame, rapidly exhausting VRAM. Our `textureCache` implementation prevents this redundant loading by reusing existing textures.

The rest of the code shows the content of `lru_list`, so you can get an idea of how the list maintains the most recently used textures:

```
  // Draw the texture
  DrawTexture(*texture, SCREEN_WIDTH / 2 - texture->width / 2, SCREEN_
HEIGHT / 2 - texture->height / 2, WHITE);
  // Draw cache info
  DrawText(TextFormat("Cache Size: %d/%d Hit:%d, Miss:%d", textureCache.
Size(), textureCache.MaxSize(), textureCache.NumHit, textureCache.
NumMiss), 10, 30, 20, WHITE);
  for (int i = 0; i < textureCache.Size(); i++) {
    DrawText(TextFormat("Texture:%s", textureCache.GetTexturePath(i).c_
str()), 15, 75 + i * 30, 20, (i == index) ? GREEN : WHITE);
  }
}
```

When running the demo, observe how the contents of `lru_list` change dynamically. Though we display 4 textures, we intentionally limit the cache size to 3. This forces the cache to continuously evict the least recently used texture once full. In *Figure 4.5*, the number of hits (successfully reuse the existing texture without loading a new one) is **403** times, and the number of misses (need to load a new texture) is **5**.

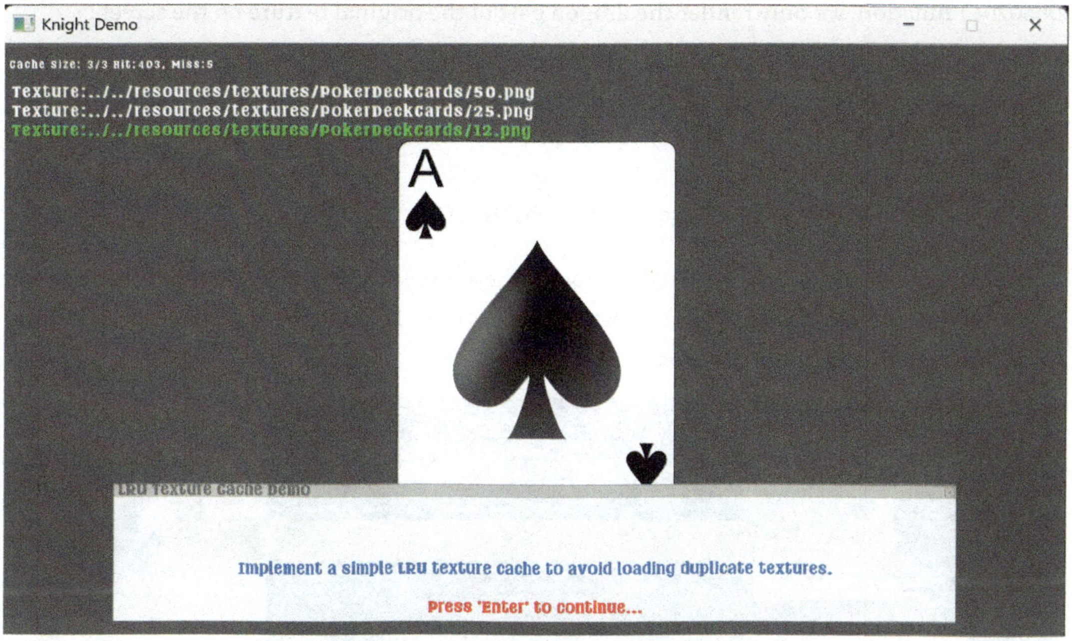

Figure 4.5 – Using texture cache to effectively manage texture resources

In the next section, let's continue to explore more 2D texture rendering features.

Working with 2D texture rendering

Until now, we have simply rendered the whole texture image to the screen. However, raylib also provides more detailed control of how a texture is rendered. In this section, we will explore the following:

- Only rendering part of a region from the source texture image
- Rotating the image with a specific angle
- Blending colors from the source and destination images

Rendering part of a region from the source texture

The next demo class, DrawPartialRotateDemo, demonstrates two more texture rendering features provided by Knight.

The first one is the ability to render part of the rectangle region inside the source texture. As in the Draw2D() function, we only render the dragon part of the original texture on the screen:

```
    Rectangle sr = {393, 6, 698-393, 431-6};
    Vector2 position = { (float)(SCREEN_WIDTH - sr.width) / 2.0f, (float)
(SCREEN_HEIGHT - sr.height) / 2.0f };
    Vector2 origin = { 0,0 };
    DrawTextureRec(texture, sr, position, WHITE);
```

The rectangle sr only includes a small region in the source texture. The position is the top-left corner of the cropped texture. The interesting part is the origin vector. It serves as the position of the pivot point inside the sub-texture.

Figure 4.6 – Rendering only a partial rectangle region from the source texture

Rotating the texture image

The second part is the ability to apply rotation to the texture:

```
    position = { 300, 300 };
    Rectangle dr = { position.x, position.y, fabs(sr.width), fabs(sr.height)
};
    currentAngle += 40 * timeDiff;
```

```
    if (currentAngle > 360) currentAngle -= 360;
    DrawTexturePro(texture, sr, dr, origin, currentAngle, WHITE);
```

In the above code, we use the more advanced version of the texture drawing function `DrawTexturePro()`. This allows us to control the rotation of the texture and specify which region of the source texture needs to be used.

Since we want to keep the texture rotating, each frame's `currentAngle` is increased by `40* timeDiff`. This is how we use the time difference between two consecutive frames to achieve a smooth rotation animation.

Of course, when the value of `currentAngle` is over 360 degrees, we need to trim the value within the valid range.

Color blending

Color blending is a technique used in computer graphics to combine two colors (a source color and a destination color) to produce a final color, based on certain blending modes or operations. It is primarily used in 2D and 3D rendering to simulate various visual effects such as transparency, lighting, shadows, and more complex graphical styles like glowing, additive effects, or darkening.

In color blending, each pixel has a source color (usually from a texture or a graphic being drawn) and a destination color (typically the color of the pixel already on the screen). The final output color is determined by combining these two colors based on a specific blend operation. The basic components for a color blending operation are:

- **Source color (SRC)**: The color of the pixel that is being drawn.
- **Destination color (DST)**: The color of the pixel already present on the screen.
- **Source alpha (SRC_ALPHA)**: The alpha (opacity) value of the source pixel, ranging from 0 (fully transparent) to 1 (fully opaque).
- **Destination alpha (DST_ALPHA)**: The alpha value of the destination pixel.

The demo class `ColorBlendingDemo` demonstrates how to use color blending to simulate the different lighting cycles from dawn to dusk for a still image. The first thing is we will need a color table in the following code snippet (defined as an array of `Color dayToNightCycle`), which contains 32 colors to represent the different times in a full dawn to dusk cycle. For any moment of the day, we can pick the color value from the array with the closest time to draw the image. This makes the final color of each pixel on the screen modulated by the color specified in the `dayToNightCycle` array.

To be able to make the color changes as smooth as possible, in the following code snippet of class `ColorBlendingDemo`, we create a table with 32 colors to represent the color changes from dawn to dusk:

```
static Color dayToNightCycle[32] = {
  // Morning (Dawn to Early Morning)
  {255, 240, 230, 255}, // Dawn (light yellow-pink)
  {250, 220, 200, 255}, // Soft sunrise
  {240, 200, 170, 255},//Early morning(warmer orange tones)
  //…
  {230, 240, 255, 255}//, // Soft blue sky (late morning)
  //{255, 255, 255}  // Midday again (completes the cycle)
};
```

We would like to animate this cycle at a steady speed by reaching the next color value in the table in 0.5-second intervals. So, we can loop through day and night in around sixteen seconds. This is done in the `Update()` function:

```
void ColorBlendingDemo::Update(float elapsed)
{
  timeDiff += elapsed;
  if (timeDiff > 0.5f) {
    currentIdx++;
    timeDiff = 0.0f;
  }
  if (currentIdx >= 32)
    currentIdx -= 32;   // loop back to first color
}
```

We use the variable `timeDiff` to determine if we need to increase the value of `currentIdx`. This ensures the change of color isn't affected by the frame rate.

The drawing function in `Draw2D()` will take the current color to blend with the texture image:

```
DrawTexture(texture, position.x, position.y, dayToNightCycle[currentIdx]);
```

In the `Draw2D()` call of each frame, we take the color indicated by the array index of `currentIdx` to draw the scene. The scene will change its color every 0.5 seconds, as shown in *Figure 4.7*:

Figure 4.7 – Transition from time of the day

Now, if you run this demo like the result shown in *Figure 4.7*, do you notice what's wrong when you run the sample on your computer?

Yes – although we have achieved the desired day-night cycle, the color transitions are not smooth.

The problem occurs because we simply pick one single color from the table. However, these colors in the table don't provide a smooth transition from one to the next. We now understand it's not enough to just pick a single color from the table. We need to interpolate between the color of `currentIdx` and the color next to `currentIdx` to create a new color in between for a better transition.

Now let's inherit the class `ColorBlendingDemo` and create a new class `SmoothColorBlendingDemo` in the following code snippet:

```
class SmoothColorBlendingDemo : public ColorBlendingDemo {
public:
  void Draw2D() override;
  SmoothColorBlendingDemo();
};
```

This new derived class in the above code will override the drawing function `Draw2D()` to implement a simple, smooth color transition:

```
void SmoothColorBlendingDemo::Draw2D()
{
  Vector2 position = { (float)(SCREEN_WIDTH - texture.width) / 2.0f,
(float)(SCREEN_HEIGHT - texture.height) / 2.0f };
  int nextIdx;
  Color c1 = dayToNightCycle[currentIdx];
  if (currentIdx < 31)
    nextIdx = currentIdx + 1;
  else
    nextIdx = 0;
  Color c2 = dayToNightCycle[nextIdx];
  float t = timeDiff / 0.5f;
```

```
    Color c = WHITE;
    c.r = (1 - t)* c1.r + t * c2.r;
    c.g = (1 - t) * c1.g + t * c2.g;
    c.b = (1 - t) * c1.b + t * c2.b;
    DrawTexture(texture, position.x, position.y, c);
}
```

In the code above, simple linear interpolation is used to calculate a transition color between the current and next colors in the table. We select two consecutive colors and use the elapsed time (stored in `timeDiff`) to determine the final color, which is then blended with the image in the `DrawTexture()` call.

Alpha blending

Alpha blending is a technique used in computer graphics to combine (or blend) two images or textures based on their alpha values, which represent the opacity or transparency of the pixels in the image. The alpha value typically ranges from 0 to 1, where:

- **0**: The pixel is fully transparent (invisible).
- **1**: The pixel is fully opaque (completely visible).
- Values between 0 and 1 represent varying degrees of transparency.
- When applying alpha blending, the colors of the foreground texture (the source) are blended with the colors of the background texture (the destination), resulting in a final image that shows a mixture of the two, depending on the transparency.

The general formula for alpha blending is:

```
FinalColor = (SourceColor * SourceAlpha) + (DestinationColor * (1 -
SourceAlpha))
```

where:

- `SourceColor` is the color of the pixel in the texture being drawn (foreground).
- `SourceAlpha` is the alpha value of the pixel in the foreground texture (determines transparency).
- `DestinationColor` is the color of the pixel in the background (destination).
- `FinalColor` is the resulting color after the blending operation.

Here's how it works:

- **Opaque pixels (Alpha = 1)**: If the source pixel is fully opaque (alpha = 1), the source color completely overwrites the destination color.
- **Transparent pixels (Alpha = 0)**: If the source pixel is fully transparent (alpha = 0), the destination color remains unchanged.
- **Semi-transparent pixels (0 < Alpha < 1)**: If the source pixel has a semi-transparent alpha value, the final color will be a mix of the source and destination colors.

In many 2D and 3D games, alpha blending is used to render transparent or translucent textures, such as:

- Glass surfaces
- Fog, smoke, or shadows
- User interface elements like windows or menus
- Particle effects, such as explosions or magic spells

Some of the common uses of alpha blending include:

- **Transparent UI elements**: Alpha blending is often used for creating transparent menus, buttons, and windows in user interfaces.
- **Particle effects**: Effects like fire, smoke, or explosions often use alpha blending to create realistic visuals.
- **Shadows and glows**: Alpha blending can be used to render soft shadows, lighting effects, or glowing auras around objects.
- **Transitions and fades**: Alpha blending is commonly used for fading objects in and out of view, creating smooth transitions.

Alpha blending is a fundamental technique in graphics programming that allows for the creation of visually rich and immersive scenes. By controlling the opacity of textures and blending them with the background, you can create effects such as transparency, semi-transparency, shadows, and more. This technique is widely used in game development, UI design, and digital art to enhance visual quality and depth.

The demo class `SceneTransitionDemo` demonstrates how to use the default alpha blending feature to create a smooth transition to switch the display of two images.

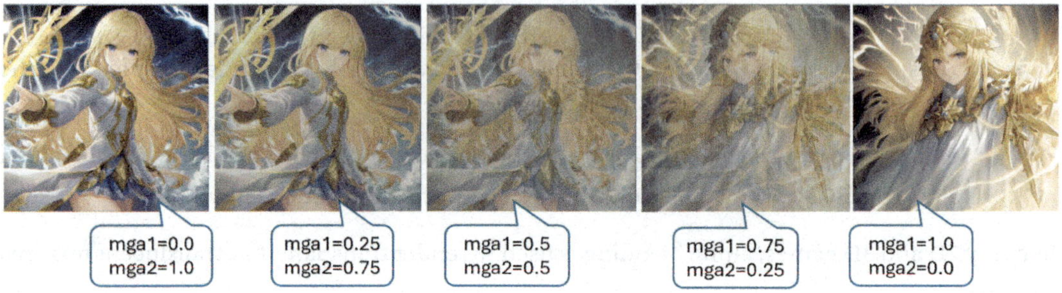

Figure 4.8 – Use alpha blending to render the transition of two images

Figure 4.8 shows five sequential screenshots illustrating the transition effect from left to right. The alpha of the first image goes from 1.0 (fully opaque) to 0.0 (fully transparent), while the alpha of the second image goes from 0.0 to 1.0. As a result, the first screenshot displays only the first image, the last shows only the second, and the middle screenshots feature both images overlapping with varying transparency.

Let's walk through the code to implement such a scene transition animation with alpha blending in `SceneTransitionDemo.cpp`. First, we will load the `scene1` and `scene2` `Texture2D` objects in the `Create()` function:

```
Image art1 = LoadImage("../../resources/textures/mga1.png");
scene1 = LoadTextureFromImage(art1);
Image art2 = LoadImage("../../resources/textures/mga2.png");
scene2 = LoadTextureFromImage(art2);
```

In order to create a ping-pong-like smooth transition effect, we can use the `sin()` function to produce the value. This is handled in the `Update()` function:

```
void SceneTransitionDemo::Update(float elapsed)
{
  elapsed_time += elapsed;
  currentProgress = (std::sin(2 * 3.14159f * 0.1f * elapsed_time) + 1) *
0.5f;
}
```

The result of `currentProgress` is used to calculate the actual alpha value for both textures in the `Draw2D()` function:

```
void SceneTransitionDemo::Draw2D()
{
  Vector2 position = { (float)(SCREEN_WIDTH - scene1.width) / 2.0f,
(float)(SCREEN_HEIGHT - scene1.height) / 2.0f };
  Color c1 = WHITE;
  c1.a = (int)(currentProgress * 255.9f);
  Color c2 = WHITE;
  c2.a = 255 - c1.a;
  DrawTexture(scene1, position.x, position.y, c1);
  DrawTexture(scene2, position.x, position.y, c2);
}
```

The final alpha component of the color value `c1` and `c2` of both images is computed from `currentProgress` in the above code snippet.

Advanced color and/or alpha blending modes

In addition to the basic blending method we discussed earlier, there are several other commonly used blending methods. Since the color usually contains the alpha channel, these methods are not only applied to color channels, but the alpha channel as well.

The most common blending methods supported by all graphics hardware are additive blending, multiplicative blending, and subtractive blending. Let's check how they work in the subsequent sections.

Additive blending

When you render a source image on the screen, the color value of each pixel from the source image will be added to the color value of the pixel on the screen, instead of just overwriting the existing color value of the destination pixel on the screen. Simply put, **additive blending** adds the source and destination colors, creating a glowing or brightening effect.

If we write pseudo code to implement the above behavior, it will look like the following:

```
FinalColor = (SourceColor * 1) + (DestinationColor * 1)
```

In a typical 24-bit color system, each color channel (red, green, and blue) is stored in 8 bits, giving each a range of 0 to 255. If the red component of `FinalColor.r` exceeds 255, it is clamped at 255.

Additive blending is often used for rendering light, fire, explosions, and particle effects where you want the combined result to appear brighter.

Multiplicative blending

Unlike additive blending, which sums the values of the source and destination pixels, **multiplicative blending** treats the red/green/blue component of each source color as a factor of the full bright value to modulate the value of the destination color to produce the final value.

Let's use the example of an 8-bit red component for the source pixel; if the value is 127, then it's treated as a factor of 0.5 (127/255). If the red component in the destination pixel is 255, the final value would be 255 * 0.5 = 127. As you can imagine, multiplicative blending results in a darker effect. The pseudo-code to achieve this is very straightforward:

```
FinalColor = SourceColor * DestinationColor
```

This is used for shadow effects, lighting, or darkening textures.

Subtractive blending

The definition of **subtractive blending** is just the opposite of additive blending. It subtracts the source color from the destination color, resulting in a darker output.

The pseudo code to achieve subtractive blending is relatively easy:

```
FinalColor = DestinationColor - SourceColor
```

If the component value of the source color is greater than the component value of the destination color, the result is clamped to zero.

It is useful for simulating darkening or reducing the brightness of certain areas.

Combining both color and alpha blending

Color and alpha blending combine two colors to produce dynamic visual effects. Using modes like alpha, additive, or multiplicative blending, you can achieve transparency, glowing particles, shadows, and lighting. The mode you choose depends on the effect you want to create.

The next demo class, `GlowDemo`, demonstrates how to use additive blending mode to render effects on top of other images. This time, let's add some shining magical spell effects to our goddess character. The glowing rays effect is made by this texture with white light rays, as shown in *Figure 4.9*:

Figure 4.9 – Using additive blending mode to render a ray light effect

By combining the features of rendering a partial region of a texture and color blending methods we introduced earlier in this chapter, we can generate a sequence of continuous action images and create an animation effect by rendering them in succession. To avoid loading multiple textures and frequently switching between them, we can merge each frame of the animation into a single large texture. For example, we can combine eleven frames of a 1024x128 lightning animation into a single 1024x1408 texture, as shown in *Figure 4.10*:

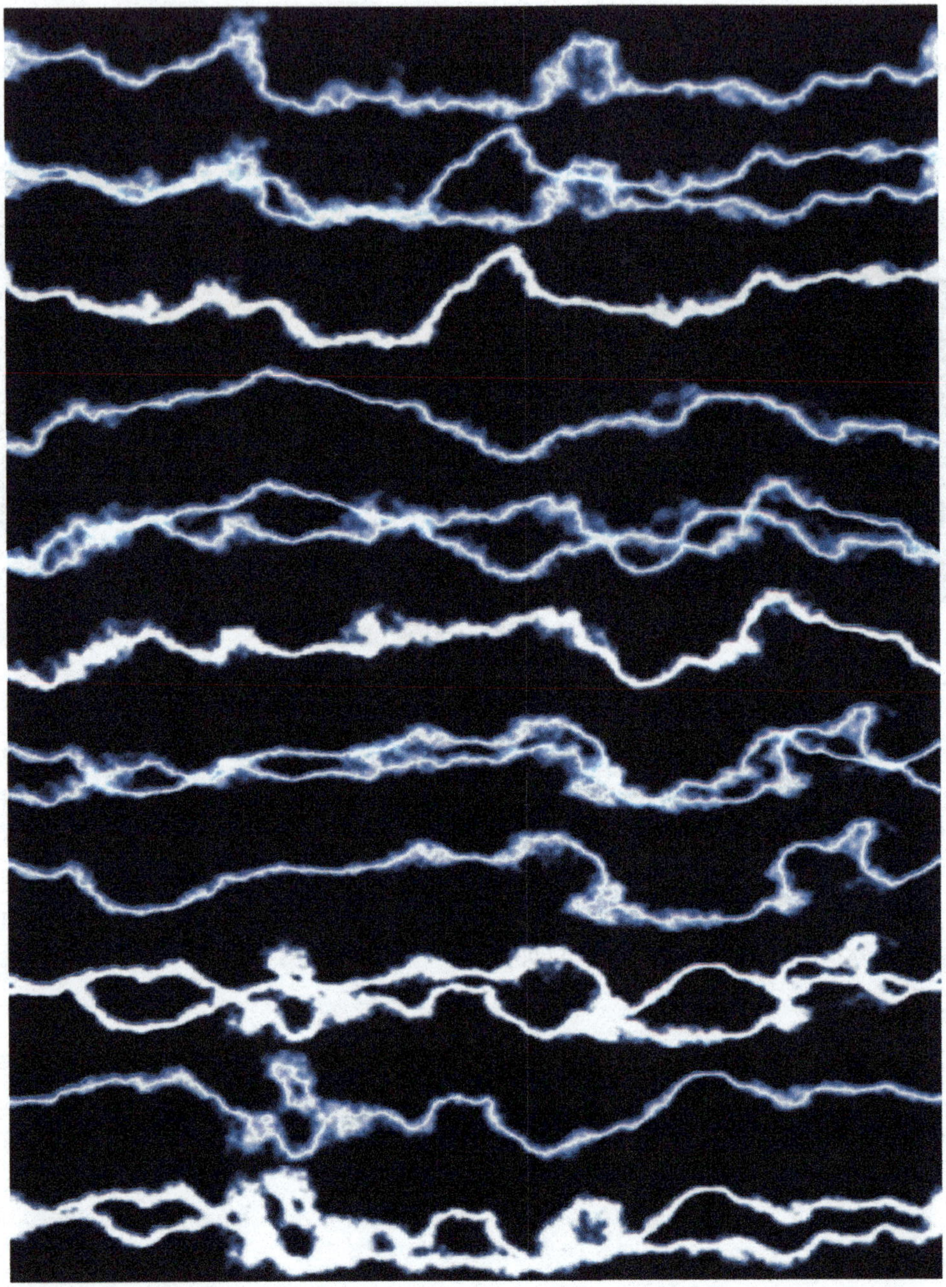

Figure 4.10 – Merging 11 1024x128 lightning textures into a 1024x1408 texture sprite sheet

The image in *Figure 4.10* is actually a combination of 11 horizontal lightning strike image strips, each with dimensions of 1024 pixels wide and 128 pixels high. It groups 11 strips into a single big 1024x1408 texture.

We sometimes refer to this kind of grouping texture as a **sprite sheet**. Depending on the nature of each frame, you can arrange the images of animation frames either row by row or in a row-major grid. For our lightning strike effect, since the dimension of each single strip is much longer in width than height, it's suitable to arrange all strips row by row.

`AnimatedTexDemo.cpp` in the sample project `Demotexops` demonstrates how we can use the grouping texture to achieve the animated lightning effect.

Let's check the demo class `AnimatedTexDemo`. It demonstrates how to render animated textures. The animation time is calculated in the `Update()` function:

```
void AnimatedTexDemo::Update(float elapsed){
    _anim_time += elapsed;
    if (_anim_time >= _anim_length)
        _anim_time -= _anim_length;
}
```

As shown in the above code, the value of `_anim_time` will loop back to the beginning when it reaches the end of the animation. Since it's a lightning effect, we choose to render it in additive blending mode in the `Draw2D()` function:

```
void AnimatedTexDemo::Draw2D(){
    int idx = (int)(_anim_time / _anim_length * 11.0f);
    Rectangle src = {0, idx * 128, 1024, 128};
    Vector2 pos = { 300,300 };
    BeginBlendMode(BLEND_ADDITIVE);
    DrawTextureRec(_spritesSheet, src, pos, WHITE);
    EndBlendMode();
}
```

The local variable `idx` is used to keep track of which strip inside the big grouping texture is currently used. We use `Rectangle src` to specify the region of the source texture to be rendered. This is a very simple yet effective way to achieve an animated effect.

N-patch texture

N-patch, also known as **9-patch** (when specifically referring to a 3x3 grid), is a technique used in graphics programming to scale images or textures in a way that preserves specific regions while allowing other regions to stretch or repeat. This is commonly used in **user interfaces (UIs)**, where you might want buttons, panels, or other visual elements to resize dynamically based on their content, while preserving the borders or corners without distortion.

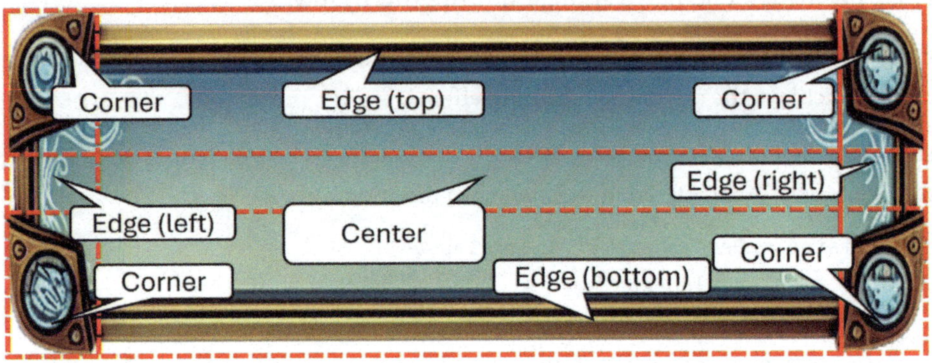

Figure 4.11 – N-patch texture is divided into 9 slices of regions.

In an N-patch like the one shown in *Figure 4.11*, it is divided into a 3x3 grid (the *red dotted lines* separate the whole image into a 3x3 grid):

- **Corners**: These regions are fixed in size and are not stretched. They are usually important for maintaining the visual integrity of the image (e.g., rounded corners or decorative edges).
- **Edges (top, bottom, left, right)**: These regions are stretched or tiled horizontally or vertically as needed to accommodate resizing.
- **Center**: This region is often the most flexible part and can be stretched or tiled both horizontally and vertically.

The N-patch texture provides the following benefits:

- **Preserve detail**: It allows you to stretch an image while preserving important visual details, like rounded corners, shadows, or borders.
- **Flexible UI elements**: UI elements like buttons, panels, and dialogue boxes can resize dynamically without losing their visual quality.
- **Efficient memory use**: You don't need to create multiple versions of an image in different sizes; instead, you create a single resizable image that adjusts as needed.

The most common usage of N-patch textures is for graphic elements in in-game user interfaces:

- **Buttons:** A 9-patch button graphic can resize dynamically as text, or the button size changes.
- **Panels and boxes:** UI panels or dialogue boxes can expand without distorting the decorative borders or corners.
- **Progress bars:** The central part of a progress bar stretches, but the ends remain fixed.

Our demo class `NPatchDemo` demonstrates how to set up the necessary information to draw an N-patch texture. In the `Create()` function:

```
void NPatchDemo::Create()
{
  Image art = LoadImage("../../resources/textures/uibkgd.png");
  _npatchTex = LoadTextureFromImage(art);
  UnloadImage(art);
  Rectangle r = { 0.0f, 0.0f, 721.0f, 289.0f };
  _ninePatchInfo = { r, 63, 54, (int)r.width - 665, (int)r.height - 239,
NPATCH_NINE_PATCH };
  //...
}
```

In the above code snippet, after we load an image as a texture and store it in `_npatchTex`, the variable of the C structure `NpatchInfo`, `_ninePatchInfo`, specifies the region in the source texture and the left/top/right/bottom offset of each side to create the slices.

Once we get the graphics image and N-patch settings ready, we can actually render it on the screen. We call the N-patch rendering API in the `Draw2D()` function in the following code snippet:

```
Vector2 origin = { _npatchTex.width * 0.5f, _npatchTex.height * 0.5f };
DrawTextureNPatch(_npatchTex, _ninePatchInfo, _dest, origin, 0.0f, WHITE);
```

Here, the `DrawTextureNPatch()` function takes `NPatchInfo` and the source texture to render the scaled result as specified in the `_dest` rectangle.

Let's draw the same UI background texture with two different sizes to show how an N-patch texture works in *Figure 4.12*:

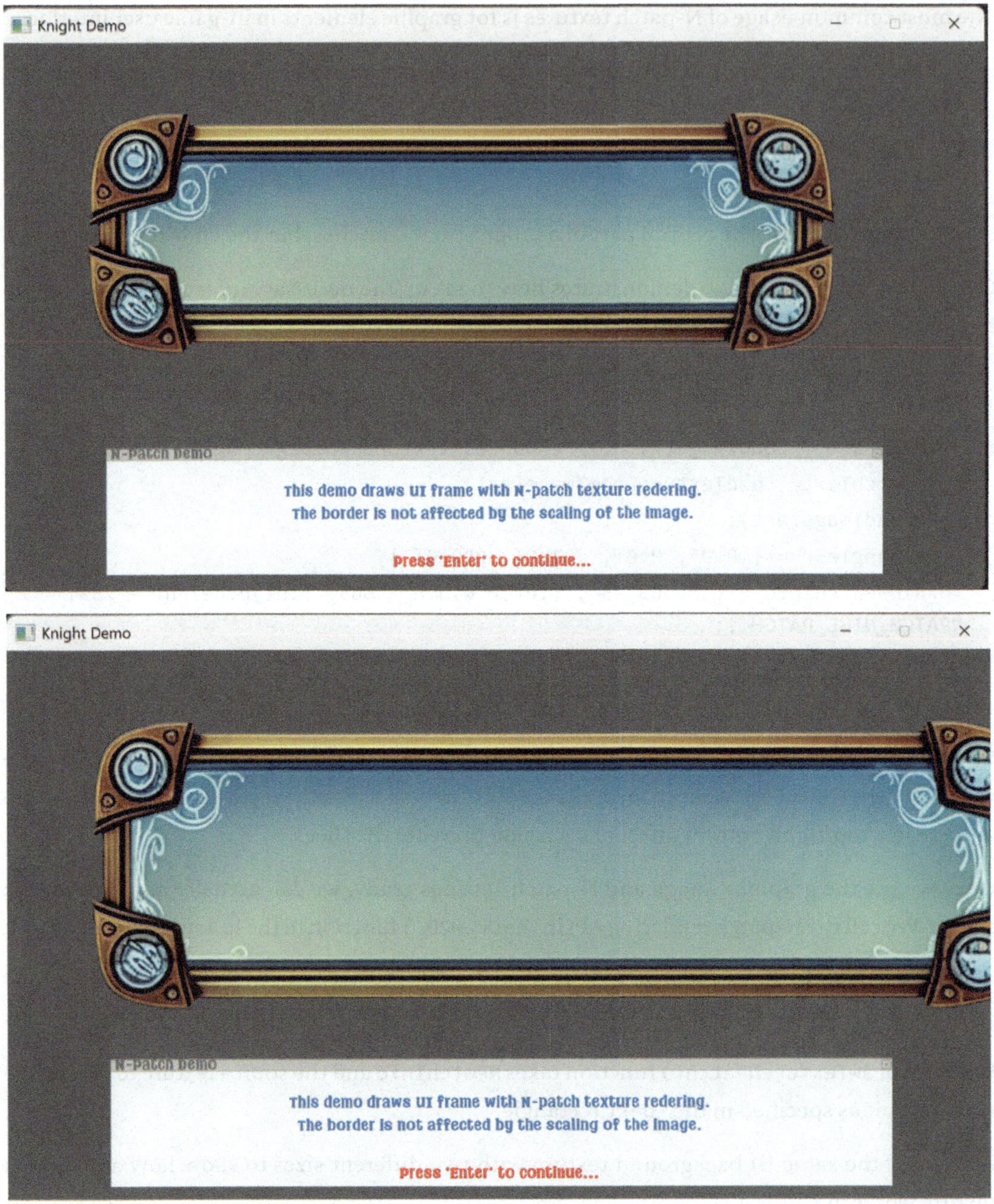

Figure 4.12 – Maintaining the proper size of the frame of the border while scaling the UI background N-patch texture up and down

As shown in *Figure 4.12*, the demo class `NPatchDemo` automatically scales the UI up and down but still maintains the correct size of the frames along the borders.

N-patch is a highly useful technique in game and UI development that allows images to scale flexibly without distorting important details. It provides a clean, efficient way to create resizable elements like buttons, panels, and progress bars while maintaining high-quality visuals.

This is also the last demo scene in the sample project `Demo4texops`. In the next section, we will explore another common feature seen in many 2D games: screen scrolling.

Using screen scrolling

In this section, we will introduce a common full-screen scrolling technique widely used in mainly side-scrolling 2D platform games like the one shown in *Figure 4.13*. This type of game usually features multiple image layers as the background, with a different scrolling speed for each layer to create a sense of depth.

Figure 4.13 – A typical side-scrolling platform game with multiple scrolled layers of background

The mouse-head main character runs in a horizontal direction, and the background graphics, like the castle and far-away mountains, are scrolled in the opposite direction to create the illusion of the character running ahead.

Parallax scrolling

Parallax scrolling is a technique used in 2D games and visual design to create an illusion of depth and immersion by having background layers move at different speeds relative to the foreground. This effect mimics how objects in the real world appear to move at different speeds depending on their distance from the viewer.

In parallax scrolling:

- Objects or layers closer to the viewer (foreground) move faster.
- Objects or layers further from the viewer (background) move more slowly.

This creates a more dynamic and immersive experience, giving a 2D scene a sense of depth, even though it is fundamentally flat.

There are certain advantages of using parallax scrolling:

- **Enhanced visual depth**: Parallax scrolling creates a more immersive experience by simulating depth, even in a 2D environment.
- **Aesthetic appeal**: It adds visual interest and dynamic movement, making static scenes come alive with background motion.
- **Versatility**: It can be used in various genres, such as platformers, side-scrolling shooters, or even adventure games, to create dynamic environments.

Parallax scrolling is widely used in 2D platformers, side-scrolling games, and even top-down games to enhance visual appeal and immersion. Some examples are:

- **2D platformers**: Games like *Super Mario Bros.* (first released in 1985) and *Rayman* (first released in 1995) use parallax scrolling to create multiple background layers (mountains, clouds, distant hills) that move at different speeds, adding depth to the gameplay environment.
- **Side-scrolling shooters**: In games like *Metal Slug* (first released in 1996), parallax scrolling is used to create a sense of speed and immersion as the player moves through different areas of the game.
- **Endless runners**: Games like *Temple Run* (first released in 2011) and *Jetpack Joyride* (2011) use parallax scrolling to simulate forward motion while maintaining a dynamic background.

How parallax scrolling works

The demo project `Demo4ss` demonstrates how to render three layers of parallax scrolling backgrounds in Knight. In a typical parallax setup, a game scene might have multiple layers, as shown in *Figure 4.14*.

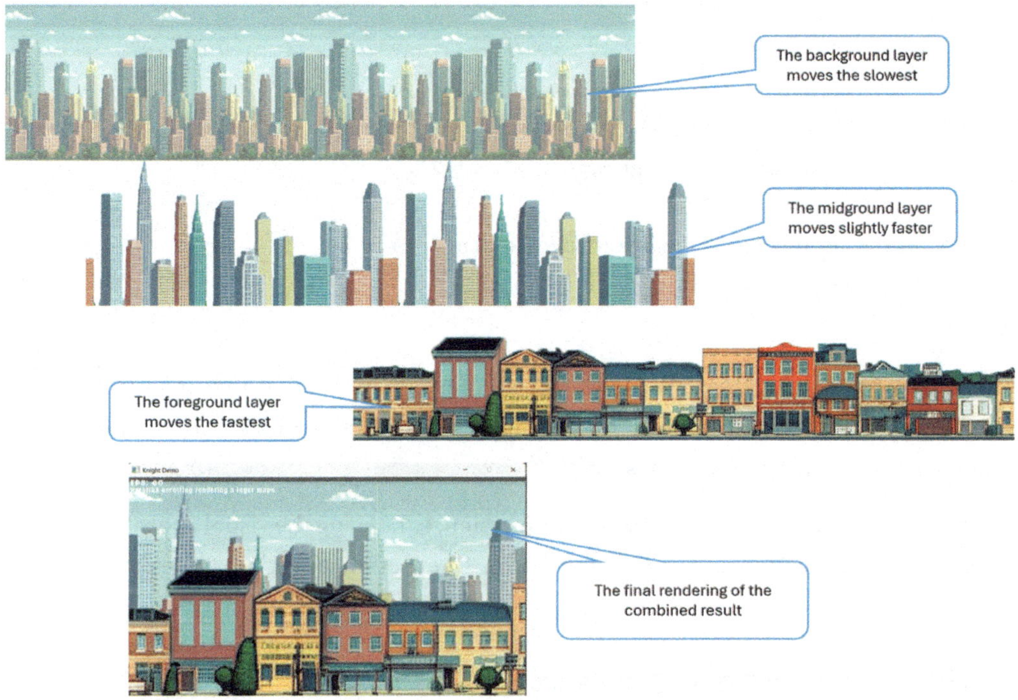

Figure 4.14 – Use 3 layers of textures with different scrolling speeds to create a parallax effect

Here are the layers:

- **Foreground layer**: The player character, platforms, or interactive objects.
- **Midground layer(s)**: Trees, buildings, or other objects closer to the player but not interactive.
- **Background layer(s)**: Mountains, sky, or clouds that are very far away.

Each of these layers moves at different speeds. For example:

- The foreground moves at full speed.
- The midground moves at half the speed of the foreground.
- The background moves even more slowly, perhaps at 1/10th the speed of the foreground.

The scrolling calculation is done in the `Update()` function (in `Demo4ss.cpp`):

```
void Demo4ss::Update(float ElapsedSeconds)
{
    __super::Update(ElapsedSeconds);
    scrollingBack -= 0.1f;
    scrollingMid -= 0.5f;
    scrollingFore -= 1.2f;
    if (scrollingBack <= -background.width * 2)
        scrollingBack = 0;
    if (scrollingMid <= -midground.width * 2)
        scrollingMid = 0;
    if (scrollingFore <= -foreground.width * 2)
        scrollingFore = 0;
}
```

The code above aligns textures to the left while accounting for the texture being scaled to twice its size, which affects scrolling. Varying scrolling speeds create an illusion of depth by making distant objects appear to move more slowly.

This parallax scrolling effect adds depth and immersion, enhancing the visual appeal of 2D games. But how can we push a 2D game to look more like a 3D experience? Let's explore that in the next section.

Rendering isometric maps

An **isometric map** is a type of 2D representation used in games and simulations to depict a 3D environment from a fixed, tilted perspective. Isometric maps create an illusion of depth without using real 3D rendering. The most common view in isometric projection is from a 30-degree angle, where objects and characters appear to have volume and depth, even though they exist on a 2D plane.

Our demo project `Demo4iso` demonstrates isometric map rendering. *Figure 4.15* shows the running of the demo. It randomly picks available tiles from the tile group texture (as shown in *Figure 4.15*) to assemble an isometric tile map at runtime.

Figure 4.15 – Rendering an isometric tile map

Here are the key features of isometric maps:

- **Tilted view**: Isometric maps show the environment from a diagonal view, usually at a 30- or 45-degree angle, making objects appear as if viewed from above and to the side.
- **No perspective foreshortening**: Unlike perspective projections, isometric projection doesn't shrink objects as they get farther from the viewer, keeping all objects the same size regardless of distance.
- **Grid representation**: Although the visual effect is 3D-like, isometric maps are typically implemented as 2D grids. This simplifies positioning, interaction, and collision detection.

Isometric maps are commonly used in 2D games to give the illusion of depth and a 3D world. They have been popular in strategy games, role-playing games (RPGs), and city-building games.

There are certain advantages of using isometric maps:

- **Depth perception**: Isometric maps provide a sense of depth while remaining in a 2D environment, making it visually appealing without the complexity of full 3D rendering.
- **Simple implementation**: While isometric projection gives a 3D-like view, the underlying logic is still based on a 2D grid, which simplifies collision detection, pathfinding, and tile-based movement.
- **Consistency**: Since isometric projection doesn't involve perspective scaling, objects remain the same size regardless of their position on the map, leading to a consistent and clean appearance.

How isometric projection works

In an isometric view, the world is usually represented on a diamond-shaped grid instead of the typical square grid. Each tile represents a cell in the game's world, and objects placed on those tiles (e.g., characters, buildings) appear in 3D, even though they are drawn in 2D.

Here, the cells have been rotated and skewed to give the illusion of depth, making the tiled map appear three-dimensional.

To render an isometric map from a 2D grid, you need to convert the grid coordinates (x, y) into screen coordinates (`screenX`, `screenY`). The following formulas are typically used for this transformation:

```
int screenX = (x - y) * TILE_WIDTH / 2;
int screenY = (x + y) * TILE_HEIGHT / 2;
```

Here's what the components of the formulae represent:

- `TILE_WIDTH` and `TILE_HEIGHT` represent the size of each isometric tile on the screen.
- The formulas account for the skew and rotation needed to create the isometric perspective.

Usually, the size of the tile is relatively small, like 256x128 pixels, so we will group all tile variations into a single texture, as seen in *Figure 4.16*:

Figure 4.16 – Grouping all tile variations into a single texture

However, there are also some challenges of rendering isometric maps:

- **Coordinate conversion**: Converting between isometric screen coordinates and grid coordinates requires additional math, especially for detecting mouse clicks or determining which tile is being interacted with. This can be done in the following code snippet:

```
tileX = (screenY/TILE_HEIGHT+screenX/TILE_WIDTH)/2;
tileY = (screenY/TILE_HEIGHT-screenX/TILE_WIDTH)/2;
```

  The calculated (`tileX`, `tileY`) is the coordinate of (row/column) of the tile.

- **Rendering order**: Overlapping tiles and objects may require careful rendering to ensure proper depth order (e.g., making sure a character is drawn in front of or behind a tree, depending on its position).

Isometric rendering in 2D games simplifies gameplay mechanics like collision detection while providing a visually engaging, pseudo-3D experience. You can extend the `Demo4iso` sample project to add characters and other props on top of the map.

Summary

In this chapter, we introduced 2D graphic techniques frequently used in game development. We provided an in-depth exploration of 2D rendering and effects for game development. It explained how 2D images are loaded from storage, transferred to the system and video memory, and then efficiently rendered onscreen. The chapter covered essential techniques such as color and alpha blending, which allow for dynamic visual effects like smooth transitions, transparency, and lighting adjustments. It also discussed various texture formats, compression methods, and memory management strategies crucial for optimizing performance in graphics-intensive applications.

This chapter further delved into advanced 2D techniques, including parallax scrolling, N-patch texture rendering for flexible UI design, and isometric map rendering to create a pseudo-3D visual experience.

Through a series of practical examples and demo projects, we illustrated how to implement these methods using Knight, emphasizing the importance of layering, scrolling speed differences, and texture manipulation to achieve depth and immersion in 2D games.

It's time for us to move on from 2D graphics into the world of 3D graphics, starting from how the player sees the game world – the 3D camera system.

5

The Camera and Camera Controls

The camera is a vital element in presenting the game world to players—it's how they view and interact with that world. Before diving into other aspects of 3D scene rendering, let's first explore the concept of cameras and their role in graphics rendering.

In *Chapters 1* and *2*, we saw examples of how the Knight uses cameras to render the game scene. This chapter introduces the principles of cameras and explores different types used across game genres, such as **first-person shooters (FPS)**, third-person action RPGs, top-down views, and cinematic storytelling. Most importantly, we'll look at how to implement these camera types using the Knight.

In this chapter, we will look at the following topics:

- Camera – how players see the game world through the 3D camera
- Defining the camera for rendering a scene
- Working with the built-in camera system
- Building a third-person follow-up camera, rail camera, and RTS camera system
- Rendering multiple split-screen cameras

By the end of this chapter, you will understand the principle of how 3D camera projection works and will have learned how to build various types of 3D camera systems frequently used by different types of 3D games, such as a first-person shooter camera, third-person follow-up camera, and a railed camera, and be able to customize Knight for your own 3D camera needs, such as rendering multiple types of camera on the screen.

Technical requirements

Download and open the project via this GitHub URL to open the example projects demonstrated in this chapter in the `Knight` solution: `https://github.com/PacktPublishing/Data-Structures-and-Algorithms-for-Game-Programming-in-CPP`. The following projects in the Visual Studio solution are used as samples for this chapter:

Project Name	Description
`Demo5FPC`	Sample code of raylib's built-in first-person camera
`Demo53PV`	Sample code of implementing a third-person follow-up camera
`Demo5Ortho`	Sample code of a 3D orthogonal project camera
`Demo5TrkCam`	Sample code of a railed camera (camera on a fixed path)
`Demo5RTSCam`	Sample code of camera navigation in an RTS-style game
`Demo5MultiCams`	Sample code to implement multiple camera viewports on a single device screen

Table 5.1 - Sample projects used in the chapter

Camera – how players see the game world

For those new to 3D game development, the first essential step is deciding how players will view the game world onscreen. Imagine an audience in a movie theater: the film uses various cinematic techniques, such as changes in camera angle and distance, to tell its story.

Similarly, designing how scenes are presented in a game is like directing a movie. In 3D game development, the game designer acts as the movie director, orchestrating different perspectives to shape the player's experience. In larger development teams, a dedicated visual director often uses storyboards to design the camera angles for each scene, creating the desired visual narrative. The following is an example storyboard of a fighting sequence.

Figure 5.1 – A typical video game storyboard for an in-game boss fight event

Some 3D games use a single fixed perspective. For instance, many popular FPS games are played entirely from the player's viewpoint because it's ideal for focusing on aiming and targeting.

Other 3D games utilize multiple perspectives to enrich the story-driven gameplay. In *Nier: Automata* (first published in 2017) players experience cinematic views while piloting a mech, in a close third-person view with sword combat, and even a top-down perspective during hacking mini-games. Each perspective provides a distinct experience and enhances the game's various gameplay mechanisms.

Common uses of cameras in video games

In many 2D and 3D games, there are several common types of camera perspectives:

First-person camera

The **first-person camera view** simulates the player's perspective from the character's eyes, creating an immersive experience ideal for FPS games and simulations. Notable titles, such as *Call of Duty* (first published in 2003), *Halo* (first published in 2001), and *Half-Life* (first published in 1998), use this view to heighten realism and support precision aiming. It dynamically rotates and moves with the player's actions, ensuring a lifelike and engaging gameplay experience.

The `Demo5FPC` project implements a first-person view camera, as shown in *Figure 5.2*:

Figure 5.2 – Knight's built-in first-person view camera

Open and run the project. You can use *WASD* keys to move yourself inside the scene. Also, you can use the *up* and *down* arrow keys or mouse to tilt and rotate the camera, just like players tilt and rotate their heads.

Third-person camera

The **third-person camera** positions the view behind and slightly above the player, offering a broad perspective of both the character and their surroundings. It's popular in action-adventure, platformer, and RPG games—such as *The Witcher 3* (2015), *Assassin's Creed* (first released in 2007), and *Uncharted* (first published in 2007)—to enhance situational awareness and highlight character animations. This camera typically follows and rotates around the player for optimal viewing during exploration and interaction.

The `Demo53PV` project implements a third-person view camera with an automatic follow feature, as shown in *Figure 5.3*:

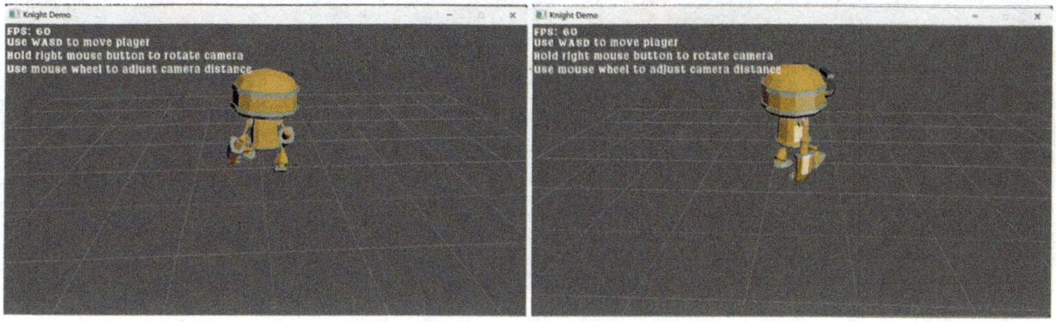

Figure 5.3 – The third-person view with the support of camera tilt and rotation

Open and run the project. You can use the *WASD* keys to control the player character and observe how the camera smoothly follows the player. You can also use the mouse to rotate the follow-up angle to see the character from different view angles while holding the *right mouse button* down.

Top-down camera

The top-down camera provides a bird's-eye view of the game world, allowing players to monitor and control multiple units and structures at once. This fixed, high-angle perspective is crucial for strategic gameplay in **real-time strategy (RTS)** games, simulation, and multiplayer RPGs, as seen in games such as *StarCraft* and *Age of Empires*. It offers a comprehensive overview of the battlefield, enabling effective management and precise control over large-scale operations.

The `Demo5RTSCam` project implements a top-down camera system designed for real-time strategy games, as shown in *Figure 5.4*:

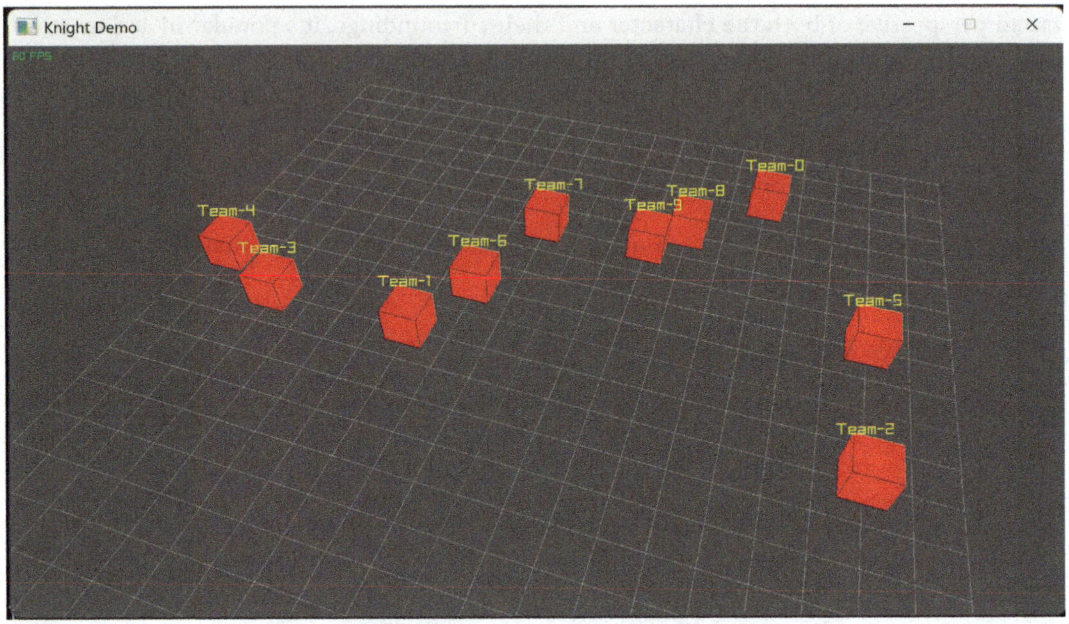

Figure 5.4 – A top-down camera with a selectable battle unit

Open and run the project. You can use the *left mouse button* to select and deselect any battle unit (represented as a *red* cube labeled with the team's name and stats). You can also hold down the *right mouse button* to rotate the camera and use *arrow keys* to move the camera around.

Rail camera

The **rail camera** follows a predetermined path, guiding the player's view along a fixed "rail" to enhance cinematic sequences and focus on key gameplay moments. Commonly used in on-rails shooters, racing games, and similar titles, this camera moves alongside or around the player, limiting control to ensure a controlled perspective. Its primary purpose is to direct attention precisely, as seen in games such as *Star Fox 64* (1997) and *Uncharted*, where it heightens the cinematic intensity of action scenes.

The `Demo5TrkCam` project demonstrates how to control camera movement along a predefined path using waypoints, while keeping the player character in view, as shown in *Figure 5.5*:

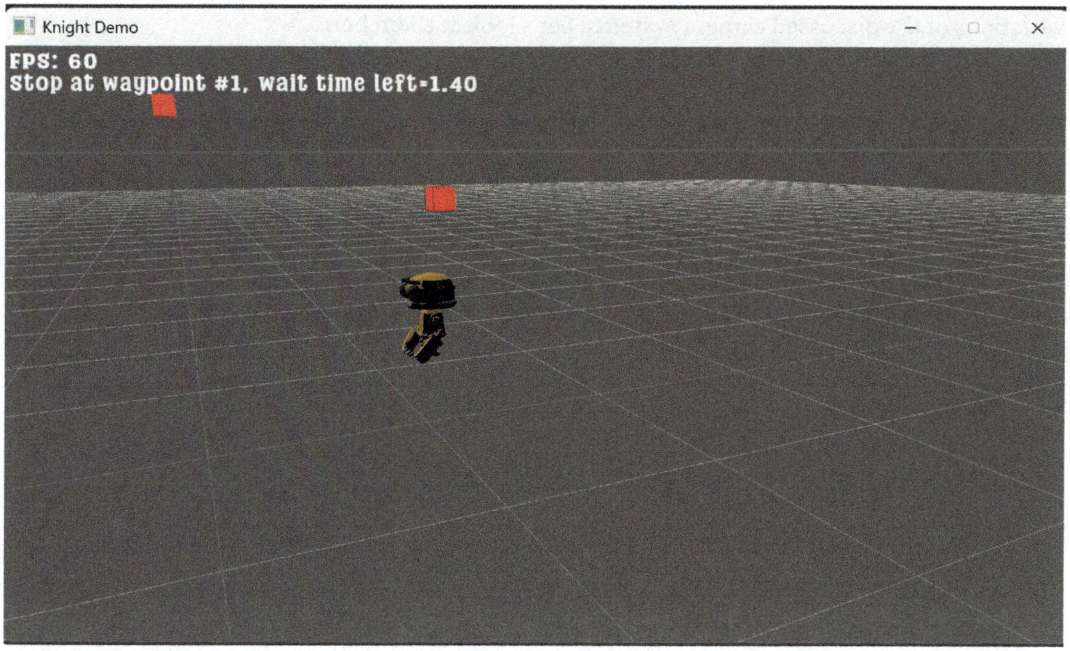

Figure 5.5 – A rail camera moves along the predefined path

Open and run the project. The camera stops at each waypoint (shown as a *red* box in the scene), allowing the game to set up challenges or trigger storytelling events.

Fly-through camera

The fly-through camera enables unrestricted movement through the game world, simulating a free-floating perspective. It's commonly used in level editors, and sandbox games (such as *Minecraft* in spectator mode), allowing users to navigate and inspect environments in detail. Its key advantage is that it isn't tied to any specific character, so it can move and rotate freely, making it ideal for exploration, debugging, and precise scene adjustments.

Other variations

Besides all the popular camera systems mentioned in the previous subsections, there are several variations of the discussed camera systems. Let's look at them here:

- **Cinematic camera**: Camera angles and movements are carefully scripted to focus on key events or characters, creating a cinematic feel to enhance immersion and storytelling.
    - **Usage**: In-game cutscenes and narrative sequences – you can combine rail, top-down, and first- or third-person views by carefully scripting them into a cohesive sequence.
    - **Purpose**: Designed to emulate real-world cinematography, it may use predefined paths, angles, and zooms to enhance the storytelling experience.
- **Orbiting camera**: The player can control the camera's angle and distance to view the object or character from multiple perspectives.
    - **Usage**: In games with detailed character or object interaction (such as *The Sims*; first released in 2000), or games that require close inspection of objects or environments.
    - **Purpose**: The camera orbits around a fixed point, typically the player character or an object of interest. It's useful for creating dynamic views of a scene.
- **Over-the-shoulder camera**: This is a special first-person-view-like camera but is often used to improve aiming or combat focus while still showing part of the character onscreen.
    - **Usage**: Tactical shooters and narrative-driven games (such as *Resident Evil 4*; released in 2005).
    - **Purpose**: A variation of the third-person camera where the camera is positioned directly behind and slightly above the player's shoulder. This camera provides a more intimate and detailed view of the character's surroundings.

- **Fixed camera**: This type of camera gives developers more control over what the player sees, creating a sense of tension, mystery, or surprise by limiting the player's view of the environment.
    - **Usage**: Early survival horror games (such as *Silent Hill*; first released in 1999), puzzle games, or platformers.
    - **Purpose**: The camera is placed in fixed positions, and the player's movement triggers a camera change based on where they move.
- **VR camera (for virtual reality)**: The camera view updates in real time to the player's head position and orientation, requiring precise tracking and rendering to avoid motion sickness and maintain immersion.
    - **Usage**: Virtual reality games and experiences (such as *Beat Saber*; released in 2019).
    - **Purpose**: The camera simulates the player's head movements in a 3D space, allowing for a fully immersive VR experience.

After introducing the various cameras commonly used in 3D games, we will now delve into how cameras are defined and implemented.

Defining the camera for rendering a scene

Before we start to implement any of the camera systems for our game, we should understand the principles and mathematics of how a camera system works.

Basic properties of a camera system

The camera can be placed, moved, rotated, and zoomed to control the player's view of the game scene. Different types of 3D cameras serve various purposes, and they are implemented depending on the gameplay style or specific needs of the game.

However, the following basic camera properties are common to the implementation of almost any kind of camera system in video game programming:

- **Position and orientation**: The camera's position and orientation (rotation) define where the player is looking. Sometimes, the term "look-at" direction is used to represent the camera's orientation.

- **Field of View (FOV)**: This controls the amount of the game world the player can see at once, simulating peripheral vision. It's important for balancing gameplay immersion and performance. *Figure 5.6* compares the same view with different FOV angles.

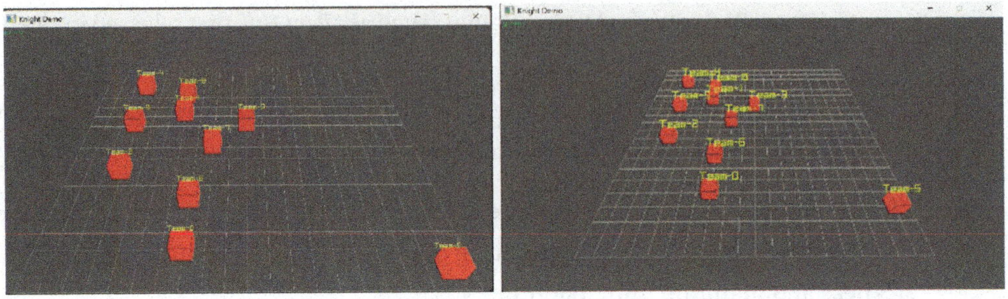

Figure 5.6 – The same top-down camera with FoV=40 (left) and FoV=80 (right)

- The **aspect ratio** is the ratio of the width to the height of the viewing area, typically represented as **width : height**. In 3D graphics, the aspect ratio defines the proportions of the camera's view and affects how the game scene is projected onto the screen. It's crucial for ensuring that objects don't appear stretched or squashed.
- **Zoom**: There is the ability to zoom in and out, adjusting how close or far away the camera is from the target (usually used in strategy games or sniper modes in FPS games). *Figure 5.7* shows the different zoom levels of the same camera:

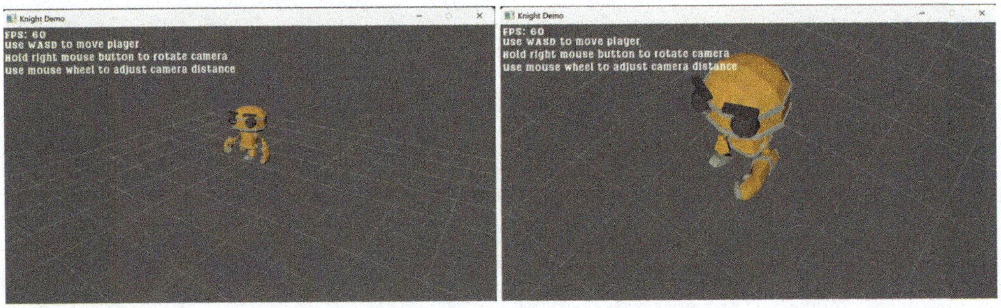

Figure 5.7 – Comparing different zoom levels

- **Clipping**: Cameras often use near and far clipping planes to determine what is visible and what is not. Anything outside the clipping planes isn't rendered. *Figure 5.8* shows how near and far planes define the visible range of the depth:

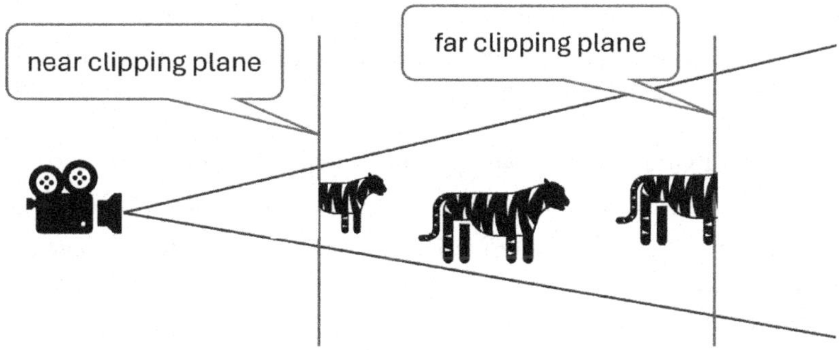

Figure 5.8 – The near and far clipping planes define the visible range of a camera

After understanding the basic properties related to cameras, in the next section, we will explore in depth how cameras project a 3D world onto a 2D plane.

Projecting a 3D world onto a 2D screen

Camera projection in 3D graphics is the process of transforming 3D coordinates into 2D coordinates, so they can be displayed on a flat screen. This transformation simulates how a camera *sees* the 3D world, and it's essential for creating a realistic or visually appropriate view of a scene.

Projecting a 3D world onto a 2D screen in Knight involves two major mathematic transformations that convert object coordinates into pixel coordinates, as we will see in the subsequent paragraphs.

The first step of transformation involves a **model-view matrix**, which positions and orients the entire scene as seen from the camera. The model-view matrix is the combination of the following:

- **Model matrix**: This transforms the object from its local coordinate space to the world coordinate space. It includes translation, rotation, and scaling transformations for each object in the scene. This process is done when the `Update()` function of the Knight app class is called. It will call the `_Scene` object's `Update()` function to traverse the entire scene hierarchy. Knight handles this calculation for you.
- **View matrix**: This transforms world coordinates into the camera's coordinate space. This matrix is created based on the camera's position, target, and up vector. Knight internally calls raylib's `BeginCamera3D()` to build the view matrix based on the camera's position and orientation, so you don't need to create the view matrix manually.

The second step of transformation continues from the result of the previous step. Using the **projection matrix** takes the camera-space coordinates and maps them into clip space, applying either perspective or orthographic projection.

In 3D graphics and video game development, perspective projection and orthogonal (or orthographic) projection are two common techniques used to project 3D objects onto a 2D screen. Both methods have different characteristics and are used in different scenarios depending on the desired visual effect.

Perspective projection

Perspective projection simulates how the human eye perceives the world, where objects appear smaller as they get farther from the camera. This type of projection introduces depth, creating a realistic sense of scale and distance. *Figure 5.2* and *Figure 5.4* are good examples of perspective projection for both a first-person view and a third-person view.

In perspective projection, each point in 3D space is scaled based on its distance from the camera. The further an object is, the more it is scaled down, resulting in a vanishing point effect.

The perspective projection can be represented by a matrix that includes the FOV, aspect ratio, and near and far clipping planes to define how much of the 3D world is visible on the screen:

$$\begin{bmatrix} \frac{1}{aspect\ ratio * \tan\left(\frac{FoV}{2}\right)} & 0 & 0 & 0 \\ 0 & \frac{1}{\tan\left(\frac{Fov}{2}\right)} & 0 & 0 \\ 0 & 0 & -\frac{far + near}{far - near} & -\frac{2 * far * near}{far - near} \\ 0 & 0 & -1 & 0 \end{bmatrix}$$

Sometimes, we may not want objects at varying distances from the camera to appear scaled differently. In such cases, we use orthographic projection.

Orthographic projection

Orthographic projection removes the effect of distance on an object's size, meaning that all objects appear the same size regardless of their distance from the camera. This projection is commonly used in CAD, architectural visualization, and certain types of games, such as 2D platformers or isometric views.

In orthographic projection, each point is mapped to the screen based on its coordinates without any scaling for distance.

The orthographic projection matrix defines a viewing box (a cuboid) where only objects within this box are visible:

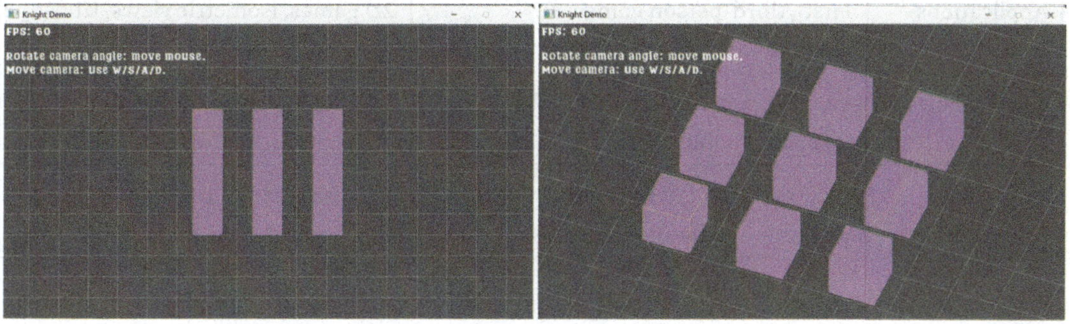

Figure 5.9 – The orthogonal project will not have any scaling effect

In orthographic projection, each point is mapped to the screen based on its coordinates without any scaling for distance.

The orthographic projection matrix defines a viewing box (a cuboid) where only objects within this box are visible:

$$\begin{bmatrix} \frac{2}{right-left} & 0 & 0 & -\frac{right+left}{right-left} \\ 0 & \frac{2}{top-bottom} & 0 & -\frac{top+bottom}{top-bottom} \\ 0 & 0 & -\frac{2}{far-near} & -\frac{far+near}{far-near} \\ 0 & 0 & 0 & 1 \end{bmatrix}$$

For a quick summary of how these two projections are different from each other, see this table:

	Perspective Projection	Orthogonal Projection
Depth Perception	Objects appear smaller as they get farther away.	Objects remain the same size regardless of distance.
Foreshortening	Yes, closer objects appear larger.	No, objects maintain their actual size.
Realism	Provides a realistic sense of depth and scale.	Provides a flat, consistent view, useful for 2D and technical views.
Applications	First-/third-person games, 3D simulations, realistic 3D environments.	2D games, isometric views, UI elements, technical drawing.
Parallel Lines	Parallel lines converge toward a vanishing point.	Parallel lines remain parallel.
Projection Matrix	Requires a field of view, aspect ratio, and near and far planes.	Requires boundaries (left, right, top, bottom, near, far).

Table 5.2 – Perspective projection versus orthographic projection

In the next section, we will put the mathematics into actual code to write our camera action.

Working with the built-in camera system

It's time to see all sorts of cameras in action. Knight comes with several handy and ready-to-use camera implementations. We will first introduce the built-in first-person-view camera and the orthogonal-view camera. Then we will take one step further to create customized control of the built-in camera.

Using the first-person-view camera

The demo project `Demo5FPC` demonstrates how to use Knight's built-in first-person-view camera.

It's simple to create a first-person-view camera with Knight:

```
FPSCamera = _Scene->CreateSceneObject<PerspectiveCamera>("Camera");
FPSCamera->SetPosition(Vector3{0.0f, 2.0f, 4.0f});
FPSCamera->SetLookAtPosition(Vector3{ 0.0f, 2.0f, 0.0f });
FPSCamera->SetFovY(60.0f);
FPSCamera->CameraMode = CAMERA_FIRST_PERSON;
```

Most of the setup code is the same as usual. However, when we assign `CameraMode` as `CAMERA_FIRST_PERSON` and add it to the scene, Knight will activate first-person mode and enable input control for first-person mode.

The first-person mode will enable the control to move the camera in the scene. You can use *WASD* to move the camera position or use the arrow key/mouse to make the camera look around.

Knight automatically calls raylib's `UpdateCamera()` API in the base class of `PerspectiveCamera`. There is no need to call `UpdateCamera()` in your Knight application as long as you create and add a `PerspectiveCamera` object in the `_Scene` object.

Using the orthogonal camera

The `Demo5Ortho` demo project demonstrates the use of the built-in orthogonal camera of Knight to display a scene:

```
OrthogonalCamera* OrthCam = NULL;
OrthCam = _Scene->CreateSceneObject<OrthogonalCamera>("Orthogonal
Camera");
OrthCam->SetUp(Vector3{ 0.0f, 15.0f, 15.0f }, Vector3{ 0.0f, 0.0f, 0.0f },
20.0f);
```

This time, we use the built-in `OrthogonalCamera` class instead of the `PerspectiveCamera` class to create the orthogonal camera.

The `Setup()` function allows you to specify the initial position of the camera, the target position it looks at, and a zoom factor.

The orthogonal camera enables mouse wheel input to adjust the zoom factor of the camera, as well as mouse moves to change the viewing angle while holding down the *right mouse button*. If you try to play around with the viewing angle, you will find the object in the scene will not distort like the perspective camera does.

The mouse and keyboard input is handled in the `Update()` function of the `OrthogonalCamera` class:

```
bool OrthogonalCamera::Update(float ElapsedSeconds){
//...
// Zoom control with mouse wheel
    cameraZoom -= GetMouseWheelMove() * 0.5f;
    if (cameraZoom < 2.0f) cameraZoom = 2.0f;    // Minimum zoom
    if (cameraZoom > 50.0f) cameraZoom = 50.0f; // Maximum zoom
    _Camera.fovy = cameraZoom;
```

This part of the code implements the zoom feature by reading the movement of the mouse wheel. It also has a minimum and maximum limits check of the zoom value. This keeps the zoom factor within a reasonable range:

```
    //Calculate the camera's position
    _Camera.position.x = _Camera.target.x -
sin(cameraHorizontalAngleShift) * cameraZoom;
    _Camera.position.z = _Camera.target.z -
cos(cameraHorizontalAngleShift) * cameraZoom;
    _Camera.position.y = cameraZoom + cameraVerticalOffset;
    // Panning with arrow keys
    if (IsKeyDown(KEY_UP)) _Camera.target.z -= panSpeed;
    if (IsKeyDown(KEY_DOWN)) _Camera.target.z += panSpeed;
    if (IsKeyDown(KEY_LEFT)) _Camera.target.x -= panSpeed;
    if (IsKeyDown(KEY_RIGHT)) _Camera.target.x += panSpeed;
```

The previous part of the code implements the control of camera move and pan. The amount of movement is controlled by the panSpeed member variable:

```
    // Rotate the camera around the player when right mouse button is held
    if (IsMouseButtonDown(MOUSE_BUTTON_RIGHT)) {
        cameraHorizontalAngleShift += GetMouseDelta().x * 0.01f;
        cameraVerticalOffset += GetMouseDelta().y * 0.01f;
    }
    return true;
}
```

The rest of the code handles the camera tilt and rotation by reading mouse movement values. So, the player can rotate and tilt the camera. This part of the code updates `cameraVerticalOffset` for the amount of tilt angle change and `cameraHorizontalAngleShift` for the amount of horizontal rotation changes. The results will be used to calculate the new camera position.

Overriding the default control for built-in cameras

Knight is built with ease of use in mind, so we provide a set of default camera controls. But what if you only want to use the camera, but not the input control? To do so, you will need to inherit from the built-in camera class and override the `Update()` function of the parent camera class. We will demonstrate how to implement this in the next follow-up camera example.

You can also use the same way to make your own camera class for your game's customized needs. In the next couple of sections, we will explore how to write our own camera system with customized behavior that still works well with the whole scene hierarchy of Knight.

Building a third-person follow-up camera

It's time for us to step forward to try implementing our own camera system for the needs of our game. Knight itself has built-in support for a third-person camera. However, it's very basic and far from the usual third-person camera you will have seen in many games.

Let's build a new third-person-view camera that supports the following behavior:

- It follows behind the main character (or any assigned `SceneActor` in Knight).
- When the main character moves, it will automatically follow the movement and change of orientation of the main character.
- The player can have control over the camera angle both horizontally and vertically.
- The player can zoom the distance between the camera and the followed `SceneActor`.

All camera types in Knight, such as `PerspectiveCamera` and `OrthogonalCamera`, inherit from the base `SceneCamera` class. This class encapsulates the `Camera3D` class provided by the underlying raylib renderer.

The `SceneCamera` constructor initializes some basic properties of the camera and, if the `IsMainCamera` parameter is set to true (default), assigns it as the "main camera" of the game scene.

In many of the example projects in *Chapter 2*, we create a camera and add it as a child `SceneObject` of `_Scene`. This setup allows the camera's `Update()` function to be automatically called when `_Scene`'s `Update()` function is invoked.

As we observed in the `OrthogonalCamera` class, which handles player input to update the camera's position and rotation, we'll also create a new `FollowUpCamera` class. This class inherits from `SceneCamera` and overrides the `Update()` function to include custom input handling. The class declaration can be found in `FollowUpCamera.h` in the `Demo5MultiCams` sample project:

```
class FollowUpCamera : public SceneCamera {
public:
  FollowUpCamera(Scene* Scene, const char* Name = nullptr, bool
IsMainCamera = true);
  virtual ~FollowUpCamera();
  void SetUp(SceneActor* pTarget, float fovY, float defaultDistance, int
projType);
  bool Update(float ElapsedSeconds) override;
  //target Actor to follow up
  SceneActor *TargetActor = NULL;
  // control the camera's distance from the player
  float cameraDistance = 5.0f;
private:
  float mCameraHorizontalAngleShift = 0.0f;
  float mCameraVerticalOffset = 0.0f;
};
```

This camera will always follow a specific target `SceneActor` (usually the one that represents the main player character of the game).

The `cameraDistance` member variable is used to specify how far the camera is behind the target `SceneActor`.

Both `mCameraHorizontalAngleShift` and `mCameraVerticalOffset` are only used for the camera tilt and rotation calculation; they are not meant to be accessed outside the class, so they are declared as private variables.

The most important part is the override `Update()` function. The first part of this function is to calculate the distance changes from mouse wheel moves:

```
bool FollowUpCamera::Update(float ElapsedSeconds) {
  if (!IsActive)return false;
  // Adjust camera distance with mouse wheel
  if (processMouseInput)
    cameraDistance -= GetMouseWheelMove();
```

```
    if (cameraDistance < 2.0f) cameraDistance = 2.0f; // Minimum distance
    if (cameraDistance > 10.0f) cameraDistance = 10.0f; // Maximum distance
```

Now we can calculate the new camera position based on the target `SceneActor`'s position and rotation. The camera always looks at the target `SceneActor`'s position:

```
    //Calculate the camera's position
    _Camera.position.x = TargetActor->Position.x -
  sin(mCameraHorizontalAngleShift + DegreesToRadians(TargetActor-
  >Rotation.y)) * cameraDistance;
    _Camera.position.z = TargetActor->Position.z -
  cos(mCameraHorizontalAngleShift + DegreesToRadians(TargetActor-
  >Rotation.y)) * cameraDistance;
    _Camera.position.y = TargetActor->Position.y + 2.0f +
  mCameraVerticalOffset; // Keep camera above the player
    _Camera.target = TargetActor->Position; // Always focus on the player
```

The final part of the code updates `mCameraHorizontalAngleShift` and `mCameraVerticalOffset` based on the changes in mouse movement since the last frame:

```
    //Rotate the camera when right mouse button is held
    if (IsMouseButtonDown(MOUSE_BUTTON_RIGHT)) {
      mCameraHorizontalAngleShift += GetMouseDelta().x * 0.01f;
      mCameraVerticalOffset += GetMouseDelta().y * 0.01f;
    }
    return true;
  }
```

Now let's go back to the main application class, `Demo53PV`. In the application's `Update()` function, we will update the `SceneActor`'s position and rotation based on player input. The change will also make `FollowUpCamera` calculate the camera's new position and view direction.

As you use the *WASD* keys to move the main character, the third-person-view camera will follow the target `SceneActor`. Meanwhile, the player can use the mouse to adjust the follow distance and angle.

Building a rail camera system

Now we want to create a different type of camera. Instead of allowing the player to control the camera's movement, a rail camera—also known as a **waypoint camera**—follows a predefined path while keeping the player character in focus.

This type of camera is commonly used in racing games, 3D side-scrollers, and platform games.

The `Demo5TrkCam` project implements the rail camera. We'll create a new `WaypointsCamera` to inherit the `SceneCamera` base class:

```
class WaypointsCamera : public SceneCamera {
public:
  WaypointsCamera(Scene* Scene, const char* Name = nullptr, bool
IsMainCamera = true);
  virtual ~WaypointsCamera();
  void SetUp(SceneActor* pTarget, float fovY, int projType);
  bool Update(float ElapsedSeconds) override;
  bool Draw() override;
  //target SceneActor to follow up
  SceneActor* TargetActor = NULL;
  int currentWaypoint = 0;  // Current waypoint index
  float moveSpeed = 1.0f; // Speed of movement
  float waypointWaitTimer = 0.0f;  // Timer to handle waiting at each
waypoint
private:
  // Define a set of waypoints for the camera to move along
  std::vector<Waypoint> waypoints = {
    {{ 0.0f, 4.0f, -10.0f }, 3.0f},
    //…  //all the way points
    {{ -5.0f, 3.0f, 5.0f }, 3.0f}
  };
};
```

Similar to a third-person-view camera, this waypoint camera has the following features:

- It moves along a path defined by the positions of the waypoints
- Each waypoint can specify a stay duration, after which the camera will continue moving to the next waypoint

The most important part is still the override `Update()` function:

```
bool WaypointsCamera::Update(float ElapsedSeconds)
{
  if (!IsActive) return false;
```

The first part is to check if we are currently stopping at some waypoint and wait for the end of the delay time to move to the next waypoint:

```
    // Check if we need to wait at the current waypoint
    if (waypointWaitTimer > 0.0f) {
      waypointWaitTimer -= GetFrameTime();
    } else {
```

If we are currently moving along the path, we need to calculate the direction and distance to the next waypoint from the current position and direction.

```
      // Calculate direction/distance to the next waypoint
      Vector3 direction = Vector3Subtract(waypoints[currentWaypoint].
  position, _Camera.position);
      float distance = Vector3Length(direction);
      // If we're close enough, move to the next one
```

If the camera is very close to the next waypoint, it should advance to the next one. If it reaches the last waypoint, it should simply move back to the first one. However, this may create a jittery effect if the last waypoint is positioned far from the first waypoint:

```
      if (distance < 0.1f) {
        currentWaypoint = (currentWaypoint + 1) % waypoints.size();
        waypointWaitTimer = waypoints[currentWaypoint].waitTime;
      } else {
```

Or, we need to calculate the camera's direction based on its current position relative to the target player character's position. The camera position should also be updated based on the frame time:

```
        // Normalize direction and move the camera
        direction = Vector3Scale(Vector3Normalize(direction), moveSpeed *
  GetFrameTime());
        _Camera.position = Vector3Add(_Camera.position, direction);
      }
      // Update camera target to follow the moving cube
      _Camera.target = Vector3Lerp(_Camera.target, TargetActor->Position,
  0.1f);
    }
    return true;
  }
```

Currently, we just store waypoints as an array of the WayPoint structure:

```
struct Waypoint {
  Vector3 position;
  float waitTime; // Optional wait time at the waypoint
};
```

In the next section, we'll learn how to build a top-down camera.

Building a top-down camera for RTS

In this section, we will build a top-down camera system, commonly used in real-time strategy and multiplayer games where the camera needs to provide a wide view of the game terrain and track the movements of multiple characters or units. This type of camera has different requirements compared to a third-person-view camera:

- The camera can move forward/backward and pan left/right
- It can zoom in to focus on a specific region of the map or zoom out for a broader view of the entire map
- The camera can tilt and rotate, allowing the player to view the map from different angles

Here is the newly created TopDownCamera camera class in TopDownCamera.h of the Demo5RTSCam project:

```
class TopDownCamera : public SceneCamera {
public:
  TopDownCamera(Scene* Scene, const char* Name = nullptr, bool
IsMainCamera = true);
  virtual ~TopDownCamera();
  void SetUp(Vector3 pos, Vector3 target, float fovY, int projType);
  bool Update(float ElapsedSeconds) override;
  float cameraZoom = 15.0f;  // Initial camera distance
  float cameraPanSpeed = 0.1f;  // Camera panning speed
  float zoomSpeed = 1.0f;  // Zoom speed
private:
  float mCameraHorizontalAngleShift = 0.0f;
  float mCameraVerticalOffset = 0.0f;
};
```

Let's check how our `Update()` function is handled. The first part also handles the camera zoom factor:

```
bool TopDownCamera::Update(float ElapsedSeconds) {
  if (!IsActive) return false;
  // Zoom control with mouse wheel
  cameraZoom -= GetMouseWheelMove() * zoomSpeed;
  if (cameraZoom < 5.0f) cameraZoom = 5.0f;
  if (cameraZoom > 25.0f) cameraZoom = 25.0f;
```

The second part is to calculate the camera position and rotation:

```
    //Calculate the camera's position
    _Camera.position.x = _Camera.target.x -
sin(mCameraHorizontalAngleShift)* cameraZoom;
    _Camera.position.z = _Camera.target.z -
cos(mCameraHorizontalAngleShift)* cameraZoom;
    _Camera.position.y = cameraZoom + mCameraVerticalOffset ;
```

The last part handles the keyboard and mouse input of the camera movement and rotation:

```
    // Pan camera with arrow keys
    if (IsKeyDown(KEY_UP)) _Camera.target.z -= cameraPanSpeed;
    if (IsKeyDown(KEY_DOWN)) _Camera.target.z += cameraPanSpeed;
    if (IsKeyDown(KEY_LEFT)) _Camera.target.x -= cameraPanSpeed;
    if (IsKeyDown(KEY_RIGHT)) _Camera.target.x += cameraPanSpeed;
    // Rotate the camera around the player when right mouse button is held
    if (IsMouseButtonDown(MOUSE_BUTTON_RIGHT)) {
        mCameraHorizontalAngleShift += GetMouseDelta().x * 0.01f;
        mCameraVerticalOffset += GetMouseDelta().y * 0.01f;
    }
    return true;
}
```

Games using a top-down camera often need to allow players to select `SceneActor` objects visible within the camera's view. To achieve this, we implement object picking in the `Update()` function of the main application class, `Demo5RTSCam`.

Since we use cubes to represent our battle units, we can calculate each cube's bounding box and cast an imaginary ray from the camera to test if the player selects any units by clicking on them with the mouse:

```
void Demo5RTSCam::Update(float ElapsedSeconds) {
  // Mouse picking: check if any unit is clicked
  if (IsMouseButtonPressed(MOUSE_LEFT_BUTTON)) {
    Ray ray = GetScreenToWorldRay(GetMousePosition(), *RTSCamera-
>GetCamera3D());
    for (auto& unit : units) {
      // Check if the ray hits the cube
      BoundingBox box = {Vector3 { unit.position.x - 0.5f, unit.position.y
- 0.5f, unit.position.z - 0.5f},Vector3 { unit.position.x + 0.5f, unit.
position.y + 0.5f, unit.position.z + 0.5f}
    };
    // Check collision between ray and cube's bounding
    RayCollision rc = GetRayCollisionBox(ray, box);
    if (rc.hit)
      unit.selected = !unit.selected;
  }
  __super::Update(ElapsedSeconds);
}
```

Sometimes it's useful to know the 2D bounding box of a 3D object. This is especially useful when we need to determine the 2D coordinate to draw the unit name of each battle unit. Knight comes with a handy API to calculate a 2D screen coordinate bounding box from a 3D cube. This is done in the `DrawGUI()` function of the `Demo5RTSCam` class (in `Demo5RTSCam.cpp`):

```
//draw all unit name on top edge of the 2D bounding box
for (auto& unit : units) {
  BoundingRect rect = Get2DBoundingRectOfCube(unit.position, 1.0f,
*RTSCamera->GetCamera3D());
  unit.LabelPos.x = rect.min.x;
  unit.LabelPos.y = rect.min.y-20;
  DrawText(unit.Name, unit.LabelPos.x, unit.LabelPos.y, 30, YELLOW);
}
```

Figure 5.10 shows the result as follows:

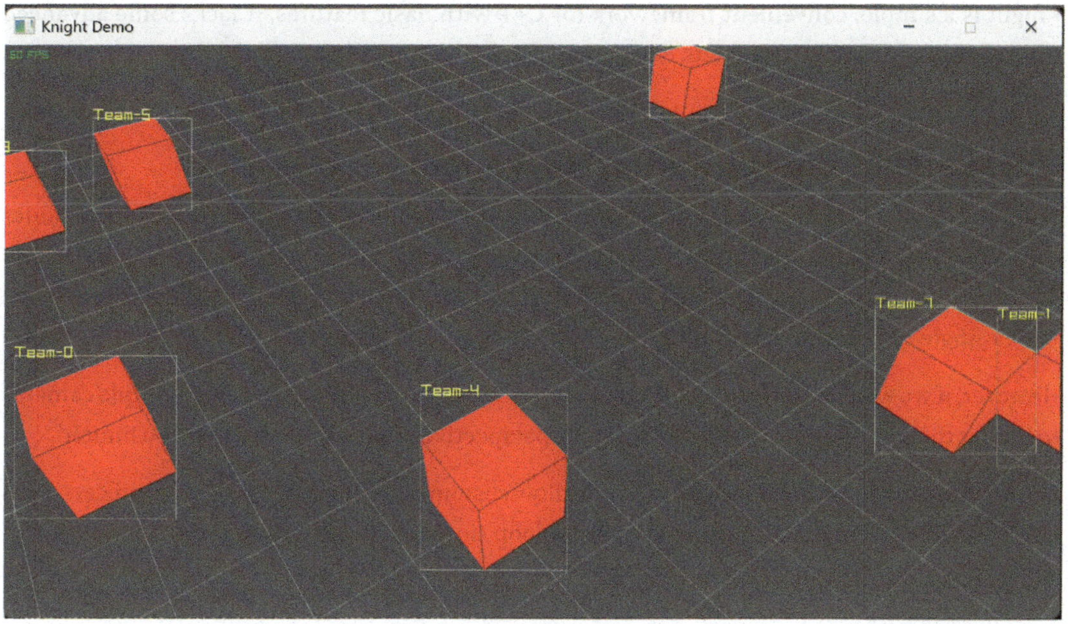

Figure 5.10 – The bounding rectangle is calculated from the cube

Moving on, let's explore rendering multiple split-screen cameras in the next section.

Rendering multiple split-screen cameras

We've seen many camera implementations. But what if we combine multiple views on one screen? Some games use split screens, while others mix perspectives—such as a third-person main view for surroundings paired with a picture-in-picture first-person view for aiming, or an FPS with a top-down map alongside the main first-person view.

So how can we implement this in Knight? Before we look at that, it's important to understand that this setup presents a couple of immediate challenges:

- Knight comes with a simple-to-use camera system, but it just directly renders onto the main display screen. If you try to render two cameras, the content rendered from the first camera will always be overwritten by content rendered from the second camera.
- Built-in camera modes in raylib come with default mouse and keyboard support, which is convenient for writing sample code. However, using two first-person cameras for different players causes input conflicts since both receive the same controls.

Before implementing multi-camera functionality, we must tackle two key issues in Knight. While Knight is a simple, convenient framework for C++ with basic features, it lacks some advanced functions. Fortunately, it also lets developers extend its capabilities. In the following sections, we'll address these challenges.

Customizing the rendering operation

Knight is designed to be simple and easy to use, so the Knight game application class includes a default `_Scene` object that allows developers to add other objects as `SceneActor` and handles basic input processing and rendering by default. This setup is useful for quickly displaying a scene with a single camera and a few 3D `SceneActor`.

However, if we want to perform more complex rendering tasks—such as using multiple cameras to render the same game scene from different perspectives—this basic setup is too limited.

Fortunately, Knight provides the flexibility to allow custom handling of the rendering process. Let's check how Knight manages the game's render loop (in `Knight.cpp` within the `Knight` project):

```
void Knight::GameLoop(){
  Vector2 v;
  while (!WindowShouldClose() && (!_shouldExitGameLoop)){
    //...
    BeginDrawing();    //prepare for rendering tasks
    ClearBackground(DARKGRAY);
    DrawOffscreen();
    SceneCamera*cameraActor=_Scene->GetMainCameraActor();
    if (cameraActor){
      BeginMode3D(cameraActor->_Camera);
      DrawFrame();
      EndMode3D();
    } else
      DrawFrame();
    DrawGUI();    //draw 2D and UI
    //...
    EndDrawing();    //finish all rendering tasks
  }
  EndGame();
}
```

In each frame, after the `Update()` function is called on all `SceneObject`, the actual rendering tasks begin with `BeginDrawing()` and end with `EndDrawing()`. The code within these two functions performs the core rendering tasks.

Knight first calls the `DrawOffscreen()` virtual function. This function is intended for any pre-rendering setup and tasks before the `_Scene` is rendered to the screen framebuffer. You can override this function to ensure it runs before `DrawFrame()` is called. We'll make use of this in the next section.

After `DrawOffscreen()` is called, Knight tries to retrieve the main camera within the `_Scene` object. In previous examples, we created a camera like this:

```
_Scene->CreateSceneObject<PerspectiveCamera>("Camera")
```

This line not only creates the camera but also designates it as the "main camera" inside the `_Scene` object. Once a camera is retrieved from `_Scene`, Knight follows the default single-camera setup and renders the game scene in `DrawFrame()`. This is the typical execution path in our previous examples with 3D objects, where `BeginMode3D()` and `EndMode3D()` are handled automatically.

However, if we don't add a camera to the `_Scene` object, Knight assumes we want to handle all rendering operations manually, so it calls `DrawFrame()` directly without setting up the scene camera with `BeginMode3D()` and `EndMode3D()`. In this case, you'll need to manage all rendering tasks yourself.

This flexibility is exactly what we need to support multiple-camera rendering. If Knight doesn't find a camera in `_Scene`, it leaves per-frame rendering entirely up to us. So, we'll create two cameras, but we won't add them to `_Scene`; instead, we'll manage their rendering ourselves. The `Demo5MultiCams` project demonstrates how to use Knight to support multiple camera rendering.

Working with RenderTexture

Let's start by rendering multiple cameras without having their outputs overwrite each other.

Until now, we've rendered the camera's view directly on the entire display screen. As discussed at the start of *Chapter 4*, the screen essentially acts as a framebuffer that displays the rendered result.

Modern graphics hardware allows us to create additional off-screen framebuffers and render content into them instead of directly to the screen framebuffer. These off-screen buffers can later be used as textures.

In modern graphics APIs, this type of texture is commonly referred to as a **RenderTexture**. It can act as a destination framebuffer and can be used like any regular texture for display or within a game scene as part of the environment or 3D models.

So how does this work with Knight? If we want a split-screen view with two different types of cameras, each looking at the same game scene, we need to create a separate `RenderTexture` for each camera. We can then render the game scene into these two `RenderTexture` separately and, as a final step, use `DrawTexture()` to display both textures on the main screen.

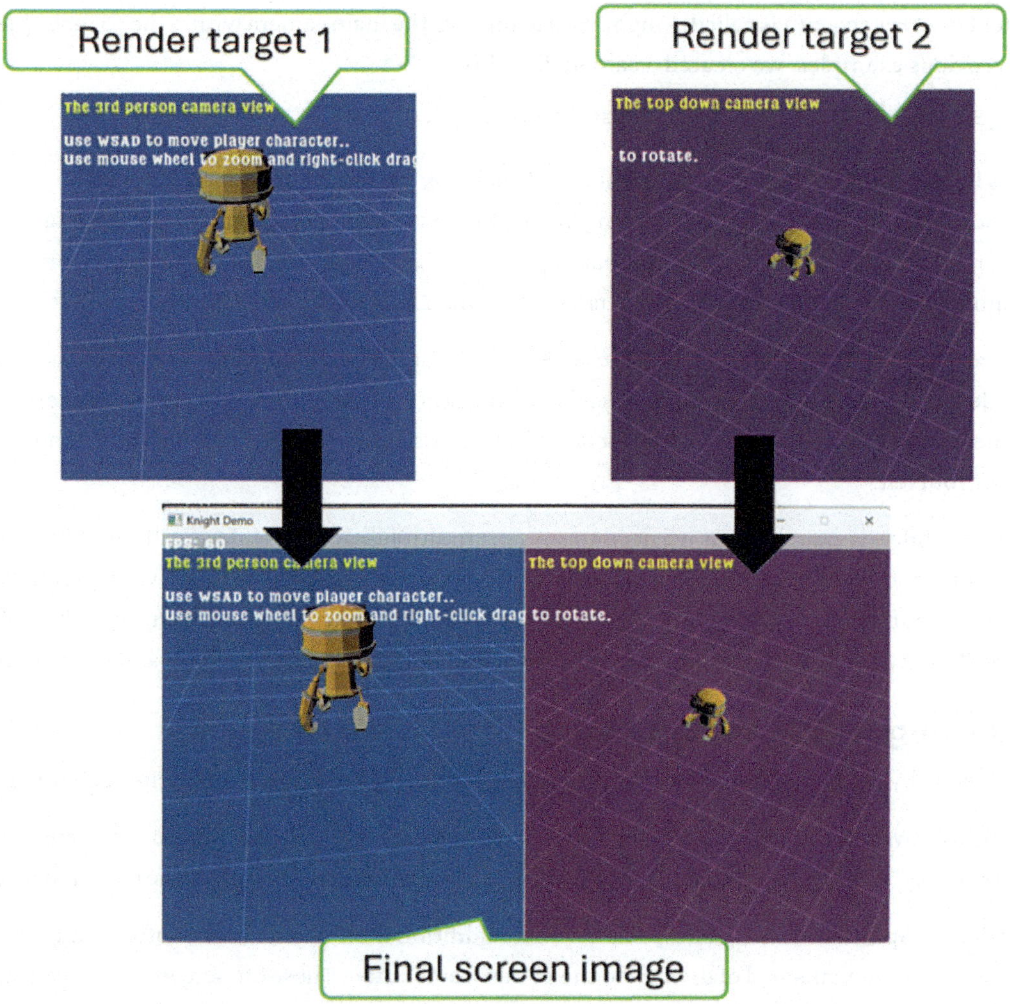

Figure 5.11 – Combining two render textures into split-screen rendering

The Demo5MultiCams project demonstrates how to work with RenderTexture in Knight. It creates a RenderTexture for a third-person follow-up camera and another RenderTexture for a top-down camera. Let's add necessary objects into the Demo5MultiCams class (in Demo5MultiCams.h):

```
FollowUpCamera* pChaseCamera = nullptr;
TopDownCamera* pTopDownCamera = nullptr;
Rectangle splitScreenRect = { 0 };
RenderTexture ChaseCamRT = { 0 };
RenderTexture TopDownCamRT = { 0 };
```

We create and initialize the cameras and RenderTexture in the Start() function of Demo5MultiCams.cpp:

```
  // Create camera for both render targets
  pChaseCamera= new FollowUpCamera(_Scene, "Chase", false);
  pTopDownCamera = new TopDownCamera(_Scene, "Map", false);
  Actor = _Scene->CreateSceneObject<SceneActor>("Player");
  //…
  // Setup player 1 camera and screen
  pChaseCamera->SetUp(Actor, 45.0f, 5.0f, CAMERA_PERSPECTIVE);
  pChaseCamera->processMouseInput = false;
  pTopDownCamera->SetUp(Vector3{ -3.0f, 3.0f, 0 }, Actor->Position, 45.0f,
CAMERA_PERSPECTIVE);
  ChaseCamRT=LoadRenderTexture(960, SCREEN_HEIGHT);
  TopDownCamRT = LoadRenderTexture(960, SCREEN_HEIGHT);
```

You might notice that this time we simply create both cameras, but don't add them into _Scene like the other examples you've seen. As we explained in the previous section, we want to handle the whole rendering task on our own so will not add them to the _Scene object.

We also create a SceneActor to represent our main player character and add it into _Scene like we're used to. Both cameras will focus on this player SceneActor but rendered from a different viewpoint.

Before we jump into any rendering operation, since we didn't add the two cameras into _Scene, this means their Update() function will not be called when Knight calls the Update() function in the main game application class, Demo5MultiCams. We will need to manually call Update() of each camera in every frame:

```
void Demo5MultiCams::Update(float ElapsedSeconds){
  //handle input to control player move
  //...
  //manually call Update() of both cameras
  pChaseCamera->Update(ElapsedSeconds);
  pTopDownCamera->SetLookAtPosition(Actor->Position);
  pTopDownCamera->Update(ElapsedSeconds);
  __super::Update(ElapsedSeconds);
}
```

In the Update() function of the Demo5MultiCams class, we will now also call the Update() function for both pChaseCamera and pTopDownCamera. Since the top-down camera doesn't automatically follow the target player SceneActor like the third-person camera, we need to set the latest "look-at" position for pTopDownCamera in every frame.

Now we're ready to perform off-screen rendering for both cameras. We'll render both cameras in the override of the DrawOffscreen() function:

```
void Demo5MultiCams::DrawOffscreen(){
  // Draw Player1 view to the render texture
  BeginTextureMode(ChaseCamRT);
  ClearBackground(DARKBLUE);
  BeginMode3D(*pChaseCamera->GetCamera3D());
  DrawGameWorld();
  //...
  EndMode3D();
  EndTextureMode();
  // Draw Player2 view to the render texture
  BeginTextureMode(TopDownCamRT);
  ClearBackground(DARKPURPLE);
  BeginMode3D(*pTopDownCamera->GetCamera3D());
  DrawGameWorld();
  //...
```

```
    EndMode3D();
    EndTextureMode();
}
```

The `BeginTextureMode()` function will make the specified `RenderTexture` ready. Any rendering operation after this call will render the result in `RenderTexture` instead of the screen. `EndTextureMode()` will flush ongoing rendering tasks and make the `RenderTexture` ready to be used as a usual texture.

You can now assign the texture to any 3D model, or simply use the handy `DrawTexture()` function to draw it on the screen. In our example, we simply draw both `RenderTexture` on the screen as a split view, so this is handled in `DrawGUI()`, where we perform all 2D drawing operations:

```
void Demo5MultiCams::DrawGUI(){
  //...
  DrawTextureRec(ChaseCamRT.texture, splitScreenRect, Vector2{ 0, 0 },
WHITE);
  DrawTextureRec(TopDownCamRT.texture, splitScreenRect, Vector2{ SCREEN_
WIDTH / 2.0f, 0 }, WHITE);
}
```

The final detail involves camera input. Since we implemented our own `FollowUpCamera`, we added a Boolean to enable or disable mouse input, ensuring it won't conflict with the mouse inputs of other cameras:

```
bool FollowUpCamera::Update(float ElapsedSeconds){
  if (!IsActive) return false;
  // Adjust camera distance with mouse wheel
  if (processMouseInput)
    cameraDistance -= GetMouseWheelMove();
  //... (omit code not related to mouse input
  // Rotate the camera around the player
  if (processMouseInput && IsMouseButtonDown(MOUSE_BUTTON_RIGHT)) {
    mCameraHorizontalAngleShift += GetMouseDelta().x * 0.01f;
    mCameraVerticalOffset += GetMouseDelta().y * 0.01f;
  }
  return true;
}
```

We can simply disable mouse input processing for one of the cameras to prevent both cameras from responding to the same input. In the `Start()` function of the `Demo5MultiCams` class (in `Demo5MultiCams.cpp`), we disable mouse input process for the chase camera. Only the top-down camera reacts to mouse input:

```
pChaseCamera->processMouseInput = false;
```

This brings us to the end of this section.

Summary

In this chapter, we explored the core principles of camera systems in 3D game development using Knight. It introduced various types of cameras, including first-person, third-person, top-down, and others, outlining how to implement and configure each for different gameplay perspectives.

Alongside this, the chapter covered important camera parameters such as position, orientation, and field of view, ensuring you understand how to manipulate and control your game's viewpoint effectively.

Additionally, the chapter demonstrated camera techniques such as following a target, panning, zooming, and rotating, providing insight into creating dynamic, user-controlled perspectives. It also touched on advanced topics, such as multi-camera rendering, using render textures for split-screen setups.

With these concepts, you can develop versatile 3D camera systems that are customizable to suit diverse gameplay mechanics and player preferences.

After understanding how to use cameras to present the game world, the next step is to explore how to utilize the power of the GPU to render a 3D game world. We'll delve into it in the next chapter.

6

3D Graphics Rendering

This chapter introduces fundamental 3D graphics rendering techniques from the modern GPU perspective and demonstrates the use of shader programming to render objects with lighting effects. Real-time 3D rendering is a broad subject, and this chapter will approach it from the viewpoint that best reflects contemporary graphics technology, serving as our foundation for learning.

The development of modern graphics hardware plays a crucial role in which algorithms we need to invest more of our time and efforts. For example, we know a graphic scene is composed of thousands of triangles. Back in the early days (such as 2000–2005), we graphics engineers spent major efforts on developing algorithms to reduce the count of triangles that actually get rendered because graphics hardware performance is limited. This is still a factor we need to consider nowadays after 20+ years, but we do not spend as much effort anymore because modern GPUs can easily handle a much larger number of triangles to render on screen. We'd rather put more effort into higher rendering quality.

The goal of this chapter is to learn how to build the main 3D graphics elements that appear in a typical 3D game scene. In *Chapter 1*, we introduced how to display 3D models, so we already know the basics of rendering the main character controlled by the player on the screen. Both in this chapter and the next chapter, we will focus on enhancing the visual representation of these objects with improved lighting effects and better realism.

In this chapter, we will cover the following topics:

- Programming with modern GPUs
- Lighting up the world
- Achieving better realism

By the end of this chapter, you will understand the detailed process stages of rendering on GPUs and know how to write efficient shader programs. Additionally, you will be able to write your own customized shader to achieve better lighting and other effects.

Technical requirements

The GitHub project for the book is located here: `https://github.com/PacktPublishing/Data-Structures-and-Algorithms-for-Game-Programming-in-CPP`.

The repo contains demo projects in the `Knight` solution (`https://github.com/PacktPublishing/Data-Structures-and-Algorithms-for-Game-Programming-in-CPP/tree/main/Knight`):

Project Name	Description
`Demo6LightShader`	Sample code of implementing the point light with shader
`Demo6Light`	Sample code of using a default lighting shader
`Demo6NormalMap`	Sample code of implementing normal mapped lighting

Table 6.1 – Sample projects in this chapter

All the sample code in this chapter is built with Knight. However, some basic understanding of the **OpenGL graphics API**, either from direct experience or from working with other graphics libraries built on top of it (such as raylib) would be useful.

Additional reading resources

Here are some great online learning resources about OpenGL:

- For general information: `https://www.khronos.org/opengl/wiki/Getting_Started`
- For tutorial-related information: `https://www.opengl-tutorial.org/`
- The official raylib website: `https://www.raylib.com/`

Let's get started!

Programming with modern GPUs

If we were to discuss the biggest difference between modern game graphics programming and that of a decade or two ago, it would be the increasing reliance on the GPU to handle more and more rendering tasks. This is achieved by writing code directly running on the GPU to handle graphics rendering tasks. These programs that run on the GPU to execute graphic rendering tasks are called *shaders*.

A **shader** is a small program written in a specialized C-like language (such as *GLSL*, *HLSL*, or *SPIR-V*) that runs directly on the GPU to define how pixels, vertices, or other graphical elements should be processed to create visual effects such as lighting, shadows, textures, and complex animations.

In the process of projecting and drawing a 3D object onto the screen, one crucial part is the transformation of the object from a 3D coordinate space into a 2D screen coordinate space.

Understanding different coordinated spaces

In *Chapter 5*, we learned the basic idea of how to project a 3D world into a 2D screen. Before diving into writing your own shader, it's crucial to understand the basic concept of **coordinate spaces**. This is often the most confusing aspect of understanding how shaders work and can be a major source of frustrating bugs in shader code.

From our experience, many shader bugs aren't caused by flawed logic but rather by the misuse or misunderstanding of coordinate spaces.

Understanding the different coordinate spaces is fundamental to 3D graphics operation. These coordinates spaces are used at various stages of rendering to position and transform objects relative to one another, the camera, and the screen. Mastery of transformation between different coordinate spaces will not only help you write effective shaders but also make it easier to debug issues when things don't work as expected.

Let's dive into the coordinate spaces mostly used in shader programming.

Model space

The first is **model space**, or **local space**. When a graphics artist makes a 3D player character in *Blender* or *3ds Max/Maya* at the origin position and exports it into a model file format, the coordinate used in the stored vertex data is in its model space.

In the following example OBJ format 3D model file, all vertex positions are in model space:

```
# Blender v2.90.0 OBJ File: ''
# www.blender.org
o BODY_Material_#24_0
v 2.545141 5.783802 -25.976692  //vertex position
v 3.235504 6.677957 -13.125248  //vertex position
...
```

Now, let's summarize the usage of model space:

- **Purpose**: Model space represents the object in its own local context before any transformations are applied.
- **Example**: A player character might have its origin at the center between the two soles of the feet. All other vertex positions are relative to this origin.
- **Transformations applied**: None at this stage. When you upload mesh data into the GPU, the coordinate used in the mesh data is usually just in its original model space.

World space

World space is a global coordinate system that represents the positions of all objects in a scene or a game world. Now, let's load the player character mentioned previously into Knight as an attached `ModelComponent` of a `SceneActor`, and set this `SceneActor's` `Position` (or world space coordinate) value as (20,10,30). However, the actual mesh data still contains the coordinates of original values related to the model space.

Let's summarize the usage of world space:

- **Purpose**: It transforms the object from its local (model) space into the scene's shared space.
- **Example**: The car model is placed in a parking lot. Its position and orientation in the parking lot (scene) are described in the world space, and the car's position in the parking lot is specified relative to the origin point of the world space.
- **Transformations applied**: In 3D graphics, a **model matrix** (a matrix defines the scaling, rotation, and translation; also referred to as *world matrix*) moves the object from model space to world space.

In Knight, we store not a single model matrix in each SceneActor; instead, we store the translation matrix, rotation matrix, and scale matrix separately:

```
Matrix _MatTranslation;
Matrix _MatRotation;
Matrix _MatScale;
```

We calculate the final matrix to transform coordinates from model space to world space in the Update() function:

```
_MatTranslation = MatrixTranslate(Position.x, Position.y, Position.z);
_MatRotation = MatrixRotateXYZ(Vector3{DEG2RAD * Rotation.x, DEG2RAD *
Rotation.y, DEG2RAD * Rotation.z });
_MatScale = MatrixScale(Scale.x, Scale.y, Scale.z);
_MatTransform = MatrixMultiply(MatrixMultiply(_MatScale, _MatRotation),
_MatTranslation);
```

The world space is calculated by multiplying the original value from model space with this _MatTransform transformation matrix to get the world space coordinate (20,10,30).

View space (camera space/eye space)

Sometimes, we need to know the coordinates relatively from the camera's viewpoint. **View space** regards the camera as the original point at (0,0,0). We use the **view matrix** to represent the transformation from the world coordinate to the coordinate of camera space.

Let's summarize the usage of view space:

- **Purpose**: It positions all objects in the scene as if they are being observed from the camera's perspective.
- **Example**: The car and parking lot are transformed so the camera sees them from their specific position and angle.
- **Transformations applied**: The view matrix moves objects from world space to view space by transforming them relative to the camera's position and orientation. The view matrix is usually calculated inside the camera handling code from the camera's position, look at position (target position), and up vector. raylib has a handy function:

  ```
  Matrix viewMat = MatrixLookAt(camera->position, camera->target,
  camera->up);
  ```

Clip space

Clip space is a normalized coordinate system used for visibility determination and perspective projection. This is where GPU drops anything that is outside the view frustum of the camera.

Let's summarize the usage of clip space:

- **Purpose**: It projects the 3D scene into a 2D view suitable for rendering on the screen.
- **Example**: After transforming the car and parking lot into clip space, they are ready for rasterization into pixels. Some areas of the parking lot may no longer be visible from the camera view and get removed from the clip space.
- **Transformations applied**: The projection matrix converts coordinates from view space to clip space. This involves perspective division, which maps 3D points to a 2D plane.

Normalized device coordinates space (NDC)

NDC space is almost like clip space, with a small difference in ranges of the coordinate values, where all coordinates are normalized to the range [-1, 1].

Let's summarize the usage of NDC space:

- **Purpose**: It prepares the scene for rendering by defining which parts of the scene are visible on the screen.
- **Example**: Objects with x, y, or z values outside the range of [-1, 1] are outside the visible area and get clipped.
- **Transformations applied**: Clip space coordinates are divided by their *w component* (perspective division) to produce NDCs.

Screen space

This coordinate system represents the actual screen position, measured in pixels.

Let's summarize the usage of screen space:

- **Purpose**: It converts normalized device coordinates into actual pixel locations on the screen.
- **Example**: A point with NDC coordinates of (0, 0) maps to the center of the screen, while (-1, -1) maps to the bottom-left corner.
- **Transformations applied**: The viewport transformation scales and translates NDCs into screen coordinates based on the screen resolution.

Now, by connecting the various coordinate spaces introduced above, we form a continuous chain of coordinate system transformations that projects and renders a 3D object from the 3D world onto the 2D screen. Each transformation step involves applying a mathematical matrix or operation:

- From model space to world space: apply model matrix
- From world space to view space: apply view matrix
- From view space to clip space: apply projection matrix
- From clip space to NDC: perform perspective division
- From NDC to screen space: apply viewport transformation

The series of transformations of the above coordinate spaces are executed as part of a series of tasks executed on modern graphics hardware. We refer to the entire series of these tasks as the *graphics rendering pipeline*. Let's investigate it in the next section.

Introducing the 3D graphics rendering pipeline

In modern 3D graphics programming, the **graphics rendering pipeline** is a series of steps that a GPU follows to convert 3D models and scenes into a 2D image on the screen. The pipeline is highly parallelized, allowing the GPU to process large amounts of data (vertices, textures, etc.) efficiently.

Stages of the graphics rendering pipeline

Let's look at key stages in the pipeline, from the initial 3D models rendering API to the final image display:

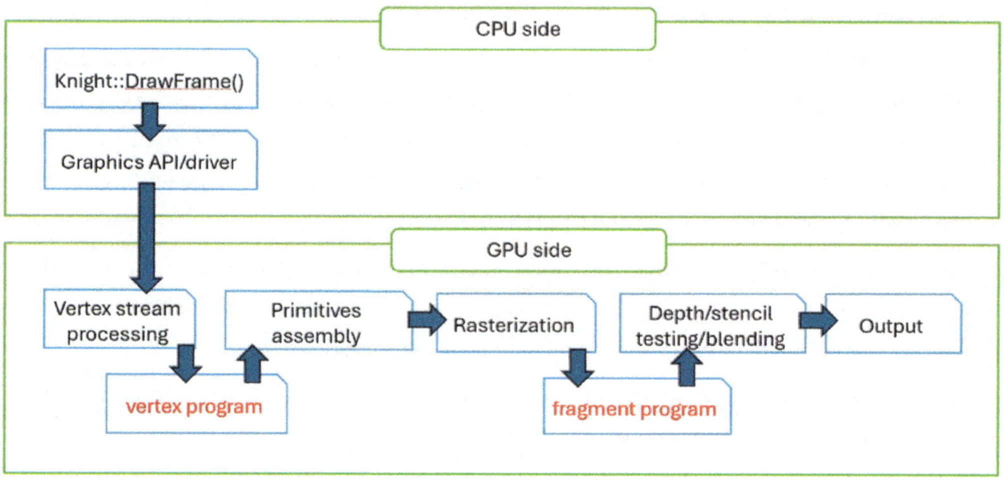

Figure 6.1 – Stages of the GPU rendering pipeline

First off, in *Figure 6.1*, you'll observe that the entire rendering pipeline process involves both the CPU and the GPU side tasks. As a software engineer, you might think that calling Knight's `DrawFrame()` function is all it takes to display the 3D game graphics. But in reality, a series of stages occur internally, from your application to the low-level graphics driver, culminating in the GPU being instructed to carry out the actual rendering:

- **Vertex stream processing**: This stage processes each vertex of the 3D models. Each vertex contains information such as position, color, texture coordinates, and normals.
- **Vertex program**: The **vertex program** (or vertex shader) is a programmable step in this stage, allowing you to apply transformations (e.g., translation, rotation, and scaling) to each vertex and calculate other properties such as lighting per vertex.
- **Primitives assembly**: After vertices are processed, they are assembled into geometric primitives, typically triangles, which are the basic building blocks of 3D models.
- **Rasterization: Rasterization** is the process of converting triangles into a 2D grid of fragments (potential pixels) on the screen. Each triangle is mapped to a 2D area on the screen, and each fragment within this area represents a sample point on the triangle. This stage includes clipping (removing parts of triangles outside the camera's view) and culling (discarding triangles that face away from the camera).
- **Fragment program**: For each fragment generated by rasterization, the GPU runs a **fragment program** (also known as the **fragment shader** or **pixel shader**). It determines the color, lighting, and texture effects of each pixel, performing calculations such as texture mapping, lighting, and color blending. This stage is where most visual effects are applied, including shadows, reflections, bump mapping, and other surface details.
- **Depth/stencil testing**: After the fragment shader computes the color of each fragment, **depth testing** checks whether the fragment is in front of or behind other fragments at the same screen location. Fragments behind others are discarded. **Stencil testing** can also be applied to create special effects such as mirrors or outlines. This stage ensures that only the visible surfaces remain in the final image.
- **Blending: Blending** combines the color of each fragment with the color of the pixel already in the framebuffer (the image being created). This is useful for effects such as transparency, where the colors of overlapping objects need to be mixed.
- **Output (to framebuffer)**: The final processed pixels are written to the framebuffer, which is then displayed on the screen as a 2D image.

When a vertex program is executed, it operates in the model space at the input stage and transforms the data through multiple coordinate spaces during its execution.

When a fragment shader is invoked, it operates in screen space or NDC space, depending on the context of the inputs it processes. The fragment program itself doesn't perform transformations but works with data passed from earlier pipeline stages.

In summary, the fragment shader typically receives interpolated world-space or view-space attributes and screen-space information such as the built-in variable `gl_FragCoord`. It uses these to compute the final color or other outputs for each pixel.

In graphics programming, the vertex program and the fragment program are essential stages in the GPU's rendering pipeline. These stages give you precise control over 3D rendering by defining how vertices are transformed and how pixels are colored.

In the next section, we'll dive into shader programming for writing vertex and fragment programs.

Working with vertex and fragment programs

As the name suggests, vertex and fragment programs function much like standard C programs. They include an entry function, `main()`, to initiate the program, and allow you to declare local variables, functions, and even simple structures to handle complex data types.

Here is a minimal example of a vertex program, which translates 3D vertex data into 2D screen coordinates, preparing it for rendering on the screen:

```
#version 330
layout(location = 0) in vec3 vertexPosition;
layout(location = 1) in vec3 vertexColor;
out vec3 fragColor;
uniform mat4 mvp;
void main()
{
  gl_Position = mvp * vec4(vertexPosition, 1.0);
  fragColor = vertexColor;
}
```

Usually, we have both a vertex program and a fragment program, where the fragment program takes output from the vertex program and then prepares the final pixel for rendering on the screen. The fragment program accompanied by the above vertex program is here:

```
#version 330
in vec3 fragColor;
out vec4 finalColor;
```

```
void main() {
  finalColor = vec4(fragColor, 1.0);
}
```

Before exploring what vertex and fragment programs do, we first need to load them into the graphics driver. These programs are then compiled and uploaded to the GPU, where they will be executed.

You can store vertex and fragment programs as simple C strings in your C/C++ source code. The following code snippet demonstrates how to compile and load these programs into the GPU:

```
// Load the vertex and fragment shaders
const char *vsCode = R"The vertex program code above";
const char *fsCode = R"The fragment program code above";
Shader shader = LoadShaderFromMemory(vsCode, fsCode);
```

Or you can put vertex program and fragment program code inside two text files and load the shader from the file:

```
Shader shader = LoadShader("vertex.vs","fragment.fs");
```

The `LoadShader()` function will load and compile the shader at runtime, making it ready to use.

We will now take a closer look at writing vertex programs and how they access the vertex data of 3D models.

Vertex program (vertex shader)

A **vertex shader** processes each vertex of a 3D model. It's responsible for:

- Transforming vertex positions from model space to screen space and setting the output position to the built-in variable `gl_Position`
- Calculating lighting values per vertex
- Passing data to the fragment shader, such as transformed positions, normals, and texture coordinates

Now let's go back to the previous minimum vertex program. In the beginning, we have:

```
#version 330
```

The first line, `#version 330`, indicates that this shader program is intended for OpenGL version 3.3 or later. If your shader is designed specifically for mobile versions of OpenGL, such as OpenGL ES 3.0, you will need to specify the appropriate version with a directive like:

```
#version 300 es
```

Typically, after the versioning statement, we declare the input and output data for the vertex program. Since a vertex program is designed to process vertex data, its input consists of one or more vertex attributes from the vertex data:

```
layout(location = 0) in vec3 vertexPosition;
layout(location = 1) in vec3 vertexColor;
```

Table 6.2 lists the vertex attributes that are commonly supported:

Attribute	**Data type**	**Description**
Vertex position	`vec3` or `vec4`	A 3-float or 4-float vector spatial position of the vertex in 3D or 4D space.
Vertex normal	`vec3`	A 3-float vector represents the direction perpendicular to the surface at the vertex, used for lighting calculations.
Vertex color	`vec3` or `vec4`	Per-vertex color data, often interpolated across surfaces for gradient effects. Either `vec3` for the `(r,g,b)` color channel or `vec4` for the `(r,g,b,a)` color channel.
Vertex texture coordinate	`vec2`	2-float UV mapping coordinates for textures, determining how textures are mapped to the vertex.
Vertex tangent	`vec3`	Used in advanced lighting and normal mapping techniques.
Vertex bitangent	`vec3`	Also used in advanced lighting and normal mapping techniques. Together with the normal, they form a **tangent space** for transforming lighting data.
Bone weight	`vec4`	Used in skeletal animation to define how much influence each bone has on a vertex.
Bone index	`vec4`	Index of bone with influence on the vertex. The maximum number is usually 4.

Table 6.2 – Vertex attributes supported by shader

In fact, you can also define any purpose of data if the data type is supported by one of the following, as categorized into groups by their dimensionality and shown in *Table 6.3*:

Categories	Supported data types
Scalar	`float`, `int`, `uint`
Vector	`vec2`, `vec3`, `vec4`, `ivec2`, `ivec3`, `ivec4`
Matrix data	`mat2`, `mat3`, `mat4`

Table 6.3 – All supported data types

The graphic API facilitates loading your vertex data into the GPU and making it accessible to your vertex program, but it's up to you to decide how to interpret and access the attributes in the vertex data. To do this, let's find out how we can access attributes in the vertex data from the vertex program.

Since you can freely name variables in your vertex program, how does the program know which input variable corresponds to which vertex attribute in the actual vertex buffer passed to the shader?

The answer lies in the *location specifier*. The following figure demonstrates how to map input variables in your vertex program to specific vertex attributes in the vertex buffer:

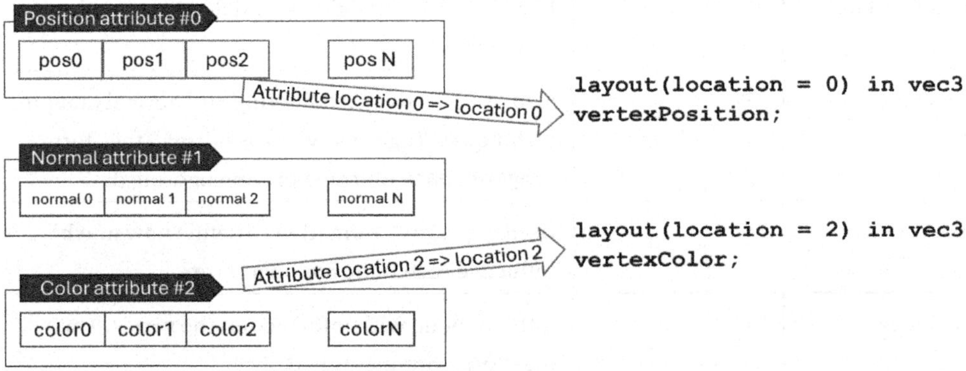

Figure 6.2 – The vertex program uses a location specifier to map vertex attributes inside the vertex buffer

This flexibility allows the vertex program to process only the attributes it needs, even if the actual vertex format contains additional attributes. For example, a raylib vertex format typically includes vertex normal. However, in this minimal vertex program example, since we are not using vertex normal, we can simply ignore them in the shader.

The output variable specifies the type of data that needs to be passed to the fragment program when a pixel is ready to be drawn on the screen. Typically, at least two types of data are required – color and coordinate (position) of the pixel:

```
out vec3 fragColor;
```

This is the *color* we want to pass to the fragment program to draw the pixel. It will become the input variable of the same name in the fragment program.

Another critical piece of data is the *coordinate* used to draw the pixel. OpenGL provides several built-in variables for vertex programs, and `gl_Position` is one of the most important. This variable allows a vertex program to store the position of the current vertex projected into clip space. Every vertex shader must write to `gl_Position` for OpenGL to render geometry correctly.

To calculate the value of `gl_Position`, additional information from the game code is required. Specifically, you need details from the current `SceneActor` to compute the model transformation matrix. You also need data from the 3D camera to calculate the view and projection matrices.

If you're building your own 3D engine, you must provide this information from your game application code. The method for passing such data from the CPU to the GPU is through uniform variables. When you define a uniform variable in a vertex or fragment program, it might look like this:

```
uniform mat4 mvp;
```

You can set the value of any uniform variable from your C/C++ code with such an API:

```
int loc = GetShaderLocation(shader, "mvp");
SetShaderValue(shader,loc,&matrix, SHADER_UNIFORM_MAT4);
```

On the main application side, we can use the handy function `GetShaderLocation()` to retrieve an ID for any uniform variable by its name. Then we can use `SetShaderValue()` to pass data from the CPU to vertex or fragment programs running on the GPU.

Even better, raylib also provides some *ready-to-use* uniform variables. Each time a vertex or fragment program is loaded, raylib will scan the code and determine whether the shader needs to use some common data from the engine. Then, raylib will automatically make these uniform variables available to your vertex and fragment program without any of your efforts to call `GetShaderLocation()` and pass the data through `SetShaderValue()` on your own.

Those "ready-to-use" uniform variables supported by raylib are listed in *Table 6.4*:

Attribute	Data type	Description
`matModel`	`mat4`	Model matrix if you are currently rendering a vertex from a raylib 3D `Model` class. (Knight uses raylib's `Model` as well.) However, if you define your own 3D model rendering and do not use the `Model` class provided by raylib, this will not be available. You need to supply your own model transformation matrix.
`matView`	`mat4`	View matrix calculated from the `Camera3D` class of raylib. The `SceneCamera` of Knight uses raylib's `Camera3D` internally, so you will have a view matrix ready to use if you work with Knight's `SceneCamera` or any camera inherited from the `SceneCamera` class.
`matProjection`	`mat4`	Projection matrix from the `Camera3D` class of raylib. Same as `matView`, you will have this ready if you work with `SceneCamera`.
`mvp`	`mat4`	Another handy model-view-projection matrix, pre-calculated and ready to use if you use Knight's `SceneCamera` and `ModelComponent`.
`matNormal`	`mat4`	This is a handy version of `transpose(inverse(matModelView))`, prepared by the CPU side and ready to use in your vertex and fragment program.
`colDiffuse`	`vec3`	When you specify a *tint* color in raylib's API, this is the tint color passed by raylib. Do not confuse it with the color assigned in each vertex.

`texture0`
`texture1`
`texture2`
	`Sampler2D`	This is specifically for ready-to-use `Sampler2D` texture sampling units for the fragment program. If you use it in the fragment program, raylib will automatically enable it.

Table 6.4 – Handy uniform variables provided by raylib

If you want to supply your own data with these predefined uniform variables, make sure the value you set is not overwritten by raylib during rendering.

Finally, the last part is the `main()` function of the vertex program:

```
    gl_Position = mvp * vec4(vertexPosition, 1.0);
    fragColor = vertexColor;
```

It simply uses the model-view-projection matrix to calculate `gl_Position` and also just passes the vertex color as the input to the fragment program.

Fragment program (fragment/pixel shader)

A **fragment shader** processes each fragment (essentially, a potential pixel on the screen) generated by rasterizing the triangles that make up a model. It determines the final color and appearance of each pixel by:

- Applying lighting calculations, colors, and textures
- Using data from the vertex shader, such as texture coordinates and normals, to color the pixel
- Applying advanced effects such as normal mapping, shadow mapping, and reflections

Let's go back to our minimum fragment shader:

```
#version 330
```

The first versioning statement is the same as the vertex program; choose the best for your target platform.

```
in vec3 fragColor;
```

This time, we will receive the `fragColor` from the vertex program.

```
out vec4 finalColor;
```

Also, we define an output variable, `finalColor`. The fragment shader only has a single output – the final color of the pixel (with alpha). The name doesn't matter and it can only have a single color output.

```
void main()
{
  finalColor = vec4(fragColor, 1.0);
}
```

The main body of the `main()` function in this fragment program only copies the color passed by the vertex program and sends it to the output of the final color. Since the input color is `vec3` but the output is `vec4`, we need to convert the format with alpha component 1.0 in the final color.

The above demonstrates a minimal fragment program. Most fragment programs involve more operations, such as sampling color from a texture map, blending, or calculating lighting. To write more complex fragment shaders, we can pass more data from the vertex program to the fragment program.

We can also pass more information from the CPU side to the vertex program of the GPU side, which we will cover in the next section.

Passing data from CPU to GPU

In shader programming, **uniform** is the variable that is passed from the CPU (application code) to the GPU (shader code) and remains constant for the duration of a single draw call. They are commonly used to provide global data to shaders that multiple vertices or fragments need to access, such as transformation matrices, lighting information, or texture samplers.

Figure 6.3 demonstrates how we can pass the color of a light to the variable `lightColor`, accessible by the vertex program and fragment program.

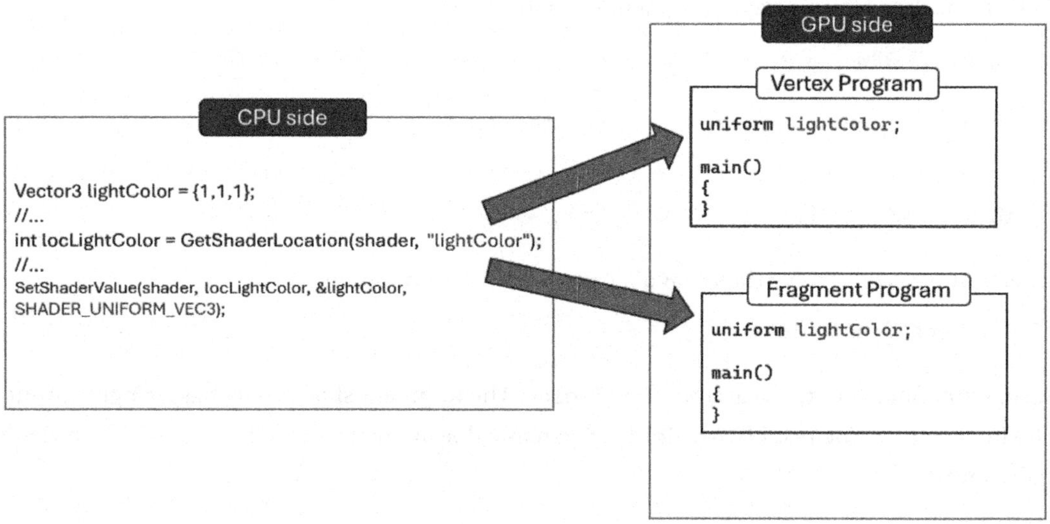

Figure 6.3 – Uniform variables pass values from CPU to GPU

The example illustrated in *Figure 6.3* is that on the CPU side, within your C++ code, we use the `GetShaderLocation()` function to obtain an integer ID representing the `lightColor` uniform variable. This ID allows us to call `SetShaderValue()` and pass a `Vector3` value to the `lightColor` uniform variable in both the vertex and fragment shaders. However, since the CPU and GPU operate as separate worlds, uniform variables come with a few limitations:

- **Read-only**: Uniform variables are read-only in shaders. They can be set by the CPU but cannot be modified within the shader code.
- **Constant per draw call**: Uniform variables retain the same value for all vertices or fragments processed during a single draw call. This makes them ideal for information that applies to an entire object or scene, rather than data that varies per vertex or per fragment.
- **Accessible by vertex and fragment shaders**: Uniform variables can be used in both vertex and fragment shaders, making them well suited for passing data that influences all stages of rendering.

`Uniform` is used in daily shader programming for passing the following information:

- **Transformation matrices**: `Uniform` variables are often used to pass transformation matrices (such as model, view, and projection matrices) to the vertex shader. This enables each vertex to be transformed from model space to screen space:

  ```
  SetShaderValueMatrix(shader, uniform_id, Matrix);
  ```

- **Lighting information**: Lighting properties, such as the direction and colors of light sources, material properties, and ambient light values, are passed as `uniform` variables. These values remain constant for all vertices or fragments of a rendered object, making `uniform` variables ideal for storing lighting data:

  ```
  SetShaderValue(shader, uniform_id, (Vector3)light_dir, SHADER_
  UNIFORM_VEC3);
  ```

- **Camera parameters**: `Uniforms` often carry camera-related data such as the camera's position, direction, or view matrix. This information can be used for calculations such as distance-based effects or environment mapping:

  ```
  SetShaderValue(shader, shader.locs[SHADER_LOC_VECTOR_VIEW],
  &cameraPos, SHADER_UNIFORM_VEC3);
  ```

- **Time and animation data**: For time-based effects or animations, the elapsed time is often passed as a `uniform`, enabling shaders to create animated effects such as waves or pulsing lights without recalculating time for each vertex or fragment individually:

```
int elapsedTimeLoc = GetShaderLocation(shader, "elapsedTime");
SetShaderValue(shader, elapsedTimeLoc, 3.0f, SHADER_UNIFORM_VEC3);
//pass value 3.0 to shader
```

- **Texture samplers**: Textures are accessed in shaders through special type of `uniform` called a sampler (e.g., `sampler2D` for 2D textures). This `uniform` variable tell the shader which texture unit to use for fetching texture data:

```
int textureLoc = GetShaderLocation(shader, "mySampler2D");
SetShaderValueTexture(shader, textureLoc, texture);
```

- **Material properties**: Properties such as color, shininess, reflectivity, and other material-specific values can be passed as `uniform` to control the appearance of objects:

```
SetShaderValue(shader, shader.locs[SHADER_LOC_COLOR_DIFFUSE],
&diffuseColor, SHADER_UNIFORM_VEC4);  //color as vec4 (r,g,b,a)
```

`Uniform` is a fundamental part of shader programming, providing a convenient way to pass constant data from the CPU to the GPU for each draw call. They play an essential role in controlling transformations, lighting, textures, and other parameters across the entire rendered object, allowing for efficient and flexible shader effects.

Now you have learned the basics of shader programming, let's start to harness its power by adding lighting effects to the game world.

Lighting up the world

In computer graphics, **directional lights** and **point lights** are two fundamental types of light sources used to simulate realistic lighting effects in 3D scenes. They each have distinct characteristics and applications based on how they emit light and interact with objects in the scene.

Understanding directional light

A **directional light** simulates a light source that is infinitely far away, such as the sun or moon. As a result, all light rays from a directional light are parallel, and the light's intensity remains consistent throughout the scene, unaffected by distance.

The key characteristics of directional lights are:

- **Parallel light rays**: Since the light source is considered infinitely far away, all rays are parallel to each other.
- **Constant intensity**: The light intensity does not decrease with distance, making it uniform across the entire scene.
- **Defined by direction**: Directional lights are specified by a direction vector, indicating where the light is coming from, rather than a specific position.

The lighting effect of a directional light on a surface is commonly calculated using the **Lambertian reflection model** (diffuse shading). Here's the basic calculation:

- **Surface normal vector** (`N`): The normal vector perpendicular to the surface at a particular point.
- **Light direction vector** (`L`): The normalized direction from which the directional light is coming, typically constant across the scene.
- **Diffuse reflection**: The diffuse component of the lighting is calculated using the dot product between the surface normal and the light direction:

  ```
  Diffuse Intensity = max(0,dot(N,-L));
  ```

  This gives a value between `0` and `1`, representing the brightness at that point.

- **Final color**: This intensity value is then multiplied by the light color and surface color to get the final color at that point.

In video game graphics rendering, since the sun and moon are far away, their light can be modeled as directional light in outdoor scenes.

`Demo6LightShader` demonstrates how to implement directional light in a shader:

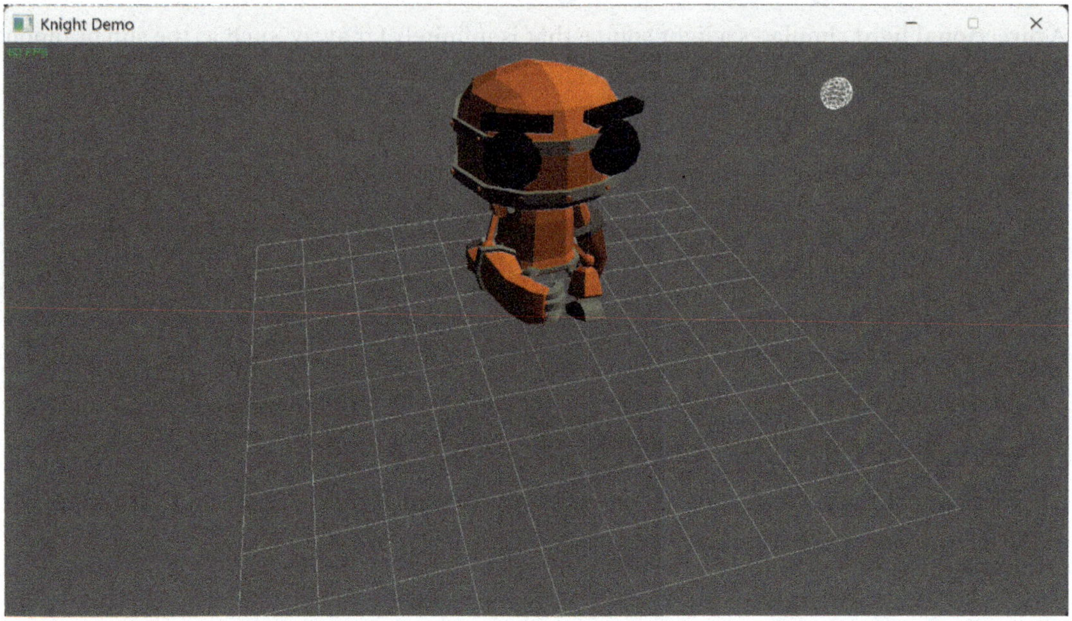

Figure 6.4 – Directional light shader demo

The input vertex attributes required for calculating directional lighting are the vertex's world-space position, normal vector, and texture coordinates (for texture-mapped objects):

```
layout(location = 0) in vec3 vertexPosition;
layout(location = 2) in vec3 vertexNormal;
layout(location = 1) in vec2 vertexTexCoord;
```

Next, to calculate directional lighting, the required input vertex attributes are the vertex's world-space position, its normal vector, and texture coordinates (if the object uses a texture map):

```
uniform mat4 matModel;
uniform mat4 matView;
uniform mat4 matProjection;
```

However, we also need to know the color and direction of our directional light source:

```
uniform vec3 lightDirection; // Directional Light direction (normalized)
uniform vec3 lightColor; // Color of the directional Light
```

The data we are going to pass to the fragment program is the world-space position, normal, and directional light. We will calculate the final lighting intensity in the fragment program:

```
// Output to fragment shader
out vec3 fragPosition;
out vec3 fragNormal;
out vec3 directionalLight;
void main() {
  // Transform vertex position to world space
  fragPosition=vec3(matModel*vec4(vertexPosition, 1.0));
  // Transform the normal to world space and normalize
fragNormal=mat3(transpose(inverse(matModel)))*vertexNormal;
  // Calculate the diffuse of directional lighting
  float diff = max(dot(fragNormal, -lightDirection), 0.0);
  directionalLight = lightColor * diff;
  // Transform vertex position for final position in screen space
  gl_Position=matProjection*matView*vec4(fragPosition,1.0);
}
```

The preceding code computes the normal and directional light and passes the value to the fragment program. In the fragment program, we calculate the final projected pixel color affected by the directional light:

```
#version 330
in vec3 directionalLight;  // Input from vertex shader
uniform vec4 colDiffuse; // The base color of the object
out vec4 fragColor;  // Output color
void main() {
    // Apply lighting to the base color
    fragColor = vec4(colDiffuse.rgb * directionalLight, colDiffuse.a);
```

The last part of the fragment program calculates the gamma correction. It adjusts color values to account for the non-linear way human eyes perceive light. It's a power-law transformation applied to color data, particularly in RGB, to map the values to how humans perceive them:

```
    //Calculate gamma correction
    fragColor = pow(fragColor, vec4(1.0/2.2));
}
```

Directional lighting works well for outdoor 3D scenes. However, it doesn't work well for confined spaces where light should fade. We will introduce another type of light source for those: point lights.

Understanding point lights

A **point light** simulates a small, localized light source, such as a light bulb, candle, or torch. Light from a point light radiates in all directions, and its intensity decreases with distance, simulating how light behaves in real life.

The key characteristics of point light are:

- **Omnidirectional**: A point light emits light equally in all directions from a single point.
- **Attenuation**: Light intensity decreases with distance, typically following an inverse square law. This effect, known as attenuation, makes nearby objects appear brighter than distant ones.
- **Defined by position**: Unlike directional light, point lights are specified by a position in 3D space, affecting objects differently based on their distance from the light.

Point light calculations include both diffuse reflection and attenuation:

- **Surface normal vector** (`N`): The normal vector perpendicular to the surface at the illuminated point.
- **Light direction vector** (`L`): The vector from the point on the surface to the light source, normalized to a unit vector.
- **Distance**: The distance between the surface point and the light source.
- **Attenuation**: Attenuation is often modeled using an inverse square law:

  ```
  float attenuation = 1.0 / (distance * distance);
  ```

  or with more customizable formulas, such as:

  ```
  float att = 1.0 / (constant + 0.5 * distance + 0.25 * (distance *
  distance));
  ```

- **Diffuse reflection**: The diffuse component is calculated using the Lambertian reflection model as with directional light, but with the additional attenuation factor:

  ```
  Diffuse Intensity=max(0,dot(N,L))×Attenuation
  ```

- **Final color**: The resulting intensity is multiplied by the light color and surface color.

Let's change Demo6LightShader a bit to support the point light. This time, we load a different fragment shader program to calculate point lighting:

```
shader = LoadShader("../../resources/shaders/glsl330/light_point.vs",
"../../resources/shaders/glsl330/light_point.fs");
//...
SetShaderValue(shader, locLightPosition, &Position, SHADER_UNIFORM_VEC3);
// if light position move
```

The light is circular around the character and you can see the change of lighting effect.

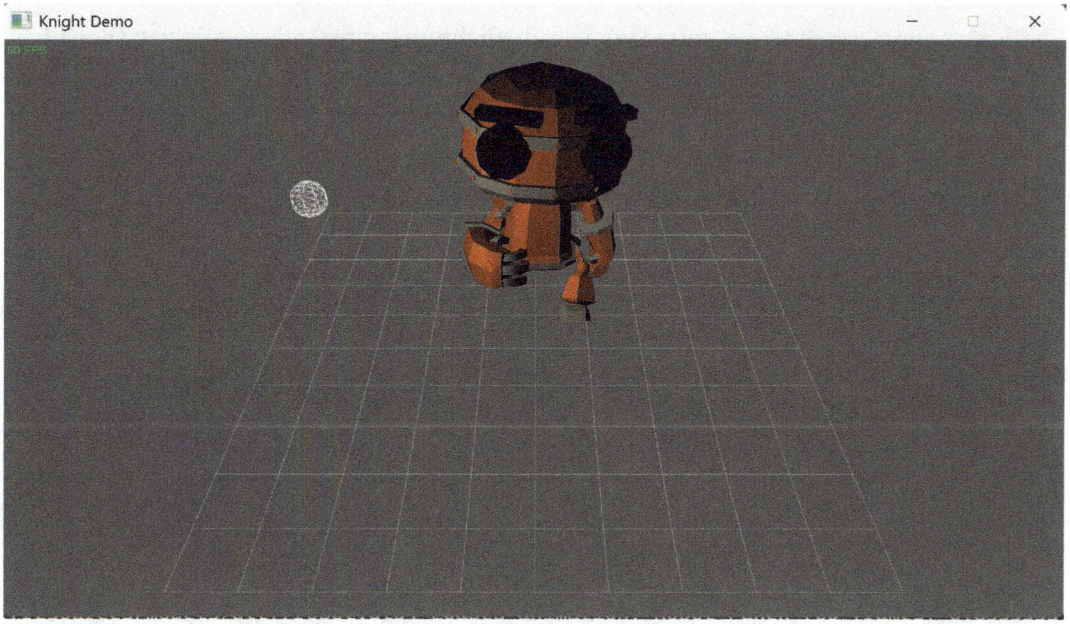

Figure 6.5 – Point light demo

When the light moves around, you can see the difference. The intensity of light changes according to the distance from the object to the light position.

Rendering with multiple lights

So far, our scene has only used a single light source. However, in real game scenes, it's common to have multiple light sources, including a combination of directional lights and point lights. In such cases, all lighting calculations must take multiple sources into account.

raylib's `rlights` module provides support for multiple light sources. It includes both a vertex shader and a fragment shader specifically for lighting calculations. To use it, you need to include the `rlights.h` header in your main program. The `rlights.h` header defines a `Light` structure, which stores information such as the position, direction, type, and properties of each light. It supports both directional and point lights. It also supply its own vertex and fragment programs. The vertex program is located at `resources/shaders/glsl330/lighting.vs`, while the corresponding fragment program is at `resources/shaders/glsl330/lighting.fs` (`https://github.com/PacktPublishing/Data-Structures-and-Algorithms-for-Game-Programming-in-CPP/tree/main/resources/shaders/glsl330`).

The demo project `Demo6Light` is ported from raylib's lighting sample code to Knight. It shows how to use the `rlights` module. In this example shown in *Figure 6.6*, four light sources are used in the scene. By holding the *right mouse button*, you can rotate the camera and observe how the lighting affects the surface of the robot model from different angles. Pressing *Y*, *R*, *G*, and *B* toggles each individual light source on or off, letting you see how each one contributes to the final lighting effect.

Figure 6.6 – Rendering with multiple light sources

Just like in our previous sample project, the main program `Demo6Light.cpp` first loads the lighting shaders, then creates four light sources:

```
void Demo6Light::Start()
{
  //…
  //Load light shaders
  shader = LoadShader(TextFormat("../../resources/shaders/glsl%i/lighting.
vs", GLSL_VERSION), TextFormat ("../../resources/shaders/glsl%i/lighting.
fs", 330));
  //…
  //create lights
  lights[0]=CreateLight(LIGHT_POINT, Vector3 { -2, 1, -2 }, Vector3Zero(),
YELLOW, shader);
  lights[1]=CreateLight(LIGHT_POINT, Vector3 { 2, 1, 2 }, Vector3Zero(),
RED, shader);
  lights[2]=CreateLight(LIGHT_POINT, Vector3 { -2, 1, 2 }, Vector3Zero(),
GREEN, shader);
  lights[3]=CreateLight(LIGHT_POINT, Vector3 { 2, 1, -2 }, Vector3Zero(),
BLUE, shader);
  //…
}
```

The raylib API `CreateLight()` initializes and returns the `Light` structure. In the `Update()` function, we will pass the current camera position to the shader:

```
float cameraPos[3]={pMainCamera->GetPosition().x, pMainCamera-
>GetPosition().y,pMainCamera->GetPosition(). z};
SetShaderValue(shader, shader.locs[SHADER_LOC_VECTOR_VIEW], cameraPos,
SHADER_UNIFORM_VEC3);
```

The vertex program is very similar to our own lighting vertex program. The magic of calculating multiple light sources happened in the program. First, we need light and camera information from the main program:

```
// Input lighting values
uniform Light lights[MAX_LIGHTS];
uniform vec3 viewPos;  //position of camera
struct Light {
    int enabled;  //non-zero means enabled
```

```
    int type; //directional or point light
    vec3 position; //world space position
    vec3 target;
    vec4 color;
};
```

The shader above also defines a simple data structure `Light` – a simplified version contains minimum information needed for lighting calculation. Do not confuse the C++ `Light` structure defined in `rlight.h`!

In the `main()` function of fragment shader, we use a loop to calculate the influence of each light and sum them up:

```
void main()
{
  // ...
    vec3 lightDot = vec3(0.0);
  vec3 normal = normalize(fragNormal);
  vec3 viewD = normalize(viewPos - fragPosition);
  for (int i = 0; i < MAX_LIGHTS; i++) {
      if (lights[i].enabled == 1){
         vec3 light = vec3(0.0);
    if (lights[i].type == LIGHT_DIRECTIONAL){
          light=-normalize(lights[i].target- lights[i].position);
        }
        if (lights[i].type == LIGHT_POINT){
          light = normalize(lights[i].position - fragPosition);
        }
        float NdotL = max(dot(normal, light), 0.0);
        lightDot += lights[i].color.rgb*NdotL;
    //...
    }
  }
  finalColor = (texelColor*((colDiffuse+vec4(specular,
1.0))*vec4(lightDot, 1.0)));
}
```

The above code snippet uses a loop to go through every light and sum up the result. It's very similar to our own lighting implementation but with additional support to ambient light and specular lighting.

In the next section, we will push the lighting effect with better realism.

Achieving better realism

In the previous section, we covered the basics of lighting. Now, let's dive deeper and explore how to extend lighting techniques to achieve greater realism.

In 3D graphics, we enhance the realism of lighting by incorporating two key properties:

- **Material**: Defines the surface's appearance by describing how it interacts with light
- **Shadow**: Adds visual depth and spatial context, helping to establish the relationships between objects in the scene

We will cover shadows, a more extensive subject, in the next chapter. For now, let's explore in more detail how materials define the properties of a surface's interaction with light.

Describing the surface properties

Materials determine properties such as color, shininess, roughness, and texture, which give objects their realistic look. A **material** can include various types of maps (or textures), which define specific surface characteristics at each point, allowing detailed control over how light affects the surface.

The following properties of materials are common to many 3D graphics engines:

- **Diffuse color**: This is the base color of the material, often controlled by a texture. It represents the color the material reflects under direct light.
- **Specular highlight**: This determines how shiny or reflective a surface appears. The specular intensity and shininess (glossiness) of a material affect the size and brightness of highlights on the surface.
- **Roughness or glossiness**: Roughness affects the spread of reflected light. A rough surface scatters light, creating a soft, matt appearance, while a glossy surface produces sharp reflections.
- **Normal map**: This is a texture that simulates fine surface details such as bumps and grooves without increasing the polygon count. The normal map affects how light interacts with the surface, creating the illusion of depth and texture on flat surfaces.

- **Bump map**: This is like a normal map but simpler. Bump maps create the illusion of depth using grayscale values to modify surface normals. They are often less detailed than normal maps.
- **Height/displacement map**: Used to adjust the actual geometry of the surface, height maps provide true depth by modifying the vertices of the mesh. They are more computationally expensive than normal maps.
- **Ambient occlusion (AO)**: This defines areas on the surface where light is less likely to reach, often used to add subtle shadows in cracks or crevices, enhancing realism.

We've already explored how diffuse color influences the lighting outcome. Now, let's take a look at a common technique for enhancing surface detail: **normal mapping**.

Rendering with normal mapping

A **normal map** is a specialized texture map used to simulate fine surface details, such as bumps or grooves, without modifying the actual geometry of a 3D model. Unlike a typical texture map that stores color information for each pixel, a normal map stores the offset of the surface normal for each pixel.

During per-pixel lighting calculations in the fragment program, instead of relying solely on the normal calculated in the vertex program, we also incorporate the normal offset from the normal map. This combination creates the illusion of a bumpy or uneven surface, enhancing visual realism without increasing geometric complexity.

By altering the direction of the surface normal on each pixel, normal maps trick the lighting calculations into thinking the surface is more complex than it actually is. In the normal map:

- **Red channel** (*X-axis*) shifts the surface normal in the left/right direction.
- **Green channel** (*Y-axis*) shifts the surface normal in the up/down direction.
- **Blue channel** (*Z-axis*) is usually close to 1, keeping the normal vector pointing outward.

Figure 6.7 shows an example of a normal map:

Figure 6.7 – A typical normal map

The offset normal coordinates stored in the normal map are usually the **tangent space coordinates**. Imagine you're standing on a sphere. The tangent space at your feet is like a perfectly flat plane that touches the sphere at that exact point (see *Figure 6.8*).

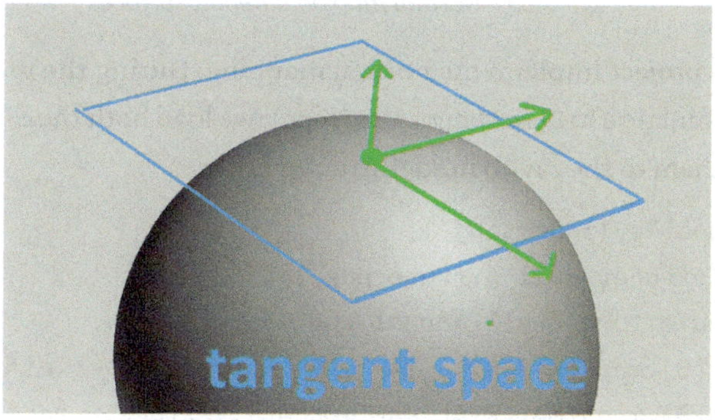

Figure 6.8 – Tangent space

This flat blue plane in *Figure 6.8* represents all the possible directions you could move on the surface of the sphere at that moment, without immediately going up or down relative to the surface at that point.

The most important reason we store the offset of normal offset in tangent space is to decouple the normal map from the specific geometry of a model. The offset information within the normal map describes the surface detail relative to the local orientation of each point on the surface (defined by the *tangent, bitangent,* and *normal vectors* at that point). This means the same tangent space normal map can be applied to different models, even if they have different overall shapes, orientations, or polygon counts.

For example, a brick texture normal map created in tangent space can be applied to a flat wall, a curved arch, or even part of a 3D model with varying surface normal, as shown in *Figure 6.9*:

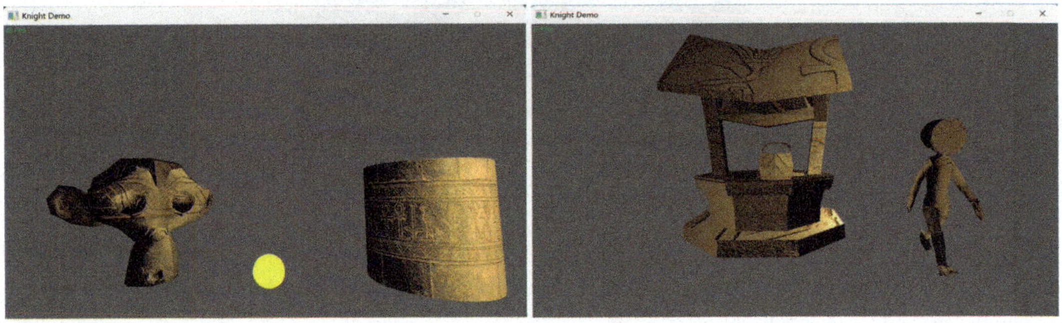

Figure 6.9 – Normal map on different surfaces

The `Demo6NormalMap` project implements normal mapping. During the program's initialization phase (the `Create()` function in `Demo6NormalMap.cpp`), we load both the diffuse and normal map textures and assign them to the raylib model structure:

```
model = LoadModel("cylinder.obj");
diffuse = LoadTexture("wall_diffuse.png");
normalMap = LoadTexture("wall_normal.png");
model.materials[0].maps[MATERIAL_MAP_DIFFUSE].texture = diffuse;
model.materials[0].maps[MATERIAL_MAP_NORMAL].texture = normalMap;
```

In the demo project, the original model does not include a normal map, so we provide one for you. You can also use tools, such as **ShaderMap** or other online normal map generators, to create your own normal map.

Additionally, most free models typically lack the necessary tangent data for each vertex. Fortunately, raylib offers a convenient function to calculate this data for us:

```
for(int i=0;i<model.meshCount;i++)
  GenMeshTangents(&model.meshes[i]);
```

Once the calculations are complete, the vertex tangent array is enabled and uploaded, allowing our vertex shader to access it at vertex attribute location 4 (as predefined by raylib):

```
#define RL_DEFAULT_SHADER_ATTRIB_LOCATION_TANGENT    4
```

We will also provide a default light source with its world position to our shader program. To better demonstrate the effect of normal mapping, we will make one of the cylinder models rotate all the time. Run the demo and rotate the camera to see how light reflection changes when the surface rotates, as in *Figure 6.10*:

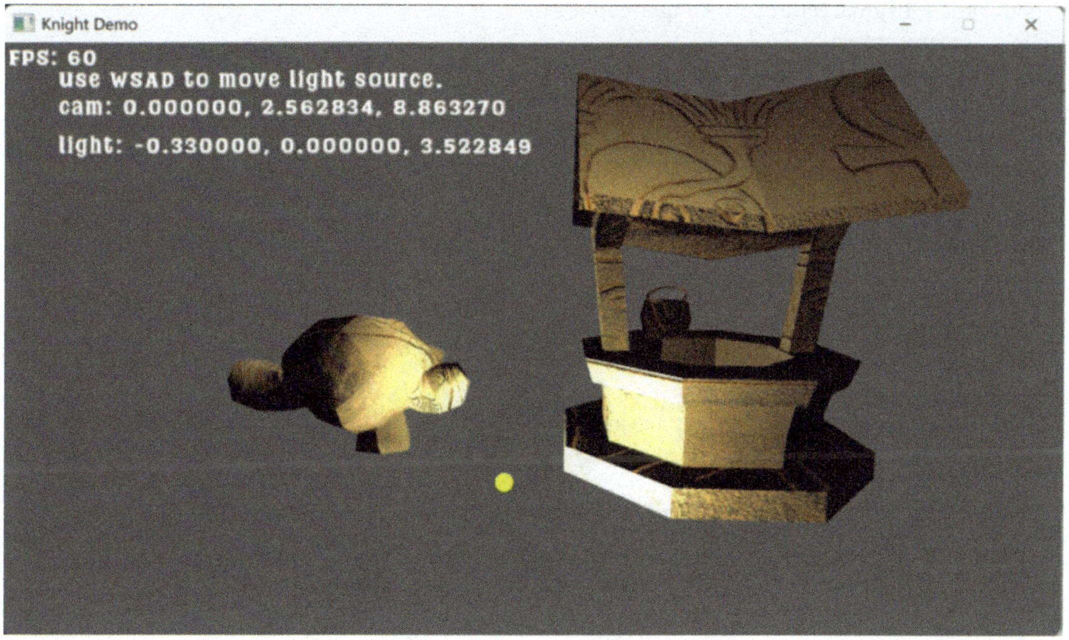

Figure 6.10 – Normal mapping rendering

Now, let's dive into the details of the magic happening inside our vertex program (`normalmap.vs`). The vertex program utilizes four input attributes:

```
layout(location = 0) in vec3 vertexPosition_modelspace;
layout(location = 2) in vec3 vertexNormal_modelspace;
layout(location = 1) in vec2 vertexUV;
layout(location = 4) in vec3 vertexTangent_modelspace;
```

Since a lot of final calculations are done at the pixel level, we will pass a lot more information than usual to the fragment program this time:

```
// Output data ; will be interpolated for each fragment.
out vec4 vcolor;
out vec2 UV;
out vec3 Position_worldspace;
out vec3 EyeDirection_cameraspace;
out vec3 LightDirection_cameraspace;
out vec3 LightDirection_tangentspace;
out vec3 EyeDirection_tangentspace;
```

We also need to leverage many uniforms provided by raylib:

```
// Values that stay constant for the whole mesh.
uniform mat4 matView;
uniform mat4 matModel;
uniform mat4 matProjection;
uniform vec3 LightPosition_worldspace;
uniform vec4 colDiffuse;
```

The first is to calculate the world-space and camera-space positions of the vertex, then compute the final `gl_Position`:

```
Position_worldspace=(matModel * vec4 (vertexPosition_modelspace,1)).xyz;
vec3 vertexPosition_cameraspace=(matView* vec4 (Position_worldspace,1)).
xyz;
gl_Position= matProjection*vec4(vertexPosition_cameraspace ,1);
```

So far, we have only performed standard 3D projection calculations. Next, we need to compute a few key elements in camera space – the direction of the eye and the light direction in camera space:

```
EyeDirection_cameraspace = vertexPosition_cameraspace;
vec3 LightPosition_cameraspace = (matView * vec4 (LightPosition_
worldspace,1)).xyz;
LightDirection_cameraspace = LightPosition_cameraspace + EyeDirection_
cameraspace;
```

Now, we can calculate the bitangent value of the vertex. While some implementations prefer to pre-calculate this value alongside the tangent during the creation of model vertices, we take advantage of the GPU's power and compute it directly in the vertex program:

```
vec3 vertexBitangent_modelspace = cross(vertexNormal_modelspace,
vertexTangent_modelspace);
mat3 MV3x3 = mat3(matView*matModel);
vec3 vertexTangent_cameraspace = MV3x3 * vertexTangent_modelspace;
vec3 vertexBitangent_cameraspace = MV3x3 * vertexBitangent_modelspace;
vec3 vertexNormal_cameraspace = MV3x3 * vertexNormal_modelspace;
mat3 TBN = transpose(mat3(vertexTangent_cameraspace,
vertexBitangent_cameraspace, vertexNormal_cameraspace));
```

The last line of the code above calculates the **Tangent-Bitangent-Normal (TBN)** matrix. The TBN matrix is a transformation 3x3 matrix used to convert vectors from tangent space to world space, or vice versa.

In *Figure 6.11*, the tangent **(T)** is aligned with the normal map texture's U direction; the bitangent **(B)** is aligned with the normal map texture's V direction; and normal **(N)** is perpendicular to the surface.

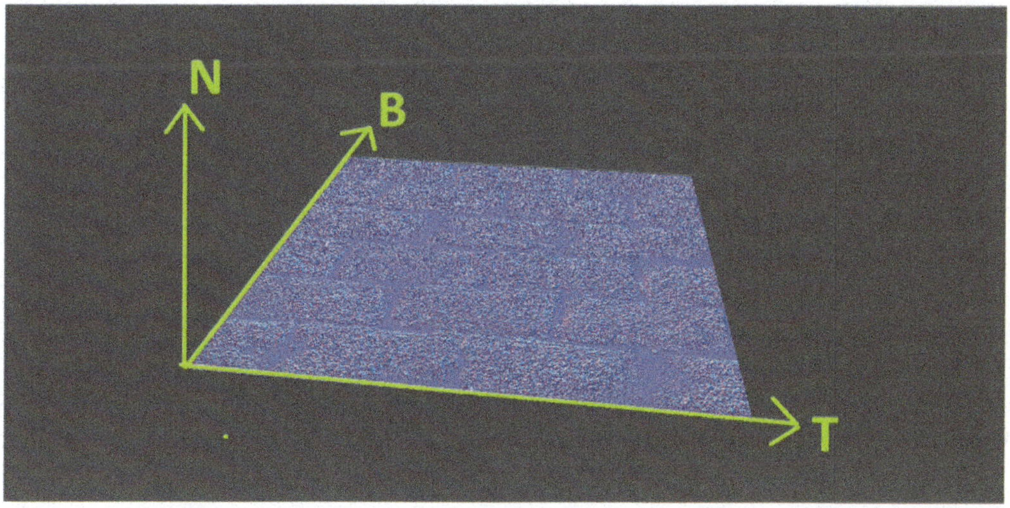

Figure 6.11 – Normal map texture and tangent/bitangent/normal axis

The normal map's RGB values (ranging from [0, 1] to [-1, 1]) tilt the default normal ([0, 0, 1]) along these axes to create the effect of a bumpy surface.

Once we have the TBN matrix, we can calculate both eye and light directions in tangent space. The benefit of calculating in tangent space is the lighting calculations stay consistent under the rotation of the object;

```
LightDirection_tangentspace = TBN * LightDirection_cameraspace;
EyeDirection_tangentspace = TBN * EyeDirection_cameraspace;
```

Wow! That's a lot of calculations! Fortunately, modern GPUs are powerful enough to handle these operations in real time.

Now, let's move on to the fragment program (`normalmap.fs`) to see how it handles the final calculations. This time, we have more data than usual being passed from the vertex program:

```
in vec4 vcolor;
in vec2 UV;
in vec3 Position_worldspace;
in vec3 EyeDirection_cameraspace;
in vec3 LightDirection_cameraspace;
in vec3 LightDirection_tangentspace;
in vec3 EyeDirection_tangentspace;
```

And we also need many uniforms passed by the CPU side:

```
uniform sampler2D texture0;
uniform sampler2D texture1;
//uniform sampler2D texture2;
uniform mat4 matView;
uniform mat4 matModel;
uniform vec3 LightPosition_worldspace;
uniform vec3 LightColor;
uniform float LightPower;
```

The first step is calculating material diffuse and ambient color. Here, we use the texture coordinate UV to locate the material diffuse RGB color:

```
vec3 MaterialDiffuseColor = texture( texture0, UV ).rgb;
vec3 MaterialAmbientColor=vec3(0.1,0.1,0.1)* MaterialDiffuseColor;
```

Now we need to calculate the angle between the normal and the light direction:

```
vec3 TextureNormal_tangentspace = normalize(texture( texture1, vec2(UV.x,
UV.y) ).rgb*2.0 - 1.0);
float distance = length( LightPosition_worldspace - Position_worldspace );
vec3 n = TextureNormal_tangentspace;
vec3 l = normalize(LightDirection_tangentspace);
float cosTheta = clamp( dot( n,l ), 0,1 );
```

The cosine of the angle between the normal and the light direction is calculated and clamped to a minimum value of `0`. This result determines the following:

- `cosTheta` = `1`: The light is directly above the triangle (at a vertical angle).
- `cosTheta` = `0`: The light is perpendicular to the triangle or positioned behind it.

The final color is then calculated using the formula shown in the last step:

```
color = vec4(MaterialAmbientColor,1) + vcolor * vec4(MaterialDiffuseColor
* LightColor * LightPower * cosTheta / (distance*distance),1);
```

For simplicity, we omit the calculation of specular. Many implementations also allow us to use another **specular map** (another texture map used to control the reflectivity and shininess of a surface at a per-pixel level). This demo project gives you a barebone implementation of normal mapping, showcasing GPU's powerful computing ability while maintaining a decent real-time rendering efficiency.

The benefits of using normal mapping instead of rendering highly detailed models with millions of triangles are obvious:

- **Realistic detail without extra geometry**: Normal maps allow detailed surface features (such as bumps and grooves) without increasing the polygon count. This improves performance while maintaining realism.
- **Versatility**: Normal maps can be applied to a wide range of surfaces, from walls and floors to characters and organic shapes, enhancing realism in games and simulations.
- **Efficient lighting**: Since normal maps modify only the lighting calculations, they're an efficient way to simulate complex textures without adding complexity to the geometry.

To sum up, a material in 3D graphics defines how surfaces interact with light, encompassing properties such as color, reflectivity, roughness, and texture. Normal mapping is a critical tool for enhancing materials by simulating surface details without additional geometry, allowing for realistic lighting and shadow effects on otherwise flat surfaces. Through shaders, normal maps alter the perceived shape and depth of surfaces, making them invaluable for achieving detailed and efficient graphics in 3D applications.

Summary

This chapter introduced the fundamentals of 3D graphics rendering, explaining how modern GPUs power real-time visuals. It detailed Knight's transformation pipeline—from model to screen space—and how vertices are processed, assembled, and rasterized. We covered vertex and fragment programs for geometry manipulation, texturing, and lighting. The chapter also gave an overview of GLSL shader programming, including data flow via uniforms, lighting models, and techniques like normal mapping. With this foundation, the next chapter will focus on rendering larger numbers of objects and full 3D scenes.

Having understood the detailed process of drawing individual 3D objects, the next chapter will explore how to render a larger number of objects and more extensive 3D game scenes on the screen.

7

Rendering a 3D Game World

Building a visually convincing 3D game world involves more than just displaying a single 3D model. It incorporates the player character, multiple NPCs, a terrain or level map, lighting, shadows, effects such as particle systems, and immersive backgrounds like the sky or distant landscapes.

The challenge comes not just from making these elements look good but from rendering them efficiently, so the game remains smooth, even in large or complex scenes.

This chapter explores several crucial 3D rendering techniques and shows how to integrate them into a coherent game scene.

In this chapter, we'll cover the following main topics:

- Rendering imposters (billboards)
- Rendering visual effects with particle systems
- Multi-pass rendering effects
- Creating a large outdoor landscape

By the end of the chapter, you will be able to render a complete game world with terrain, skybox, player and NPCs, and scene props (like trees and buildings) with visual effects animated by particle systems.

Technical requirements

Download the `Knight` Visual Studio solution from GitHub. Here is the link to the repository:

`https://github.com/PacktPublishing/Data-Structures-and-Algorithms-for-Game-Programming-in-CPP`

The demo projects for this chapter are located within the `Knight` Visual Studio solution (`https://github.com/PacktPublishing/Data-Structures-and-Algorithms-for-Game-Programming-in-CPP/tree/main/Knight`), specifically under these project names, for rendering features introduced in this chapter:

Project Name	Description
`Demo7Billboard`	This project implements a billboard `Component` in Knight.
`Demo7Particle`	This sample project implements a particle system.
`Demo7PCFShadow`	This sample project implements a real-time shadow with a soft edge.
`Demo7HMap`	This project implements a terrain created from a height map.
`Demo7QuadTreeTerrain`	This sample demonstrates how to render large-scale terrain with level of detail.
`Demo7SkyBox`	This project implements the rendering of a skybox.

Table 7.1 – Sample projects used in this chapter

Rendering imposters (billboards)

Many mobile survival games render thousands of *zombies*, and real-time strategy games render lots of armies smoothly by not using full 3D models for each one. Instead, they rely on **billboards**—flat, camera-facing quads with textures. A billboard's surface normally always aligns with the camera, creating a 3D illusion while keeping geometry simple and performance high.

Billboards are commonly used in the following scenarios:

- **Particles**: Each particle (smoke, fire, explosions, dust) is a small, camera-facing quad, providing a volumetric look without heavy geometry.
- **Foliage/trees**: Distant plants are rendered as quads to reduce rendering costs; from afar, the difference is barely noticeable.

- **Light flares/glows:** Sun glare or headlight glow can be a simple billboard with an additive texture, delivering realistic effects inexpensively.
- **Crowds:** Large, distant groups are easily represented by billboards when great detail isn't essential.
- **UI overlays in 3D:** Health bars and icons remain readable at any angle by always facing the camera.

Figure 7.1 – Rendering a large number of objects with billboards to achieve high performance

Billboarding is a simple and effective optimization for rendering a large amount of object instances. In the next section, we will learn how to implement it in Knight.

Making 2D look like 3D

When using billboards, the object's orientation is constantly updated to ensure it faces the camera. This can be achieved either:

- On the CPU, by directly adjusting the orientation of the billboard in each frame based on the camera's position.
- Through shader calculations on the GPU, where the rotation is handled in the vertex or geometry shader.

The billboarding technique can be implemented in different ways depending on the application:

- **Axis-aligned billboard**: Only rotates around a specific axis (e.g., vertical) to face the camera, making it useful for objects that should stay upright even when the camera tilt angle changes, like trees or grass in open-world environments.
- **Screen-aligned billboard**: Always faces the camera and ignores world orientation.

`Demo7Billboard` demonstrates the basic use of the billboard technique. Run the demo and hold the *right mouse button* to rotate the camera around. The demo defaults to an axis-aligned billboard, like the left side of *Figure 7.2*.

Open `Demo7Billboard.cpp` and uncomment line **74**:

```
//billboard->AlignType = SCREEN_ALIGNED;
```

This will change the alignment mode to the screen-aligned billboard. Now run the demo and rotate around the camera. The billboard will always face the camera and align with the screen like a 2D image, like the right side of the screenshot shown in *Figure 7.2*:

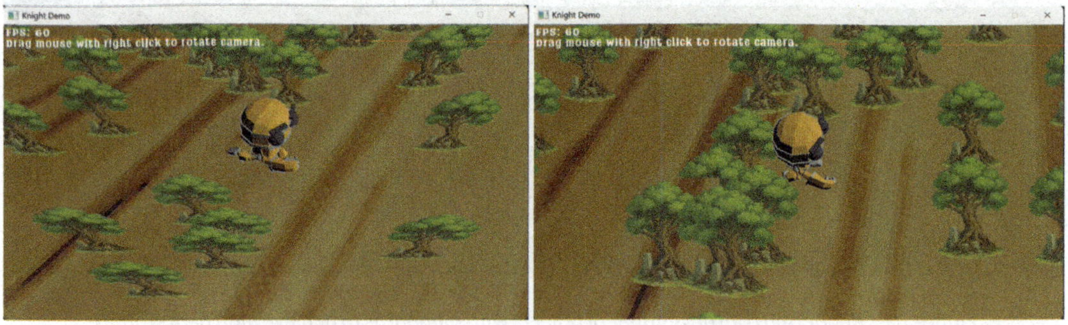

Figure 7.2 – Screen-aligned billboard (left) versus axis-aligned billboard (right)

Now it's time to learn how to implement billboard rendering in Knight. Do you remember in *Chapter 1* we introduced the `Component` class – the foundational graphical unit in Knight?

In this example, we will demonstrate how to extend the `Component` base class to render billboards. This serves as an excellent opportunity to get hands-on experience with expanding the functionality of Knight. By the end of this example, you'll have a clearer understanding of how to customize and enhance Knight to meet your specific needs.

We define our `BillboardComponent` class by extending the `Component` base class (in `BillboardComponent.h`):

```
class BillboardComponent : public Component {
public:
    BillboardComponent();
    ~BillboardComponent();
    void Update(float ElapsedSeconds) override;
    void Draw() override;
    Texture2D texture = { 0 };  //billboard texture
    Rectangle source = { 0 };  //source rectangle
    Vector2 size = { 0 };   //size of billboard
    Vector2 origin = { 0 };     //the "pivot" point
    Color tint = WHITE;  //tint color
     BillboardAlignType AlignType = UPWARD_ALIGNED;
    friend SceneActor;   //for quick access related class
};
```

The workflow of `Component` is consistent with the main program structure used in all our previous demo projects. The `Component` class includes its own `Update()` function, which allows the CPU to handle tasks such as updating logic or managing state changes.

`Component` also includes a `Draw()` function, which is invoked when the `SceneObject` or `SceneActor` that owns this `Component` calls its own `Draw()` function as part of Knight's rendering process.

The code implementation is in `BillboardComponent.cpp`. In the following code snippet, we use `billUp` vector `{0,1,0}` as the default to render the Y-axis-aligned billboard. However, if it is set to `SCREEN_ALIGNED`, we will get the up vector from the view matrix. We need to use raylib's `DrawBillboardPro()` function to draw billboards, so we can control how alignment is properly specified:

```
void BillboardComponent::Draw()
{
  Vector3 billUp = { 0, 1, 0 };
  SceneCamera* pSC = this->_SceneActor->GetMainCamera();
  if (pSC != NULL) {
    if (AlignType == SCREEN_ALIGNED) {
      Matrix matView = rlGetMatrixModelview();
      billUp = { matView.m1, matView.m5, matView.m9 };
```

```
    }
    DrawBillboardPro(*pSC->GetCamera3D(), texture, source, this->_
SceneActor->Position, billUp, size, origin, 0, tint);
  }
}
```

The billboard cannot function without knowing where the current camera is facing. So, we will get it from the SceneActor this billboard component is attached to. Knight uses raylib's handy API DrawBillboardPro() to draw a billboard. We need to supply camera information, position, scale, and a tint color.

Since Knight automatically handles the rendering of all components in the scene, there's no need for us to explicitly call its Draw() function in the main application class like other demo projects we did before. We only need to handle the creation of the billboard SceneActor and BillboardComponent and set up the initial values in the Start() function of Demo7Billboard.cpp.

In this example, we want to create 100 billboards at random positions. We can use the standard library's random generator uniform_real_distribution for this purpose, as follows:

```
std::random_device rd;
std::mt19937 gen(rd());
std::uniform_real_distribution<float> dist(-5.0f, 5.0f);
```

The preceding code will prepare us a random number distributor, dist, which generates random values between [-5,5). Let's look at the code implementation:

```
for (int i = 0; i < 100; i++) {
  SceneActor* imposter = _Scene->CreateSceneObject <SceneActor>("Billboard
Object");
  imposter->Scale = Vector3{ 1, 1, 1 };
  imposter->Position = Vector3{ dist(gen),0.5f, dist(gen)};
  imposter->Rotation = Vector3{ 0,0,0 };
  BillboardComponent* billboard = imposter->
CreateAndAddComponent<BillboardComponent>();
  //initialize billboard
  billboard->texture = billboardImage;
  // Entire billboard texture, source is used to take a segment from a
larger texture.
  billboard->source = { 0.0f, 0.0f, (float)billboard->texture.width,
(float)billboard->texture.height };
```

```
    billboard->size = { billboard->source.width / billboard->source.height,
  1.0f };
    billboard->origin = Vector2Scale(billboard->size, 0.5f);
    billboard->blendingMode = BLEND_ADDITIVE;
    billboard->renderQueue= Component::eRenderQueueType::AlphaBlend;
    imposters.push_back(imposter);
  }
```

In the above example, we created an empty `SceneActor` called `imposter` first, and then we created and added a `BillboardComponent` to the `SceneActor`. Now it's part of the scene. The `Scene` class handles the update and rendering of all `SceneActor` automatically.

One important setting is the `blendingMode` from the above code example. This is a good time to refresh the various blending modes we learned about in *Chapter 4*. For brighter and shinier effects, we use the *additive blending mode*. For other effects, such as raindrops or floating dust, we can use *multiplicative blending*.

Despite the heavy use of billboards in many 3D games, they're not without some drawbacks:

- **Lack of depth**: Since they are flat, billboards do not convey depth accurately from all angles, which can be noticeable when viewed closely or from the side.
- **Limited detail**: Billboards work best for distant objects or effects; up close, the illusion of 3D may break.
- **Overdraw**: Using many overlapping billboards (such as in dense particle effects) can lead to overdrawing, which can impact performance.

However, billboard rendering is still an effective technique and is widely used in 3D game scenes. One particularly popular use case of billboards is to render particle effects. We will explore the implementation in the next section.

Rendering visual effects with particle systems

In many gameplay scenes, we render and manage large numbers of billboards to create effects such as explosions (assembled from multiple firelight quads), raindrops, or water splashes—often involving hundreds or thousands of small images. These effects typically rely on a **particle system**, a manager class that generates, animates, and recycles individual particles over time.

The basic concept to achieve visually stunning effects is all about how to animate key properties mathematically and procedurally. The common *key properties* of these particles include, but are not limited to, the following:

Property	Description
`position`	Each particle's position can change due to physics (wind, gravity, etc.), mathematical formulas (explosions, magic attacks), or manually authored paths—often combining all these methods.
`velocity`	A 3D vector (x, y, z) defining the particle's path. For example, (1,0,0) moves it along X while (0,1,0) moves it upward.
`initialColor`	This is the particle's tint at creation. Additional properties (e.g., a `dimSpeed` float property) often control how this color fades over time.
`initialSpeed`	This sets the particle's movement rate along its velocity, influenced by factors like wind or water resistance.
`lifetime`	The lifetime is the duration the particle remains active. Once it expires, the particle disappears, and new ones may spawn to maintain the effect.

Table 7.2 – Common example properties to animate a particle

Modern game engines provide a large set of properties available for tweaking the most complex effects. They even allow particles to interact with other physical objects in the scene – like allowing particles to bounce on the ground, or be affected by the gravity of the game world, and so on.

Implementing particle animation effects

`Demo7Particle` demonstrates the use of rendering thousands of billboards as a fountain-like particle effect (see *Figure 7.3*). Again, we will implement a particle system as a component so we can reuse it later.

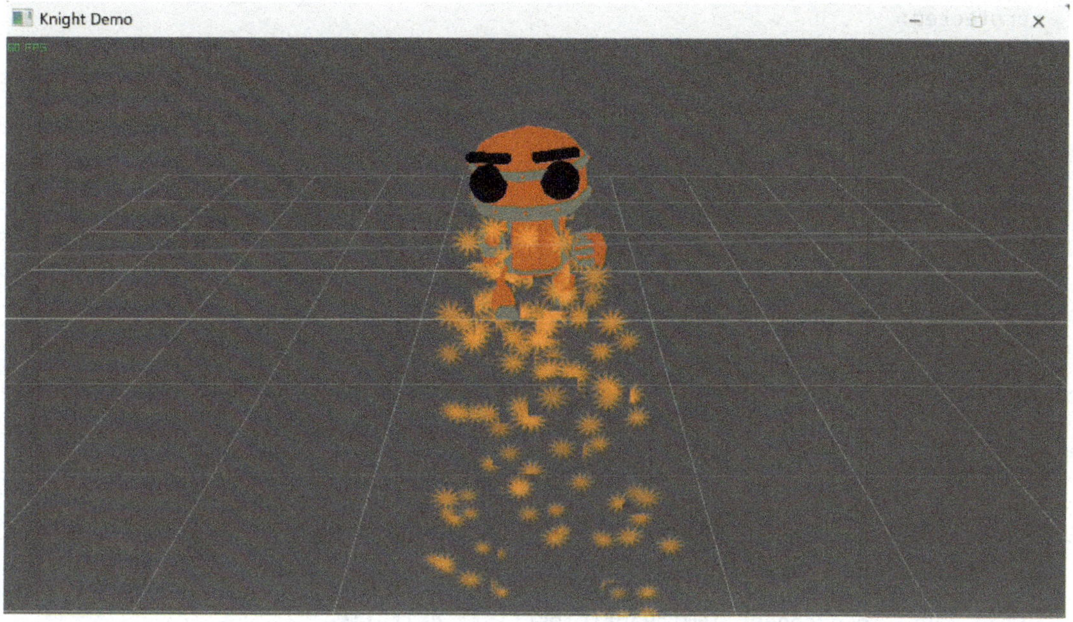

Figure 7.3 – Using billboards to render particles

Let's start with the definition of a single particle (in `ParticleComponent.h`):

```
struct Particle { // Struct to represent a particle
    Vector3 position;  //position in 3D world
    Vector3 velocity;   //the moving velocity
    float life;        // Remaining life of the particle
    float maxLife;     // Total life duration of the particle
    Color color;       // Particle color
};
```

In this code snippet, each particle is defined as a C++ `struct Particle`, which contains the necessary properties to animate it.

Here is the new `Component` as the management class for each particle effect:

```
class ParticleComponent : public Component {
public:
  bool CreateFromFile(const char* path, int maxp, Vector3 v, Color ic =
WHITE, Vector3 isp = {0,0,0});
  void Update(float deltaTime) override;
  void Draw(void) override;
```

```
protected:
  int maxParticles = 500;
  Vector3 offset = Vector3{ 0,0,0 };
  Color initialColor = Color{255,255,255,255};
  Vector3 initialSpeed = Vector3{0,0,0};
  Texture2D texture = { 0 };
  std::vector<Particle> particles;
  virtual void EmitParticles(float deltaTime);
};
```

Each particle stream has a `particles` array (declared as `vector`) to store all active particles. The default value of `maxParticles` is set to `500` to control how many particles can be generated per particle system.

The virtual function `EmitParticles()` in `ParticleComponent.cpp` is the controller for how to generate new particles if needed:

```
void ParticleComponent::EmitParticles(float deltaTime) {
    int particlesToEmit = 5; // Emit rate
    Vector3 origin = Vector3Add(_SceneActor->Position, offset);
    for (int i = 0; i < particlesToEmit && particles.size() <
maxParticles; i++) {
        Particle particle;
        particle.position = origin;
        // Random velocity with some upward direction
        particle.velocity.x = (float(rand()) / RAND_MAX - 0.5f) * 2.0f;
        particle.velocity.y = (float(rand()) / RAND_MAX) * 2.0f + 2.0f; //
Upward velocity
        particle.velocity.z = (float(rand()) / RAND_MAX - 0.5f) * 2.0f;
        Vector3Add(particle.velocity, initialSpeed);
        particle.life = particle.maxLife = 2.0f + float(rand()) / RAND_MAX
* 2.0f; // Life in seconds
        particle.color = initialColor; // Initial color
        particles.push_back(particle);
    }
}
```

In the above code snippet, new particle creation is limited to a maximum of 5 new particles in each frame and new particles will not be created if the maximum number of particles is reached.

> **Note**
>
> In the preceding code, you could also make the variable `particlesToEmit` a configurable property of the particle system.

The spawn position of all particles is based on the `original` variable. It's the position of `SceneActor` plus an `offset` variable. This gives flexibility to spawn particles in some particular position specified by caller code.

This is very useful when you need to spawn particles at some specified position relative to the position of `SceneActor` and the `offset` variable may change over time. For example, if you have a player character, a mage represented by a 3D character model of `SceneActor`, you can calculate the offset position of the mage's right hand in every frame and add a fireball particle effect, which will be attached to the mage character's right hand all the time.

Next, we animate the particles in the `Update()` function:

```
void ParticleComponent::Update(float deltaTime)
{
  for (auto& particle : particles) {
    // Update particle position based on velocity
    particle.position.x += particle.velocity.x * deltaTime;
    particle.position.y += particle.velocity.y * deltaTime;
    particle.position.z += particle.velocity.z * deltaTime;
    // Apply gravity
    particle.velocity.y -= 9.8f * deltaTime;
    // Decrease particle life
    particle.life -= deltaTime;
    float lifeRatio = particle.life / particle.maxLife;
    // Fade out as life decreases
    particle.color.a = static_cast<unsigned char>(255 * lifeRatio);
  }
```

The `Update()` function is responsible for calculating all particles' new positions based on their `velocity`, applying gravity to the vertical velocity, and updating life by the `deltaTime`. Particles gradually fade out towards the end of their lifetime by calculating the alpha component of the particle `color`.

For particles reaching the duration limit of their lifetime, they are recycled here:

```
    // Remove dead particles
    particles.erase(remove_if(
      particles.begin(), particles.end(),
      [](const Particle& p){return p.life<=0;}),
      particles.end());
```

When some particles get removed, we might need to spawn some new ones:

```
    // Emit new particles
    EmitParticles(deltaTime);
  }
```

In the preceding code snippet, some particles reach the end of their lifetime and get removed, but we will continue to emit new particles so the total number of particles will not reduce to zero.

Multi-pass rendering effects

In *Chapter 6*, we learned how to use **material** for better realism of lighting results and techniques like normal mapping. Now, let's dive deeper and explore how to use **shadow** to achieve greater realism. However, we will need to learn a new rendering technique for rendering the same object multiple times but with different settings for each rendering pass. Shadow is one of the graphic effects that need to use multi-pass rendering.

Rendering shadows

Shadows add depth, realism, and spatial awareness but are computationally expensive. A common approach is **shadow mapping**, which uses a depth texture to check if each point on a surface is lit or blocked by an object from the light source. This method requires understanding the relationships between light, shadow-casting objects, and shadow-receiving surfaces.

Unlike single-pass rendering, which produces the final image in one go for all our previous projects, casting real-time shadows generally demands multiple passes in each frame—one from the light's perspective to build a shadow map, then another from the camera's viewpoint. Such multi-pass rendering also underpins effects like bloom or motion blur.

Shadow mapping is one such technique, typically performed in two main rendering passes, as we will examine in the following sections.

Shadow map creation (first pass)

The first pass is sometimes referred to as the light pass, which involves rendering the scene from the light source(s) into a depth texture called a shadow map:

- Render the scene from the light's perspective and store the depth of each fragment relative to the light in a shadow map (a depth texture).
- This shadow map records the closest distance from the light to any object in the scene at each point, essentially capturing a *snapshot* of the scene from the light's perspective.

Shadow application (second pass)

This is the actual pass to render shadow based on depth information produced from the first rendering pass. It includes the following steps:

1. Render the scene from the camera's perspective as we did before.
2. For each fragment (pixel), transform its position into the light's coordinate space: compare the fragment's depth from the light's perspective to the corresponding value in the shadow map. If the fragment's depth is *greater* than the depth stored in the shadow map, it means the fragment is behind another object and is therefore in shadow. If the fragment's depth is *equal to* or *less than* the depth in the shadow map, it is visible to the light and is therefore illuminated.

The `Demo7PCFShadow` project implements a shadow mapping algorithm in Knight. Since this process requires rendering the scene twice—with different cameras, shaders, and settings—we handle this type of multi-pass rendering using the `SceneRenderPass` class in Knight.

Using Knight's SceneRenderPass class

The `SceneRenderPass` class is responsible for managing all the detailed tasks involved in rendering a scene with specific settings—such as the camera, light, shaders, textures, and more. It ensures that all necessary settings and resources are prepared for a particular rendering pass. The base class is structured as follows:

```
class SceneRenderPass{
  public:
    virtual bool Create(Scene *sc) = 0;
    virtual void Release() = 0;
```

```
    virtual void BeginScene(SceneCamera *cam = NULL) = 0;
    virtual void Render();
    virtual void EndScene() = 0;
    virtual void BuildRenderQueue(SceneObject *pR, Shader* pShaderOverride
= nullptr);
    virtual void ClearRenderQueue();
  protected:
    RenderQueues renderQueue;
    Scene* pScene = NULL;
    SceneCamera* pActiveCamera = NULL;
};
```

For any specific rendering pass, you should initialize and load the required resources (such as shaders, textures, and other settings) by overriding the default `Create()` function. Similarly, make sure to delete and release these resources by overriding the `Release()` function.

The `BeginScene()` function is where you prepare all the necessary settings and resources for a rendering pass. It also allows you to pass an optional `SceneCamera` if you need to override the default main camera for the scene.

The true magic lies in the `BuildRenderQueue()` function. This function, invoked by `BeginScene()` by default, builds the lists of components that need to be rendered during this pass. It provides the flexibility to:

- **Separate different types of components**: For instance, transparent objects are typically rendered in sorted order based on their distance from the camera, starting with the most distant object to ensure proper transparency rendering.
- **Select only the components needed**: Instead of rendering all components, you can include only those required for the current pass.

The default implementation of the `Render()` function loops through all the lists of components and renders them sequentially.

The `SceneRenderPass` class is an ideal solution for managing the need to render the same scene multiple times with different settings for each pass. By encapsulating the details of a single rendering pass, it prevents your Knight application class from becoming cluttered with various camera, texture, and shader settings all mixed together.

Implementing the depth rendering pass of shadow mapping

The first step of rendering a shadow effect is defining the light data structure that will project the shadows:

```
class ShadowSceneLight : public SceneActor
{
  public:
ShadowSceneLight(Scene* Scene, const char* Name = nullptr);
    bool Update(float ElapsedSeconds) override;
    virtual void SetLight(Vector3 dir, Color col);
    // Record the Light matrices for future use!
    Matrix lightView = { 0 };
    Matrix lightProj = { 0 };
    Matrix lightViewProj = { 0 };
    Vector3 lightDir = { 0 };
    Color lightColor = WHITE;
    float ambient[4] = {0.1f,0.1f,0.1f,1.0f};
};
```

In the preceding code snippet, we declare a new class, `ShadowSceneLight`, inherited from the common `SceneActor` base class. So, it acts like all other `SceneActor` classes in the game scene and also holds extra lighting information.

In the main Knight application class, we need to create two derived `SceneRenderPass` classes to handle the two rendering passes described earlier. This is implemented in `Demo7PCFShadow.cpp`:

```
ShadowMapRenderPass* pShadowMapRenderer = nullptr;
DepthRenderPass* pDepthRenderer = nullptr;
//…
  sceneLight = _Scene->CreateSceneObject<ShadowSceneLight> ("Light");
  pDepthRenderer = new DepthRenderPass(sceneLight);
  pDepthRenderer->Create(_Scene);
  pShadowMapRenderer = new ShadowMapRenderPass(sceneLight, pDepthRenderer-
>shadowMap.depth.id);
  pShadowMapRenderer->Create(_Scene);
```

In this code snippet, both `DepthRenderPass` and `ShadowMapRenderPass` access the `sceneLight` class.

The first rendering pass, the depth rendering pass, is implemented in the `DepthRenderPass` class. This pass renders the scene from the light's viewpoint to produce a depth texture map (representing the relative distance between the light and each pixel), utilizing the render-to-texture feature introduced in *Chapter 5*. For this rendering pass, we are only concerned with the depth information of each pixel, not the color components (RGB). Therefore, the render target texture is created as a depth texture, rather than a full texture map with color components (such as the RGBA texture introduced in *Chapter 4*).

A customized fragment shader, `shadow_depth.fs`, is used that renders only depth information and nothing else:

```
#version 330
void main() {
    gl_FragDepth = gl_FragCoord.z;  //Save depth value
}
```

This depth rendering pass is implemented in `DepthRenderPass.cpp`. Here is the overridden `Create()` function:

```
bool DepthRenderPass::Create(Scene* sc)
{
  __super::Create(sc);
  depthShader = LoadShader(NULL, "shadow_depth.fs");
  shadowMap = LoadShadowmapRenderTexture
(SHADOWMAP_RESOLUTION, SHADOWMAP_RESOLUTION);
  lightCam.position = Vector3Scale(pLight->lightDir, -15.0f);
  lightCam.target = Vector3Zero();
  lightCam.projection = CAMERA_ORTHOGRAPHIC;
  lightCam.up = Vector3{ 0.0f, 1.0f, 0.0f };
  lightCam.fovy = 20.0f;
  return true;
}
```

For this depth rendering pass, the first parameter of the `LoadShader()`function is `NULL` because we will use raylib's default vertex program. We also create a camera for rendering purposes. The position of the light camera will be set as the position of light later in every frame, so we don't assign a position for the `lightCam` here.

We also need an offscreen rendering buffer to store the rendered depth information. The code to create `RenderTexture2D` object as the render buffer is implemented in `DepthRenderPass::LoadShadowmapRenderTexture()`:

```
RenderTexture2D DepthRenderPass::LoadShadowmapRenderTexture(int width, int
height)
{
  RenderTexture2D target = { 0 };
  target.id=rlLoadFramebuffer();//Load an empty framebuffer
  target.texture.width = width;
  target.texture.height = height;
  if (target.id > 0){
    rlEnableFramebuffer(target.id);
    //Create depth texture. Don't need a color texture
    target.depth.id = rlLoadTextureDepth(width, height, false);
    target.depth.width = width;
    target.depth.height = height;
    target.depth.format = 19;
    target.depth.mipmaps = 1;
    // Attach depth texture to FBO
    rlFramebufferAttach(target.id, target.depth.id, RL_ATTACHMENT_DEPTH,
RL_ATTACHMENT_TEXTURE2D, 0);
    // Check if fbo is complete with attachments (valid)
    if (rlFramebufferComplete(target.id)) TRACELOG(LOG_INFO, "FBO: [ID %i]
Framebuffer object created successfully", target.id);
    rlDisableFramebuffer();
  } else
    return { 0 };
  return target;
}
```

The preceding code snippet uses some low-level raylib APIs to create a customized `RenderTexture2D` object, which only contains a depth texture. Unfortunately, raylib doesn't have a convenient wrapper for creating a depth-only `RenderTexture2D` object, so we need to manually create one for our purpose with the following steps:

1. The low-level API `rlLoadFramebuffer()` allocates an empty framebuffer from the OpenGL graphics driver.
2. The `rlLoadTextureDepth()` API allocates a GPU texture that stores depth values.
3. Use `rlFramebufferAttach()` to attach the just-created depth buffer with the frame buffer object.

Now we have a customized `RenderTexture2D` object that only contains a depth buffer. We are ready to do some rendering!

The depth rendering pass is performed in `DrawOffscreen()` in `Demo7PCFShadow.cpp`:

```
void Demo7PCFShadow::DrawOffscreen()
{
  pDepthRenderer->BeginShadowMap(_Scene);
  pDepthRenderer->BeginScene();
  pDepthRenderer->Render();
  pDepthRenderer->EndScene();
  pDepthRenderer->EndShadowMap();
}
```

The `BeginShadowMap()` function in `DepthRenderPass.cpp` prepares the render buffer texture and uses another `Camera3D` object `lightCam`, which looks at the scene from the direction of light. Let's look at what it does:

```
void DepthRenderPass::BeginShadowMap(Scene* sc, SceneCamera*
pOverrideCamera)
{
  BeginTextureMode(shadowMap);
  ClearBackground(WHITE);
  BeginMode3D(lightCam);
  pLight->lightView = rlGetMatrixModelview();
  pLight->lightProj = rlGetMatrixProjection();
}
```

After the first rendering pass completes, we obtain a depth map that stores the "depth" values from the light's perspective. Now it's ready to proceed to the next rendering pass.

Implementing the shadow rendering pass of shadow mapping

Once the depth rendering pass is complete, the second pass requires the offscreen depth buffer produced by the previous pass. This is handled in the overridden `BeginScene()` function of the second scene render pass class, `ShadowMapRenderPass`, implemented in `ShadowMapRenderPass.cpp`:

```
void ShadowMapRenderPass::BeginScene(SceneCamera* pOverrideCamera)
{
  pLight->lightViewProj = MatrixMultiply(pLight->lightView, pLight-
>lightProj);
  SetShaderValueMatrix(shadowShader, lightVPLoc, pLight->lightViewProj);
  //Make shadow map referenced texture as 5th texture, the first four
textures are commonly used by other effects
  int slot = 4;
  rlActiveTextureSlot(slot);
  rlEnableTexture(depthTextureId);
  rlSetUniform(shadowMapLoc, &slot, SHADER_UNIFORM_INT, 1);
  pScene->_CurrentRenderPass = this;
  pActiveCamera = pScene->GetMainCameraActor();
  if (pOverrideCamera!= nullptr)
    pActiveCamera = pOverrideCamera;
  BuildRenderQueue(pScene->SceneRoot, &shadowShader);
}
```

In the preceding code snippet, we enable the depth texture in the 5th texture `slot` (value = 4). Since most graphics applications typically use the first four slots, assigning it to the fifth slot is generally safe.

This time, we perform rendering using the usual active main camera but with a new shadow mapping vertex program (in `shadowmap.vs`).

The vertex program is straightforward. It calculates the `gl_Position` and passes the following attributes to the fragment shader:

```
out vec3 fragPosition;  //world position of the vertex
out vec2 fragTexCoord;  //texture uv coordinates
out vec4 fragColor;  //vertex color (if any)
out vec3 fragNormal;    //normal in world space
```

The actual heavy-lifting part is in the fragment program (in `shadowmap.fs`). The fragment program relies on the following information passed as uniform from the main application class:

```
uniform vec3 lightDir;  //Light direction
uniform vec4 lightColor;   //color
uniform vec4 ambient;   //the ambient light
uniform vec3 viewPos;   //the camera position
uniform mat4 lightVP; //Light source view-projection matrix
uniform sampler2D shadowMap;//the depth texture in 1st pass
uniform int shadowMapResolution; //size of depth texture
```

Since there is still a directional light in the scene, the first task is still calculating the lighting:

```
vec3 lightDot = vec3(0.0);
vec3 viewD = normalize(viewPos - fragPosition);
vec3 specular = vec3(0.0);
vec3 normal = normalize(fragNormal);
vec3 l = -lightDir;
float NdotL = max(dot(normal, l), 0.0);
lightDot += lightColor.rgb*NdotL;
float specCo = 0.0;
if (NdotL > 0.0) specCo = pow(max(0.0, dot(viewD, reflect(-(l), normal))),
16.0);
specular += specCo;
finalColor = (texelColor*((colDiffuse + vec4(specular,
1.0))*vec4(lightDot, 1.0)));
```

In the shader, we determine whether each pixel is visible to the light by comparing its depth value. If another object obstructs the light, we know that the pixel is within the shadow.

The following code transforms the world-space position into the light camera's clip space. This allows us to determine where the vertex is visible from the light source's perspective:

```
// Find out the position in lighting camera space
vec4 fragPosLightSpace = lightVP * vec4(fragPosition, 1);
// Perform the perspective division
fragPosLightSpace.xyz /= fragPosLightSpace.w;
```

Since the light camera's clip space ranges from `-1` to `1`, it differs from the texture map's UV coordinate range of `0` to `1`. To address this, we need to shift and scale the value range, enabling the texture map sampler to locate the depth value at the corresponding position:

```
// Transform from [-1, 1] range to [0, 1] range
fragPosLightSpace.xyz = (fragPosLightSpace.xyz + 1.0f) / 2.0f;
vec2 sampleCoords = fragPosLightSpace.xy;
```

Now we can use a texture map sampler to get the depth value:

```
float sampleDepth = texture(shadowMap, sampleCoords).r;
float curDepth = fragPosLightSpace.z;
if (curDepth > sampleDepth)
  finalColor = vec4(0, 0, 0, 1);
```

By comparing the current pixel's depth with the stored depth, we can determine if the pixel is in shadow. If the current depth is greater than the stored depth, it means the vertex is blocked by another object and cannot be seen by the light source:

```
if (curDepth > sampleDepth)
  finalColor = vec4(0,0,0,1);  //under shadow
```

Before you run the `Demo7PCFShadow` project, we want to make a small temporary change to one line of the code. We want to show you how we refine the same shadow mapping fragment program and fix some issues along the way.

Now let's open `ShadowMapRenderPass.cpp`. In the function `Create()`, we use `LoadShader()` to load the fragment program `shadowmap-pcf.fs` by default.

We have 3 different versions of the same fragment programs:

- `shadowmap.fs`: First try rendering shadow, but with unwanted visual defects.
- `shadowmap-bias.fs`: Improved version to fix shadow acne effects.
- `shadowmap-pcf.fs`: Final version with soft shadow rendering.

Let's change to the first version of the fragment program `shadowmap.fs`, as follows:

```
shadowShader = LoadShader("../../resources/shaders/glsl330/shadowmap.vs",
"../../resources/shaders/glsl330/shadowmap.fs");
```

Now we get the first working shadow map demo:

Figure 7.4 – The shadow mapping with acne effect

Yes! We see shadow now but with very strange black triangle strips appearing on the surface of all objects.

However, this strange artifact, known as **shadow acne**, is caused by precision errors in depth calculations. A common technique to mitigate this issue is to apply a bias value.

The `Shadowmap-bias.fs` is our second implementation to apply a bias for mitigating the precision error. There are several ways to determine this bias, the most common one of which is the **slope-scaled bias**—a bias proportional to the angle between the surface normal and the light direction:

```
float bias = max(0.0002 * (1.0 - dot(normal, l)), 0.00002) + 0.00001;
```

Then, compare the depth value with bias:

```
if (curDepth - bias > sampleDepth)
  finalColor = vec4(0, 0, 0, 1);
```

Now please open `ShadowMapRenderPass.cpp` and replace the fragment program `shadowmap.fs` with `shadowmap-bias.fs` in line **17**:

```
shadowShader = LoadShader("../../resources/shaders/glsl330/shadowmap.vs",
"../../resources/shaders/glsl330/shadowmap-bias.fs");
```

Save the changes and run the project again. Now it looks a lot better:

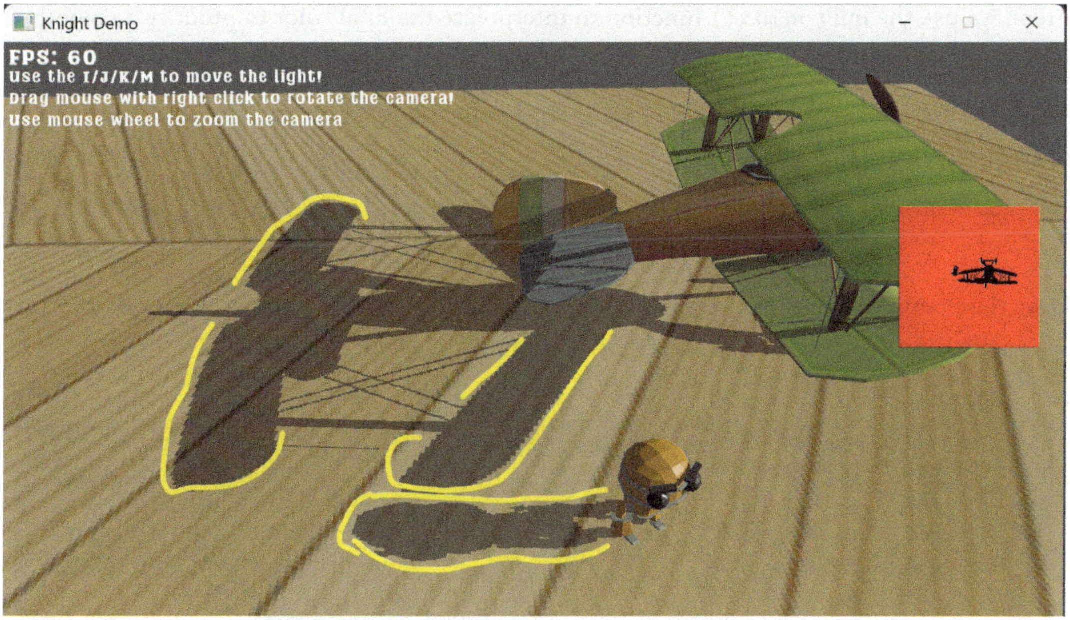

Figure 7.5 – The shadow edge is too sharp

The edges of the shadow currently appear too sharp, which can make them look unnatural. To enhance the visual quality, we can soften the shadow edges.

Softening the shadow edges

A commonly used technique in real-time applications is **Percentage-Closer Filtering (PCF) shadow mapping** to soften the edges of shadows. This approach averages the shadow value of the current pixel with those of its neighboring pixels.

For this implementation, we average the surrounding 8 pixels along with the center pixel, resulting in a total of 9 pixels. The code needs to be refined using a double loop:

```
vec2 texelSize = vec2(1.0f / float(shadowMapResolution));
for (int x = -1; x <= 1; x++)
  for (int y = -1; y <= 1; y++) {
    float sampleDepth = texture(shadowMap, sampleCoords + texelSize *
vec2(x, y)).r;
    if (curDepth - bias > sampleDepth) shadowCounter++;
  }
finalColor = mix(finalColor, vec4(0,0,0,1), float(shadowCounter) /
float(numSamples));
```

Here, we use the built-in `mix()` function to interpolate the final color to produce a smoothed shadow edge.

Now open `ShadowMapRenderPass.cpp` and replace the fragment program `shadowmap-bias.fs` with `shadowmap-pcf.fs` in line **17**:

```
shadowShader = LoadShader("../../resources/shaders/glsl330/shadowmap.vs",
"../../resources/shaders/glsl330/shadowmap-pcf.fs");
```

Save the changes and run the project again, you can now see the edge of the shadow improves a lot – with the cost of sampling an additional 8 pixels and averaging them.

Figure 7.6 – Using the Percentage-Closer Filtering algorithm to soften the shadow

In the demo project `Demo7PCFShadow`, we also render a debug view of the depth texture on the right side of the screen. You can also use the *I*, *J*, *K*, and *L* keys to move the light source around and see the different shadow effects.

The PCF shadow mapping algorithm has some immediate benefits:

- **Flexible**: PCF works with various types of light sources (directional, point, and spotlights).
- **Real-time performance**: It's relatively fast and efficient, making it suitable for real-time applications like video games.

However, shadow mapping isn't flawless:

- **Aliasing**: Low-resolution maps or large shadowed areas can introduce jagged edges; techniques like PCF help soften them.
- **Perspective artifacts**: Objects near the camera but far from the light can show distortions due to non-uniform depth sampling. **Cascaded Shadow Maps (CSMs)** alleviate this by splitting the shadow map into segments for more precise detail.

Shadow mapping is widely used due to its flexibility and compatibility with various types of lights, though it has limitations like aliasing and precision issues that require additional techniques to mitigate. Despite these challenges, shadow mapping remains one of the most popular and practical shadow techniques in real-time 3D rendering.

Thus far, we have explored rendering techniques applicable to individual elements within the scene, like player characters, props, and buildings. Now, we will broaden our scope to learn the rendering techniques necessary for handling terrain.

Creating a large outdoor landscape

In 3D game development, several common methods are used to create 3D landscapes. For relatively small terrains, the terrain can be modeled directly as a 3D object. The rendering of small terrain is no different than rendering other objects in the game. This section will focus on creating and rendering larger outdoor terrain.

Let's start with something simple: instead of manually constructing the 3D terrain model, a flat image can be used to generate uneven and rolling 3D terrain. This technique is known as **height mapping**.

Height-mapping 3D terrain

A **height-mapped** 3D terrain uses a 2D grayscale image to set surface elevations: each pixel's brightness defines the height of a corresponding grid vertex, as shown in *Figure 7.7*:

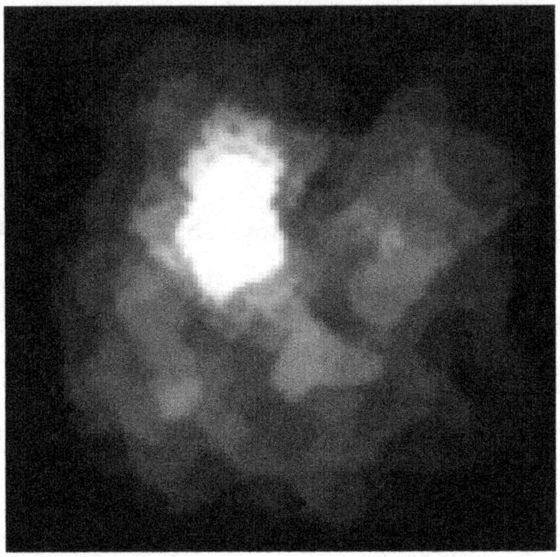

Figure 7.7 – The height map uses the grayscale value to represent height

In *Figure 7.7*, *lighter* pixels represent higher elevations, *darker* ones lower. By scaling these values, you can adjust vertical exaggeration. This method is both efficient and popular for realistic terrain since it generates complex shapes from simple data structures.

The sample project `Demo7HMap` implements the height-mapped terrain.

The following code in `HMapTerrainModelComponent.h` makes the terrain a `Component` so we can reuse it later:

```
class HMapTerrainModelComponent : public Component
{
public:
  HMapTerrainModelComponent();
  ~HMapTerrainModelComponent();
  bool CreateFromFile(Vector3 terrainDimension, Vector2 texTileSize, const
char* pHeightmapFilePath, const char* pTerrainTexurePath);
  void Update(float ElapsedSeconds) override;
  void Draw() override;
  Image heightMapImage;
  Model model;
```

```
    Mesh mesh;
    Color tint = WHITE;
    friend SceneActor;
protected:
    Mesh GenMeshHeightmapEx(Image heightmap, Vector3 size, Vector2
texPatchSize);
};
```

The component is implemented in `HMapTerrainModelComponent.cpp`. The `CreateFromFile()` function loads the height map from the image file into the `Image` object `heightMapImage`. We will use this height map to create the actual 3D `Mesh` object to build our 3D terrain `Model` object.

In this project, we will build a terrain feature partially supported by raylib, so we will try to customize it to our needs but still make the best use of raylib. The first thing is to create the terrain. It's implemented in `CreateFromFile()` and here is a simplified version (with some error-checking code removed):

```
bool HMapTerrainModelComponent::CreateFromFile(Vector3 terrainDimension,
Vector2 texTileSize, const char* pHeightmapFilePath, const char*
pTerrainTexurePath)
{
    heightMapImage = LoadImage(pHeightmapFilePath);
    Texture2D texture = LoadTextureFromImage(heightMapImage);
    mesh = GenMeshHeightmapEx(heightMapImage, terrainDimension,
texTileSize);
    model = LoadModelFromMesh(mesh);
    model.materials[0].maps[MATERIAL_MAP_DIFFUSE].texture =
LoadTexture(pTerrainTexurePath);
    return true;
}
```

In the above snippet, the most important part of the code lies in our custom function, `GenMeshHeightmapEx()`. raylib already provides a convenient function, `GenMeshHeightmap()`, which we initially used for the first implementation of this project. However, there's a limitation: the texture coordinates generated by `GenMeshHeightmap()` are designed for a single large texture that covers the entire terrain.

This approach works fine for a quick height map terrain demo, but it introduces a significant drawback when scaling the terrain bigger. As the terrain size increases, the single texture becomes stretched and blurred, reducing visual quality, as shown in *Figure 7.8*:

Figure 7.8 – The terrain texture gets blurry if we scale the size of the terrain up

To address this limitation, a more flexible implementation was needed—one that provides control over texture tiling. To achieve this, we develop our own implementation, `GenMeshHeightmapEx()`, which overcomes this limitation and offers finer control over texture mapping for larger terrains.

The key difference from the original function provided by raylib is the addition of a parameter to control the texture patch size for tiling. This allows for tiling repeatable textures on the terrain surface, rather than using a single large texture for the entire terrain. As a result, the texture quality is much less affected by changes to the terrain's scale.

Below is a highlight of the changes made to the original function in `HMapTerrainModelComponent.cpp` of the `Demo7HMap` project:

```
Mesh HMapTerrainModelComponent::GenMeshHeightmapEx(Image heightmap,
Vector3 size, Vector2 texPatchSize)
{
#define GRAY_VALUE(c) ((float)(c.r + c.g + c.b)/3.0f)
```

```
    Mesh mesh = { 0 };
    int mapX = heightmap.width;
    int mapZ = heightmap.height;
    //…
    int px = mapX / (int)texPatchSize.x;
    int pz = mapZ / (int)texPatchSize.y;
    for (int z = 0; z < mapZ - 1; z++)
      for (int x = 0; x < mapX - 1; x++){
        // Fill vertices array with data
        // …
        mesh.texcoords[tcCounter] = (float)x / (px - 1);
        mesh.texcoords[tcCounter + 1] = (float)z / (pz - 1);
        mesh.texcoords[tcCounter + 2] = (float)x / (px - 1);
        mesh.texcoords[tcCounter+3]=(float)(z+1)/(pz - 1);
        mesh.texcoords[tcCounter + 4]=(float)(x+1)/(px - 1);
        mesh.texcoords[tcCounter + 5] = (float)z / (pz - 1);
     mesh.texcoords[tcCounter+6]=mesh.texcoords[tcCounter+4];
     mesh.texcoords[tcCounter+7]=mesh.texcoords[tcCounter+5];
     mesh.texcoords[tcCounter+8]=mesh.texcoords[tcCounter+2];
     mesh.texcoords[tcCounter+9]=mesh.texcoords[tcCounter+3];
     mesh.texcoords[tcCounter+10]=(float)(x + 1) / (px - 1);
     mesh.texcoords[tcCounter+11]=(float)(z + 1) / (pz - 1);
        tcCounter += 12;    // 6 texcoords, 12 floats
        //…
      }
    UnloadImageColors(pixels);  // Unload pixels color data
     UploadMesh(&mesh, false);
    return mesh;
}
```

The patch size is specified as a `Vector2` with X-axis patch size and Z-axis patch size. Each patch has 6 vertices (2 triangles). We manually build the mesh data in the double `for` loop of the preceding code snippet.

You can adjust the texture patch size to make it look good in your game:

```
HMapTerrainModelComponent* heightMap = pTerrain->CreateAndAddComponent<HMa
pTerrainModelComponent>();
Vector3 terrainDimension = Vector3{32,8,32};
```

```
bool success = heightMap->CreateFromFile(terrainDimension, Vector2{ 4,4
}, "../../resources/textures/heightmap.png", "../../resources/textures/
terrain_map.png");
```

We set the terrain size as 32x32 and used a repeatable grass texture with a tile size of 4x4:

Figure 7.9 – Improving texture quality by introducing tiling

A good exercise for you is to extend this to allow more than a single type of texture used for terrain tiling. You can have repeatable tiles of sand, river, grass textures, etc.

Since we made the terrain a standard `Model`, we can use the handy `DrawModel` function to render the terrain:

```
void HMapTerrainModelComponent::Draw()
{ DrawModel(model,this->_SceneActor->Position,1.0f, tint);}
```

This is the simplest way to create a bigger terrain with a single `Model`. In the next section, we will discuss various ways to build bigger terrain.

Rendering terrain with level of detail (LOD)

Imagine exploring a vast, breathtaking 3D terrain stretching as far as the eye can see in an open-world MMORPG. Rolling hills, towering mountains, and deep valleys – all rendered in stunning detail. Now imagine your computer trying to draw every single tiny rock, blade of grass, and pebble across that entire landscape *all the time*. The result? A sluggish, unresponsive mess, even with very powerful modern hardware.

Well, the secret is you do not even need to draw them all. This is where **Level of Detail** (**LOD**) comes to the rescue.

Figure 7.10 – Even in a large open-world game, only scenery near the main characters matters (created with ChatGPT by the author)

Look at the imaginary open-world game with your player character facing vast scenery in *Figure 7.10*. Only those trees near the player character need to be real 3D objects. For those trees far away, and even the mountain, rather than a real 3D model, billboards can be used, which were introduced at the beginning of the chapter. This significantly reduces the number of triangles to be rendered by the GPU. The same also goes for the terrain. We only need to render the terrain near the player character the greatest detail. Distant terrain can be rendered with less detail.

LOD is a technique used to dynamically adjust the complexity of a 3D model based on its distance from the viewer. This approach is essential when scaling up to render larger terrains and more complex scenes with numerous objects and effects. LOD allows distant terrain patches to be rendered with fewer triangles and reduced detail, depending on their distance from the camera. In many open-world games, LOD also helps manage memory efficiently by loading and keeping in memory only the necessary level of detail for the currently visible terrain, thereby reducing the memory footprint.

In the previous height map terrain sample, we loaded the entire terrain as a single 3D model into the GPU. While this method works for small environments, it is not suitable for games that require rendering expansive open-world terrains. In the next section, we will introduce the quadtree — a data structure specifically designed to implement LOD efficiently.

Implementing level of detail with quadtree

Quadtree is a tree data structure used to partition a 2D space by recursively subdividing it into four quadrants or regions. This structure is especially useful for efficiently managing spatial data and is well-suited for 3D terrain represented as a 2D height map.

Figure 7.11 shows an example of a quadtree data structure. Each element in the tree is called a **node**, and each node can be subdivided into a maximum of four child nodes. The topmost node serves as the single entry point, known as the **root node** of the entire quadtree. Traversal always starts from the root node and proceeds down to each child node. A node without any child nodes is considered a **leaf node**.

The **depth** of a node indicates the number of parent nodes that must be traversed to reach that node. For instance, the depth of nodes **E**, **F**, and **G** is 2, meaning two levels of traversal are required from the root to these nodes.

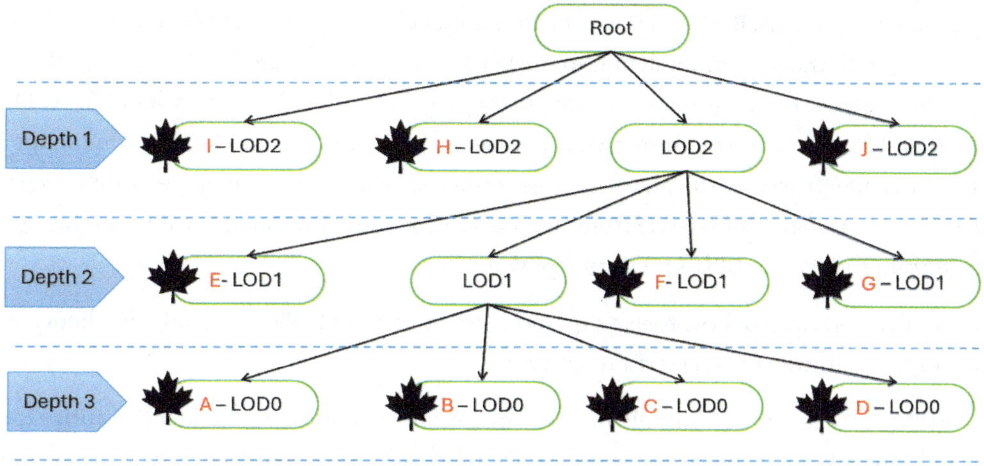

Figure 7.11 – Using the depth of quadtree to represent level of detail

However, when we mention LOD, it usually works in the opposite way. LOD 0 means the highest detail level or full detail level. LOD 1 is less detailed, followed by level 2, level 3, etc. Now look back to *Figure 7.10*. Suppose the player character (shown as the camera icon) is standing at the bottom-right of the terrain and looking diagonally at the top-left corner of the game terrain, like *Figure 7.12*:

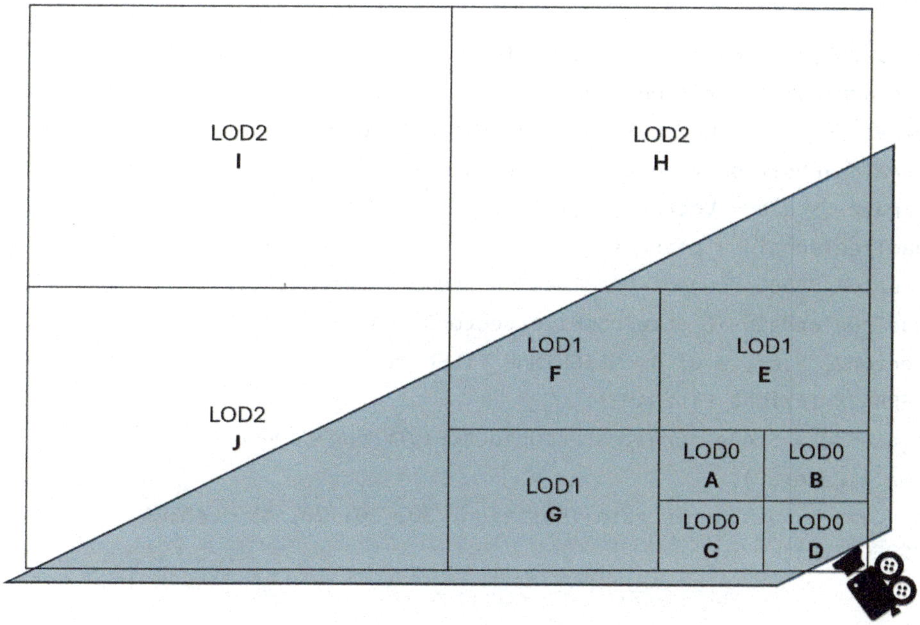

Figure 7.12 – The relationship between LOD and quadtree

We can observe nodes **A**, **B**, **C**, and **D** are the four nodes closest to the player camera. They should be rendered with the maximum detail, so the LOD of these four nodes is level 0. Nodes **E**, **F**, and **G** are behind nodes **A-D** in the camera view, so they can be rendered with less detail (level 1 LOD). Nodes **H** and **J** are even further from the camera view, so their LOD is 2. The blue cone shape area means the range (frustum) the player can see through a perspective camera; we don't even need to render node **I** since it's invisible from the player's location. We can drop at least one-quarter of the terrain to save the GPU's rendering power.

As we get the basic idea of how to use a quadtree to implement LOD, let's apply the theory above to the implementation of LOD terrain rendering.

The `Demo7QuadTreeTerrain` sample project implements a quadtree to render the entire terrain with a different LOD. It reuses the same height map from the previous demo. However, unlike the previous approach where the entire terrain was treated as a single 3D model, this time the terrain's triangle structure is dynamically generated on the fly during the rendering process. This approach enables more efficient rendering, particularly for large terrains, by adjusting the level of detail based on the camera's distance from different terrain patches.

The first part is the main Knight application class in `Demo7QuadTreeTerrain.cpp`. We override the `Create()` function to initialize a camera and a quadtree terrain model `SceneActor` in the following code snippet:

```
void Demo7QuadTreeTerrain::Start(){
//… other initialization code
pTerrain =_Scene->CreateSceneObject<SceneActor>("Terrain");
pTerrain->Position = Vector3{ 0.0f, 0.0f, 0.0f };
pTerrain->Scale = Vector3{ 1,1,1 };
pQuadTreeTerrain = pTerrain->
  CreateAndAddComponent<QuadTreeTerrainModelComponent>();
pQuadTreeTerrain->CreateFromFile(Vector3{ 64, 13, 64 },
  Vector2{ 8.0f, 8.0f }, HEIGHTMAP_FILENAME,
  TERRAIN_TEXTURE_FILENAME);
pMainCamera=_Scene->CreateSceneObject<FlyThroughCamera>(
  "Main Camera");
pMainCamera->SetUp(pTerrain->Position, 30, 20, 20, 45, CAMERA_
PERSPECTIVE);
}
```

Let's create our own `QuadTreeTerrainModelComponent`, just like we did for `HMapTerrainModelComponent` in the previous example. The code is organized into three parts in `QuadTreeTerrainModelComponent.cpp`. The first part is easy: loading the grayscale image and converting it to the height map:

```
bool LoadHeightmapFromImage(const char* fileName)
{
//file name checking …
Image image = LoadImage(fileName);
// Store actual dimensions from the loaded image
HeightMapWidth = image.width;
HeightMapDepth = image.height;
heightmap.resize(HeightMapWidth * HeightMapDepth);
for (int z = 0; z < HeightMapDepth; ++z) {
  for (int x = 0; x < HeightMapWidth; ++x) {
    Color pixelColor = GetImageColor(image, x, z);
    heightmap[z * HeightMapWidth + x] = (float)pixelColor.r / 255.0f;
  }
}
UnloadImage(image); // Free image data from RAM
return true;
}
```

Like the previous example, the main difference here is that the height map is stored as a normalized float value ranging from 0.0 to 1.0. This representation ensures that the height data is both compact and easily scalable, making it more efficient for terrain rendering calculations.

The most significant difference from the previous example is that we no longer create a model with fixed vertices and triangles. Instead, the triangles to be rendered are dynamically selected by each frame. This means that the set of triangles may vary from frame to frame, depending on the traversal results of the quadtree that we will build in the next steps. This approach allows for more adaptive and efficient rendering, especially in large, complex terrains.

Building a quadtree for the terrain

The second part of QuadTreeTerrainModelComponent.cpp is focused on building the quadtree data structure for the height map terrain we just created. First is the class definition in QuadTreeTerrainModelComponent.h:

```
struct QuadTreeNode {
  BoundingBox bounds;
  QuadTreeNode* children[4];
  Vector2 center;
  float size;
  int depth;  // Depth in the tree (0 = root)
  bool isLeaf;  // Is this node a leaf?
  QuadTreeNode(BoundingBox b, int d) : bounds(b), depth(d), isLeaf(true)
  {
    for (int i = 0; i < 4; ++i) children[i] = nullptr;
    // Calculate center and size from bounds
    center.x=bounds.min.x+(bounds.max.x-bounds.min.x)/2.0;
    center.y=bounds.min.z+(bounds.max.z-bounds.min.z)/2.0f;
    size = bounds.max.x - bounds.min.x;
  }
  // Recursive destructor
  ~QuadTreeNode() {
    for (int i = 0; i < 4; ++i) {
      delete children[i]; // recursively delete children
      children[i] = nullptr;
    }
  }
};
```

In the above class definition, each node records its own depth and a bool isLeaf for quickly identifying a leaf node. Let's take a look at how we build the quadtree:

```
void BuildQuadtreeNode(QuadTreeNode* node)
{
  // Stop subdividing if max depth is reached
  if (node->depth >= MaxQuadTreeDepth) {
      node->isLeaf = true;
      return;
```

```
    }
    // Calculate the size of potential children
    float halfSize = node->size / 2.0f;
    // Stop subdividing if the node's area is very small
    if (halfSize < terrainScale.x || halfSize < terrainScale.z)
    {
      node->isLeaf = true;
      return;
    }
    //If we are here, the node is not a leaf yet and can be subdivided
    node->isLeaf = false;
    // Get parent bounds
    Vector3 min = node->bounds.min;
    Vector3 max = node->bounds.max; // Y component of max is max terrain
  height
    // Define bounds for the four children
    // Child 0: Top-Left (NW)
    BoundingBox childBounds0 = { {min.x, min.y, min.z}, {min.x + halfSize,
  max.y, min.z + halfSize} };
    // Child 1: Top-Right (NE)
    BoundingBox childBounds1 = { {min.x + halfSize, min.y, min.z}, {max.x,
  max.y, min.z + halfSize} };
    // Child 2: Bottom-Left (SW)
    BoundingBox childBounds2 = { {min.x, min.y, min.z + halfSize}, {min.x +
  halfSize, max.y, max.z} };
    // Child 3: Bottom-Right (SE)
    BoundingBox childBounds3 = { {min.x + halfSize, min.y, min.z +
  halfSize}, {max.x, max.y, max.z} };
    node->children[0] = new QuadTreeNode(childBounds0, node->depth + 1);
    node->children[1] = new QuadTreeNode(childBounds1, node->depth + 1);
    node->children[2] = new QuadTreeNode(childBounds2, node->depth + 1);
    node->children[3] = new QuadTreeNode(childBounds3, node->depth + 1);
    // Recursively build children
    for (int i = 0; i < 4; ++i) {
      BuildQuadtreeNode(node->children[i]);
    }
  }
```

The most crucial part of the above code is determining whether the current node is a leaf node (reaching the maximum depth) and correctly calculating each child's bounding box. It is important to note that the quadtree is built only once during the terrain initialization process, not in every frame. Once the quadtree structure is established, it remains static, and we can proceed to render the terrain efficiently.

Traversing the quadtree for terrain rendering

The third part is rendering a quadtree terrain. The `Draw()` function of `QuadTreeTerrainModelComponent` is the starting point:

```
void QuadTreeTerrainModelComponent::Draw()
{
  __super::Draw(); // Call base class draw
  FrustumPlane frustumPlanes[6]; // Array to hold the frustum planes
  NumTriangles = 0;
  _SceneActor->GetMainCamera()-> ExtractFrustumPlanes(frustumPlanes);
  DrawQuadtreeNode(rootNode, _SceneActor->GetMainCamera(),
DebugShowBounds, frustumPlanes);
}
```

One important part is we retrieve the frustum of the current main camera by calling Knight's function `SceneCamera::ExtractFrustumPlanes()`. We then pass this camera frustum data into the recursive function `DrawQuadtreeNode()`:

```
void DrawQuadtreeNode(QuadTreeNode* node, SceneCamera *pCamera, bool
drawBounds, const FrustumPlane frustumPlanes[6])
{
  if (!node) return;
  if (!pCamera->IsBoundingBoxInFrustum(node->bounds, frustumPlanes)) {
    return; // Node is outside the frustum, so skip
  }
```

The above code calls Knight's `SceneCamera:: IsBoundingBoxInFrustum()` function to determine if the bounding box of the current node is visible from the camera. Let's go back to *Figure 7.12*. Remember we mentioned node I is completely falling outside the frustum (light blue region) of the main camera and can be excluded from rendering? This `SceneCamera` function tests if the bounding box of the current node is visible. If it's completely invisible, we simply skip rendering it.

The next part of the code is also essential as it calculates the distance between the main camera and the current node. This distance is used to determine whether the current node's depth matches the required LOD. If the depth is not sufficient, the function recursively calls itself with the four possible child nodes. If the depth is appropriate, it directly calls `DrawTerrainChunk()`, which performs the actual rendering task:

```
  Camera3D camera=*pCamera->GetCamera3D(); //Get the camera
  float dx = camera.position.x - node->center.x;
  float dz = camera.position.z - node->center.y; // node->center.y stores
the Z-coordinate of the node's center
  float distanceToNode = sqrtf(dx * dx + dz * dz);
  //LOD Threshold: if distance is greater than node_size * factor, or if
it's a leaf, or max depth draw it.
  //Otherwise, recurse into children.
  float lodThreshold = node->size * LevelOfDetailDistance;
  if (node->isLeaf || distanceToNode > lodThreshold || node->depth >=
MaxQuadTreeDepth - 1) { // -1 to ensure leaves at max depth are drawn
    DrawTerrainChunk(node);
    // Optionally draw the bounding box for debugging …
  } else {
    //Recursively draw children
    for (int i = 0; i < 4; ++i) {
      if (node->children[i]) {   // Check if child exists
        DrawQuadtreeNode(node->children[i], pCamera, drawBounds,
frustumPlanes);
      }
    }
    // Optionally draw bounds of the parent node …
  }
}
```

Finally, the below code snippet pushes triangles into the GPU to render a single node:

```
void DrawTerrainChunk(QuadTreeNode* node)
{
  //Some check …
  //Calculate the dimensions of the terrain in world space
  float worldTotalWidth = HeightMapWidth * terrainScale.x;
  float worldTotalDepth = HeightMapDepth * terrainScale.z;
```

```
float worldOriginX = -worldTotalWidth / 2.0f;
float worldOriginZ = -worldTotalDepth / 2.0f;
//Convert node's bounds to heightmap grid coordinates
int mapStartX = Clamp((int)roundf((node->bounds.min.x - worldOriginX) / 
terrainScale.x), 0, HeightMapWidth - 1);
int mapStartZ = Clamp((int)roundf((node->bounds.min.z - worldOriginZ) / 
terrainScale.z), 0, HeightMapDepth - 1);
int mapEndX = Clamp((int)roundf((node->bounds.max.x - worldOriginX) / 
terrainScale.x), 0, HeightMapWidth) +1;
int mapEndZ = Clamp((int)roundf((node->bounds.max.z - worldOriginZ) / 
terrainScale.z), 0, HeightMapDepth) +1;
//Ensure there's at least one quad to draw
if (mapEndX <= mapStartX || mapEndZ <= mapStartZ)
  return;
//Step determines the resolution of this chunk.
int step = 2;
```

Unlike the previous Demo7HMap example, we simply call raylib's DrawModel() to render a whole terrain mesh in the 3D model. In the following code, we will use raylib's immediate-mode low-level API to stream raw triangle data to the GPU. The reason we do so is because, each frame, we only pick a few subsets of nodes to render, so the triangle data is dynamically assembled frame by frame:

```
rlEnableTexture(terrainTexture.id); // Enable texturing
rlBegin(RL_TRIANGLES); // Start drawing triangles
rlColor4ub(255, 255, 255, 255); // Set vertex color to white to show 
original texture colors
rlSetTexture(terrainTexture.id); // Bind the texture
for(int z = mapStartZ; z < mapEndZ - step; z += step){
  for (int x = mapStartX; x < mapEndX - step; x += step){
    //Get normalized height values for the four corners
    float h1 = GetHeightmapValue(x, z); // Top-left
    float h2 = GetHeightmapValue(x + step, z);//Top-right
    float h3 = GetHeightmapValue(x,z+step);//Bottom-left
    float h4 =GetHeightmapValue(x+step,z+step);// Bottom-right
    // Calculate world coordinates for the four corners
    Vector3 p1 = { worldOriginX + x * terrainScale.x ,                h1 * 
terrainScale.y, worldOriginZ + z * terrainScale.z };
    Vector3 p2 = { worldOriginX + (x + step) * terrainScale.x, h2 * 
terrainScale.y, worldOriginZ + z * terrainScale.z };
```

```
        Vector3 p3 = { worldOriginX + x * terrainScale.x ,              h3 *
terrainScale.y, worldOriginZ + (z + step) * terrainScale.z };
        Vector3 p4 = { worldOriginX + (x + step) * terrainScale.x, h4 *
terrainScale.y, worldOriginZ + (z + step) * terrainScale.z };
        //Calculate UV coordinates for each vertex
        //These map the texture across the entire terrain, tiled by
tilingFactor
        float u1 = (float)x / (HeightMapWidth - 1.0f) * tilingFactor.x;
        float v1 = (float)z / (HeightMapDepth - 1.0f) * tilingFactor.y;
        float u2 = (float)(x + step) / (HeightMapWidth - 1.0f) *
tilingFactor.x;
        float v2 = v1;
        float u3 = u1;
        float v3 = (float)(z + step) / (HeightMapWidth - 1.0f) *
tilingFactor.y;
        float u4 = u2;
        float v4 = v3;
        // Triangle 1: p1, p3, p4
        Vector3 n1 = Vector3Normalize(Vector3CrossProduct(Vector3Subtract(p3,
p1), Vector3Subtract(p4, p1)));
        rlNormal3f(n1.x, n1.y, n1.z);
        rlTexCoord2f(u1, v1);
        rlVertex3f(p1.x, p1.y, p1.z); // p1
        rlTexCoord2f(u3, v3);
        rlVertex3f(p3.x, p3.y, p3.z); // p3
        rlTexCoord2f(u4, v4);
        rlVertex3f(p4.x, p4.y, p4.z); // p4
        // Triangle 2: p1, p4, p2
        Vector3 n2 = Vector3Normalize(Vector3CrossProduct(Vector3Subtract(p4,
p1), Vector3Subtract(p2, p1)));
        rlNormal3f(n2.x, n2.y, n2.z);
        rlTexCoord2f(u1, v1);
        rlVertex3f(p1.x, p1.y, p1.z); // p1
        rlTexCoord2f(u4, v4);
        rlVertex3f(p4.x, p4.y, p4.z); // p4
        rlTexCoord2f(u2, v2);
        rlVertex3f(p2.x, p2.y, p2.z); // p2
        NumTriangles += 2;
```

```
        }
    }
    rlEnd(); // Finish drawing triangles
    rlDisableTexture(); // Disable texturing
}
```

The preceding code is long but easy to understand. It builds the terrain's triangle data based on the current depth of the node and streams it into GPU.

> **Important note**
>
> If you are not familiar with how raylib's low-level graphics APIs work, here are some additional internet resources:
>
> - Quick reference document: `https://www.raylib.com/cheatsheet/cheatsheet.html`
> - Architecture overview: `https://github.com/raysan5/raylib/wiki/raylib-architecture`

We have introduced the primary part of the `QuadTreeTerrainModelComponent` class. For the rest of the class, there are two important member variables:

```
    int MaxQuadTreeDepth = 7;
```

This value represents the *maximum depth* allowed for the quadtree. You can adjust it based on the map size and terrain complexity. However, it is not recommended to set the quadtree depth too deep, as this can significantly increase the *traversal cost*, leading to reduced performance:

```
    float LevelOfDetailDistance = 4.5f;
```

This value acts as a threshold that determines how quickly the quadtree needs to traverse to deeper levels. A lower threshold value means the tree will descend more quickly, resulting in the entire terrain being rendered with the highest detail.

The best way to understand how to choose `LevelOfDetailDistance` is to run the sample project and see the different visual results. To be able to see the quadtree and LOD in action, toggle the *B* key to turn on the drawing of each node's bounding box, like in *Figure 7.13*:

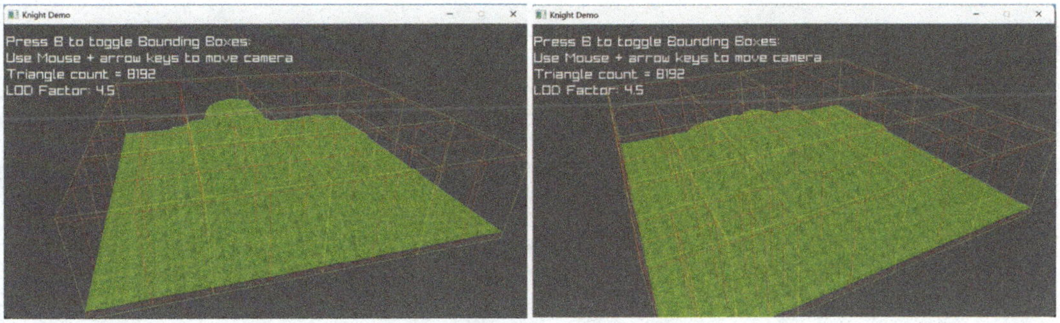

Figure 7.13 – Bounding boxes show a different LOD based on the distance of the camera from each node

By scrolling the mouse wheel and using arrow keys to move the camera, you can observe how different LOD are used to render the terrain dynamically. The quadtree technique is highly effective for rendering large terrains and is widely used in many games.

In addition to terrain rendering, the next section will cover how to render the sky, completing your game environment for a more immersive experience.

Rendering a skybox

A **skybox** is a large, cube-shaped enclosure that creates the illusion of a distant background for skies, landscapes, or space scenes. It typically uses a **cubemap**—six images mapped to the cube's faces—forming a seamless panorama, or six 2D texture maps. Rendered as if infinitely far away, the skybox rotates with the camera but never appears closer or farther.

`Demo7SkyBox` demonstrates a simple use case to use shaders to render a skybox cubemap, as shown in *Figure 7.14*. Use your mouse to rotate the camera:

Figure 7.14 – Using a cubemap for a skybox

The vertex program is mostly identical to the default one, except, for the skybox, it will always keep the same distance from the camera view. So, we need to remove the *translation* part of the view matrix:

```
// Remove translation from the view matrix
mat4 rotV = mat4(mat3(matView));
gl_Position = matProjection*rotV*vec4(vertexPosition,1.0);
```

The fragment program uses a cube mapping sampler instead of our usual `sampler2D` to sample the pixel from a cubic texture map:

```
uniform samplerCube environmentMap;
color = texture(environmentMap, fragPosition).rgb;
```

By adding the skybox with the terrain introduced in this chapter, we can create a complete outdoor game scene environment.

Summary

This chapter tackled several core techniques for constructing a full, performant 3D game world. It started by explaining billboards—flat, camera-facing quads that reduce geometry complexity, making it possible to render large crowds, distant foliage, or effects with minimal overhead. Particle systems build on billboards by simulating hundreds or thousands of small, short-lived elements (e.g., sparks, smoke) under a simple physics model, showcasing how multiple, lightweight billboards can create lively visual effects.

Next, we introduced multi-pass rendering, focusing on shadow mapping. Rather than drawing everything in a single pass, modern engines generate a shadow map from the light's perspective, which captures object depth. Each pixel in the main pass is then tested against the shadow map to determine whether it is lit or occluded. Common issues like shadow acne are addressed through biasing, and *PCF* helps soften hard shadow edges.

For large outdoor scenes, we demonstrated how to generate height-mapped terrain from a grayscale image, where each pixel's brightness corresponds to vertex elevation. This method efficiently produces realistic landscape shapes with minimal data. The skybox was also introduced, which involves wrapping the scene in a large textured cube that simulates an infinitely distant horizon.

While each feature—billboards, particles, shadows, terrain, and the skybox—can be demonstrated individually, a real-world 3D game must combine them. You are encouraged to understand the trade-offs of each method and choose those that best match your project requirements.

Moving into the next chapter, we will focus on character animation. Just as the particle effects introduced in this chapter contribute to a lively game scene, animation plays a crucial role in making characters feel real and dynamic.

Part 3

Breathing Life into Your Games

In this part, the focus shifts to two essential pillars of modern game development—character animation and **artificial intelligence (AI)**. Together, these systems bring game worlds to life, transforming static models and scripted behaviors into immersive, responsive, and intelligent experiences.

You'll begin by exploring core animation techniques, including keyframe animation, skeletal hierarchies, and interpolation methods that create smooth, natural transitions between movements. The chapter also introduces **inverse kinematics (IK)**, a real-time technique that allows characters to adapt their animations dynamically to the environment—essential for realism and player immersion.

From animation, you'll move into the field of game AI, starting with foundational systems such as **finite state machines (FSMs)**, behavior trees, and steering behaviors. These techniques provide the logic behind NPC decisions, movement, and interactions. You'll also learn about A* pathfinding—one of the most widely used algorithms in games—for enabling intelligent navigation through game worlds.

Finally, the journey leads to modern AI approaches, including neural networks, shadow learning, and deep learning. You'll explore how these advanced techniques can be used to build adaptable and intelligent agents capable of learning from data. With hands-on C++ examples, you'll train a neural network and integrate it into an AI-controlled turret defense game, providing a complete, real-world application of machine learning in games.

This part includes the following chapters:

- *Chapter 8, Animating Your Characters*
- *Chapter 9, Building AI Opponents*
- *Chapter 10, Machine Learning Algorithms for Game AI*

8

Animating Your Characters

This chapter delves into key methods for enhancing the animation process, offering insights into techniques that can significantly elevate the quality and immersive experience of character animations in games. It explores three main topics, each essential to creating smooth, responsive, and realistic animations.

The first section introduces fundamental animation transition methods, focusing on interpolation and extrapolation. These techniques help smoothly transition between different animations, ensuring a seamless flow that enhances gameplay. We discuss various types of interpolation, such as linear, ease in/out, and exponential transitions. These approaches allow developers to maintain smooth animations, even when the rendering frame rate fluctuates.

The second section moves on to the skeletal hierarchy, explaining how character models are structured and animated. A solid skeletal foundation is crucial for smoothly transitioning between animations, especially when using the previously discussed interpolation methods. The section addresses common challenges, such as *jittering* or *misalignments* during transitions, and offers techniques to avoid these issues.

The final section covers a powerful real-time animation technique: **Inverse Kinematics (IK)**. This method allows characters to adapt their movements to the environment dynamically, adding another layer of realism to the game. This adaptability creates a more engaging and immersive experience for the player.

The topics covered in this chapter are:

- Understanding keyframe animation
- Learning about skeletal animation
- Using inverse kinematics

Let's get into it!

Technical requirements

Download the `Knight` Visual Studio solution from GitHub. Here is the link to the repository:

`https://github.com/PacktPublishing/Data-Structures-and-Algorithms-for-Game-Programming-in-CPP`

The demo projects for this chapter are located within the `Knight` Visual Studio solution (`https://github.com/PacktPublishing/Data-Structures-and-Algorithms-for-Game-Programming-in-CPP/tree/main/Knight`), specifically under the project names:

Project Name	Description
`Demo8a`	Playing animation with interpolations
`Demo8b`	Transitioning animations with two channels
`Demo8c`	Using IK to simulate a robotic arm

Table 8.1 – Sample projects used in this chapter

These projects demonstrate the implementation of concepts covered in this chapter and are integral to understanding the practical application of the discussed algorithms.

Understanding keyframe animation

Animations are crucial to creating lifelike and immersive experiences in games. These animations bring characters, objects, and environments to life, making interactions dynamic and visually engaging. Implementing animation in game development typically involves the manipulation of an object's position, rotation, scale, or other properties over time. By continuously updating these properties in real time, characters can walk, jump, attack, or perform any number of complex actions, and objects can respond to player interactions or environmental forces.

We'll begin by introducing keyframe animation, one of the most commonly used methods for animating characters and objects.

Keyframe animation is a technique used to animate objects by moving, rotating, or resizing them. Animations are defined by crucial frames known as *keyframes*. An object's movement typically includes a starting point (P1) and an ending point (P2).

For example, to move a box from **P1 (-1, 0.5, 0)** to **P2 (1, 0.5, 0)** over two seconds (see *Figure 8.1*) with a rendering frame rate of 100 frames per second, we have two possible approaches:

- **Frame-by-frame animation**: Create an array of positions that specifies the box's location at each frame, ensuring it is drawn in the correct position throughout the animation. The positions of the box's motion for the 100 frames are (-1, 0.5, 0), (-0.09, 0.5, 0), (-0.08, 0.5, 0), ..., (0.08, .0.5, 0), (0.09, 0.5, 0), and (1, 0.5, 0).
- **Keyframe animation**: Define just two keyframes, one for the starting point and one for the ending point. The positions between these points are then calculated based on the time the box has traveled. The positions of the box's motion are only two keyframes: (-1, 0, 0) and (1, 0, 0).

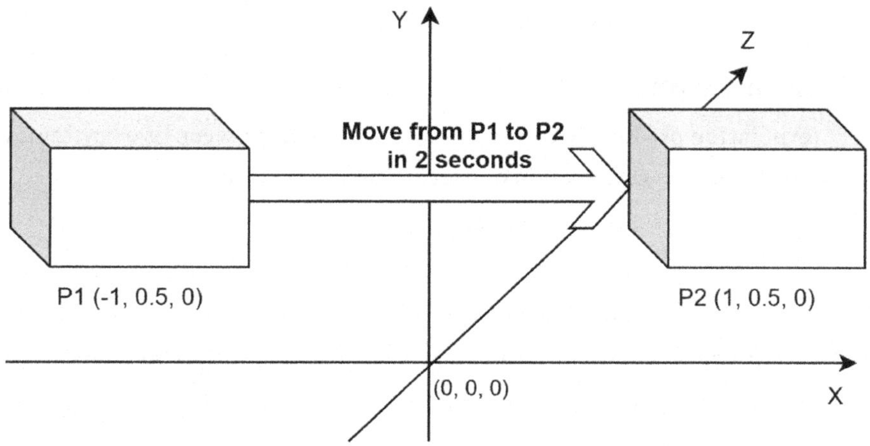

Figure 8.1 – Moving a box from P1 to P2 in a 3D space

In comparison with frame-by-frame animation, keyframe animation needs less data storage and reduces the workload involved in creating and adjusting animations. It also enables the generation of intermediate frames, resulting in smoother and more consistent animations.

Now, the question arises: how do we determine the positions between frames? The next topic will introduce the motion techniques that can be used to achieve this.

Understanding motion techniques

In animation, two primary motion techniques are frequently used: **interpolation** and **extrapolation**. Interpolation is used to create smooth transitions between keyframes over time, making it ideal for blending animations and calculating gradual changes. Integration, a fundamental concept in both mathematics and computer science, involves computing an object's position over time using its velocity. It is particularly suitable for speed-based movements and physics simulations. In this chapter, we will focus on the interpolation method, as it is primarily used in skeletal character animations.

Different interpolation methods can influence how an object moves or how values change over time. Let's explore the two most common interpolation techniques in animation: linear interpolation and ease-in/ease-out interpolation.

Linear interpolation

Linear interpolation produces a consistent rate of change between two keyframes, resulting in a transition without any acceleration or deceleration. Here is the formula:

$$P = P0 * (1 - t) + P1 * t$$

where:

- t is the interpolated value of time. The value of t falls within the range of [0, 1].
- $P0$ is the starting position when $t=0$.
- $P1$ is the end position when $t=1$.
- P represents the in-between position at time t.

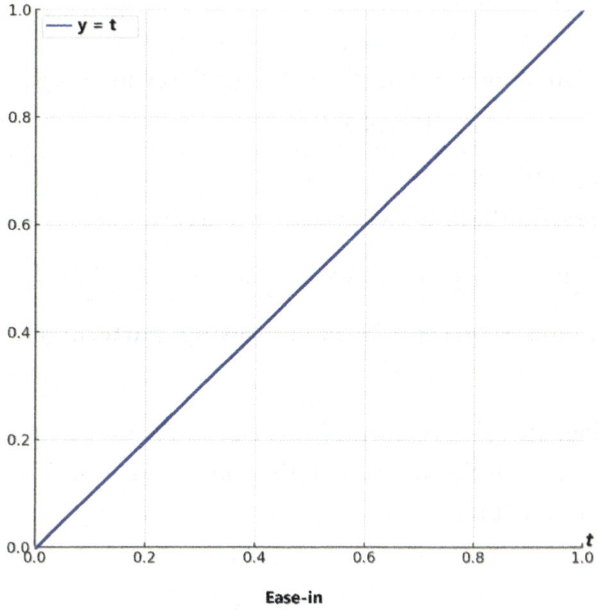

Figure 8.2 – Linear interpolation

The object travels at a constant speed from the starting point `P0` to the midpoint `Pi`, and then to the endpoint `P1`.

Ease-in/ease-out interpolation

Ease-in/ease-out (or **exponential**) interpolation adds a gradual acceleration or deceleration to the movement. The transition starts or ends more slowly compared to the middle of the animation. Here are the formulas.

Here's the ease-in formula:

$$P_{in} = P0 * t^n$$

And the ease-out formula:

$$P_{out} = P0 * (1 - t)^n$$

where:

- t is the interpolated value of time. The value of t falls within the range of [0, 1].
- *P0* is the starting position when *t=0*.
- *P1* is the end position when *t=1*.
- P_{in} and P_{out} represent the in-between ease-in and ease-out positions at time t.

When *n=2*, the formula follows a **quadratic easing pattern:** $P_{in} = P0 * t^2$ and $P_{out} = P0 * (1-t)^2$.

When *n=3*, the formula represents a **cubic easing pattern**: $P_{out} = P0 * (1-t)^3$ and $P_{out} = P0 * (1-t)^3$.

In ease-in interpolation, the cubic version starts even slower and accelerates more rapidly than the quadratic version. Conversely, in ease-out, the cubic version begins faster and decelerates more smoothly than the quadratic version.

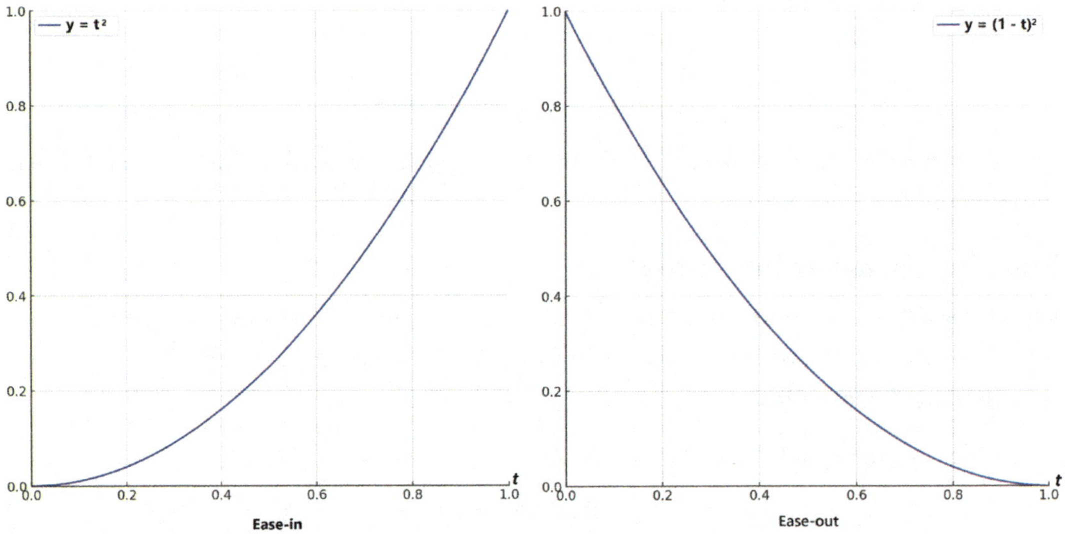

Figure 8.3 – Ease-in and ease-out interpolation curves

While ease-in and ease-out provide smooth acceleration and deceleration separately, some animations and movements require a combination of both. This leads us to ease-in-out, which blends the two to create a more natural transition.

Ease-in-out

This is a combined process that integrates both ease-in and ease-out effects. It can be used in character transitions from one animation (such as idle) to another (like running). During this transition, two animation timeline channels can be used: one for the previous animation with ease-out interpolation and another for the new animation with ease-in interpolation. Eventually, these two channels' animation data are blended to achieve a smooth transition.

In the earlier discussion of interpolation methods, we used examples of moving objects from an initial position **P1** to a destination position **P2**. However, these methods can also be applied to rotation and scaling animations. For instance, an object can be rotated along one or more axes from an initial angle **R1** to a target angle **R2** or scaled from an original size **S1** to a target size **S2**. When an operation involves the combined processes of scaling, rotating, and translating (or moving) objects, it is referred to as a transformation. *Figure 8.4* provides an example of a transformation that scales the character from size **S1** to **S2**, rotates its facing angle along the Y axis from **R1** to **R2**, and moves the character from position **P1** to **P2**.

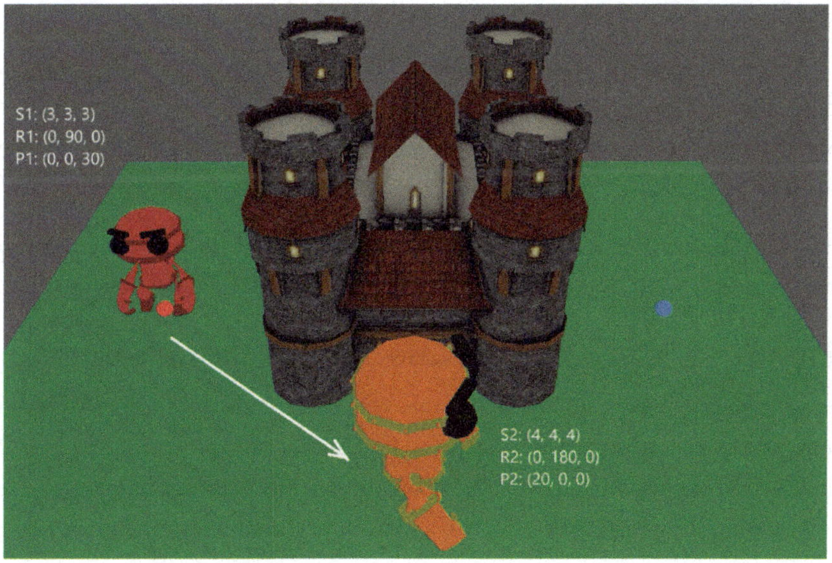

Figure 8.4 – Transforming a character

While keyframe animation is effective for simple transformations, more complex and dynamic character movements require a more advanced approach. This brings us to skeletal animation, a technique that allows for greater flexibility and realism in character animation.

Learning about skeletal animation

In **3D skeletal animation**, several key concepts form the foundation of how characters move and deform realistically. These concepts include bones, skeletons, and skin. Let's look at them in depth here before we move on to the more practical aspects of skeletal animation:

- **Bone** is a transformable object that acts as the primary control structure for character movement. Bones are not visible in the final rendered model but are essential in defining the movement of specific parts of a character, such as the head, arms, legs, etc. Each bone controls a portion of the character's mesh, and they are often arranged in a hierarchical manner. When a bone moves, it influences the mesh linked to it.
- **Skeleton** is the complete system of interconnected bones that defines the overall structure of a 3D model. Each bone in the skeleton is connected in a parent-child relationship, where movement in one bone affects the bones connected to it. For example, rotating the upper arm affects the lower arm and hand bones. The skeleton determines how the model behaves when animated.
- **Skin** refers to the outer mesh or surface of the character model that is visible to the viewer. It is the appearance of the character, including meshes, materials, and textures. The process of attaching the skin to the skeleton is known as **skinning**. Skinning ensures that when the skeleton moves, the skin follows the same motion. Proper skinning is crucial for maintaining the natural look of the character as it bends or stretches.

Now that we've covered the basic concepts of skeletal animation, let's dive into some fundamental mathematics essential for a deeper understanding of how skeletal animation works.

Understanding 3D motion related to mathematics

The mathematical foundations essential for animations include concepts like vectors, quaternions, and matrices. These tools are crucial for understanding motion, rotation, and transformations in animation. Before diving into the details of key animation techniques, we provide a clear introduction to these fundamentals to ensure a solid understanding of the underlying principles.

Vector

In 3D space, a 3D vector is a mathematical entity defined by three components (x, y, z), which can represent a point, direction, scale, or **Euler** angles in three-dimensional space. Vectors can be used to mathematically represent an object's scale, rotation, and position relative to the axes of a coordinate system, where x represents the horizontal axis, y the vertical axis, and z the depth axis.

Quaternion

A more advanced way to represent rotation is through a quaternion, which can express a combination of multiple rotations, including those around any axis, not just the x, y, or z axes. To compute a combined rotation, we simply multiply the individual rotation quaternions together.

An example of a complex rotational and orbital relationship is the sun, Earth, and moon system. The Earth rotates on its axis while orbiting the sun, and at the same time, the moon orbits the Earth.

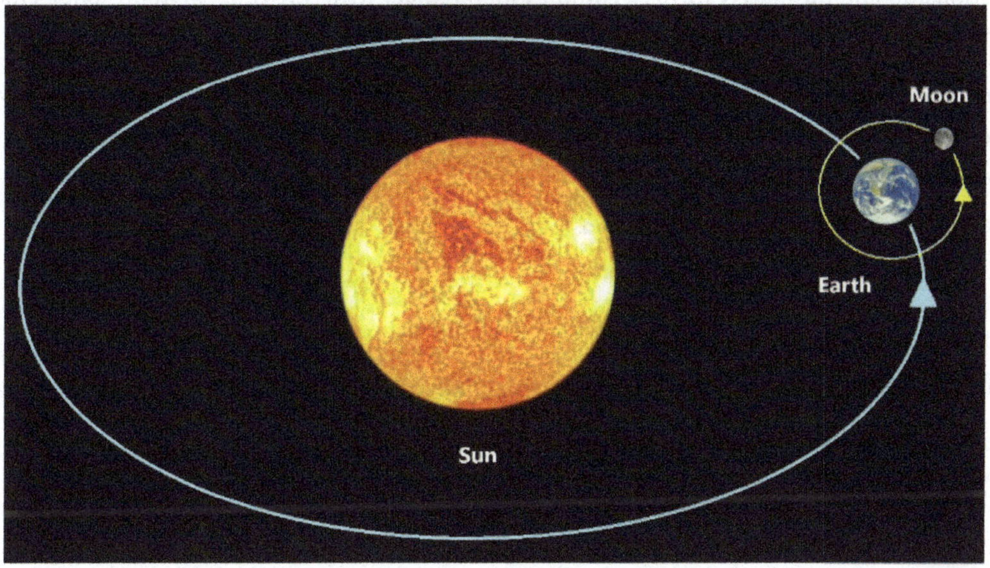

Figure 8.5 – The relationship between the sun, Earth, and moon in the solar system

The quaternion of the moon can be calculated with the following expression:

$$q_{moon} = q_{sun} * q_{earth} * q_{relative\ moon}$$

where:

- q_{sun}: Represents the sun's rotation.
- q_{earth}: Represents the Earth's rotation relative to the sun.
- $q_{relative\ moon}$: Represents the moon's rotation relative to the Earth.

Matrix

A **matrix** is commonly used to represent a transformation that combines translation, rotation, and scaling into a single mathematical entity in 3D space. Transformations can be linked up, so the next transformation based on the previous transformation can be stacked up like a joint linking up two objects. Any motion on the first transformation affects the next transformation, and the next transformation is based on the first transformation. This creates a parent-child movement relationship and ultimately forms a complex hierarchical structure that can represent a character's skeletal system.

In game development, 4x4 matrices are widely used to perform transformations. They provide a compact mathematical representation that combines multiple transformations into a single operation:

$$M = \begin{bmatrix} s_x * \cos(\theta) & -s_y * \sin(\theta) & 0 & x \\ s_x * \sin(\theta) & s_y * \cos(\theta) & 0 & y \\ 0 & 0 & s_z & z \\ 0 & 0 & 0 & 1 \end{bmatrix}$$

where:

- s_x, s_y, s_z represents scales along the X, Y, and Z axes.
- θ represents rotation around the Z axis.
- (x, y, z) represents position offsets along the X, Y, and Z axes.

Now that we've covered the fundamentals of 3D mathematics, we can apply these concepts to skeletal character animation.

Skeletal animation keyframes

In skeletal animation, a keyframe holds the transformation data for each bone in the character's skeleton. An animation clip consists of a sequence of these keyframes, capturing different poses over time. When animating a character using a specific clip, two main techniques can be employed: frame-by-frame animation, where the character moves exactly according to the keyframes, and interpolation animation, where the transitions between keyframes are smoothed by calculating intermediate positions. Since interpolation allows for fluid and natural movement, it makes it a common technique in modern game development.

Let's dive into the C++ project `Demo8a` to explore and compare the differences between the two animation techniques: frame-by-frame and interpolated animation. This hands-on example will help illustrate how each method affects character movement and animation quality in real time.

Demo8a – playing animation with interpolation

When you compile and run `Demo8`, you can see a character walking in the middle of the screen. Here is the screenshot of what that should look like:

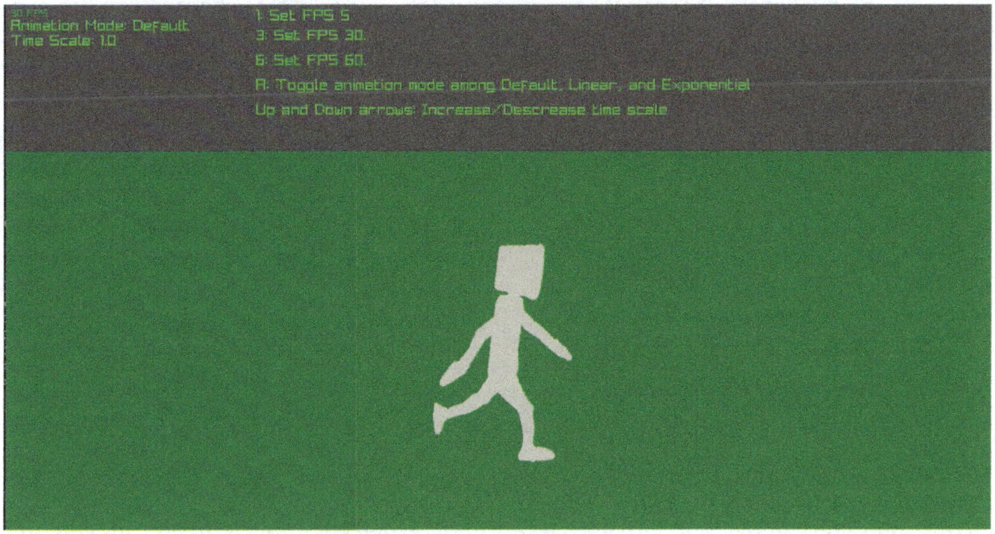

Figure 8.6 – Using frame-by-frame and interpolated methods to animate the character

`Demo8a` showcases a character walking animation using two playback techniques: **frame-by-frame** and **interpolation**. You can toggle between these two techniques by pressing the *A* key, allowing you to observe the differences in animation speed and smoothness. Press the *1*, *3*, and *6* keys to switch between different frame rates (**5**, **30**, **60**, respectively), and use the *up* and *down* arrow keys to adjust the time scale for faster or slower motion. The following matrix compares two playback techniques and shows the difference in animation speed and smoothness.

	Frame-by-Frame (Default)	**Interpolation (Linear)**	**Interpolation (Exponential)**
Framerate-Dependent Animation Speed	Yes	No	No
Animation smoothness	Slightly jerky all the time	Smooth	Smooth

Table 8.2 – Comparison of animation playback techniques

Let's take a closer look at how the frame-by-frame playback is implemented in `Demo8a`.

Frame-by-frame animation implementation

The raylib library provides a function called UpdateModelAnimation, which calculates bone transformations based on the current keyframe information and updates the skin meshes. While the inner workings of UpdateModelAnimation are beyond the scope of this chapter, you can explore the details in the models.c source code file of the raylib project.

To see how the animation is updated, open the ModelComponent.cpp file within the Knight project. In the Update function, it gets the next keyframe's index and calls UpdateModelAnimation to refresh the skin meshes:

```
void ModelComponent::Update(float ElapsedSeconds) {
  __super::Update(ElapsedSeconds);
  ......
  _CurrentFrame = GetNextFrame();
  UpdateModelAnimation(_Model,
    _Animations[_AnimationIndex], _CurrentFrame);
}
```

From this code, you can see that with each frame update, one keyframe is advanced. This applies the frame-by-frame playback strategy.

Interpolation playback implementation

To interpolate animation keyframes, we introduced a new member function, UpdateModelAnimationWithInterpolation, to the ModelComponent class. This function interpolates between the current frame and the next frame as time progresses from 0 to the designated frame duration. This new function is a modified and enhanced version of raylib's UpdateModelAnimation function.

The main difference between the UpdateModelAnimationWithInterpolation function and the original UpdateModelAnimation function is that the former does not merely advance the keyframe and apply the bone transformations to the skin meshes. Instead, it interpolates the bone transformations of the current and next keyframes using weights calculated by dividing the interpolation time of the frame by its duration, thereby generating an in-between frame, so two variables are used to indicate the frame's interpolation time and duration in seconds: _InterpolationTime and _FrameDuration.

_InterpolationTime is initialized to 0 at the start of transitioning from one keyframe to the next. Meanwhile, it accumulates the elapsed time from frame updates. When its value reaches the frame's duration, it resets to 0, and the current keyframe index is updated to the next keyframe index.

In this case, we make a slight modification to the Update function of the ModelComponent class to call UpdateModelAnimation when the current animation playback mode is set to Default (frame-by-frame) and to call UpdateModelAnimationWithInterpolation when the current animation mode is either linear or exponential:

```
void ModelComponent::Update(float ElapsedSeconds) {
  __super::Update(ElapsedSeconds);
  ......
  if (_AnimationMode == eAnimMode::Default) {
    _CurrentFrame[0] = GetNextFrame();
    UpdateModelAnimation(_Model,
      _Animations[_AnimationIndex], _CurrentFrame[0]);
  }
  else {//Linear_interpolation or_Exponential_interpolation
    UpdateModelAnimationWithInterpolation(ElapsedSeconds);
    _InterpolationTime += ElapsedTime;
    If(_InterpolationTime > _FrameDuration) {
      _CurrentFrame = GetNextFrame();
      _InterpolationTime = 0.0f;
}
  }
}
```

Important note

The code block above differs slightly from the actual source code, as the full implementation includes additional logic to support multi-channel interpolation. For clarity, this example highlights only the initial stage, where the system transitions to the next frame once the transition timeout is reached.

Now, let's explore the core of the interpolation technique in the above code snippet. First, we need to calculate the value of `t`. Then, it checks whether the animation mode is set to use exponential interpolation. If so, `t` is squared to facilitate an ease-in interpolation process. Finally, the function utilizes the `t` value along with the `Vector3Lerp` and `QuaternionLerp` functions to compute and output the translation, rotation, and scale data components for the in-between frame:

```
t = (float)_InterpolationTime / _FrameDuration;
if (_AnimationMode == eAnimMode:: Exponential_interpolation)
{
  t *= t; //Square of t for exponential interpolation
}
Transform* preFrameTransform =
  &(anim.framePoses[_PrevFrame][boneId]);
Transform* currentFrameTransform =
  &(anim.framePoses[_CurrentFrame][boneId]);
outTranslation = Vector3Lerp(
  preFrameTransform->translation,
  currentFrameTransform->translation, t);
outRotation = QuaternionLerp(
  preFrameTransform->rotation,
  currentFrameTransform->rotation, t);
outScale = Vector3Lerp(
  preFrameTransform->scale,
  currentFrameTransform->scale, t);
```

This code snippet ultimately stores the interpolated translation, rotation, and scale data in `outTranslation`, `outRotation`, and `outScale`, which will be used to transform the mesh vertices for rendering.

Having discussed the techniques for interpolating between two animation keyframes to create smoother and consistent speed animations, we will now explore how to apply interpolation techniques to transition from one animation state to another.

Transiting between animations

An animated character is typically controlled by a **Finite State Machine** (**FSM**), a computational model that controls the character's behavior by transitioning between predefined states, such as idle, walking, attacking, or jumping. FSM will be introduced in detail in the next chapter.

To transition a character's animation from one state to another, such as from `Idle` to `Walking`, you can simply pass the currently playing animation ID as a parameter when calling the `UpdateModelAnimation` function in raylib. The following code snippet demonstrates an immediate animation transition from `Idle` (`animationIndex = 4`) to `Walking` (`animationIndex = 6`):

```
Model model = Loadmodel(…);
ModelAnimation *_Animations = LoadModelAnimations(…);
animationIndex = 6;
  //current value 4 which indicates the Idle animation
  //6 is the Id that indicates the Walking animation
ModelAnimation animation = _Animations[animationIndex];
frameIndex = 0;
UpdateModelAnimation(model, animation, frameIndex);
```

The transition method in this code has two key shortcomings. First, the transition occurs abruptly, without any smooth blending between animations, leading to a choppy visual effect. Second, the transition can happen at any point during the `Idle` animation, potentially cutting it off mid-action, resulting in a disjointed and unnatural player experience.

To achieve smoother transitions between animations, a two-channel strategy is utilized. In this approach, the current animation clip continues to play on channel one. Simultaneously, when a transition is initiated, the next animation clip begins playing on channel two. This method ensures that the transition from one animation to the next is seamless.

The transition itself has a specified duration, during which both animations overlap. On channel one, the current animation gradually fades out over this transition time. At the same time, the new animation on channel two fades in. The two channels are used to generate the final blended animation. The fading process can be controlled using either linear interpolation or an ease-in/ease-out interpolation, depending on the desired effect for smoothness and pacing. This technique provides a flexible and visually appealing way to handle animation blending in various applications, particularly in game development.

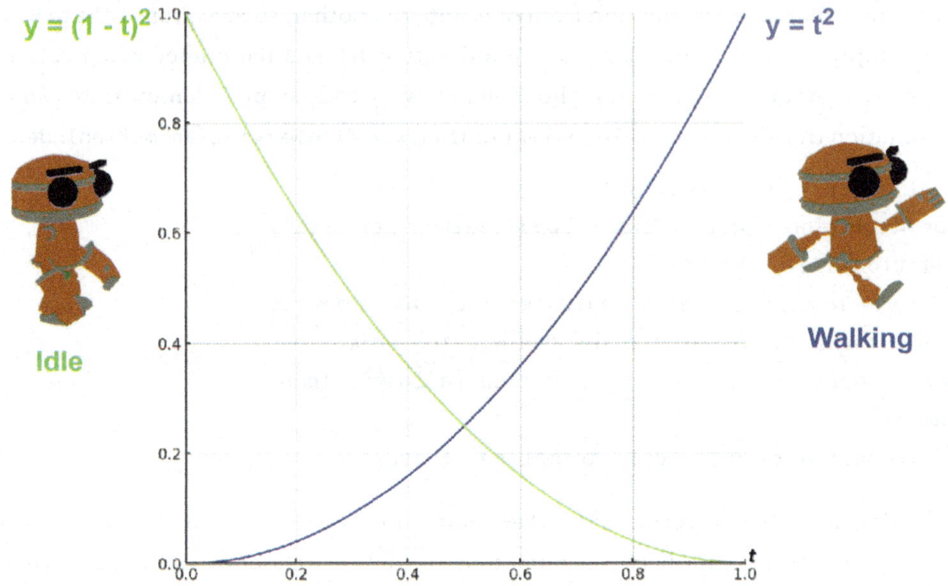

Figure 8.7 – Transitioning from Idle to Walking animations with two channels

Figure 8.7 demonstrates an example of transitioning the character from the `Idle` animation to the `Walking` animation. The transition employs the ease-out method on channel one for the `Idle` animation and the ease-in method on channel two for the `Walking` animation. As shown, the green curve representing the weight of the `Idle` animation decreases from `1` to `0`, while the blue curve representing the weight of the `Walking` animation increases from `0` to `1`. `Demo8b` provides an in-depth view of the actual implementation.

Demo8b – transitioning animations with two channels

`Demo8b` demonstrates three different modes for transitioning the character from the `Idle` animation to the `Walking` animation: immediate, linear interpolation, and ease-in/ease-out interpolation.

Figure 8.8 – Demo8b character animation

In `Demo8b`, you can press the *A* key to initiate the transition between the `Idle` and `Walking` animations. Use *left and right arrow* keys to rotate. Pressing +/- increases or decreases the time scale. Use the *T* key to toggle between the different transition modes: immediate, linear, and ease-in/ease-out. The smooth animation transition using two channels is only applied for the `Linear` and `Exponential` interpolation modes. The following steps outline the implementation of the two-channel transition mechanism:

1. In the `ModelComponent.h` header file, the states of each channel are represented using two-element arrays. The first element contains the current animation state, and the second element holds the next animation state:

```
int _CurrentFrame[2];    //Current frame indices for the current and next animations
int _PrevFrame[2];      //Previous frame indices for the current and next animations
float _InterpolationTime[2]; //Interpolation times for the current and next animations
```

In the ModelComponent.h header file, define the enum type eAnimTransitionMode and the variable _AnimTransitionMode to indicate the currently active transition mode:

```
enum eAnimTransitionMode {
  Immediate = 0,
  Linear,
  EaseInEaseOut
};
eAnimTransitionMode _AnimTransitionMode;
```

2. Declare the member functions, SetTransitionMode and TransitionAnimation, in the ModelComponent.h header file for the ModelComponent class, and implement them in the ModelComponent.cpp source file:

   - The SetTransitionMode function sets the current active animation transition mode
   - The TransitionAnimation function starts transitioning the current animation to a new animation with the current transition mode:

```
//ModelComponent.h
void SetTransitionMode(eAnimTransitionMode TransitionMode);
bool TransiteAnimation(int AnimationIndex, float
TransitionSeconds = 0.1f);
//ModelComponent.cpp
void ModelComponent::SetTransitionMode(eAnimTransitionMode
TransitionMode) {
  _AnimTransitionMode = TransitionMode;
}
bool ModelComponent::TransitionAnimation(int AnimationIndex,
float TransitionSeconds) {
  if (_AnimTransitionMode == Immediate) {
    SetAnimation(AnimationIndex); //Transition immediately
    return true;
  }
  if (AnimationIndex >= 0 && AnimationIndex < _
AnimationsCount) {
    //Initialize transition variables
    _TransiteToAnimationIndex = AnimationIndex;
```

```
        _TransitionDuration = TransitionSeconds;
    _TransitionTime = 0.0f;

    //Start playing the next animation on channel 1
        _PrevFrame[1] = 0;
        _CurrentFrame[1] = _Animations[_TransiteToAnimationIndex].
    frameCount > 1 ? 1 : 0;
        _InterpolationTime[1] = 0.0f;
        return true;
      }
      return false;
    }
```

3. Modify the `InterpolateAnimation` function to support two-channel animation transitions. The changes primarily involve the following tasks:

    1. During the animation transition, interpolate animations for both channels.
    2. Calculate the normalized transition time `t`.
    3. Blend the animations of the two channels. Use either the linear or ease-in/ease-out formula to calculate the weights for each channel, and then combine their animations.

    The process is divided into two parts: animation channel interpolation and animation blending between two channels. The code snippet below illustrates animation interpolation for the first and second channels when they are in use:

```
//Interpolate animations for the effective channels
for(int channel = 0; channel < ChannelCount; ++channel) {
  anim = channel == 0 ? _Animations[_AnimationIndex] : _Animations[_
TransiteToAnimationIndex];
  t = (float)_InterpolationTime[channel] / _FrameDuration;
  if (_AnimationMode == Exponential_interpolation) {
    t *= t; //Square of t for exponential interpolation
  }
  Transform* preFrameTransform = &(anim.framePoses[_
PrevFrame[channel]][boneId]);
  Transform* currentFrameTransform = &(anim.framePoses[_
CurrentFrame[channel]][boneId]);
```

```
  channelOutTranslation[channel] = Vector3Lerp(preFrameTransform->translation, currentFrameTransform->translation, t);
  channelOutRotation[channel] = QuaternionLerp(preFrameTransform->rotation, currentFrameTransform->rotation, t);
  channelOutScale[channel] = Vector3Lerp(preFrameTransform->scale, currentFrameTransform->scale, t);
}
```

The second part of the code utilizes the interpolated animation when only one channel is active. Otherwise, it blends the animations from both channels using a weight calculated with either the linear or ease-in-ease-out strategy:

```
if (ChannelCount == 1) {    //No animation transition
  outTranslation = channelOutTranslation[0];
  outRotation = channelOutRotation[0];
  outScale = channelOutScale[0];
}
else {//ChannelCount == 2. Process the animation transition
  //Calculate the normalized transitioning time
  t = Clamp(_TransitionTime / _TransitionDuration, 0.0f, 1.0f);
  //Blend the two channels' animations with t
  if (_AnimTransitionMode == Linear) {    //Linear transition animation blending
    outTranslation = Vector3Lerp(channelOutTranslation[0], channelOutTranslation[1], t);
    outRotation = QuaternionLerp(channelOutRotation[0], channelOutRotation[1], t);
    outScale = Vector3Lerp(channelOutScale[0], channelOutScale[1], t);
  }
  else {//Easy-in/Easy-out tranisiton animation blending
    float n = 2.0f;
    float easeInOut = t < 0.5 ?  (float)(pow(2.0 * t, n) / 2.0) : (float)(1.0 - pow(-2.0 * t + 2.0, n) / 2.0);
    outTranslation = Vector3Add(channelOutTranslation[0], Vector3Scale(Vector3Subtract(channelOutTranslation[1], channelOutTranslation[0]),easeInOut));
    outRotation = QuaternionAdd(channelOutRotation[0], QuaternionScale(QuaternionSubtract(channelOutRotation[1],
```

```
channelOutRotation[0]), easeInOut));
        outScale = Vector3Add(channelOutScale[0],
Vector3Scale(Vector3Subtract(channelOutScale[1],
channelOutScale[0]), easeInOut));
    }
}
```

To ensure `Demo8b` functions properly, we made some minor adjustments to other function implementations within the `ModelComponent` class. Please refer to the project source code (see the *Technical requirements* section) for further details on the implementation.

Congratulations! You've grasped the concept of how keyframe animations are implemented and transitioned. Now, let's shift our focus to a new topic: inverse kinematics. This technique allows us to adapt animations dynamically in response to the environment, ensuring that movements are realistic and responsive. By exploring inverse kinematics, we can enhance our animations further, enabling characters to interact more naturally with their surroundings.

Using inverse kinematics

A character skeleton can be visualized as a tree structure, where each bone represents a node connected to its parent and child bones. To calculate bone transformations, the process begins at the root and traverses through all child bones, determining their transformations based on the parent bone's transform. This hierarchical approach is known as **Forward Kinematics (FK)**, which computes the position of the end effector by considering the current joint angles and the lengths of the links. By applying FK, we can effectively build the skeleton's poses for animations.

In real life, there are instances where we have a clear endpoint that a character's limb should reach, such as when an animated character stretches out its arm to grab a box on a table. In this scenario, it's essential that the grab animation precisely aligns the character's hand with the position of the box, rather than relying on a fixed offset. This level of adaptability enhances the realism of the player's experience, making interactions feel more intuitive and believable. Similar cases can be observed in various animations, like ensuring a character's footsteps align with the contours of stairs or positioning a fighter's punches accurately against an opponent's body. These dynamic adjustments highlight the significance of using IK, a technique that is used in robotics and animation to calculate the necessary joint angles to achieve a specific position or orientation of a connected object and improve overall immersion.

A typical use case of IK is in robotic arms, where the end effector needs to reach a specific target. In this section, we will introduce a commonly employed method, **Jacobian transpose**. Before delving into the algorithm, it's essential to present a robotic arm scenario and introduce fundamental terms and mathematical concepts.

Understanding the robotic arm scenario

To facilitate a better understanding of the application of the IK algorithm, we will narrow the focus to a concrete example—a robotic arm scenario (see *Figure 8.9*):

- We have a 2-joint robotic arm.
- Each joint is capable of rotating in 3D space (around the X, Y, and Z axes), providing a total of 6 degrees of freedom (2 joints × 3 angles per joint).
- Joint 1 is located at the base of the robot and has a link length of 5 units.
- Joint 2 is situated at the end of the first link and has a link length of 4 units.
- We want the end effector to move toward the target position.

Let's look at some important terms now.

Learning the fundamental terms and mathematical concepts

The following are the fundamental terms and mathematical representations related to the Jacobian transform algorithm.

- **End effector** refers to the component at the tip of the arm that interacts with the environment.
- **Target position** is the position in 3D space the the end effector is trying to reach.
- **Error (error vector)** represents the difference on each axis (X, Y, Z) between the target position and the current end effector position:

$$\text{Error} = \begin{pmatrix} error_x \\ error_y \\ error_z \end{pmatrix}$$

- **Jacobian transpose algorithm** is a method that iteratively adjusts a robotic arm's joint angles to make the end effector reach a desired position in space, minimizing the error between the current end effector position and the target.

- **Jacobian matrix** describes the relationship between joint angles and the position of the end effector. It consists of 3 rows—corresponding to each spatial dimension (x, y, z)—and 6 columns, representing the two joints, each of which has 3 rotational degrees of freedom. The values within the matrix indicate how much the end effector's position changes in the x, y, and z directions in response to small adjustments in one of the joint angles:

$$J = \begin{pmatrix} J_{11} & J_{12} & J_{13} & J_{14} & J_{15} & J_{16} \\ J_{21} & J_{22} & J_{23} & J_{24} & J_{25} & J_{26} \\ J_{31} & J_{32} & J_{33} & J_{34} & J_{35} & J_{36} \end{pmatrix} = \begin{pmatrix} \frac{\partial x}{\partial \theta_{x1}} & \frac{\partial x}{\partial \theta_{y1}} & \frac{\partial x}{\partial \theta_{z1}} & \frac{\partial x}{\partial \theta_{x2}} & \frac{\partial x}{\partial \theta_{y2}} & \frac{\partial x}{\partial \theta_{z2}} \\ \frac{\partial y}{\partial \theta_{x1}} & \frac{\partial y}{\partial \theta_{y1}} & \frac{\partial y}{\partial \theta_{z1}} & \frac{\partial y}{\partial \theta_{x2}} & \frac{\partial y}{\partial \theta_{y2}} & \frac{\partial y}{\partial \theta_{z2}} \\ \frac{\partial z}{\partial \theta_{x1}} & \frac{\partial z}{\partial \theta_{y1}} & \frac{\partial z}{\partial \theta_{z1}} & \frac{\partial z}{\partial \theta_{x2}} & \frac{\partial z}{\partial \theta_{y2}} & \frac{\partial z}{\partial \theta_{z2}} \end{pmatrix}$$

  - Each *row* corresponds to a different spatial coordinate (x, y, z) of the end effector.
  - Each *column* corresponds to how a specific joint angle affects those coordinates. Since each joint has 3 rotational axes (around X, Y, and Z), the columns are grouped into sets of 3 for each joint.

- **Jacobian transpose** is the transpose of the original Jacobian matrix for solving the joint angles in inverse kinematics problems. It turns a mapping from joint velocities to end effector velocities into a mapping from end effector velocity to joint velocity changes:

$$J^T = \begin{pmatrix} J_{11} & J_{21} & J_{31} \\ J_{12} & J_{22} & J_{32} \\ J_{13} & J_{23} & J_{33} \\ J_{14} & J_{24} & J_{34} \\ J_{15} & J_{25} & J_{35} \\ J_{16} & J_{26} & J_{36} \end{pmatrix}$$

- **Delta angles** indicate how much each joint's angles (in X, Y, Z) should change to reduce the error:

$$DeltaAngles = J^T * Error$$

Now that we have covered the IK essential terms and mathematical foundations, we can move on to understanding how the algorithm works in practice.

Understanding the algorithm

The key process of the algorithm is to adjust joint angles based on the current error and the relationship described by the Jacobian transpose iteratively and refine the position of the end effector step by step:

1. Compute the current position of the end effector using the forward kinematics function.
2. Calculate the errors.
3. Compute the Jacobian matrix for the current joint angles.
4. Transpose the Jacobian matrix and multiply by the error to compute the delta angles.
5. Update the joint angles using delta angles to reduce the error.

Now that we've introduced the Jacobian transpose method and its underlying principles, we can see how this algorithm is applied in practice. To better illustrate how the method works, let's turn to `Demo8c`, a project that simulates a robotic arm with two joints.

Demo8c – using IK to simulate a robotic arm

The `Demo8c` project showcases a straightforward two-joint arm that attempts to reach a red target ball (see *Figure 8.9*). The robotic arm uses the Jacobian transpose algorithm to move its end effector toward a target. By adjusting the joint angles iteratively, the arm demonstrates how the method efficiently minimizes the error between its current position and the target.

While running the demo, you can use the arrow keys to move the ball left and right, as well as up and down, and the *W* and *S* keys to move the ball forward and backward. You'll notice that the arm's end point (or end effector) adjusts its joint angles to reach the ball.

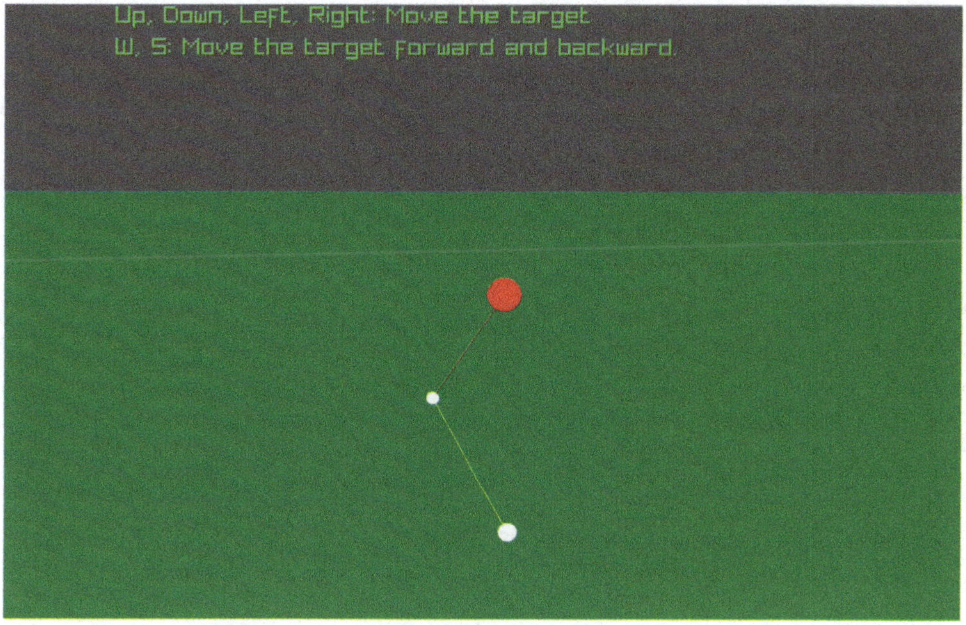

Figure 8.9 – Using IK to simulate a robotic arm

Let's begin by exploring the `Demo8c` header file to understand the key variable definitions and function declarations:

- `_JointAngles`: An array that stores the two joint angles
- `_JointLength`: An array that represents the length vectors for the two joints
- `_JacobianMatrix`: An array representing the Jacobian matrix. The array has a fixed length, determined by the matrix's 3 rows (corresponding to the X, Y, and Z axes) and 3 columns (representing rotations around these axes) for each of the 2 joints.
- `_TargetPosition`: The position of the red ball, which represents the target position.
- `_DeltaAngles`: An array that stores the delta angles for the two joints.
- `InverseKinematics`: The function that applies the Jacobian transpose method to compute and adjust the two joint angles.
- `ForwardKinematics`: The function that computes the end effector position based on current joint angles.
- `ComputeJacobinaMatrix`: The function that computes and fills up the Jacobian matrix.

Let's look at the code now!

```
#pragma once
#include "Knight.h"
#define IK_NUMBER_OF_JOINTS 2
#define IK_MAX_ITERATIONS 5000
#define IK_TOLERANCE 0.01f
#define IK_LEARNING_RATE 0.1f
#define IK_MIN_ERROR 1.0f
class Demo8c : public Knight {
private:
  Vector3 _JointAngles[IK_NUMBER_OF_JOINTS] = {
    Vector3{ 0.0f, 0.0f, 0.0f },    Vector3{ 0.0f, 0.0f, 0.0f }
  };
  Vector3 _JointLengths[IK_NUMBER_OF_JOINTS] = {
    Vector3{ 5.0f, 0.0f, 0.0f },    Vector3{ 4.0f, 0.0f, 0.0f }
  };
  float _JacobianMatrix[18]; //3 rows * (3 angles * 2 joints)
  Vector3 _TargetPosition;
private:
  float _MinErrorLength;
  Vector3 _DeltaAngles[2];
  Vector3 _BestJointAngles[2];
protected:
  void InverseKinematics();
  Vector3 ForwardKinematics(Vector3 *Angles = nullptr);
  void ComputeJacobianMatrix();
  void DrawRoboticArm();
  ......
};
```

The implementation of the `InverseKinematics` function iterates up to `MAX_ITERATIONS`. In each iteration, it calls the `ForwardKinematics` function to compute and retrieve the end effector's position, then calculates the error vector using vector subtraction. Next, it calls the `ComputeJacobianMatrix` function to generate the Jacobian matrix and uses it to compute the `DeltaAngles`. Throughout the iterations, the function keeps track of the best `DeltaAngles` found and applies these adjustments to the `JointAngles` once the loop is complete:

```
void Demo8c::InverseKinematics() {
  for (int i = 0; i < IK_MAX_ITERATIONS; ++i) {
    Vector3 endEffector = ForwardKinematics();
    Vector3 error = Vector3Subtract(_TargetPosition, endEffector);
    float errorLength = Vector3Length(error);
    if (errorLength <= IK_MIN_ERROR) {
      break;
    }
    if (i == 0 || _MinErrorLength > errorLength) {
      _MinErrorLength = errorLength;
      _BestJointAngles[0] = _JointAngles[0];
      _BestJointAngles[1] = _JointAngles[1];
    }
    ComputeJacobianMatrix();
    _DeltaAngles[0] = Vector3 {
      error.x * _JacobianMatrix[0] + error.y * _JacobianMatrix[1] +
error.z * _JacobianMatrix[2],
      error.y * _JacobianMatrix[3] + error.y * _JacobianMatrix[4] +
error.z * _JacobianMatrix[5],
      error.z * _JacobianMatrix[6] + error.y * _JacobianMatrix[7] +
error.z * _JacobianMatrix[8]
    };
    _DeltaAngles[1] = Vector3 {
      error.x * _JacobianMatrix[9] + error.y * _JacobianMatrix[10] +
error.z * _JacobianMatrix[11],
      error.y * _JacobianMatrix[12] + error.y * _JacobianMatrix[13] +
error.z * _JacobianMatrix[14],
      error.z * _JacobianMatrix[15] + error.y * _JacobianMatrix[16] +
error.z * _JacobianMatrix[17]
    };
```

```
    for (int i = 0; i < IK_NUMBER_OF_JOINTS; ++i) {
      _JointAngles[i] = Vector3Add(_JointAngles[i], Vector3Scale(_
DeltaAngles[i], IK_LEARNING_RATE));
    }
  }
  _JointAngles[0] = _BestJointAngles[0];
  _JointAngles[1] = _BestJointAngles[1];
}
```

In the sample code for the `InverseKinematics` function, we didn't explicitly transpose the matrix. Instead, we directly calculated the delta angles from the array, as we already know the formula to obtain the result without needing to perform the transpose operation.

Refer to the following formulas for a clearer understanding of the calculation details for the rotation angles of each joint:

- First joint:

$$\Delta\theta_{x1} = J_{11} * error_x + J_{21} * error_y + J_{31} * error_z$$

$$\Delta\theta_{y1} = J_{12} * error_x + J_{22} * error_y + J_{32} * error_z$$

$$\Delta\theta_{z1} = J_{13} * error_x + J_{23} * error_y + J_{33} * error_z$$

- Second joint:

$$\Delta\theta_{x2} = J_{14} * error_x + J_{24} * error_y + J_{34} * error_z$$

$$\Delta\theta_{y2} = J_{15} * error_x + J_{25} * error_y + J_{35} * error_z$$

$$\Delta\theta_{z2} = J_{16} * error_x + J_{26} * error_y + J_{36} * error_z$$

For the remaining implementation details, please refer to the source code in `Demo8c.cpp`. It primarily consists of the mathematical computations and logic needed to control the robotic arm and the visualization. This demo code can easily be adapted for more complex 3D configurations by adjusting the number of joints, joint limits, or constraints.

Summary

This chapter covered essential topics and techniques related to character animations, providing a comprehensive understanding of how to create engaging and fluid animations for games.

In the first section, we explored keyframe animation, beginning with the foundational concept of simple frame-by-frame animation. We learned about keyframes and how various interpolation methods, such as linear and ease-in/ease-out, are employed to smooth out animations and maintain consistent animation speeds. These techniques are crucial for achieving a polished look in your character movements, ensuring they flow seamlessly and enhance the overall visual experience.

The second part delved into the structural aspects of character animation, focusing on how a character's skeleton is constructed and animated using bone transformations and keyframes. Two demos, `Demo8a` and `Demo8b`, showcased the implementation of the interpolation techniques to smooth animations and facilitate transitions between them. Additionally, a two-channel mechanism was introduced for blending animations, enabling more complex and realistic animation transitions.

In the final section, we examined the application of inverse kinematics for adapting animations to the environment. The Jacobian transpose method was introduced and applied in `Demo8c`, which demonstrated the functionality of a two-joint robotic arm. This technique allows for dynamic adjustments in character movements, enhancing realism and interaction with the game world.

By mastering these animation techniques, you can significantly elevate the quality and immersion of your game's character animations, creating smoother transitions, realistic movements, and dynamic interactions with the environment.

In the next chapter, we will explore useful and widely utilized AI algorithms that can further enhance gameplay and character behaviors.

9

Building AI Opponents

Artificial Intelligence (AI) plays a pivotal role in shaping the player's experience in modern games. From enemies that react to player actions to NPCs with lifelike behaviors, AI is the cornerstone of making game worlds feel alive and dynamic. At its core, AI in games involves creating systems that simulate decision-making, movement, and problem-solving, enabling virtual agents to perform tasks intelligently and efficiently.

Unlike AI in other domains, such as autonomous vehicles or robotics, game AI emphasizes creating engaging and entertaining behavior rather than achieving perfect solutions. For example, an enemy in a stealth game might deliberately miss spotting the player to build suspense, whereas in real-world AI, avoiding mistakes would be the priority. This unique requirement calls for algorithms tailored to gaming scenarios.

This chapter will delve into some of the most widely used AI techniques in games, including:

- Understanding Finite State Machines
- Demo9a: Controlling character animation with an FSM
- Using a behavior tree to make decisions
- Steering for movement
- Demo9b: Using an FSM and BT to control the NPC
- Understanding pathfinding
- Exploring A* pathfinding
- Demo9c: Pathfinding in action with character movement

Each technique has its strengths, and understanding their implementation and use cases will empower you to design intelligent, adaptable AI systems for your games. Through detailed explanations and C++ code examples, this chapter aims to provide a solid foundation in game AI programming.

Technical requirements

The book's GitHub repo at `https://github.com/PacktPublishing/Data-Structures-and-Algorithms-for-Game-Programming-in-CPP` contains demo projects in the `Knight` solution (`https://github.com/PacktPublishing/Data-Structures-and-Algorithms-for-Game-Programming-in-CPP/tree/main/Knight`):

Project Name	Description
`Demo9a`	Controls character animation using a Finite State Machine
`Demo9b`	Implements a Behavior Tree to manage decision-making for the NPC
`Demo9c`	Utilizes the A* pathfinding algorithm to enable the NPC to navigate through the maze

Table 9.1 – Sample projects used in this chapter

Understanding Finite State Machines

A **Finite State Machine** (**FSM**) is one of the most fundamental tools for implementing decision-making logic in game AI. FSMs are widely used in game development. They provide a clear, organized structure for managing an agent's behavior, making them ideal for straightforward AI systems.

An FSM provides a computational model that represents and controls the behavior of a system. It consists of a finite number of states, transitions, and actions, where:

- **State** represents the current condition or behavior of an AI agent.
- **Transition** defines the conditions for switching from one state to another.
- **Action** is the task performed while in a particular state or during a transition.

Example of an FSM

Let's explore an FSM example that manages animation transitions for a player character (see *Figure 9.1*). In this example, the FSM controls the character's transitions among three animations: **Idle** (`state = 0`), **Walk** (`state = 1`), and **Attack** (`state = 2`). A `state` variable serves as the condition that triggers transitions between these states.

For instance, when the value of `state` is changed from `0` to `1`, the FSM transitions from the **Idle** state to the **Walk** state. Similarly, if the `state` variable changes, the FSM switches from the present state to a new state. This simple structure demonstrates how an FSM can effectively manage animation states in a clear and logical manner.

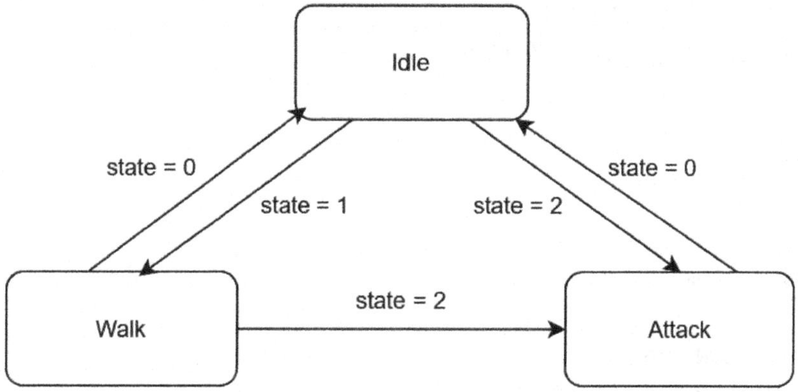

Figure 9.1 – A simple character animation control FSM

Each state in an FSM can have specific actions associated with it, either when entering the state or while remaining in it. For example, consider the **Idle** state: if the player presses and holds the *W* key, the FSM changes the state value from `0` (**Idle**) to `1` (**Walk**) and transitions to the **Walk** state. During this transition, an action is performed to switch the character's animation from **Idle** to **Walk**.

Implementing an FSM

Based on the concept of an FSM, we can design an FSM class that manages multiple predefined states and handles transitions between them. In this case, we need three states that represent the Idle, Walk, and Attack states. The FSM transitions from one state to another when certain conditions are met.

Let's write code to implement an FSM along with its three states. To begin with, we can define an `FSMState` class to serve as the base class for individual states and an `FSM` class to represent the finite-state machine:

```
//FSM.h
class FSMState
{
public:
virtual void Enter(FSM* FiniteStateMachine) = 0;
        //is called when entering this state
virtual void Update(FSM* FiniteStateMachine, float DeltaTime) = 0;
        //is called every frame
    virtual ~FSMState() = default;
};

class FSM
{
public:
    typedef enum
{
        UNKNOWN = 0,
        IDLE= 2,
        ATTACK = 5,
        WALK = 10,
    } ECharacterState;        //The enum of animation states
public:
    FSM(SceneActor* Character, ModelComponent* AnimController);
    virtual ~FSM();
    void SetState(ECharacterState NewState);
    void Update(float DeltaTime);
    ECharacterState GetPrevState() { return _PrevState; }
    ECharacterState GetCurrentState() { return _CurrentState; }
    SceneActor* GetCharacter() { return _Character; }
    ModelComponent* GetAnimController() { return _AnimController; }
protected:
    FSMState* _States[15];     //Stores the 15 animation states
    ECharacterState _PrevState = UNKNOWN;
    ECharacterState _CurrentState = UNKNOWN;
```

```
    SceneActor* _Character;//The controlled character
    ModelComponent* _AnimController;
};
```

Since the FSM in this demo only handles transitions between three states—*Idle*, *Walk*, and *Attack*—only these three values from the ECharacterState enum are used, even though the character model includes more animations.

The two key functions are SetState and Update. The SetState function handles transitioning to a new state, replacing the current one, while the Update function simply calls the Update function of the current state:

```
void FSM::SetState(ECharacterState NewState)
{
    _PrevState = _CurrentState;
    _CurrentState = NewState;
    _States[_CurrentState]->Enter(this);
}

void FSM::Update(float DeltaTime)
{
    _States[_CurrentState]->Update(this, DeltaTime);
}
```

Next, we can define three states—PlayerIdleState, PlayerWalkState, and PlayerAttackState—that inherit from the FSMState class to represent the **Idle**, **Walk**, and **Attack** states. Additionally, we'll create a dedicated state machine for the player character, named PlayerFSM, which will be a subclass of the FSM class:

```
class PlayerFSM : public FSM
{
public:
    PlayerFSM(SceneActor* Character, ModelComponent* AnimController);
};

class PlayerIdleState : public FSMState
{
public:
    void Enter(FSM* FiniteStateMachine) override;
```

```
    void Update(FSM* FiniteStateMachine, float DeltaTime) override;
};

class PlayerWalkState : public FSMState
{
public:
    void Enter(FSM* FiniteStateMachine) override;
    void Update(FSM* FiniteStateMachine, float DeltaTime) override;
};

class PlayerAttackState : public FSMState
{
private:
    float _Timer = 0.0f;
public:
    void Enter(FSM* FiniteStateMachine) override;
    void Update(FSM* FiniteStateMachine, float DeltaTime) override;
};
```

The constructor of the `PlayerFSM` class performs three initial tasks:

- It sets the character and its animation controller to the `_Character` and `_AnimController` variables.
- It instantiates the animation states for the `IDLE`, `WALK`, and `ATTACK` states.
- It sets the current state to `IDLE`.

Let's look at the implementation, as follows:

```
PlayerFSM::PlayerFSM(SceneActor* Character, ModelComponent*
AnimController)
    : FSM(Character, AnimController)
{
    _Character = Character;
    _AnimController = AnimController;
    _States[IDLE] = new PlayerIdleState();
    _States[WALK] = new PlayerWalkState();
    _States[ATTACK] = new PlayerAttackState();
    SetState(IDLE);
}
```

Based on the code above, each state's `Enter` function is responsible for transitioning the character to the corresponding animation. In the `Update` functions, we can define conditions that trigger transitions from the current state to the next based on specific actions.

To see how actions and conditions are implemented within these state functions, let's delve into the example project, `Demo9a`, in the next section.

Demo9a: Controlling character animation with an FSM

`Demo9a` showcases a player-controlled character. The player can navigate the character around the terrain using the *WASD* keys. Pressing the *spacebar* triggers an attack.

The screenshot below shows an animated character that the player can control to move and perform attacks. The control keys are indicated in *green* text in the top-left corner of the screen.

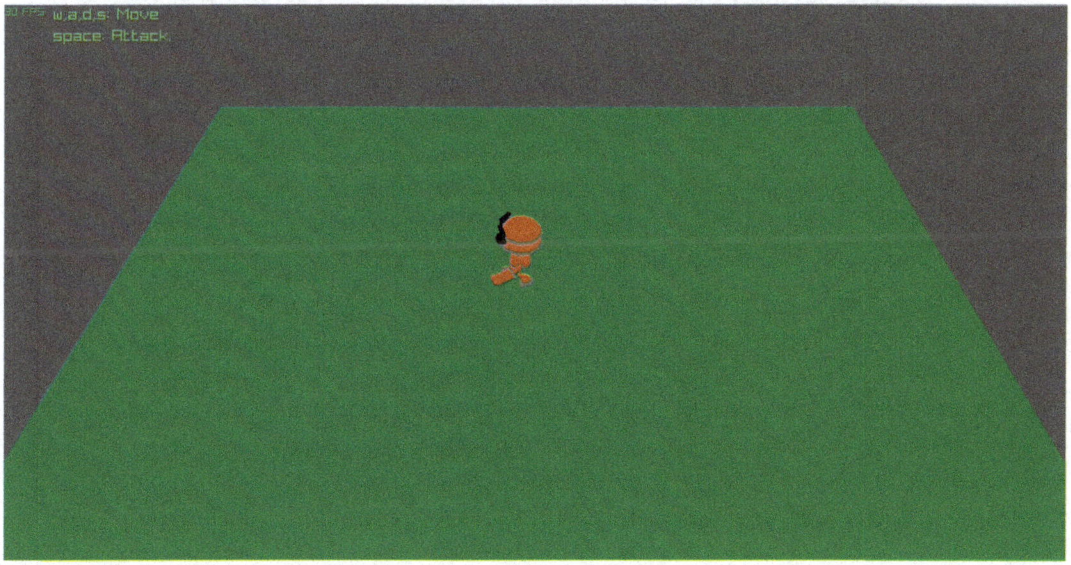

Figure 9.2 – The player-controlled character based on an FSM

Building on `PlayerFSM` and the `PlayerIdle`, `PlayerWalk`, and `PlayerAttack` states defined in the earlier section, we can now implement the state functions. For the `Enter` functions, as mentioned previously, we simply invoke the character's animation controller's `TransitionAnimation` function. This ensures that the appropriate animation is played when entering each state:

```
void PlayerIdleState::Enter(FSM* FiniteStateMachine)
{
    if (FiniteStateMachine->GetPrevState() == PlayerFSM::UNKNOWN)
    {
        FiniteStateMachine->GetAnimController()-
>SetAnimation(PlayerFSM::IDLE);
    }
    else
    {
        FiniteStateMachine->GetAnimController()->TransitionAnimation(Playe
rFSM::IDLE);
    }
}
......
void PlayerWalkState::Enter(FSM* FiniteStateMachine)
{
    FiniteStateMachine->GetAnimController()->TransitionAnimation(PlayerFSM
::WALK);
}
......
void PlayerAttackState::Enter(FSM* FiniteStateMachine)
{
    _Timer = 0.5f;
    FiniteStateMachine->GetAnimController()->TransitionAnimation(FSM::ATTA
CK);
}
```

Here, notice that the implementation of the `Enter` function in the `PlayerIdleState` class differs slightly from the others. This is because the `IDLE` state is initially set from the `UNKNOWN` state at the beginning, requiring a special process to handle this initial transition.

The final and crucial step is implementing the `Update` functions for each state. These functions handle the conditions for state transitions, which are structured based on the following matrix:

Current State	Condition	Enter State
IDLE	Pressed the *spacebar*	ATTACK
IDLE	Pressed *A*, *W*, *D*, or *S*	WALK
WALK	Pressed the *spacebar*	ATTACK
WALK	Released *A*, *W*, *D*, or *S*	IDLE
ATTACK	Timeout (`_Timer <= 0.0f`)	IDLE

Table 9.2 – Demo9a: State transition matrix

To change from the current state to another, we can call the `SetState` function of the FSM instance. To transition the character to a specific animation, we retrieve the character's animation controller from the FSM instance and invoke its `TransitionAnimation` function.

Here's an example of the `Update` function for the `PlayerIdleState` class:

```
void PlayerIdleState::Update(FSM* FiniteStateMachine, float DeltaTime)
{
    if (IsKeyPressed(KEY_SPACE))
    {
        FiniteStateMachine->SetState(PlayerFSM::ATTACK);
        return;
    }

    SceneActor* character = FiniteStateMachine->GetCharacter();
    if (IsKeyDown(KEY_A))
    {
        character->Rotation.y = 90.0f;
        FiniteStateMachine->SetState(PlayerFSM::WALK);
    }
    else if (IsKeyDown(KEY_W))
    {
        character->Rotation.y = 0.0f;
        FiniteStateMachine->SetState(PlayerFSM::WALK);
    }
    else if (IsKeyDown(KEY_D))
    {
        character->Rotation.y = -90.0f;
        FiniteStateMachine->SetState(PlayerFSM::WALK);
```

```
        }
        else if (IsKeyDown(KEY_S))
        {
            character->Rotation.y = 180.0f;
            FiniteStateMachine->SetState(PlayerFSM::WALK);
        }
    }
```

The Demo9a project includes the complete source code for reference. You can compile and run the demo to explore the full implementation.

Now, you have a solid understanding of the core concepts of an FSM, demonstrated through the player character animation control example. It's important to note that the FSM method is not limited to player animation systems; it can also be applied to a variety of AI behavior simulations. These include enemy AI, game mechanics, dialog systems, game state management, and flow control, among others. FSMs are a versatile option to consider whenever you need to design a new AI control system, offering a clear and structured approach to managing state transitions.

After learning how FSMs are used to control character animations, we can now move on to exploring Behavior Trees, which offer a more flexible and scalable solution for handling complex decision-making processes in game AI.

Using a behavior tree to make decisions

In the previous section, we introduced an FSM to control the player's character animation, where decisions on movement and attack were made by the player. But how does an NPC make decisions? In this section, we will explore Behavior Trees, a powerful tool for handling NPC AI decision-making.

A **Behavior Tree (BT)** is a hierarchical structure decision-making model used primarily in AI systems. The basic structure consists of *nodes* that can be of different types: **composite** (e.g., selectors and sequences), **decorators**, and **leaf** nodes (e.g., tasks and conditions). These nodes are organized in a tree-like structure, where each node represents a specific action or condition in the decision-making process.

Here is a breakdown of the key components that make up a BT:

- **Action nodes** perform tasks such as moving, attacking, or interacting with objects.
- **Condition nodes** check whether certain conditions are met, such as whether an NPC can see the player or an object is within range.

- **Composite nodes** control the flow of the tree by managing the execution of child nodes. The most common types of composite nodes are *Sequence* and *Selector*.
    - A **Sequence node** runs its child nodes in order, one after another, and only succeeds if all child nodes succeed. If any child node fails, the entire sequence fails.
    - A **Selector node** runs its child nodes in order but succeeds as soon as one of the child nodes succeeds.
- **Decorator nodes** modify the behavior of other nodes, often by adding conditions or altering the flow of execution.
- **Blackboard** is an important concept in BTs. It acts as a shared memory storage system that holds information relevant to the BT's decision-making process. The blackboard stores variables, such as the NPC's position, target, health, or the state of the environment, which can be accessed and modified by nodes throughout the tree. This allows the tree to make decisions based on dynamic conditions, enabling more flexible and adaptive behaviors.

BTs combine different types of nodes along with a shared blackboard and enable NPCs to make complex decisions according to changing conditions in the game world.

Example of a BT

Let's use a simple BT example (see *Figure 9.3*) to illustrate how an NPC leverages the BT to make decisions:

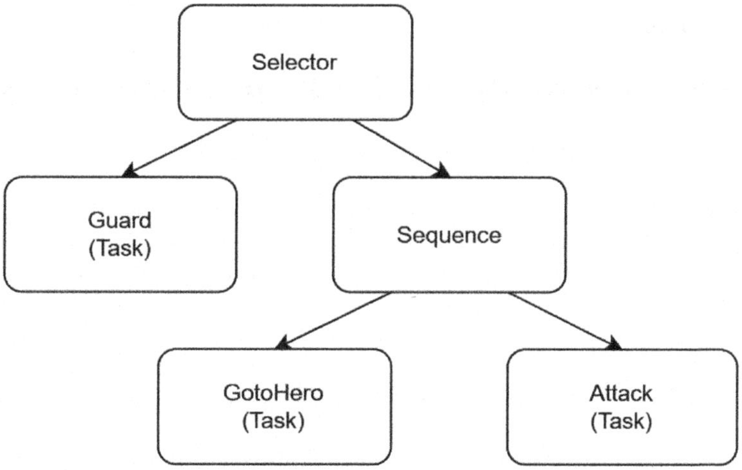

Figure 9.3 – A BT used for the NPC decision-making

Now, let's understand the working of the BT in *Figure 9.3*.

The root node of the BT is a **Selector** node. During game updates, the evaluation begins at the root node and proceeds from the leftmost child node (**Guard**) to the rightmost child node (**Sequence**). If the **Guard** node succeeds, the **Selector** node also succeeds; otherwise, the **Sequence** node is evaluated.

The **Guard** node calculates the distance between itself and the player. It succeeds if the player is within a specified range; otherwise, it fails.

If the **Guard** node fails, the next child (which, in this case, is the **Sequence** node) begins its evaluation. The **Sequence** node also processes its children sequentially, starting with the leftmost node (**GotoHero**) and proceeding to the rightmost node (**Attack**). The sequence evaluation terminates and returns a failure as soon as any child node fails.

The **GotoHero** node controls the character's movement toward the player and checks whether the player is within attack range. If the player is outside the attack range, the node fails. However, when the player enters the attack range, the node succeeds.

When the **GotoHero** node succeeds, the sequence proceeds to the next node, the **Attack** node, which directs the NPC to execute an attack.

This process repeats with each frame update, continuously refreshing the NPC's state.

Implementation of a BT

Now that you should have some idea about how the BT works, let's explore the code implementations for more details.

First, we need to create a `TreeNode` class to serve as the base for other node types:

```
typedef enum
{
    BT_SUCCESS,
    BT_FAILURE,
    BT_RUNNING
} ETreeStatus;

class TreeNode
{
public:
    TreeNode() : _BT(nullptr) {}
    TreeNode(BehaviourTree* BT);
```

```
    virtual ~TreeNode();
    virtual ETreeStatus Update(float DeltaTime);
    BehaviourTree* GetBehaviourTree() { return _BT; }

protected:
    BehaviourTree* _BT;
};
```

Next, we can define the subclasses, starting with the composite class and its child classes, `Sequence` and `Selector`, as shown in *Figure 9.4*. Following that, we can implement the task classes, as shown in the following class diagram:

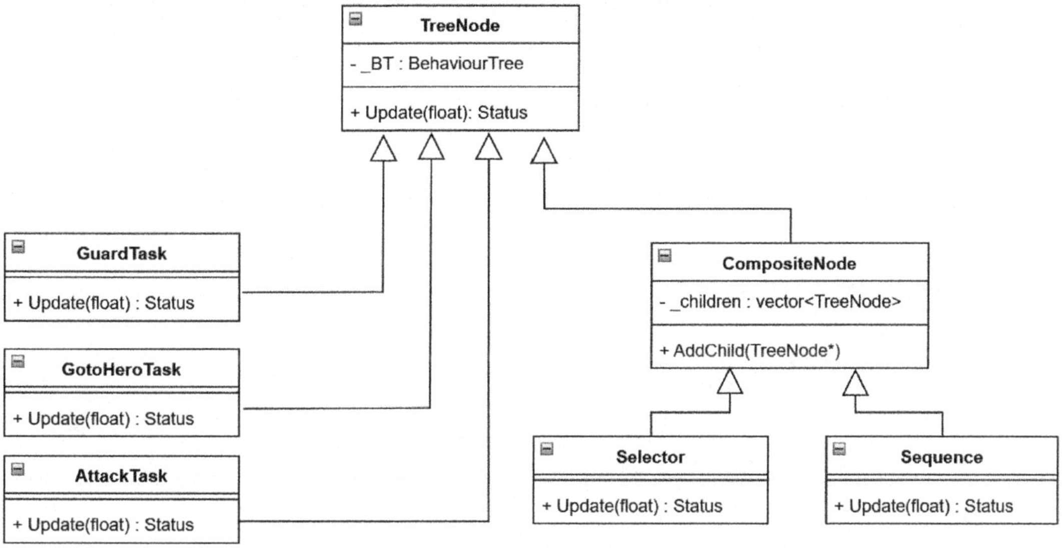

Figure 9.4 – BT nodes class diagram

For the declarations of the `TreeNode` subclasses, refer to the following C++ code:

```
class CompositeNode : public TreeNode
{
protected:
  vector<std::shared_ptr<TreeNode>> _children;
public:
  void AddChild(shared_ptr<TreeNode> childNode);
};
class Sequence : public CompositeNode
{
```

```
public:
  ETreeStatus Update(float DeltaTime) override;
};
class Selector : public CompositeNode
{
public:
    ETreeStatus Update(float DeltaTime) override;
};
```

In the above class declaration code, the `CompositeNode` class contains a vector variable, `_children`, which holds its child nodes. It also includes an `AddChild` function for adding child nodes. The implementations of the `AddChild` function and the `Update` functions for the two subclasses, `Sequence` and `Selector`, are provided as follows:

```
void CompositeNode::AddChild(std::shared_ptr<TreeNode> childNode)
{
  _children.push_back(childNode);
}

ETreeStatus Sequence::Update(float DeltaTime)
{
  for (const auto& child : _children)
  {
    ETreeStatus status = child->Update(DeltaTime);
    if (status == BT_FAILURE || status == BT_RUNNING)
    {
      return status;
    }
  }
  return BT_SUCCESS;
}

ETreeStatus Selector::Update(float DeltaTime)
{
  for (const auto& child : _children)
  {
    ETreeStatus status = child->Update(DeltaTime);
```

```
        if (status == BT_SUCCESS || status == BT_RUNNING)
        {
            return status;
        }
    }
    return BT_FAILURE;
}
```

The implementations of the task functions will be covered in the *Demo9b: Using FSM and BT to control the NPC* section.

Now, let's move on to the final step—defining the `BehaviourTree` class and the `Blackboard` class:

```
class Blackboard
{
public:
  float DistanceFromPlayer;
  SceneActor* NPC;
  EnemyFSM* FSM;
  SceneActor* Player;
  Vector3 Velocity;
  float WalkSpeed;
  float MaxSpeed;
};
......
class BehaviourTree
{
private:
  Blackboard _blackboard;
  shared_ptr<Selector> _root;
private:
  void Steering(float DeltaTime);
public:
  BehaviourTree(SceneActor* NPC, EnemyFSM* NPC_FSM, SceneActor* Player);
  void Update(float DeltaTime);
  Blackboard& GetBlackboard() { return _blackboard; }
};
```

The BehaviourTree class holds the instance of Blackboard, which serves as a container for shared data and the root node of the tree. The GetBlackboard function provides an interface for nodes to access the blackboard.

Now, let's take a closer look at the function implementations of the BehaviourTree class:

```
BehaviourTree::BehaviourTree(SceneActor* NPC, EnemyFSM* NPC_FSM,
SceneActor* Player)
{
  //Initialize the blackboard
  _blackboard.NPC = NPC;
  _blackboard.FSM = NPC_FSM;
  _blackboard.Player = Player;
  _blackboard.Velocity = Vector3Zero();
  _blackboard.WalkSpeed = 1.5f;
  _blackboard.MaxSpeed = 3.0f;
  //Build up the behaviour tree
  _root = make_shared<Selector>();
  _root->AddChild(make_shared<GuardTask>(this));
  auto sequence = make_shared<Sequence>();
  sequence->AddChild(make_shared<GotoHeroTask>(this));
  sequence->AddChild(make_shared<AttackTask>(this));
  _root->AddChild(sequence);
}
void BehaviourTree::Update(float DeltaTime)
{
  //Calculate the distance from the player and the enemy
  _blackboard.DistanceFromPlayer = Vector3Distance(_blackboard.NPC-
>Position, _blackboard.Player->Position);
  //Update the tree
  _root->Update(DeltaTime);
  //Update the finite state machine for animation control
  _blackboard.FSM->Update(DeltaTime);
  //Steering process
  Steering(DeltaTime);
}
```

The `BehaviourTree` constructor is responsible for initializing the blackboard and constructing the tree by adding child nodes. This setup ensures that the tree structure is ready for evaluation during game updates.

The `Update` function performs the following tasks:

1. It calculates the current distance between the player and the NPC and stores this value in the blackboard. This distance information helps the enemy NPC determine whether to chase the player or execute an attack.
2. It updates both the BT and the FSM, ensuring smooth transitions between animations for the NPC.
3. The final step is performing the steering process.

The steering process is used to control and adjust the NPC's movement. One apparent outcome is that it prevents characters from overlapping with one another. Let's explore how this process works in the next section.

Steering for movement

Steering behaviors are widely used in games to manage the dynamic and smooth movement of characters, such as NPCs or vehicles. Typical steering behaviors include tasks such as seeking, fleeing, arriving, and wandering, where an AI character adapts its movement based on environmental factors or specific objectives.

To better understand how steering controls an NPC's movement and maneuvering, we use *Figure 9.5* to illustrate an example of an NPC avoiding overlapping with the player character:

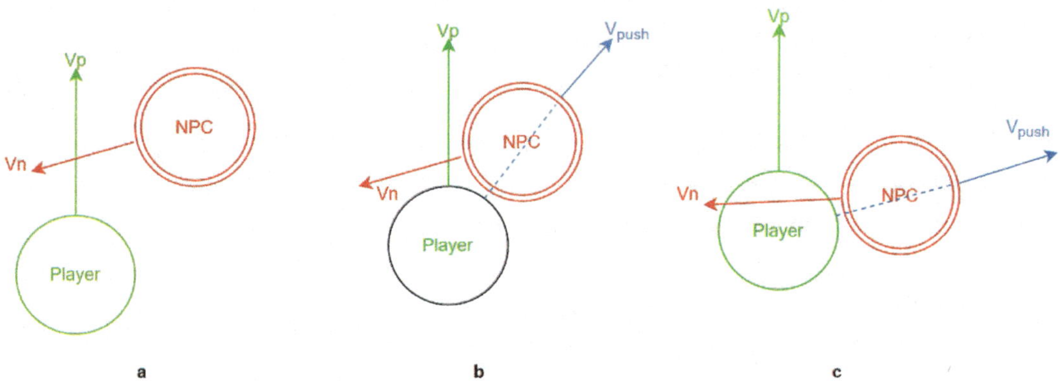

Figure 9.5 – An NPC steering move example

Let's understand what's going on in *Figure 9.5*, as follows:

1. **a**: Both the player and the NPC are moving at speeds $\mathbf{V_p}$ and $\mathbf{V_n}$, respectively, and their paths intersect, leading to a potential collision.
2. **b**: When the player and NPC come close enough to block each other's movement, a push-away velocity ($\mathbf{V_{push}}$) is applied to the NPC to resolve the obstruction.
3. **c**: The player continues moving along its path, while the NPC is pushed to the right to clear the way for the player. The push-away velocity ($\mathbf{V_{push}}$) remains applied to the NPC until it has completely moved away from the player.

Refer to the following code snippet for a detailed implementation of the `Steering` function, which demonstrates how to calculate and apply steering behaviors to control NPC movement effectively:

```
void BehaviourTree::Steering(float DeltaTime)
{
  auto modelComponent = _blackboard.NPC->GetComponent<ModelComponent>();
  FSM::ECharacterState animState = (FSM::ECharacterState)modelComponent-
>GetAnimation();
  //Get the vector from Player to NPC
  Vector3 dir = Vector3Subtract(
    _blackboard.Player->Position,
    _blackboard.NPC->Position);
  _blackboard.Velocity = Vector3Zero();
  if (Vector3Equals(dir, Vector3Zero())) {
    dir = Vector3{ 0.0f, 0.0f, 1.0f };
  }
  //Calculate the movement velocity
  if (animState == FSM::WALK)
  {
    dir = Vector3Normalize(dir);
    _blackboard.Velocity = Vector3Scale(
      dir, _blackboard.WalkSpeed * DeltaTime);
  }
  //Add Vpush when NPC and Player are close
  if (_blackboard.DistanceFromPlayer < 2.6f)
  {
    Auto Vpush = Vector3Scale(Vector3Negate(dir),
        _blackboard.MaxSpeed * DeltaTime);
```

```
        _blackboard.Velocity = Vector3Add(_blackboard.Velocity,
            Vpush);
    }
    //Move NPC to the new Location
    _blackboard.NPC->Position = Vector3Add(_blackboard.NPC->Position, _
blackboard.Velocity);
    //Rotate NPC to face Player
    _blackboard.NPC->Rotation.y = RAD2DEG * atan2f(dir.x, dir.z);
}
```

The code snippet above illustrates the five steps involved in applying the steering process to character movement. It begins by calculating the movement velocity using the vector from the player to the enemy. If the enemy is close enough, a push-back velocity (`Vpush`) is applied to create distance. The enemy is then moved and rotated to achieve the correct position and orientation.

With a clear understanding of BTs and steering and how they guide NPC movement, we can now move on to the practical application of these concepts. In the next section, `Demo9b` presents a demo project that brings these ideas to life.

Demo9b: Using an FSM and BT to control the NPC

`Demo9b` builds upon the foundation of `Demo9a` adding new elements to enhance the gameplay. In this demo, the player can control the protagonist to move around and attack. Additionally, an NPC is introduced on the battlefield. The NPC leverages a BT to determine its actions, such as remaining in the *guard* state, going to the player, or attacking the player. Its animation transitions are seamlessly managed using an FSM.

Let's explore a typical gameplay scenario to understand the NPC's behavior. Initially, the NPC remains *stationary*, observing its surroundings. When the player character enters the NPC's vision range, the NPC transitions into *pursuit mode*, running toward the player to close the distance and move within *attack range* to launch an attack. However, if the player character successfully leaves the NPC's vision range, the NPC halts its pursuit and returns to its *guard* state. This scenario highlights the seamless interaction between the NPC's BT and FSM, creating dynamic and engaging gameplay.

Figure 9.6 illustrates this gameplay scenario, as follows:

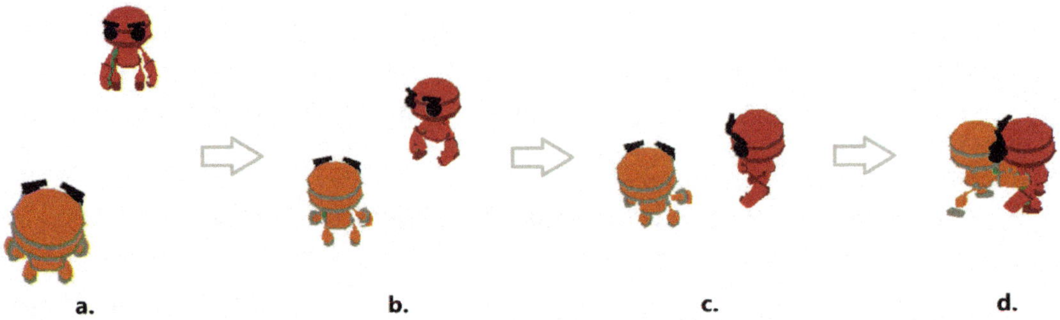

Figure 9.6 – NPC decision-making with a BT

Here:

1. **a**: The player moves closer to the NPC.
2. **b**: The NPC sees the player.
3. **c**: The NPC goes toward the player.
4. **d**: The NPC and the player attack.

In the previous sections, we covered most of the essential code implementations for the BT. To get `Demo9b` to work, the final step is to define the three task nodes: `GuardTask`, `GotoHeroTask`, and `AttackTask`. The class declarations for these task nodes are provided in the code snippet as follows:

```
class GuardTask : public TreeNode
{
public:
  GuardTask(BehaviourTree* BT) : TreeNode(BT) {};
  ETreeStatus Update(float DeltaTime) override;
};
class GotoHeroTask : public TreeNode
{
public:
  GotoHeroTask(BehaviourTree* BT) : TreeNode(BT) {};
  ETreeStatus Update(float DeltaTime) override;
};
class AttackTask : public TreeNode
{
private:
```

```
  float _Interval = 0.0f;
public:
  AttackTask(BehaviourTree* BT) : TreeNode(BT) {};
  ETreeStatus Update(float DeltaTime) override;
};
```

Next, the `Update` function of the `GuardTask` class performs a simple distance check between the player and the NPC. If the distance is less than or equal to `15` (the vision range), the node returns `BT_FAILURE`, prompting the BT to evaluate the next sibling node (the `Sequence` node). Otherwise, it returns `BT_RUNNING` to stop the tree evaluation. The implementation of the `Update` function is shown here:

```
ETreeStatus GuardTask::Update(float DeltaTime)
{
  auto modelComponent = _BT->GetBlackboard().NPC->GetComponent<ModelCompon
ent>();
  FSM::ECharacterState animState = (FSM::ECharacterState)modelComponent-
>GetAnimation();
  if (_BT->GetBlackboard().DistanceFromPlayer <= 15.0f)
  {
    return BT_FAILURE;
  }
  else if (animState != EnemyFSM::ECharacterState::IDLE)
  {
    auto bt = _BT->GetBlackboard().FSM;
    bt->SetState(EnemyFSM::ECharacterState::IDLE);
  }
  return BT_RUNNING;
}
```

Then, the `Update` function of the `GotoHeroTask` class evaluates the distance between the player and the NPC. If the distance is less than or equal to `3` (the attack range), it returns `BT_SUCCESS`, allowing the BT to proceed to the next sibling node (the `AttackTask` node). Otherwise, it returns `BT_RUNNING`, halting further tree evaluation:

```
ETreeStatus GotoHeroTask::Update(float DeltaTime)
{
  auto blackboard = _BT->GetBlackboard();
  auto player = blackboard.Player;
```

```
  auto npc = blackboard.NPC;
  auto modelComponent = npc->GetComponent<ModelComponent>();
  FSM::ECharacterState animState = (FSM::ECharacterState)modelComponent-
>GetAnimation();
  auto fsm = blackboard.FSM;
  if (blackboard.DistanceFromPlayer <= 3.0f)
  {
    return BT_SUCCESS;
  }
  else
  {
    if (animState != EnemyFSM::ECharacterState::WALK)
    {
      fsm->SetState(EnemyFSM::ECharacterState::WALK);
    }
    return BT_RUNNING;
  }
}
```

Finally, the `Update` function of the `AttackTask` class utilizes the `_Interval` variable as a timer to track the duration of the attack animation. While the timer is counting down, the function returns `BT_RUNNING`. Once `_Interval` reaches `0`, indicating the attack animation has finished, the function returns `BT_SUCCESS`:

```
ETreeStatus AttackTask::Update(float DeltaTime)
{
  auto blackboard = _BT->GetBlackboard();
  auto modelComponent = blackboard.NPC->GetComponent<ModelComponent>();
  FSM::ECharacterState animState = (FSM::ECharacterState)modelComponent-
>GetAnimation();
  auto fsm = blackboard.FSM;
  if (animState != FSM::ECharacterState::ATTACK)
  {
    if (_Interval <= 0.0f)
    {
      fsm->SetState(FSM::ECharacterState::ATTACK);
      _Interval = 1.5f;
    }
```

```
        else
        {
            _Interval -= DeltaTime;
            if (_Interval <= 0.0f)
            {
                return BT_SUCCESS;
            }
        }
    }
    return BT_RUNNING;
}
```

Now that you understand how to control character animations and how an NPC makes decisions, a new challenge arises: *navigation*. When the NPC moves toward the player, it naturally takes the shortest straight path. However, in most games, obstacles often block the direct route. How can the NPC navigate around these obstacles, follow accessible paths, and determine the best route to the target position?

This challenge introduces the concept of **pathfinding**, a fundamental aspect of game AI. Among the various pathfinding algorithms, the widely used A* (A-star) algorithm will be our next focus.

Understanding pathfinding

In game development and AI, finding the shortest path between two points is a fundamental problem. A **pathfinding algorithm** is a computational method that enables game objects—including player-controlled characters and NPCs—to determine an optimal or feasible route between a start and an end point within a game environment, which is often represented as a graph. In essence, it calculates how a game object moves from its current location to a target location in the shortest way.

Game worlds are typically represented as graphs, where nodes correspond to locations in the game space and edges define possible paths between them. These edges can be *bidirectional* or *unidirectional* and may carry equal or weighted distances (or costs) that influence pathfinding.

Figure 9.7 shows a city transportation map, where the map nodes are connected by streets with different distances. In this example, a car travels from the house to the bank, finding a path from point **1** to point **6**.

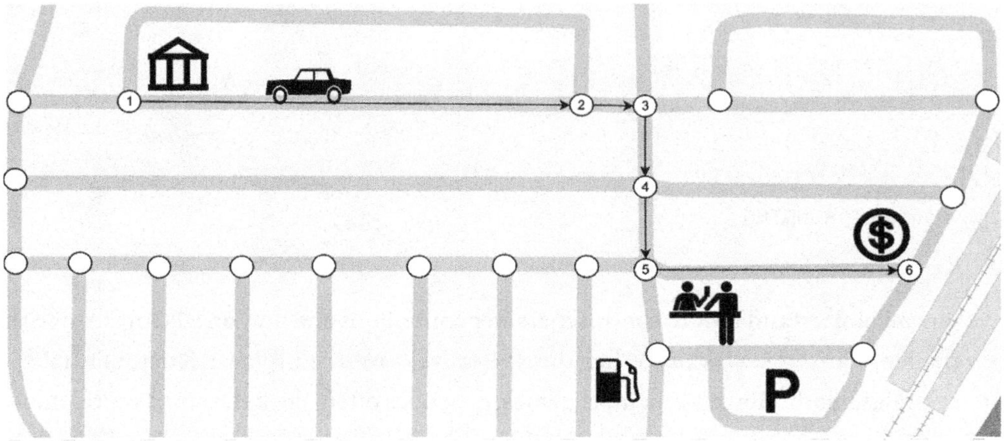

Figure 9.7 – A city transportation graph map

There are three common types of navigation maps that serve as the foundation for pathfinding:

- **Grid-based map**: Each square is a node; edges connect adjacent squares. This kind of map is ideal for tile-based games where characters navigate a 2D plane.
- **Graph map**: These kinds of maps are suitable for scenarios involving connections and edges, such as transportation networks.
- **Navigation Mesh (NavMesh) map**: Polygons are used to represent walkable areas. Nodes are points on the meshes. NavMeshes are perfect for 3D worlds, allowing characters to navigate on surfaces, avoid obstacles, and adhere to terrain constraints.

Some commonly used pathfinding algorithms in games include Breadth-First Search (BFS), Dijkstra's algorithm, and A*. Let's understand these in greater detail in the subsequent sections.

Breadth-First Search (BFS)

BFS is a simple graph traversal algorithm that explores nodes level by level. It guarantees the shortest path in unweighted graphs, where every edge is considered to have the same cost. The steps of the algorithm are described below:

1. Start from the starting point node.
2. Visit all immediate neighbors, then neighbors' neighbors, and so on.
3. Track distance by counting the number of edges traversed.

Dijkstra's algorithm

Dijkstra's algorithm is one that travels graph nodes based on weighted edges. While BFS is sufficient for unweighted graphs, most real-world problems require weighted graphs, where edges have different distance costs. The steps of the algorithm are described below:

1. Initialize distances:
    - *dist[start] = 0*
    - *dist[all other nodes] = ∞*
2. Maintain a set of unvisited nodes.
3. Select the unvisited node with the smallest distance.
4. Update distances of all neighbors of the selected node.
5. Mark the current node as visited.
6. Repeat until all nodes are visited or the remaining unvisited nodes are inaccessible.

A*

A* introduces a *heuristic* (e.g., straight-line distance) to guide the search. Unlike BFS and Dijkstra, which systematically explore all reachable nodes in a graph, A* uses a heuristic to intelligently prioritize nodes that are more likely to lead to the goal. By estimating the remaining cost to the target, A* can often bypass unnecessary nodes, making it a more efficient choice for pathfinding in large or complex game maps.

Table 9.3 compares the key differences among the BFS, Dijkstra, and A* algorithms:

Algorithm	Graph type	Time complexity	Use cases
BFS	Unweighted	$O(V + E)$	Grids, maze
Dijkstra	Weighted	$O((V + E)\ Log(E))$	Terrain, roads
A*	Weighted + heuristic Unweighted + heuristic	$O((V + E)\ Log(E))$	Grids, maze, terrain, roads

Table 9.3 – Comparison of the BFS, Dijkstra, and A pathfinding algorithms*

In the next section, we will take a closer look at the A* algorithm and explore how it efficiently finds optimal paths.

Exploring A* pathfinding

A* (A-star) is a widely used algorithm in game development for pathfinding and decision-making. It helps characters, such as NPCs, navigate around obstacles to reach a target efficiently. The algorithm combines two essential strategies: *graph traversal* and *heuristic search*, enabling it to find the shortest and most cost-effective path to a destination.

How A* works

At its core, A* explores a search space, such as a grid, graph, or navigation mesh, to find the best path from a starting point to a target. It evaluates paths by considering both the cost to reach a given node and an estimate of the cost to get from that node to the target.

In the next section, we'll start by introducing the concept of a **priority queue** (also known as the open list) and its function, which is a basic data structure used by the A* algorithm.

Processing data with a priority queue

Before diving into the details of the A* algorithm, it's essential to understand the concept of a priority queue.

A **priority queue** is a specialized data structure where elements are arranged based on their priority values. Unlike a standard queue, where elements are processed with the **First-In, First-Out (FIFO)** strategy, a priority queue retrieves or removes elements with the highest priority first. Each element in a priority queue is associated with a priority value that determines its order in the queue. When a new item is added to the queue, it is positioned according to its priority value.

To better understand how data items are added to and retrieved from a priority queue, let's consider an example. Imagine we have three paths from point **A** to point **B**, each with a distance that serves as its priority value, as shown in *Figure 9.8*:

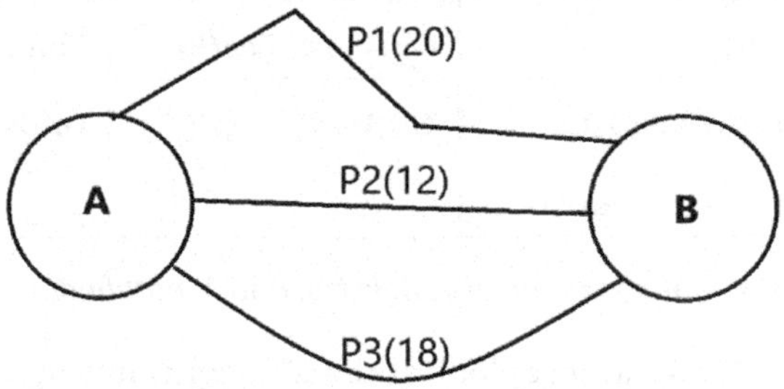

Figure 9.8 – Three paths from point A to point B

Here, **P1**, **P2**, and **P3** are the three paths, with distances of **20**, **12**, and **18**, respectively. *Figure 9.9* illustrates how each path is discovered and enqueued, followed by the dequeuing of the paths in ascending order of **P2**, **P3**, **P1** based on their distances:

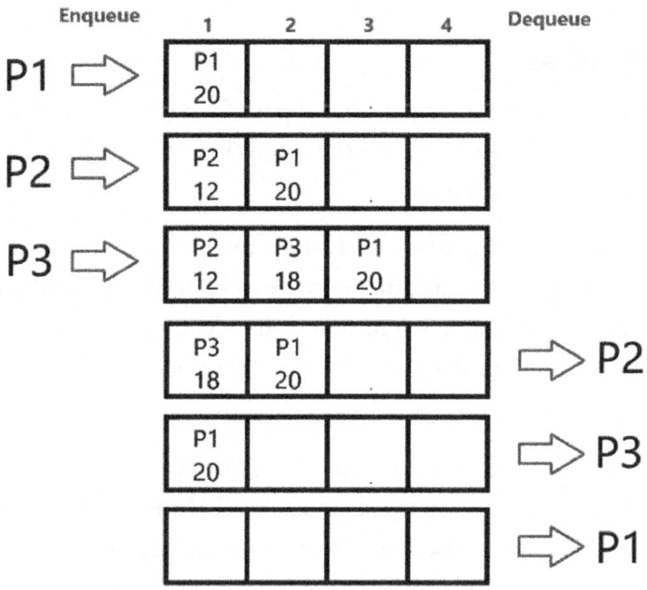

Figure 9.9 – Processing P1, P2, and P3 paths with a priority queue

A priority queue is used to sort the found paths in ascending order based on their distances. This means that when dequeuing the first path from the queue, it will always be the shortest among the found paths.

Calculating path node priority values

The A* algorithm maintains a priority queue of path nodes, with each assigned a score calculated as:

$$f(n) = g(n) + h(n)$$

where,

- $g(n)$ is the cost of reaching the node, n, from the starting point.
- $h(n)$ is the heuristic estimate of the cost to reach the target from n.
- $f(n)$ is the total estimated cost of the path through n.

A* prioritizes nodes with the lowest *f(n)*, ensuring it explores the most promising paths first.

The question now is, how do we sample and calculate node values in different environments? This leads us to discuss the versatility of the A* algorithm.

The versatility of A*

The A* algorithm is highly adaptable to various types of environments and applications, showcasing its versatility. This adaptability stems from its ability to customize the heuristic function and cost metrics to fit specific scenarios.

A* can also be combined with graph traversal algorithms, such as DFS or Dijkstra's algorithm, and applied to different types of maps, including unweighted (e.g., grids) and weighted (e.g., NavMesh) graph maps. A **NavMesh (navigation mesh)** is a polygonal representation of walkable areas in a game world. Each polygon is treated as a node in a weighted graph, and the edges carry traversal costs such as distance.

A* is not limited to physical navigation. It can also be applied to decision-making scenarios based on graph models. For instance, in a strategy game, A* can help an AI determine the best sequence of actions to achieve a goal (e.g., gathering resources or building units).

Building on the above explanation, we will now explore an example to better understand how A* identifies the best path on a navigation map, delving deeper into the process details.

Delving into an A* on a grid example

Imagine an NPC navigating a grid-based game world filled with obstacles such as walls that block direct paths. The NPC must travel from point **A** to point **B** (see *Figure 9.10*). Each grid cell has an associated movement cost; for instance, moving from one cell to an adjacent cell incurs a cost of 1:

1. The algorithm begins at point **A**, calculates *f(n)* for all reachable cells (e.g., cells *(2, 1)* and *(2, 2)*), and adds these cells to the priority queue.
2. It then selects the node with the lowest *f(n)*, calculates *g(n)* and *h(n)* for its neighbors, and updates the path.
3. The process repeats until the target (point **B**) is reached, and the path is reconstructed by tracing back through the nodes.

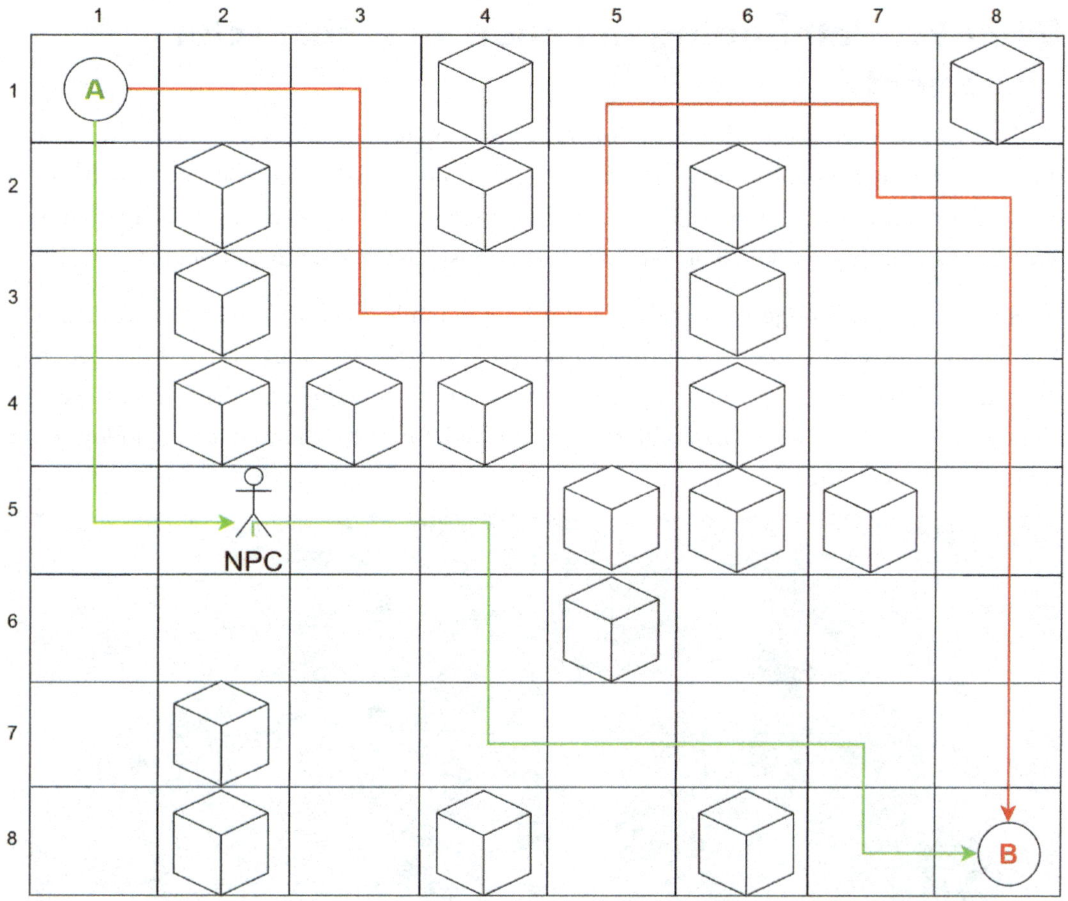

Figure 9.10 – An NPC walks from point A to point B on a grid map

There are often multiple possible paths to reach the target position, but A* ensures that the optimal path is selected. In *Figure 9.10*, the *green* path is shorter than the red path, making it the optimal choice.

We have covered the essential concepts and core mechanics of the A* algorithm. To gain a comprehensive understanding and effectively apply this pathfinding method, it is best to explore its actual implementation and source code in the `Demo9c` project, which is the focus of the next section.

Demo9c: Pathfinding in action with character movement

The best way to learn about A* pathfinding is by applying it to a real project. `Demo9c` illustrates this with a scenario where a character must navigate from a starting point in the top-left corner to a target point in the bottom-right corner. The environment is a grid-based navigation map featuring randomly placed wall blockers that act as obstacles, preventing direct paths.

Pressing the *spacebar* triggers the maze generation, randomly placing blockers on the map. The pathfinding function then calculates the shortest path from the starting point to the target point. Once the path is determined, the character follows the path, moving from the start to the target point. *Figure 9.11* shows a screenshot illustrating the path found for the character to follow while navigating through the maze.

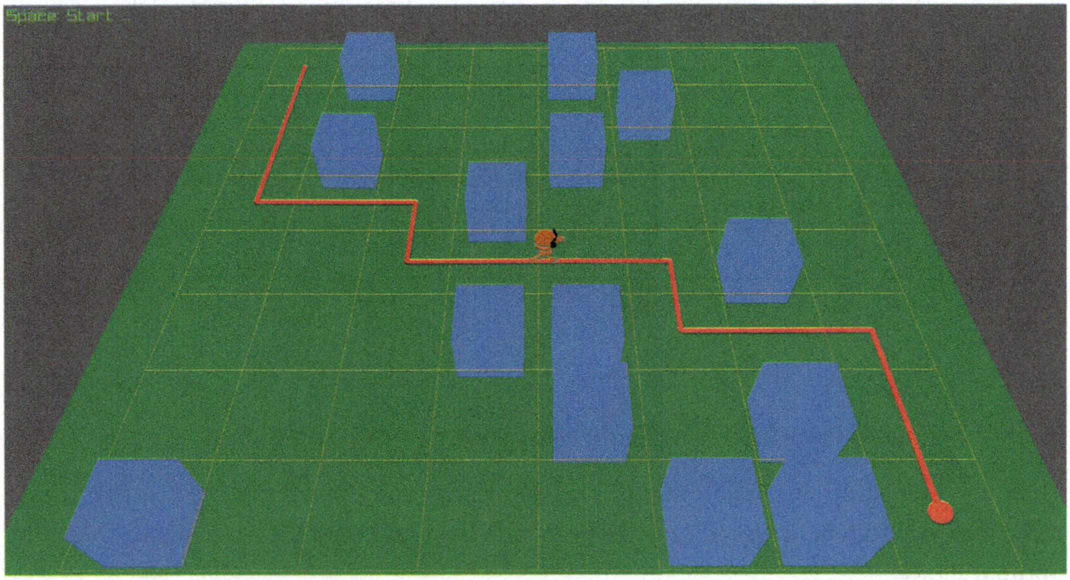

Figure 9.11 – Moving the character on the maze with A-star pathfinding

The foundational class we need to define first is the `Node` struct in the `A-Star.h` header file. A **node** represents a waypoint in the navigation grid and stores the information needed for pathfinding. Each node serves as a potential candidate for constructing the optimal path:

```
struct Node
{
  Vector3 Position;       //Position of a grid cell
  int GridPos[2];         //Grid position on the grids
```

```
    float GCost, HCost;  //stores G and H values
    Node* Parent;        //The previous waypoint node
    Node(Vector3 pos, Node* parent = nullptr)
      : Position(pos)
      , GridPos{0, 0}
      , GCost(0)
      , HCost(0)
      , Parent(parent) {}
    //The function which calculates the F value
    float FCost() const
    {
      return GCost + HCost;
    }
};
```

Second, we need two helper functions. The `ManhattanDistance` function calculates the heuristic metric, representing the shortest path between two points in a grid-based system by summing only vertical and horizontal movements. The `ReconstructPath` function constructs the final path by backtracking from the target node to the start node using parent pointers once the target is reached. Let's implement these as follows:

```
float ManhattanDistance(Node* p1, Node* p2)
{
  return (float)(abs(p1->GridPos[0] - p2->GridPos[0]) +
  abs(p1->GridPos[1] - p2->GridPos[1]));
}

vector<Vector3> ReconstructPath(Node* node)
{
  vector<Vector3> path;
  while (node != nullptr)
  {
    path.push_back(node->Position);
    node = node->Parent;
  }
  reverse(path.begin(), path.end());
  return path;
}
```

The third step is to define the `NodeComparer` structure for the priority queue, which will compare the `FCost()` values of two nodes to establish their order, determining which has the lower or higher priority:

```
struct NodeComparer
{
  bool operator()(Node* a, Node* b)
  {
    return a->FCost() > b->FCost();
  }
};
```

The final step is to implement the `FindPath` function, which is the core of the A* algorithm. This function iteratively explores nodes, calculates their costs, and maintains priority-based traversal using a priority queue. The `FindPath` function starts at the start node, evaluates potential paths by computing *g-cost* (actual cost), *h-cost* (heuristic estimate), and *f-cost* ($f=g+h$), and dynamically updates the open and closed lists. Once the target node is reached, the function reconstructs and returns the optimal path.

We'll implement this as follows:

```
vector<Vector3> AStarPathFinder::FindPath(Vector3& Start, Vector3& Target)
{
  //A priority queue containing all travelled nodes
  priority_queue<Node*, vector<Node*>, NodeComparer> OpenList;
  //A matrix indicating if a grid node has been visited
  vector<vector<bool>> ClosedList(GridsSize,
    vector<bool>(GridsSize, false));
  Node* startNode = new Node(Start);
  Node* targetNode = new Node(Target);
  Maze::GetMazeCellRowCol(Start, startNode->GridPos[0], startNode-
>GridPos[1]);
  Maze::GetMazeCellRowCol(Target, targetNode->GridPos[0], targetNode-
>GridPos[1]);
```

The code above initializes the necessary data structures, including `OpenList` (a priority queue), `ClosedList` (a two-dimensional Boolean matrix to track whether each grid cell has been accessed), and `StartNode` and `TargetNode` used for path generation.

Before pathfinding begins, the following code initializes the start node's `GCost` and `HCost`, then adds the `StartNode` to the `OpenList`, which is implemented as a priority queue:

```
//Set the start node's G value to be 0
startNode->GCost = 0;
//Calculate the H value
startNode->HCost = ManhattanDistance(startNode, targetNode);
OpenList.push(startNode);       //Enqueue the start node

int directions[4][2] = {
  {-1, 0}, {1, 0}, {0, -1}, {0, 1} };
      //These four vectors help lead to the left,
      //right, down, and up adjacent neighbours
```

Here, the `directions` array defines vectors used to locate the eight neighboring cells around the current node.

With these initial steps complete, the pathfinding process can begin in the following code:

```
while (!OpenList.empty())
{
  //Get the shortest found neighbour node
  Node* currentNode = OpenList.top();
  OpenList.pop();

  int row = currentNode->GridPos[0];
  int col = currentNode->GridPos[1];
  ClosedList[row][col] = true;     //Mark as a visited node

  //If it reaches the target node, return the found path
if (currentNode->GridPos[0] == targetNode->GridPos[0]
  && currentNode->GridPos[1] == targetNode->GridPos[1])
  {
    return ReconstructPath(currentNode);
  }
  //Visit the four neighbour nodes
  for (const auto& dir : directions)
  {
    int row = currentNode->GridPos[0] + dir[0];
```

```
            int col = currentNode->GridPos[1] + dir[1];
            //If the neighbour node is valid and has not been visited
            if (Maze::IsValidNode(row, col)
              && !ClosedList[row][col])
            {
              float newGCost = currentNode->GCost + 1;
              Vector3 pos = Maze::GetCellPosition(row, col);
              Node* neighborNode = new Node(pos, currentNode);
              neighborNode->GridPos[0] = row;
              neighborNode->GridPos[1] = col;
              neighborNode->GCost = newGCost;
              neighborNode->HCost =
                   ManhattanDistance(neighborNode, targetNode);
              //Add the new visited node to the priority queue
              OpenList.push(neighborNode);
            }
        }
    }
    return {};
}
```

The code block above performs the pathfinding process. The `FindPath` function marks the current node as accessed, and then iterates through its neighboring nodes. For each neighbor, it calculates the `GCost` and `HCost` and adds the node to the `OpenList`. The node with the lowest total cost is then popped from the `OpenList` and set as the new current node. This process continues until the target node becomes the current node. Finally, the `ReconstructPath` function is called to return the found path.

You have now explored the core principles of the A* pathfinding algorithm, including how it operates and how it applies to navigation in grid-based environments. These concepts lay a strong foundation for understanding pathfinding in games. As a next step, you are encouraged to download and explore the `Demo9c` project to examine and trace through the source code, which will further solidify your understanding and provide practical insights into how the algorithm is implemented in a real scenario.

Summary

This chapter provided an exploration of traditional AI algorithms and their applications in game development. It began by introducing FSMs to control player character animations, enabling seamless transitions for walking and attacking actions, as demonstrated in the `Demo9a` project.

The second section focused on BTs, which were used to guide NPC decision-making. NPCs could guard areas, chase the player, or attack when the player entered specific ranges. `Demo9b` showcased the integration of a BT with an FSM and steering movement techniques, combining these tools to manage decision-making, animation transitions, and movement.

Finally, the chapter introduced the DFS, Dijkstra, and A* pathfinding algorithms. Using `Demo9c`, you learned how to generate a grid-based maze, apply the A* algorithm to find the optimal path, and utilize a priority queue as the open list to explore neighboring nodes. The demo also illustrated how to move the character along the determined path from the start to the target point.

In the next chapter, we will delve into modern AI technologies, exploring how machine learning and deep learning are transforming game development.

10

Machine Learning Algorithms for Game AI

The rapid evolution of AI has unlocked immense potential and opened new possibilities across various industries, and the game industry is no exception. AI technology has advanced from basic rule-based systems to more sophisticated methods such as machine learning and deep learning, allowing developers to create more dynamic, responsive, and intelligent game environments. The application of AI in games has shifted from traditional NPC behaviors to more complex systems that can adapt to player actions, predict strategies, and even generate content. This evolution has not only enhanced the realism and immersion of games but also introduced new gameplay mechanics that were previously unthinkable.

Neural networks can be trained to simulate intricate decision-making processes, while **deep learning algorithms** can process vast amounts of data to improve gameplay and character interaction. The trend in the game industry is increasingly shifting toward using these AI models to power NPCs, procedural content generation, and even game design elements. As a result, players can now experience games that feel alive and reactive, constantly adapting to their strategies and actions.

This chapter delves into modern AI technologies, focusing on introducing neural networks, shadow learning, and deep learning. Through an actual C++ implementation code of a neural network, the chapter provides a real-world application of these technologies covering the topics of:

- Reviewing the evolution of AI
- Learning the basic concepts of a neural network

- Understanding how neural networks predict
- Understanding how neural networks learn
- `Demo10`: An AI-controlled turret defense game

By the end of this chapter, you will have a solid understanding of how to apply neural networks in your games. This includes constructing network models, generating training data, training AI models, and utilizing the trained models in games to control NPCs.

Technical requirements

Download the `Knight` Visual Studio solution from GitHub. Here is the link to the repository:

`https://github.com/PacktPublishing/Data-Structures-and-Algorithms-for-Game-Programming-in-CPP`

The demo projects for this chapter are located within the `Knight` Visual Studio solution (`https://github.com/PacktPublishing/Data-Structures-and-Algorithms-for-Game-Programming-in-CPP/tree/main/Knight`), specifically under this project name:

Project Name	Description
`Demo10`	AI-controlled turret

Table 10.1 – Sample project used in this chapter

This project demonstrates the implementation of concepts covered in this chapter and is integral to understanding the practical application of the discussed algorithms.

Reviewing the evolution of AI

Artificial intelligence (**AI**) has evolved from early rule-based systems into powerful technologies that shape today's world. In the mid-20th century, AI began with symbolic reasoning and expert systems—machines that followed human-defined rules to simulate decision-making in limited contexts.

However, these early systems were constrained by limited computing power and data, making them suitable only for narrow, specialized tasks. A major shift occurred in the 1980s and 1990s, as faster processors, increased storage, and the rise of GPUs enabled AI to handle complex computations and large datasets.

This progress laid the groundwork for the machine learning techniques you're about to explore in this chapter—systems that learn from data rather than relying solely on pre-programmed rules.

Advancements in computing power and access to data opened the door to a new era of AI: **Machine learning** (**ML**). A major breakthrough came when Geoffrey Hinton introduced the idea of designing AI systems inspired by the mechanism of the human brain. This idea led to the development of neural networks, which simulate how neurons in the brain process information. Unlike traditional rule-based AI, ML systems learn from data to recognize patterns and make predictions. This ability to learn and improve over time means ML systems don't need to be manually programmed for every situation, making them much more flexible and powerful.

Deep learning (**DL**), a subset of ML, uses multi-layered neural networks to handle large amounts of unstructured data, including images, audio, and text. These advanced networks can identify complex patterns and make highly accurate predictions. This capability has enabled innovative applications, such as generative models like ChatGPT and DALL·E, which can produce creative outputs such as written content and visual art.

The upcoming section will explore how neural networks are applied in gaming. By examining their foundational concepts and implementation, this section seeks to offer insights into how neural networks enhance AI systems in games, driving smarter behaviors and more immersive interactions.

Before learning how a neural network functions, it's essential to understand its fundamental building blocks, including neurons, layers, and the way they interact to process data.

Learning the basic concepts of a neural network

A **neural network**, also known as an **artificial neural network** (**ANN**), is an AI model designed to process information in a way similar to the human brain. It transmits signals between interconnected neurons, enabling the network to learn patterns and make decisions based on input data.

A neural network is made up of layers of interconnected nodes, called **neurons**. A neuron connection can also be called a **synapse**. Each connection between neurons has a *weight*, which adjusts as the network learns from data. Signals are transmitted between neurons, enabling the network to learn patterns and make decisions based on input data.

A neural network basically has three layers:

- **Input layer**: This layer receives the raw data or inputs, such as images, text, or numbers.
- **Hidden layers**: These layers process the input data through mathematical operations and extract patterns or features. A network can have multiple hidden layers, and the term *deep learning* refers to networks with many such layers.
- **Output layer**: This layer outputs the final result based on the input data, such as an image, a text, or a set of values.

Let's explore an example to dissect a simple **shadow learning** neural network—a neural network that contains only one hidden layer—with two input values, a single output value, and the hidden layer containing just one neuron:

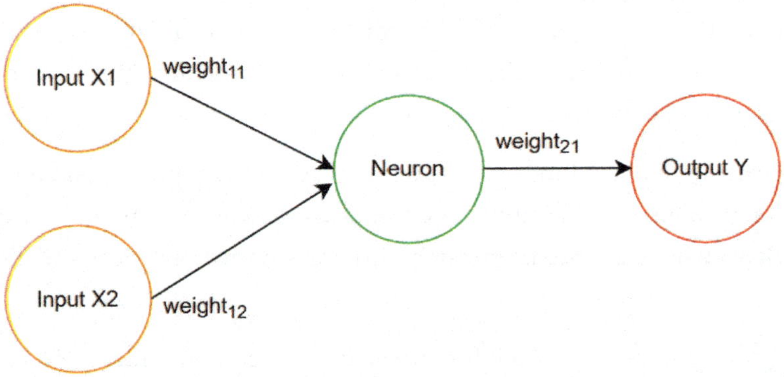

Figure 10.1 – A simple neural network

Based on the concept shown in *Figure 10.1*, we can define the `Neuron` class in C++ as follows:

```
class Neuron {
private:
  vector<float> _Weights;      //Weights for the inputs
  float _Error;                //Error
  float _Activation;           //Activation
  float _Output;               //Output
  float _Bias;                 //Bias
public:
  Neuron(size_t InputSize);
  void Activate(vector<float> inputs);
public:
  vector<float>& GetWeights() { return _Weights; }
```

```
    float GetActivation() { return _Activation; }
    float GetOutput() { return _Output; }
    float GetError() { return _Error; }
    void SetError(float Error) { _Error = Error; }
    float GetBias() { return _Bias; }
    void SetBias(float Bias) { _Bias = Bias; }
};
```

Within the class definition, the `private` section here declares the key variables required for a neuron, including `_Weights`, `_Error`, `_Activation`, `_Output`, and `_Bias`. You can refer to the implementation of the `Activate` function in the next paragraph to understand how these variables are used to adjust the network during prediction. The second `public` section primarily consists of the class's setter and getter methods, which provide access to and control over these internal variables.

The following is the code for the implementation of the class constructor and the `Activate` function:

```
Neuron::Neuron(size_t InputSize) {
  //Using random values to initialize the weights and bias.
  for (int i = 0; i < InputSize; ++i) {
    _Weights.push_back((float)((double)rand()) / RAND_MAX);
  }
  _Bias = (float)((double)rand() / RAND_MAX);
}
void Neuron::Activate(vector<float> Inputs) {
  //The number of inputs must match the weights' size
  assert(Inputs.size() == _Weights.size());
  //Calculate the activation value
  _Activation = _Bias;
  for (int i = 0; i < _Weights.size(); ++i) {
    _Activation += _Weights[i] * Inputs[i];
  }
  //Apply the activation function
  _Output = NeuralNetwork::Sigmoid(_Activation);
}
```

The class constructor simply initializes the `_Weights` array and the `_Bias` variable with random numbers. The `Activate` method calculates the output based on the inputs, the weights, and the bias values.

Since a neural network consists of layers, including an input layer, an output layer, and one or more hidden layers, we can define the `Layer` class as follows:

```
class Layer
{
private:
  vector<Neuron> _Neurons;     //Neurons on this Layer
public:
  Layer(size_t NeuronSize, size_t InputSize);
  vector<Neuron>& GetNeurons() { return _Neurons; }
};
```

Lastly, we define the `NeuralNetwork` class. The number of layers and the number of neurons in each layer can be customized based on specific requirements. Additionally, we can declare the `Sigmoid` and `SigmoidDerivative` functions as public static members of the class for convenient access:

```
class NeuralNetwork
{
public:
  static float Sigmoid(float x);
  static float SigmoidDerivative(float x);
private:
  vector<Layer> _Layers; //The hidden and output Layers
  float _LearningRate = 0.5f;
  vector<float> ForwardPropagate(vector<float>& Inputs);
  void BackPropagate(vector<float>& Targets);
  void UpdateWeights(vector<float>& Inputs);
public:
  NeuralNetwork(vector<size_t>& LayerSizes, float LearningRate = 0.5f);
  void Train(vector<float>& Inputs, vector<float>& Targets);
  vector<float> Predict(vector<float>& Inputs);
};
```

Let's clarify a few points from the preceding code snippet:

- The `Sigmoid` and `SigmoidDerivative` activation functions will be explained and implemented in the next section.
- The `_LearningRate` variable is a hyperparameter that determines the extent of weight adjustments in response to the error during each update. Its value ranges from `0` to `1` and influences the model's adaptation speed. Smaller learning rates lead to *slower but more precise* updates, requiring more training epochs (a single pass of the training process with an entire dataset), while larger learning rates result in *faster updates with fewer epochs*. More details on this will be covered in the *Training the models* section, along with the concept of **gradient descent**.
- The `ForwardPropagate`, `BackPropagate`, and `UpdateWeights` functions represent the three key steps of training a neural network. These steps are executed within the `Train` function, and their detailed implementation will be discussed in the next section.
- The `Predict` function calls the `BackPropagate` function to generate outputs based on the given inputs.

Now that you understand the basic components and structure of a neural network, we'll move on to explaining how a neural network processes input values to predict and generate outputs.

Understanding how neural networks predict

The prediction process used to generate the output value in a neural network is known as **forward propagation**. During this process, input values are passed through the network's layers, where each neuron applies a mathematical operation to the data, such as multiplication by weights and the addition of biases. The result of each operation is passed to the next layer until the output is produced.

This process is essential for making predictions or decisions based on the given inputs and is a key mechanism in neural networks. Therefore, the weights of each neuron play a crucial role in the prediction process.

Imagine a turret on a battlefield tasked to defend the gate of a base from the player. The turret's system takes two inputs:

- Distance of the player from the turret
- Angular difference required for the turret to aim at the player

Based on these inputs, the system produces an output value between `0` and `1`, indicating the likelihood of the turret firing:

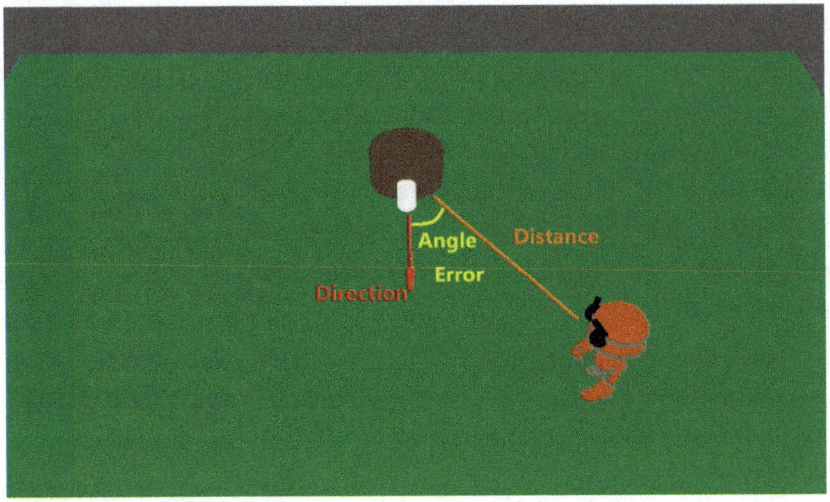

Figure 10.2 – The screenshot of the turret defense game

Inputs fed into a neural network are typically normalized to improve convergence and training stability. **Normalization** ensures a consistent scale and reduces the impact of varying feature magnitudes.

Let's define the equations used to calculate the two inputs:

1. The equation for *Input X1* normalizes the player's distance to the turret into a range between 0 and 1. Here's how it works:

$$Input\ X1 = \text{clamp}(\frac{Distance}{Vision\ Range}, 0, 1)$$

   where:

   - *Distance* is the current distance between the player and the turret.
   - *Input X1* is calculated by dividing *Distance* by *Vision Range* and clamping the normalized distance to a range of *[0, 1]*, where *0* means the player is at the turret's position, and *1* means the player is at or out of the maximum vision range.

2. The equation for *Input X2* normalizes the angular difference required for the turret to aim at the player into a range between 0 and 1. Here's how it works:

$$Input\ X2 = \text{Clamp}(\frac{Angular\ Error}{180}, -1, 1)$$

   where:

   - *Angular Error* is the angle between the turret's forward direction and the vector pointing from the turret toward the player character.
   - *Input X2* is calculated by dividing the *Angular Error* by the 180-degree scales and clamping the normalized angular error to a range of *[-1, 1]*.

A neuron's `Activate` function uses the two inputs to calculate the activation value using the following formula:

$$y = b + \sigma(\sum_{i=1}^{n} w_i x_i)$$

where:

- y is the *Output Y* value, which is the sum of all the input values multiplied by their connection weights.
- b is the bias.
- w_i is the weights for each connection.
- x_i is the input values.
- σ indicates the **Sigmoid function** used as the rate of change with respect to its input. The Sigmoid function is defined with the following formula:

$$\sigma(x) = \frac{1}{1 + e^{-x}}$$

Refer to the graph shown in *Figure 10.3*, which illustrates the curve of the Sigmoid function. The function compresses input values into a range between **0** and **1**. As input values move further away from **0** (either positively or negatively), the output values approach **1** or **0**, respectively, creating an S-shaped curve. This behavior makes the Sigmoid function useful for transforming inputs into probabilities or bounded activations.

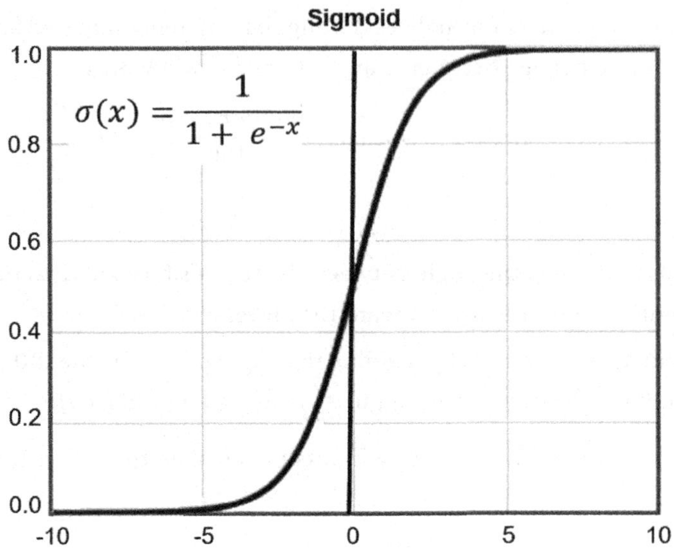

Figure 10.3 – Sigmoid function graph

> **Additional reading**
>
> For more details about activation functions, refer to this article on *Geeks for Geeks*: `https://www.geeksforgeeks.org/activation-functions-neural-networks/`

The following code implements the `Predict`, `ForwardPropagation`, `Activate`, and `Sigmoid` functions:

```
vector<float> Predict(vector<float>& Inputs) {
  return ForwardPropagate(Inputs);
}
vector<float> ForwardPropagate(vector<float>& Inputs){
  vector<float> outputs;
  vector<float> inputs = Inputs;
  for (size_t layer = 0; layer < _Layers.size(); ++layer) {
    outputs.clear();
    vector<Neuron>& neurons = _Layers[layer].GetNeurons();
    for (size_t i = 0; i < neurons.size(); ++i) {
      neurons[i].Activate(inputs);
      outputs.push_back(neurons[i].GetOutput());
```

```
    }
    inputs = outputs;
  }
  return outputs;
}
void Neuron::Activate(vector<float> Inputs) {
  _Activation = _Bias;
  for (int i = 0; i < _Weights.size(); ++i) {
    _Activation += _Weights[i] * Inputs[i];
  }
  _Output = Sigmoid(_Activation);
}
float Sigmoid(float x) {
  return (float)(1.0 / (1.0 + exp(-x)));
}
```

This code snippet implements four key functions used in the prediction process:

- The `Predict` function simply calls the `ForwardPropagate` function to process the input values and generate the corresponding output.
- The `ForwardPropagate` function takes the input values and processes them layer by layer—starting from the first layer and continuing through to the final layer. At each layer, it calls the `Activate` function to compute the value of each neuron based on the outputs from the previous layer. This process continues until the final output values are produced by the last layer of neurons.
- The `Activate` function multiplies the input values by their corresponding weights, sums the results, and then applies the `Sigmoid` function to produce the neuron's output.
- The `Sigmoid` function applies to the sigmoid formula to regulate the activation strength of the neuron.

In the example shown in *Figure 10.2*, the single predicted output is used to control the turret's firing mechanism. For instance, we can specify that if the output value falls between `0.6` and `1.0`, the turret will be triggered to fire.

A neural network can generate outputs from given inputs, but these outputs may not always meet real-world requirements due to errors. How can we improve its accuracy to better align with actual needs? The solution lies in using training data to train the neural network, which actually adjusts the neurons' weights and enhances the network's ability to make more precise predictions.

Understanding how neural networks learn

The prediction process shows that a neural network's outputs are determined by the weights of its input connections. Adjusting these weights to better align with different input values improves the network's accuracy and performance. This adjustment forms the core of the learning process, where the network iteratively updates its weights to minimize prediction errors. This iterative refinement of weights is known as **training**.

To train a neural network, the **backpropagation** algorithm is used to adjust the weights effectively. The process involves four key steps, which we'll examine in the subsequent sections.

Step 1: Predicting outputs

In this step, a set of training data inputs is used by the neural network to predict the corresponding outputs. For instance, with reference to *Figure 10.2*, if the training data consists of the distance from the turret to the player and the firing angle error, the normalized inputs are processed by the network to predict whether the turret should fire or not.

Step 2: Calculating the output errors

For each predicted output value, use the target value in the training data to calculate the errors. The errors can be evaluated with the following formula:

$$\delta_{output} = \hat{y} - y$$

where:

- δ_{output} is the error of an output
- $\hat{y}$ is the actual target value
- y is the predicted output value

Step 3: Propagating errors backward

The backpropagation process starts with the output error(s) and propagates the error(s) backward, layer by layer, through all the neurons, ultimately reaching the input layer.

The formula below illustrates the process for hidden layer neurons *j*, where the error is propagated backward from the output layer. The error for each neuron in the hidden layer is computed as the sum of the errors in the subsequent layer, weighted by the corresponding weights, and then multiplied by the derivative of the sigmoid function:

$$\delta_j = \sigma'(\sum_{i=1}^{n} (\hat{y}_i - y_i) * w_i)$$

where:

- δ_j is the error of neuron *j* in the current layer, which could be the input layer or a hidden layer.
- $(\hat{y}_i - y_i)$ is the error of neuron *i* in the subsequent layer, which could be a hidden layer or the output layer.
- w_i is the weight between neuron *j* in the current layer and neuron *k* in the next layer.
- σ' is the `SigmoidDerivative` function defined as:

$$\sigma'(x) = x * (1 - x)$$

The `Backpropagation` and `SigmoidDerivative` functions can be implemented using the following code:

```
void BackPropagate(vector<float>& Targets) {
  size_t i;
  float error, output;
  vector<Neuron>& outputs = _Layers.back().GetNeurons();
  assert(Targets.size() == outputs.size());
  //Calculate the errors for the outputs
  for (i = 0; i < outputs.size(); ++i) {
    output = outputs[i].GetOutput();
    float derivative = SigmoidDerivative(output);
    error = Targets[i] - output;
    outputs[i].SetError(error * derivative);
  }
  //Calculate errors for hidden layers' neurons
  for (int layer = (int)_Layers.size() - 2; layer >= 0; --layer) {
    vector<Neuron>& neurons = _Layers[layer].GetNeurons();
```

```
    for (size_t i = 0; i < neurons.size(); ++i) {
      error = 0.0f;
      vector<Neuron>& nextLayerNeurons = _Layers[layer + 1].GetNeurons();
      for (size_t j = 0; j < nextLayerNeurons.size(); ++j){
        error += nextLayerNeurons[j].GetWeights()[i] *
nextLayerNeurons[j].GetError();
      }
      output = neurons[i].GetOutput();
      float derivative = SigmoidDerivative(output);
      neurons[i].SetError(error * derivative);
    }
  }
}
float SigmoidDerivative(float x) {
  return (float)(x * (1.0 - x));
}
```

The preceding code snippet primarily implements the `BackPropagate` function, which starts from the neurons in the last layer and works backward to the first hidden layer. It uses the known output values to calculate the error for each neuron during this process.

The `SigmoidDerivative` function computes the derivative by multiplying the sigmoid value by one minus the sigmoid value, following the standard formula.

Step 4: Updating the weights

The process of updating weights in a neural network involves adjusting the weights based on the errors propagated backward through the network during backpropagation. *Figure 10.4* illustrates how the backpropagation process updates neuron weights for two neural networks – the upper one has only one hidden layer and the lower one has two hidden layers:

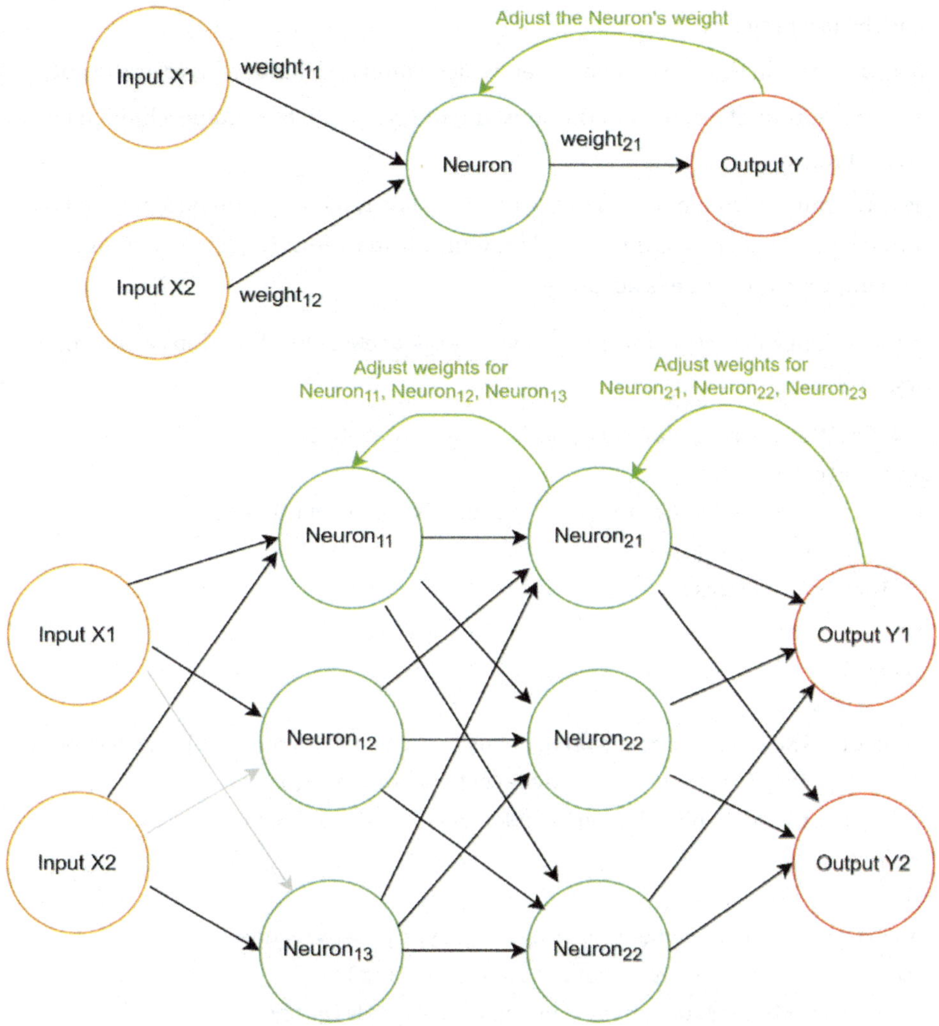

Figure 10.4 – Updating neuron weights through backpropagation

What the process does is update each weight *wij*, which connects neuron *i* in layer *l - 1* to neuron *j* in layer *l*, according to a formula derived from the gradient of the loss function with respect to that weight:

$$w'_{ij} = w_{ij} + \eta * \delta_j * y_i$$

where:

- w'_{ij} is the new weight for the connection between neuron *i* and neuron *j*.
- w_{ij} is the old weight for the connection between neuron *i* and neuron *j*.

- η is the learning rate.
- δ_j is the error in the subsequent layer, which could be a hidden layer or the output layer.
- y_j is the output of neuron j in the subsequent layer, which could be a hidden layer or the output layer.
- y_i is the output from neuron i in the previous layer, which could be a hidden layer or the input layer. This process is repeated for multiple iterations (epochs) to minimize the error and improve the model's accuracy.

Based on the weight calculation formula above, the `UpdateWeights` function can be implemented as follows:

```
void NeuralNetwork::UpdateWeights(vector<float>& Inputs) {
  vector<float> inputs;
  for (size_t layer = 0; layer < _Layers.size(); ++layer) {
    if (layer == 0) {
      inputs = Inputs;
    }
    Else {
      inputs.clear();
      vector<Neuron>& prevLayerNeurons = _Layers[layer - 1].GetNeurons();
      for (size_t i = 0; i < prevLayerNeurons.size(); ++i){
        inputs.push_back(prevLayerNeurons[i].GetOutput());
      }
    }
    vector<Neuron>& neurons = _Layers[layer].GetNeurons();
    for (size_t i = 0; i < neurons.size(); ++i) {
      vector<float>& weights = neurons[i].GetWeights();
      for (size_t j = 0; j < inputs.size(); ++j) {
        weights[j] += _LearningRate * neurons[i].GetError() * inputs[j];
      }
      neurons[i].SetBias(neurons[i].GetBias() +_LearningRate * neurons[i].
GetError());
    }
  }
}
```

The `UpdateWeight` function iterates through all the neurons in each layer, using the errors calculated during the backpropagation process to update the input weights for each neuron.

We have examined the details of implementing a neural network, including the theory behind how it learns and predicts outcomes. To gain a deeper understanding of how a neural network is applied in game development, we'll explore `Demo10`, which will be presented in the next section.

Demo10: An AI-controlled turret defense game

`Demo10` demonstrates how to use a neural network model to control a turret within a game scene. This demo provides a foundation for exploring not only the shadow learning model but also a more advanced DL model, which leverages multiple hidden layers and can manage multiple outputs to predict and control more complex systems.

In this demo, the turret can rotate and aim at the player when the player enters its vision range. If the player comes within the turret's attack range, it begins firing.

To meet these requirements, a new neural network model (see *Figure 10.5*) is designed with two inputs: the *distance to the player* and the *aiming angle error*. The model also includes two outputs: one to determine whether the turret should fire and another to control the turret's rotation.

To adapt to the more complex controls required for this scenario, the model is enhanced with two hidden layers (*Neuron1x* and *Neuron2x*). Each of the two hidden layers contains three neurons, providing the neural network with a suitable capacity to process and respond to the inputs effectively.

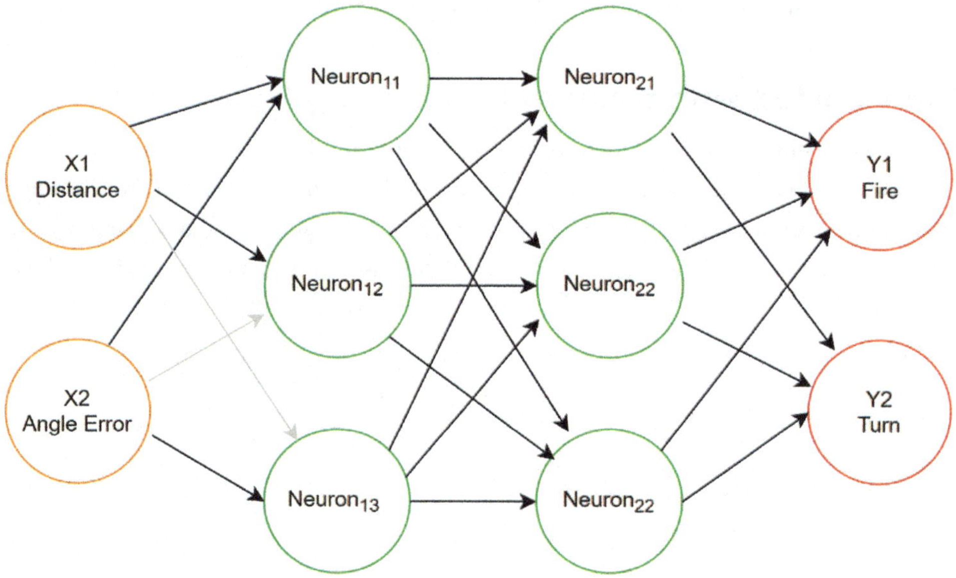

Figure 10.5 – The DL neural network for turret control

In the network model shown in *Figure 10.5*, the neurons in the first layer can be analyzed as follows:

- **Neuron$_{11}$** This neuron considers both the **Distance** and **Angle Error** factors, reflecting its interest in the combined influence of these inputs.
- **Neuron$_{12}$**: This neuron is focused solely on the **Distance** factor and disregards the **Angle Error** factor. To achieve this, the weight of the connection between **X2** (representing **Angle Error**) and **Neuron$_{12}$** is set to a very low value or even zero.
- **Neuron$_{13}$**: Conversely, this neuron is exclusively interested in the **Angle Error** factor and ignores the **Distance** factor. To reflect this, the weight of the connection between **X1** (representing **Distance**) and **Neuron$_{13}$** is set to a very small value or zero.

The purpose of analyzing these connection weights is to provide insight into how the neurons in the first layer function and the rationale behind including three neurons in this layer. This understanding serves as a foundation for designing your own neural network models in the future.

> **Important note**
>
> There is no fixed standard or rule to determine the number of layers and neurons in a neural network. The architecture depends on the specific problem and data characteristics. The general idea is to begin with a shadow network, do experiments, test, and iteratively improve the network structure.

Getting started with training and playing Demo10

`Demo10` offers two options upon launch, accessible by pressing *F1* or *F2*. These options allow you to choose between using the shadow learning model or the DL model. The *shadow learning model* enables the turret to fire only when the player is within its attack range and firing arc. Besides the control of firing, the *DL model* adds functionality for the turret to rotate and aim at the player.

While playing the game, use the *WASD* keys to navigate the player character across the game map:

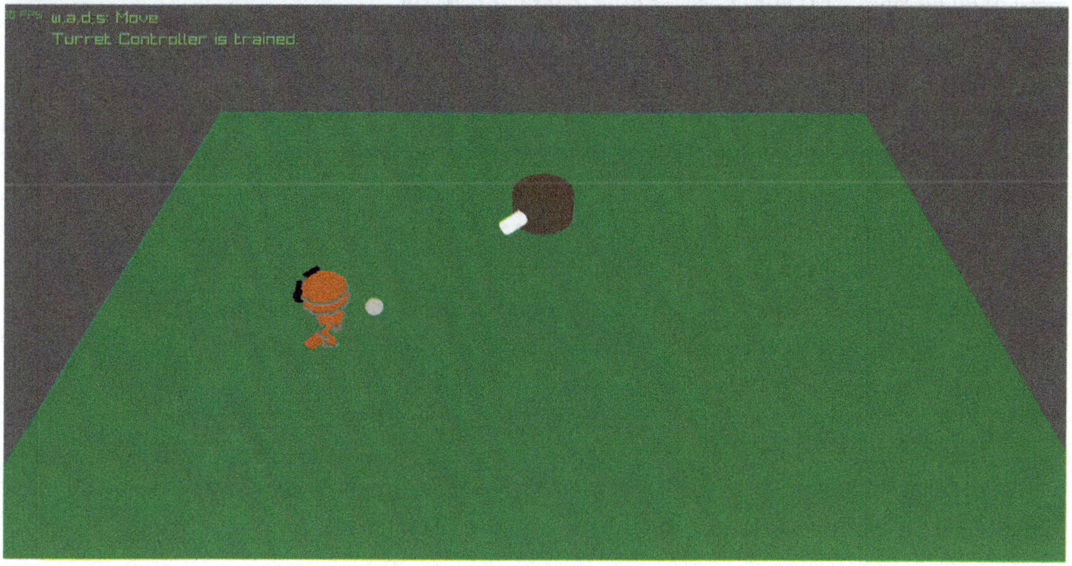

Figure 10.6 – AI-controlled turret defense

Let's start by writing the code to define the `TurretController` class.

Controlling the turret with the TurretController class

To process the training and control over the turret, the core class added to `Demo10` is the `TurretController` class. Here is the code snippet that declares the `TurretController` class:

```
class TurretController {
private:
  NeuralNetwork* _ANN;  //Artificial Neural Network
  Scene* _Scene;        //The game scene
  SceneActor* _Cannon;  //The turret cannon
  Vector3 _CannonDir = Vector3{ 0.0f, 0.0f, -1.0f }; //The cannon's aiming 
direction
  float _CannonRotAngle = 0.0f;  //The cannon's rotation angle
  float _AttackRange = 15.0f;  //The turret's attack range
  float _FiringArc = 20.0f;         //The turret's firing arc in degrees
  float _TurnSpeed = 8.0f;  //The turret's turning speed
  float _VisionRange;       //The turret's vision range
  Vector3 _FiringDir;       //The firing direction
private:
```

```
    float _IsLoaded;             //The cannon is loaded or not
    SceneActor* _Fireball;     //The Fireball actor
    float _FireballDuration = 1.5f; //The fireball's lifetime
    float _FireballSpeed = 15.0f;    //The fireball's speed
  public:
    int Trained = 0;  //Indicates whether the ANN is trined
  public:
    TurretController(Scene* Scene, SceneActor* Cannon);
    ~TurretController();
    void InitANN(int Method);         //1-shadow learning, 2-deep learning
    void Train(int Method, int SampleCount = 100000, int epochs = 1);
    void Update(float DeltaTime);
  };
```

The code snippet above defines the `TurretController` class, including its variables and member functions such as the constructor, destructor, and the `InitANN` and `Train` methods.

Now, let's examine the `InitANN` function to understand how it initializes the network models for both the shadow learning and DL approaches:

```
void TurretController::InitANN(int Method) {
  srand(time(NULL));
  if (Method == 1) {
    vector<size_t> layerSizes;
    layerSizes.push_back(2);       //Input layers: 2 inputs
    layerSizes.push_back(1);       //Hidden layer: 1 neural
    layerSizes.push_back(1);       //Output layer: 1 neural
    _ANN = new NeuralNetwork(layerSizes, 0.3f, false);
  }
  else if (Method == 2) {
    vector<size_t> layerSizes;
    layerSizes.push_back(2);       //Input layers: 2 inputs
    layerSizes.push_back(3);       //Hidden layer 1: 3 neurals
    layerSizes.push_back(3);       //Hidden layer 2: 3 neurals
    layerSizes.push_back(2);       //Output layers: 2 outputs
    _ANN = new NeuralNetwork(layerSizes, 0.1f, true);
  }
}
```

The `InitANN` function initializes the network model based on the selected method:

- `Method == 1`: This creates a shadow learning model with 2 inputs, 1 output, and a single hidden layer containing just 1 neuron.
- `Method == 2`: This generates a deep learning model with 2 inputs, 2 outputs, and two hidden layers, each containing 3 neurons.

Further, the constructor of the `NeuralNetwork` class accepts the following three parameters:

- `LayerSizes`: Specifies the size of each layer and the number of neurons in each layer, which is used to define the network architecture.
- `LearningRate`: Controls how quickly the model is adapted to the problem. We will discuss it further in the next section.
- `MinusActivation`: Refers to the activation function applied to the network. It determines whether the input and output range should be [0, 1] (if set to `false`) or [-1, 1] (if set to `true`).

While the `Sigmoid` activation function is well-suited for outputs ranging from 0 to 1, certain scenarios require outputs in the range of [-1 to 1]. In such cases, activation functions such as `TanH` and its derivative, `TanHDerivative`, are used in this case:

```
static float TanH(float x) {
    return tanh(x);
}

static float TanHDerivative(float x) {
    return 1.0f - x * x;
}
```

Figure 10.7 displays the curve of the `TanH` activation function. As shown in the figure, when the input value (**x**) is less than **-0.25**, the output approaches **-1**. Conversely, when **x** exceeds **0.25**, the output approaches **+1**. This function transforms the linear input signal into a non-linear output ranging between -1 and +1. It shows the curve of the `TanH` activation function.

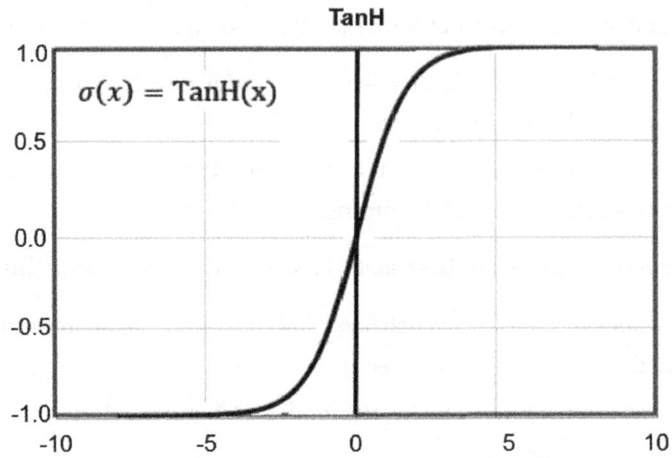

Figure 10.7 – TanH activation function graph

After completing the implementation of all the `TurretController` member functions, we are ready to begin training the AI model. However, before starting the training process, it's important to discuss how to control the training and evaluate the results using an appropriate learning rate. We'll explore this topic next.

Understanding learning rate, epochs, and training cost

DL neural networks are trained using the *gradient descent approach*, an iterative learning algorithm that updates the model using a training dataset.

The **learning rate** is a crucial hyperparameter in neural network training, typically ranging between `0.0` and `1.0`. It determines how quickly the model adapts to the problem. Selecting the appropriate learning rate is one of the most critical challenges in training DL models, as it significantly impacts the model's performance.

When choosing the learning rate, it is also important to learn and understand a little bit more about the two related concepts – **batches** and **epochs**:

- **Batch size:** This is a hyperparameter that represents the number of training samples walked through before updating weights.
- **Number of epochs:** This is a hyperparameter that represents the total number that the learning process will walk through the entire training dataset.

A *smaller learning rate* results in smaller updates to the weights during each step, requiring more epochs for training. In contrast, a *larger learning rate* leads to rapid weight updates, which may cause the model to converge too quickly or even miss the optimal solution, though it typically requires fewer training epochs.

Now that you understand the concepts of adjusting the learning rate, batch size, and epochs to train a model, the next step is to learn how to assess and evaluate your training process effectively. Therefore, it is essential to understand how to achieve your goals with optimal cost. This introduces the concepts of **training cost** and **gradient descent**.

Understanding training cost and gradient descent

During backpropagation in the training of a neural network model, the process of learning involves a technique called **gradient descent**. This method optimizes the weights and biases by minimizing the **cost**, which measures the difference between the actual and predicted outputs.

The following formula is commonly used to calculate the cost for one training iteration of weight updates, guiding the model toward achieving the goal of minimized cost:

$$C = \sum_{i=1}^{n} \frac{(\hat{y}_i - y_i)^2}{2}$$

where:

- C is the overall cost
- $\hat{y}$ is the actual target value
- y is the predicted output value

Figure 10.8 illustrates how training iterations progressively descend (repeatedly following the slope or tangent at each point to move toward a lower point) to reach the desired goal:

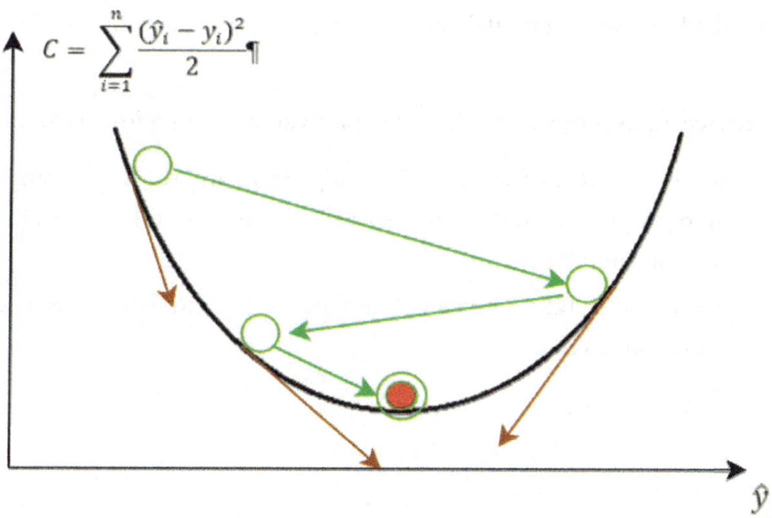

Figure 10.8 – Gradient descent approach

With a solid understanding of training models, let's now explore how the `TurretController` generates training datasets and utilizes them to train the models.

Training the models

To train a model, the first step is to obtain training data. Since the turret's control logic can be defined programmatically, we can write code to randomly generate two sample training datasets that cover various scenarios, ensuring the turret adheres to the following rules:

- For both **Method 1** and **Method 2**, the turret fires at the player only when the player is within its attack range and firing arc.
- For **Method 2**, the turret also turns to aim at the player when the player is within its vision range.

First, let's take a closer look at the arguments passed to the `Train` function of the `TurretController` class:

```
Void Train(int Method, int SampleCount, int epochs);
```

Let's break down the elements as follows:

- `Method`: A flag set to either 1 or 2, indicating whether the shadow learning model or the DL model will be trained and utilized
- `SampleCount`: Specifies the number of sample data points to be generated for training
- `Epochs`: Defines the number of epochs to be used for training the model

For training the shadow learning model, each training data sample consists of two inputs and one output:

- The **Distance** input is the normalized distance value, ranging from 0 to 1:
    - For instance, if the turret's vision range is 30 and the attack range is 15, then a randomly generated distance between 0 and 15 will be normalized to a value between 0 and 0.5.
    - If the distance falls between 15 and 30 (or beyond), the normalized value will range from 0.5 to 1.

- The **Angle Error** input is the normalized angle error:
    - For example, if the turret's firing arc is 20 degrees, a randomly generated angle between 0 and 20 will have a normalized value between 0 and 0.11 (calculated as 20/180).
    - Any angle outside this range will have a normalized value greater than 0.11, up to 1.
- The **Output** has two possible values: 1 or 0:
    - A value of 1 indicates the turret should fire, while 0 indicates it should not fire.
    - This output is determined by evaluating whether the randomly generated distance and angle error meet the firing conditions.

First, let's look at the overall structure of the implementation of the `Train` function:

```
Void Train(int Method, int SampleCount, int epochs) {
  vector<float> inputs;
  vector<float> targets;
  vector<float> sampleData;
  vector<vector<float>> dataset;
  InitANN(Method);
  if (Method == 1) {
    //Methods 1 process
  }
  else if (Method == 2) {
    //Method 2 process
  }
  Trained = Method;
}
```

The `Train` function performs three main tasks:

1. It first defines four vector datasets used to build the neural network and initializes the network by calling the `InitANN` function.
2. It then checks the value of `Method` to determine whether to use **Shadow Learning** (when `Method == 1`) or DL (when `Method == 2`) for training the model.
3. Finally, it sets the `Trained` flag to the value of the training method, indicating that the model has been successfully trained.

Now, let's dive into the actual code implementation for generating the test data that will be used for **Method 1**:

```
for (int i = 0; i < SampleCount; ++i) {
  inputs.clear();
  targets.clear();
  sampleData.clear();
  //Generate the distance input
  int distance = rand() % (int)_VisionRange;
  float distanceInput = Clamp((float)distance / _VisionRange, 0.0f, 1.0f);
  //Generate the angle error input
  int angleError;
  if (i % 3 == 0) {
    angleError = rand() % 181;
  }
  else {
    int firingArc = (int)_FiringArc;
    angleError = rand() % ((int)firingArc / 2 + 1);
  }
  float angleErrorInput = Clamp((float)angleError / 180.0f, 0.0f, 1.0f);
  inputs.push_back(distanceInput);
  inputs.push_back(angleErrorInput);
  //Determine the output value for firing
  if (distance >= 0 && distance <= _AttackRange && angleError <= _
FiringArc * 0.5f) {
    targets.push_back(1.0);
  }
  else {
    targets.push_back(0.0);
  }
  //Push the sample data into the dataset
  sampleData.clear();
  sampleData.push_back(inputs[0]);
  sampleData.push_back(inputs[1]);
  sampleData.push_back(targets[0]);
  dataset.push_back(sampleData);
}
```

The code snippet above generates training data for training the network using the shadow learning model. It uses a loop to iterate through all sample data and includes the following four steps within the loop body:

1. It randomly generates values for `distanceInput` and `angleErrorInput` and pushes them into the `inputs` datasets.
2. It randomly generates the corresponding `targets` output values.
3. It pushes the generated `inputs` and `target` pairs into `sampleData`.
4. It pushes all the `sampleData` rows into the `dataset` matrix preparing them for use in training the model.

Generating training data for **Method 2** is similar to **Method 1**, with a few key differences:

- An angle error input ranges from -180 to 180 degrees, so the normalized input will range from -1 to 1.
- The second output controls the turret's aim towards the player using three values: -1 for turning counter-clockwise, 1 for turning clockwise, and 0 for no movement.

Here is the code illustrating this difference:

```
//Generate the distance input
int distance = rand() % (int)_VisionRange;
float distanceInput = Clamp((float)distance / _VisionRange, 0.0f, 1.0f);
//Generate the angle error input
int angleError;
if (i % 2 == 0) {
   angleError = 180 - rand() % 361;
}
else {
  int firingArc = (int)_FiringArc;
  angleError = firingArc / 2 - (rand() % ((int)firingArc + 1));
}
float angleErrorInput = Clamp((float)angleError / 180.0f, -1.0f, 1.0f);
inputs.push_back(distanceInput);
inputs.push_back(angleErrorInput);
//Determine the first output value for firing
float halfFiringArc = _FiringArc * 0.5f;
```

```
if (distance >= 0 && distance <= _AttackRange &&
  angleError >= -halfFiringArc && angleError <= halfFiringArc) {
  targets.push_back(1.0);
}
Else {
  targets.push_back(0.0);
}
//Determine the second output value for turning the turret
targets.push_back((float)sign(angleError));
//Push the sample data into the dataset
sampleData.clear();
sampleData.push_back(inputs[0]);
sampleData.push_back(inputs[1]);
sampleData.push_back(targets[0]);
sampleData.push_back(targets[1]);
dataset.push_back(sampleData);
```

The code snippet above demonstrates the training data generation for **Method 2**. Lines that differ from **Method 1** are highlighted in bold to emphasize the changes.

> **Note**
>
> There are many different ways to collect training data beyond simply writing code to generate it. Depending on the project, data can be gathered through manual labeling, user interaction logs, simulation environments, or even real-world sensors. The method chosen often depends on the type of model being trained and the context in which it will be used.

By running the preceding code, we can get the training data. Now, all that is left to do is use loops to feed the training data into the model, train it, and then evaluate the cost values for each epoch:

```
for (int epoch = 0; epoch < epochs; ++epoch) {
  //Train the model
  for (int i = 0; i < dataset.size(); ++i) {
    inputs.clear();
    targets.clear();
    inputs.push_back(dataset[i][0]);
    inputs.push_back(dataset[i][1]);
    targets.push_back(dataset[i][2]);
```

```
      if (Method == 2) {
        targets.push_back(dataset[i][3]);
      }
      _ANN->Train(inputs, targets);
    }
    //Evaluate the cost
    double overallCost = 0.0;
    for (int i = 0; i < dataset.size(); ++i) {
      inputs.clear();
      inputs.push_back(dataset[i][0]);
      inputs.push_back(dataset[i][1]);
      targets.clear();
      targets.push_back(dataset[i][2]);
      if (Method == 2) {
        targets.push_back(dataset[i][3]);
      }
      vector<float> outputs = _ANN->Predict(inputs);
      float cost = (targets[0] - outputs[0]) * (targets[0] - outputs[0]) *
  0.5f;
      if (Method == 1) {
        overallCost += cost;
      }
      else if (Method == 2) {
        float cost1 = (targets[1] - outputs[1]) * (targets[1] - outputs[1])
  * 0.5f;
        targets.push_back(dataset[i][3]);
        overallCost += cost + cost1;
      }
    }
  }
```

The preceding code snippet uses the generated training data to train the AI model. It runs for a specified number of epochs, iterating through each row in the dataset. For each training sample, it performs the following steps:

1. Calls the ANN's Train function to update the model.
2. Calls the Predict function to obtain the model's prediction.
3. Compares the predicted output with the target value to calculate the cost.

Launch the game and give it a try. When you press *F1*, **Method 1** will be selected to train the shadow learning model, and when you press *F2*, **Method 2** will be chosen to train the DL model. The models are initialized and trained differently, so refer to the following matrix to compare the differences:

Method #	**1**	**2**
Learning Type	Shadow learning	Deep learning
Inputs	2	2
Outputs	1	2
Hidden Layers	1 (Neurons: 1)	2 (Neurons: 3, 3)
Learning Rate	0.3	0.1
Training Samples	10000	10000
Epochs	1	3

Table 10.2 – Comparison matrix for the two different training methods

For more implementation details of `Demo10`, please refer to the downloaded `Knight` solution and review the source code of the `Demo10` project.

The trained model in `Demo10` effectively controls the turret as intended. To further optimize performance, it is recommended to adjust the learning rate, epochs, number of layers, and neurons, as well as analyze the costs to enhance training accuracy, improve prediction performance, and minimize the cost.

Summary

This chapter explored one of the most prominent AI technologies, deep learning, and introduced essential concepts such as neural networks, shadow learning, training evaluation, and gradient descent.

We began by reviewing the history and evolution of modern AI, providing context for the current state of AI technology and its vast potential. Next, we covered the basic elements and structure of a neural network and implemented a `NeuralNetwork` class in C++ to demonstrate these concepts.

We then examined how a network makes predictions based on input data. Detailed explanations of forward propagation and the activation function were provided to illustrate how the neural network calculates outputs for each neuron.

A critical aspect of AI model development is training the neural network. We introduced the backpropagation process and the derivative `Sigmoid` function to explain how errors are computed and used to update the weights during training.

Finally, we explored the `Demo10` project, showing how training data can be generated for this demo and how learning rate, batch size, and epochs impact the training process. We also introduced the cost calculation formula and the application of gradient descent in training AI models.

Although this chapter covered foundational aspects of modern AI, many advanced topics worth exploring are outside the scope of this book. We encourage you to continue learning and exploring online resources to delve deeper into the field of AI.

With the completion of all the technical chapters, you've now built a comprehensive toolkit of practical skills and theoretical knowledge essential for modern game development. Next chapter will reflect on everything you've accomplished and explore how you can continue growing as a game developer in the future.

Part 4

Reflecting and Moving Forward

In this final part of the book, it's time to step back and reflect on the journey you've taken—from building a strong foundation in data structures and algorithms to diving into graphics, animation, and artificial intelligence in game development. This part serves as both a recap of what you've learned and a roadmap for your continued growth as a developer.

You'll revisit key milestones from each chapter, gaining a broader perspective on how the individual topics connect to form a complete, practical skillset. More importantly, this chapter looks ahead, offering strategies to deepen your expertise, explore next-level challenges, and remain engaged in the ever-evolving world of game development.

Whether you aim to specialize in AI, develop skills in real-time rendering, or lead a development team, the lessons in this part are designed to inspire your next steps and encourage a mindset of continuous learning.

This part includes the following chapter:

- *Chapter 11, Continuing Your Learning Journey*

11

Continuing Your Learning Journey

As we reach the final chapter of *Data Structures and Algorithms for Game Programming in C++*, it's time to reflect on the journey we have taken together, review the wealth of knowledge and skills you have acquired, and look ahead toward the future of your game development career.

This chapter serves not only as a summary of what you have learned but also as a guide for expanding your expertise, exploring new horizons in game development, and staying motivated in your continuous learning journey.

In this chapter, we'll cover the following key aspects:

- Recapping your journey
- Extending Knight for your game project
- Integrating features into a cohesive game
- Taking it further: Performance optimization
- Looking forward

Technical requirements

Download the `Knight` Visual Studio solution from GitHub. Here is the link to the repository:

`https://github.com/PacktPublishing/Data-Structures-and-Algorithms-for-Game-Programming-in-CPP`

The demo projects for this chapter are located within the `Knight` Visual Studio solution (`https://github.com/PacktPublishing/Data-Structures-and-Algorithms-for-Game-Programming-in-CPP/tree/main/Knight`), specifically under these project names, for rendering features introduced in this chapter:

Project Name	Description
`BonusGameWorld01`	This project integrates the individual features we learned in the previous chapters into a comprehensive demo that includes a scene, a main character, and NPCs.
`BonusGameWorld02`	Based on the `BonusGameWorld01` project, it demonstrates two quick performance optimization tricks to boost the rendering performance.

Table 11.1 - Sample projects used in this chapter

Recapping your journey

We have just gone through a comprehensive journey of modern game development using C++, raylib, and the Knight framework. *Chapter 1* set the stage by guiding you through the essential setup of a C++ game development environment. By introducing the raylib graphics library and Knight—a custom, object-oriented C++ game framework—the opening chapter ensured that you were equipped with both the technical context and hands-on tools necessary to engage deeply with the chapters that follow.

The adventure continued with an exploration of core data structures in *Chapter 2*. We discovered how arrays, lists, stacks, and queues form the backbone of gameplay logic, even in the most basic playable prototype. Through sample projects, the book demonstrated how these data structures integrate with the `Entity` system, enabling the creation of responsive gameplay, real-time input handling, and simple pop-up-style UI navigation.

Building upon these foundations, *Chapter 3* delved into essential algorithms that breathe life into games. Randomization, selection, shuffling, sorting, and procedural generation were covered in detail, each accompanied by C++ examples projects. Here, we learned how the unpredictability and variety that make games engaging are underpinned by robust algorithmic thinking and implementation.

As you delved into the realms of graphics and rendering, you gained an understanding of both 2D and 3D techniques (see *Chapters 4–7*).

Visual storytelling is at the heart of game development, and the transition into 2D graphics techniques underscored this. *Chapter 4* offered an in-depth look at how images are loaded, processed, and rendered efficiently using modern GPUs. It explained the critical importance of texture formats and memory management, equipping you with the knowledge to optimize both performance and quality. Techniques such as color and alpha blending, parallax scrolling, isometric rendering, and dynamic UI elements were brought to life, giving you the power to craft vibrant, visually compelling 2D worlds.

With a firm grasp of 2D graphics, you were then introduced to the immersive realm of 3D graphics. *Chapter 5* explained the mathematics and implementation of camera systems, from the first-person perspective to cinematic rail and top-down strategy cameras. Each camera system was explored both conceptually and practically, showing how thoughtful viewpoint design shapes the player's experience and navigational possibilities within the game world.

At the core of 3D rendering, *Chapter 6* offered a thorough examination of the graphics pipeline, from vertex transformations to fragment shading. You learned how data flows from the CPU to the GPU, how shaders are written and utilized, and how lighting and surface details are calculated and displayed. Special attention was given to shader programming, teaching you how to write both vertex and fragment shaders, manage coordinate spaces, and implement effects such as normal mapping for added realism.

As the complexity of rendered scenes grows, so do the technical challenges. *Chapter 7* guided you through building complete 3D game worlds, teaching how to efficiently render large scenes with multiple objects, terrain generated from height maps, atmospheric effects via skyboxes, and realistic lighting and shadow techniques using multi-pass rendering. Techniques such as billboards and particle systems were integrated seamlessly to create worlds that are both performant and visually rich.

Characters, of course, are the heart of any interactive story. *Chapter 8* introduced the principles and implementation of character animation, from basic keyframe systems to advanced skeletal animation and inverse kinematics. By mastering animation blending and smooth transitions, you gained the ability to create lifelike, expressive characters whose movements are both natural and dynamic.

No game is complete without intelligent behavior. In *Chapter 9*, we introduced several classic game AI implementations: FSMs, behavior trees, and A* pathfinding. They provide robust frameworks for developing believable NPCs and challenging game scenarios. By building AI systems that control character behaviors, transitions, and navigation, you acquired the skills to create engaging and responsive gameplay experiences.

Finally, *Chapter 10* opened the door to the world of modern AI. By introducing the fundamentals of neural networks, training processes, and gradient descent—all implemented in C++—the chapter laid the groundwork for incorporating machine learning into games. We saw firsthand how to implement, train, and evaluate simple neural networks, understanding the impact of parameters such as learning rate, batch size, and epochs.

By the end of *Chapter 10*, you had developed not only a theoretical understanding but also a practical command of every major discipline in game development:

- Setting up and using a C++ game development environment with raylib and Knight
- Applying core data structures and algorithms to real game scenarios
- Implementing both 2D and 3D rendering pipelines, optimizing performance and visual quality
- Developing complex camera systems for immersive gameplay
- Writing and debugging shaders for advanced graphics effects
- Constructing complete 3D scenes, including terrain, lighting, shadows, particles, and skyboxes
- Animating characters with skeletal and procedural techniques
- Building AI with both traditional and modern approaches
- Applying deep learning principles and neural network programming in games

Taken together, these key learnings provide readers with a solid foundation, equipping them with the skills needed to grow into more confident and well-rounded developers.

From the low-level handling of graphics hardware and memory to the high-level orchestration of AI-driven gameplay, this book offers a holistic education in building modern, interactive, and visually stunning games. Whether crafting 2D or 3D worlds, animating characters, or integrating both traditional and deep learning AI, you will emerge with the confidence and expertise to tackle any contemporary game development challenge.

However, this is far from the end of the journey. There is still a lot for us to explore further.

Extending Knight for your game project

The best way to continue your learning journey is to extend Knight for your game project. Let's now bring all your learning together to build your game project.

Extending the rendering feature through a component

In *Chapter 1*, we introduced the purpose of Knight's `Component` class, and in *Chapter 7*, we demonstrated how to extend the `Component` class to implement various rendering techniques.

The `Component` class serves as the foundation for creating visual elements that appear on the screen. Both Knight's built-in components and those we created in the aforementioned chapters provide support for a range of rendering features, including the following:

Component Name	Description

`PlaneComponent`
`CubeComponent`
`SphereComponent`
`CylinderComponent`
	These are primitive components

`ModelComponent`	Supports rendering of the raylib `Model` class
`BillboardComponent`	Supports billboard and particle effect rendering
`ParticleComponent`	Supports particle effect rendering and simulation
`HMapTerrainModelComponent`	Supports height map terrain rendering
`QuadTreeTerrainComponent`	Supports quadtree rendering

Table 11.2 – Summary of available components

These components cover the most common rendering needs, and by leveraging the hierarchical structure of the scene, you can combine them to create even more complex effects.

Want your game's wizard to hold a magical fireball in their hand? Or have your main character stand on a flying magic carpet? These effects can be achieved by attaching a fireball particle component to a specific hand `Mesh` of the wizard's `ModelComponent`, or by parenting the character's `ModelComponent` to the magic carpet's `ModelComponent`.

Of course, your own game project may also require importing FBX 3D models (a popular 3D model format supported by **Maya** and **Motion Builder**). In such a case, you'll need to use a third-party library such as **Assimp** and write your own code to support FBX file loading – either by creating a new `FBXModelComponent` to support FBX loading or by inheriting a new child class from `ModelComponent`.

Separating gameplay logic and rendering

Games are not just about rendering visual elements on the screen—they must also handle input and the logic that drives these visual elements during gameplay. Many of the demo projects in this book focus on particular rendering features and therefore do not include full gameplay logic handling.

In these demos, we often place user input handling and the corresponding logic directly within each `Component` or `SceneActor`'s `Update()` function. This approach is fine for small, focused sample projects throughout this book.

However, when you begin adding more and more visual elements to your dream game world, separating gameplay logic from the rendering part of the code (handled in the various `Component` objects) offers key benefits:

- **Improving the readability of your code base**: Games are complex systems, often involving hundreds of classes interacting to bring gameplay and visuals to life. Mixing gameplay logic and rendering code makes it easy to lose track of where things are handled.

  For example, when a character takes damage from an enemy, you need to update the health points (*logic*) and trigger the damage animation (*visuals*). Initially, it might seem convenient to handle both in the same place where you first wrote them, but as the project grows, you may soon forget whether the health point is updated in the character's `SceneActor::Update()` function? the `Draw()` function, or the enemy's `SceneActor::Update()` function? or even a UI class where a health bar is rendered?

  By separating gameplay logic and visual reactions, the code structure becomes clear and easy to understand. Instead of trying to remember where every piece of logic resides, you can rely on simple, consistent rules, making the code base much more readable and maintainable.

  This is especially important for one-man developers who need to keep track of where to locate code pieces from the entire code base. It's okay to mix everything when you write gameplay logic and render code together for quick experiments or proofs of concept. However, at some point, you should start to refactor your code to separate gameplay logic and rendering code for better clarity. Some code design patterns such as **MVC** or **MVVM** can also help.

- **Greater independence within a team**: Sometimes, you'll work on a game as part of a small team, such as a school coding club or simply your best video game buddy. Maybe your collaborator is skilled in graphics programming, while you prefer to handle gameplay mechanics. With this structure, you can focus on implementing `Entity` (gameplay logic), while your teammate concentrates on `SceneActor` and `Component` (graphics and rendering). As long as you both agree on how logic and visuals interact, the code overlaps and conflicts are minimized, enabling greater independence and smoother collaboration.
- **Better multi-threading adaptability**: Modern hardware—whether desktop, mobile, or console—offers increasingly powerful parallel processing capabilities. This means your logic and rendering code may run on different threads or even separate CPU cores. Just as *Chapter 6* describes how the CPU and GPU cooperate, your C++ code may be executing on different cores simultaneously. By clearly separating gameplay logic from rendering code, it becomes much easier to implement multi-threaded processing and take full advantage of modern hardware.

For real game development, we strongly recommend separating gameplay logic from rendering code.

Decoupling gameplay logic and rendering – the approaches

There are two simple ways to clearly separate gameplay logic from rendering code. As you saw in all the sample projects in *Chapter 2*, one approach is to define a dedicated `Entity` class to handle the gameplay logic for each character or object in the game. When each `Entity` is created, a corresponding `SceneActor` is also created to represent the entity visually in the game. The `Entity` handles user input and gameplay logic, while its corresponding `SceneActor` takes care of rendering and visual updates, as shown in *Figure 11.1*:

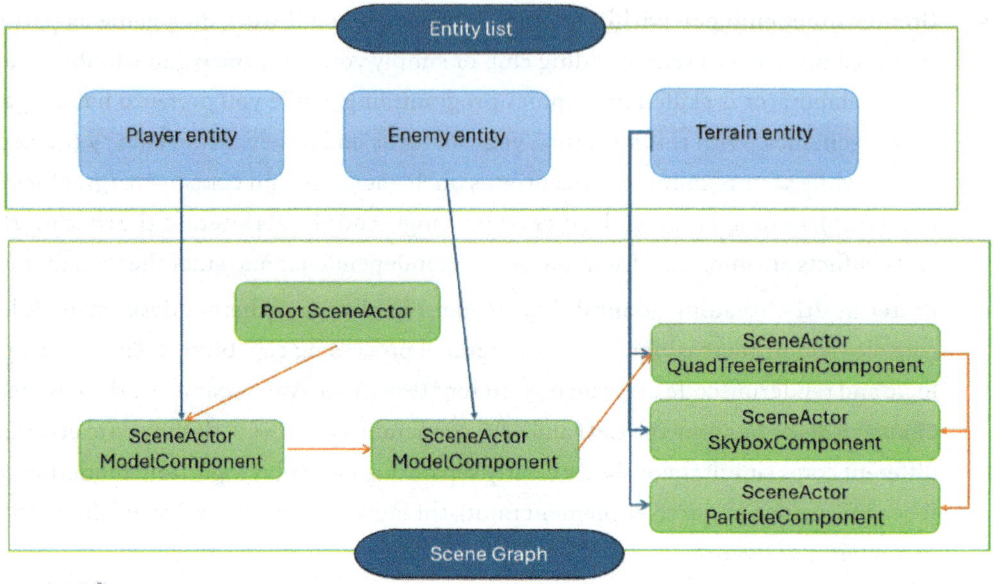

Figure 11.1 – Decoupling gameplay logic from rendering code

Another approach does not require creating a separate `Entity` data structure. Instead, you can reuse the `Component` class by creating a specialized `Component` dedicated to handling user input and gameplay logic. This gameplay logic `Component` class is then added to each `SceneActor`. As long as you ensure that the gameplay logic component is the first one added, it will always execute first in the component update sequence. This is illustrated in *Figure 11.2*, as follows:

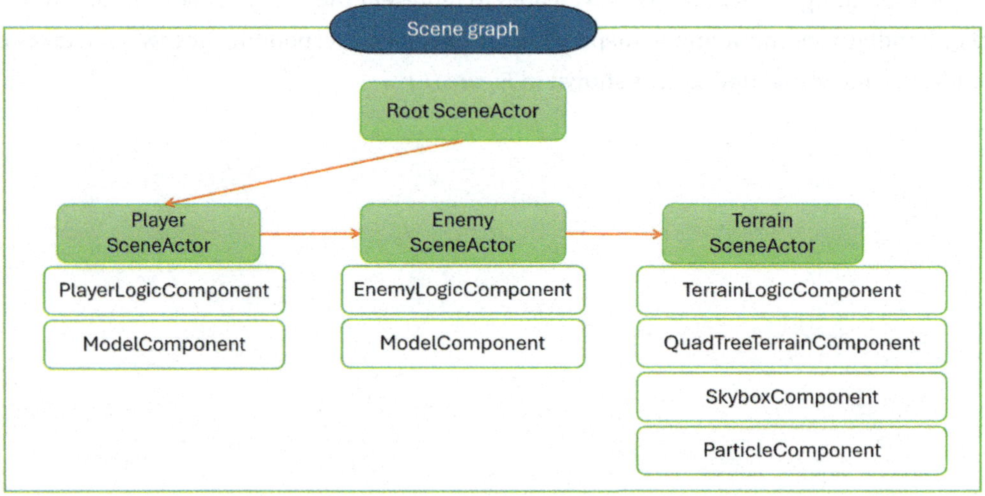

Figure 11.2 – Implementing gameplay logic as a component

This naturally raises the question: what are the pros and cons of these two approaches?

Using a separate `Entity` list data structure gives you greater flexibility in managing the relationships between `Entity` and `SceneActor`. For example, sometimes `Entity` and `SceneActor` are not strictly in a one-to-one relationship. Consider the case of terrain in a 3D MMORPG: a terrain `Entity` in Knight might manage three separate `SceneActor` objects: one with a `QuadTreeTerrainComponent` for rendering the terrain, another with a `SkyboxComponent` for the sky, and a third with a `ParticleComponent` to create falling snow for a winter scene. As shown in *Figure 11.1*, a single terrain-managing `Entity` must coordinate the state of all three `SceneActor` objects, updating them based on world time to simulate seasonal changes and activating the `ParticleComponent` snow particle system during the winter season.

As discussed in *Chapter 1*, all `SceneActor` objects in a scene are updated in the order determined by the scene's hierarchical structure: siblings are updated before their children. If your game design requires precise control over the order in which gameplay logic is processed, separating the gameplay logic into an independent `Entity` list lets you update `Entity` in any order you choose, rather than being limited to the update order of `SceneActor` objects in the scene graph.

On the other hand, handling gameplay logic through `Component` is more common in game engines that use a scene graph as the primary data structure to build the game world. Such a game engine usually has an editor to allow you to build the game scene from `SceneActor` objects representing visual elements, with both gameplay logic and rendering handled by attaching different `Component` objects to the same `SceneActor`.

For example, in the Unity game engine, the user creates and edits `GameObject` instances, which are analogous to Knight's `SceneActor`. Both gameplay logic components and rendering components can be attached to the same `GameObject`. To handle the earlier terrain example with this approach, you could implement a `TerrainLogicComponent` to manage gameplay logic for the terrain and attach it alongside a `QuadTreeTerrainComponent`, `SkyboxComponent`, and `ParticleComponent` to the same `SceneActor` representing the terrain (see *Figure 11.2*).

As for which approach is better, it ultimately depends on the specific needs of your game design. In the demo game from *Chapter 2*, we used the independent `Entity` list approach. However, you are encouraged to experiment by modifying the *Chapter 2* sample projects to implement game logic using `Component` instead, so you can compare the differences for yourself.

Use the `Entity` list or a separate `Component` object to expand gameplay functionality and avoid mixing gameplay logic into your rendering components. This will better prepare you for the increasing complexities of advanced game development.

Integrating features into a cohesive game world

From *Chapter 2* to *Chapter 10*, we focused on introducing various features commonly used in game development. In those chapters, each demo project was designed specifically to demonstrate how to implement an individual feature. Now it's time to bring all those features together.

Chances are, as you've been reading this book, you've already started building your own game project and experimenting with integrating the features we introduced into your own work.

During this process, you may have noticed something important: combining multiple features into a single project often requires additional hidden effort and problem-solving.

The sample project in this chapter, `BonusGameWorld01`, shown in *Figure 11.3*, was created with that exact purpose in mind. It integrates many of the features we covered in earlier chapters to build a game scene similar to an open-world game. This includes a scene where the player can freely move around and explore, along with other decorative objects, and visual effects that enrich the environment.

Figure 11.3 – The BonusGameWorld01 sample project

Build and run the project. You can use *WASD* to move the player character, rotate the camera with the mouse while holding the *right mouse button*, or use the *spacebar* to fire attacking magic.

This project differs from the other samples in the book. While the other samples focus on explaining and demonstrating a single feature at a time, this sample project attempts to integrate multiple features into one cohesive experience. It incorporates the following features we previously introduced and implemented:

- **The Knight application architecture**: The project overall follows the same Knight application architecture introduced in *Chapters 1* and *2*, with `Entity` classes handling gameplay logic and using the scene graph components (`SceneActor` class) to handle rendering of objects, such as in *Figure 11.1*.

  The demo only has four entities. The `TerrainEntity` handles not only the Quad-tree terrain, but also 600 decorative `SceneActor` objects (trees and other props) on the terrain.

- **Simulation of daylight changes**: The color blending technique introduced in *Chapter 4* is used in class to simulate daylight changes in the `TerrainEntity` class. We use the blended color as the diffuse color of the scene directional light and set it in the `Update()` function of the `BonusGameWorld01` main application class.

  ```
  //change of sky Light
  sceneLight->lightColor = pMainCamera->
  GetComponent<SkyboxComponent>()->_SkyColor;
  ```

- **Billboards of trees and other props**: We chose to use the Billboard technique to render lots of trees and other props in the scene. The `BillboardComponent` class is explained in *Chapter 7*.
- **Third-person view camera control**: We chose the third-person follow-up camera to render the game scene from behind the player character. This camera also allows the player to further rotate around to get the surrounding views. We use the `FollowUpCamera` class introduced in *Chapter 5*.
- **Lighting and shadow**: A directional light is used to simulate sky light. It's also used as a primary light to cast shadows. Many objects, including Billboard-rendered trees and props, cast and receive shadows. We use the same `DepthRenderPass` class and `ShadowRenderPass` class introduced in *Chapters 6* and *7* to handle multi-pass rendering tasks.
- **Attacking and other scene effects**: The magic fountain and the player character's magic attack effects are created using the particle system introduced in *Chapter 7*. In this project, we demonstrate the use of multiple independent particle systems simultaneously. The particles for the magic fountains persist in the scene, while the particle streams for the player's attacks die out quickly with each strike.

- **Open world outdoor terrain**: We use the same height map with the Quadtree terrain rendering algorithm introduced in *Chapter 7*.
- **Rendering skybox**: We use the `SkyboxComponent` class introduced in *Chapter 7* to handle seamless sky rendering. It's attached under the camera `SceneActor`, so it always moves with the camera and appears infinitely far from the viewpoint.
- **Character model and animation states**: The player model's animations are controlled by the FSM introduced in *Chapter 9*. For this sample project, the states are customized in the `PlayerFSM` class, located in the `BonusGameWorld01` project folder.

To assemble all the existing components to work together, it also takes more effort than just ripping the code from each individual sample project.

- **Adjusting shadow rendering:** In the sample code of `Demo7PCFShadow`, the `ShadowSceneLight` orthogonal projection size is set to a constant value of `20` in the `Create()` function of the `DepthRenderPass` class. This configuration restricts shadow rendering to a relatively small, focused area.

  In contrast, the third-person view camera in this example covers a much larger portion of the terrain. As a result, all shadows cast onto any objects within the camera's view must be rendered. To accommodate this larger region, the orthogonal projection scale is increased to `100` in this sample (in the `Create()` function of the `DepthRenderPass` class of this sample project):

  ```
  // Orthographic projection for directional light
  lightCam.projection = CAMERA_ORTHOGRAPHIC;
  lightCam.fovy = 100.0f;
  //...
  ```

  In your own project, you may need to adjust this value to achieve the best visual quality. If the orthogonal projection scale is set *too large*, shadows will appear overly blurred. Conversely, if the scale is set *too small*, parts of the shadows may be clipped by the boundaries of the shadow map texture, resulting in visually incorrect artifacts.

Figure 11.4 – Adjusting the shadow camera to achieve acceptable shadow quality

- **Placing objects on the terrain**: To enable other components to query the elevation of a specific world-space position, we implemented an additional function, `GetTerrainY()`, in the `QuadTreeTerrainComponent` class. This function also takes into consideration the scale of the terrain.

  The `TerrainEntity` class relies on this function to align all trees and other props with the terrain elevation in world space.

- **Moving player character**: The character's movement also depends on `GetTerrainY()` to update the player character's position, ensuring the character properly follows the terrain's contours.
- **Moving camera around**: The third-person follow-up camera must adjust its height (*Y*-axis position in world space) according to the terrain elevation at its current world position. This ensures that the camera does not move beneath the terrain surface, which would otherwise result in visual artifacts.

  Additionally, the vertical offset between the player character and the camera should not be rigidly constrained. Enforcing such a lock can cause noticeable jitters in vertical movement when the player moves on very steep slopes. This implementation detail is illustrated in the `Update()` function of the main application class, `BonusGameWorld01`.

- **Simplifying the calculation**: For simplicity, we create nearly all `SceneActor` graphic objects at the top level of the scene graph. This makes them direct descendants of the `SceneRoot` node, with their world positions the same as their local positions. In this way, we can simply assign the local position of a `SceneActor` to make it move to the same world position.

  If you place a player `SceneActor` as the child of another `SceneActor`, you must update its local position and then call the `GetWorldPosition()` function in the `SceneActor` class to obtain the final world position.

  If you need to move a `SceneActor` to a specified world position, you must reverse-calculate and update the local position in the `SceneActor` after moving it. You can check how this is done in the handy `TranslateWS()` function in the `SceneActor` class of Knight.

  This approach simplifies the calculation of object transformations in world space and is sufficient for the current demonstration.

Through this sample, we want to illustrate the kinds of issues and programming considerations you may encounter when combining individual features into a complete project.

You may have also noticed that once we place terrain, the main character, and many decorative objects into the scene, the rendering performance drops significantly. In the next section, we will introduce techniques for optimizing rendering performance.

Optimizing rendering performance

As we continue adding more objects into a game scene, we will inevitably face significant rendering performance issues. Performance is an unavoidable challenge in game development, and the key lies in analyzing the primary causes of slowdowns and applying effective strategies to address them.

In the game industry, profiling tools (such as **RenderDoc** or **Pix**) are commonly used to identify performance bottlenecks in the code. However, you don't always need to rely on such specialized tools. Sometimes simply inserting timing measurements directly into your program, or even adjusting the number of objects being rendered, can provide enough insight to perform effective optimizations.

In this section, we'll walk through an example of how to approach optimization in a game project.

Let's recall the `BonusGameWorld01` project, where we placed 600 decorative objects in the scene—far more than the earlier sample codes that demonstrated individual features. Our first step is to verify whether the sheer number of objects is the main reason for the performance drop.

The simplest way to test this is to reduce the number of objects from 600 to just 60 and then observe whether performance improves significantly. This code can be found in `TerrainEntity.cpp` (line **34**):

```
for (int i = 0; i < 60; i++)  //change from 600 to 60
```

After saving the changes, recompiling, and running the program, we can observe that the frame rate (FPS), which reflects rendering performance, jumps significantly—from the previous 30 FPS up to 55 FPS.

Figure 11.5 - The rendering performance is much better with fewer decorative trees

This is easy to understand—each decorative object also casts a shadow, meaning it must be rendered at least twice: once into the depth texture for shadow mapping, and once onto the final screen. As a result, 600 shadow-casting objects are effectively equivalent to rendering around 1,200 objects!

However, reducing the scene to just 60 trees makes it look sparse and unconvincing. The real challenge, then, is how to maintain better performance even with 600 decorative objects in the game scene.

Two possible optimization strategies quickly come to mind:

- Render only the objects that are visible to the camera.
- Use simplified, faster rendering techniques for decorative objects that appear far away from the camera.

In the following sections, we will test both of these ideas to see how much they improve performance.

Rendering only the visible SceneActor

So far, all the sample projects in this book have simply rendered every `SceneActor` in the scene. This approach works fine for small demo projects and keeps the code straightforward.

However, when dealing with 600 decorative objects, we need a way to avoid sending all of them to the GPU for rendering. Instead, we should only render the objects that are visible to the camera.

We want to check whether each `SceneActor` is visible to the current active camera before calling the `Draw()` function of its attached components. If a `SceneActor` is completely outside the camera's visible range, we can simply skip it.

In fact, we already used a similar idea in *Chapter 7* when we introduced QuadTree-based terrain rendering. A terrain may consist of tens of thousands of triangles, but we only render a small portion that is visible to the camera, keeping the triangle count around 3,000 at any given time. Our implementation relied on the `SceneCamera` class's `IsBoundingBoxInFrustum()` function, using each quad tree node's bounding box to determine visibility.

We can apply the same approach here: before rendering each `SceneActor`, we check whether it falls entirely outside the camera's frustum. If it does, we skip the actor along with all its attached `Component` instances.

Although we haven't needed it so far, the `SceneActor` class defines the following member variable:

```
BoundingBox WorldBoundingBox; //in world space
```

Now comes the question: how is this `WorldBoundingBox` variable calculated?

The answer lies in the `Component` class. It contains the following member variable:

```
BoundingBox LocalBoundingBox; //in local coordinate space
```

The `LocalBoundingBox` is initialized to zero in the `Component` constructor. Each `Component` that needs to calculate and update its own bounding box can set this value inside its `Update()` function. For example, our 3D robot main character changes shape every frame due to animation. As a result, its bounding box also changes every frame and must be recalculated based on the current animation.

When the `Update()` function of a `SceneActor` is called, it will, at the end, gather the bounding regions from all of its attached `Component` instances and calculate a bounding region that encloses them. This result is then stored in the `WorldBoundingBox` variable.

If a `SceneActor` has no attached `Component`, or if none of its `Component` instances have assigned the `LocalBoundingBox` any value, then the `WorldBoundingBox` will remain in its default zero-initialized state.

Since this new code will be used by every `SceneRenderPass`, it serves as a general-purpose optimization trick in 3D rendering. Therefore, we've implemented it directly in the `BuildRenderQueue()` function of `SceneRenderPass.cpp`:

```
void SceneRenderPass::BuildRenderQueue(SceneObject* pRoot) {
    SceneActor* pActor = dynamic_cast<SceneActor*>(pRoot);
    if (pActiveCamera != nullptr && pActor != nullptr) {
        if (!(pActor->WorldBoundingBox.min.z == pActor->WorldBoundingBox.
max.z)) {
            FrustumPlane frustumPlanes[6];
            pActiveCamera->ExtractFrustumPlanes(frustumPlanes);
            if (pActiveCamera->IsBoundingBoxInFrustum(pActor-
>WorldBoundingBox, frustumPlanes) == false) {
                bAddComponents = false;
                ++NumComponentsSkipped;
            }
        }
    }
    if (bAddComponents == true) {
        //Send all components of this SceneActor
        // to GPU to draw…
    }
    //…
}
```

In the code above, once we confirm that the `WorldBoundingBox` of the `SceneActor` is valid, we check whether the camera can see it. If the `SceneActor` lies completely outside the camera's view, it will be skipped and not rendered.

Therefore, to ensure that the `WorldBoundingBox` of a `SceneActor` is valid, each Component must define at least one or more proper `LocalBoundingBox`.

Here is an example from our modified `BillboardComponent`:

```
void BillboardComponent::Update(float ElapsedTime, RenderHints* pRH) {
    __super::Update(ElapsedTime, pRH);
    SceneCamera* pSC = this->_SceneActor->GetMainCamera();
    if (pSC != nullptr) {
        if (AlignType == SCREEN_ALIGNED) {
            Matrix matView = rlGetMatrixModelview();
            billUp = { matView.m1, matView.m5, matView.m9 };
        }
        LocalBoundingBox = { -size.x / 2, -size.y / 2, -0.1f,
                              size.x / 2,  size.y / 2,  0.1f };
    }
}
```

In the original `Demo7Billboard`, the `BillboardComponent` did not include an `Update()` function. Here, we modified the `BillboardComponent` to add an `Update()` function, where the billboard's size is used to define the `LocalBoundingBox`. With this change, once the `Update()` function of `SceneActor` finishes, it will automatically call the internal `UpdateCachedWorldBoundingBox()` function to update the actor's `WorldBoundingBox`.

By adding this code to the `SceneRenderPass` base class, all classes that inherit from `SceneRenderPass` automatically gain this optimization if they use the base class's `BuildRenderQueue()` function.

For example, recall our shadow mapping algorithm: we implemented both `DepthRenderPass` and `ShadowMapRenderPass` as custom render passes, and each of them inherits from `SceneRenderPass`:

- When the `DepthRenderPass` uses the shadow-casting light as a camera to render the shadow map texture, any objects outside the shadow map's range are automatically culled.
- When the `ShadowMapRenderPass` renders the final frame, all objects that are not visible to the view camera are also skipped and not sent to the GPU.

Now compile and run the `BonusGameWorld02` project with the same 600 scene objects, resulting in a performance boost of nearly 30%!

Rendering less detail for distant objects

In addition to optimizing with camera visibility, we can also reduce the complexity of objects that are farther away from the camera.

The simplest idea is that objects beyond a certain distance from the view camera (main camera) don't need to render shadows at all. We can simply skip the shadow rendering process, including the PCF shadow mapping steps that soften shadow edges using neighboring texture samples.

To achieve this, we can extend the existing `DepthRenderPass` and `ShadowMapRenderPass` classes to support distance-based optimizations that reduce rendering complexity.

Let's extend our current depth rendering pass with a new `LoDDepthRenderPass` class:

```
#include "DepthRenderPass.h"
class LoDDepthRenderPass : public DepthRenderPass {
  public:
    LoDDepthRenderPass(float cutoff, ShadowSceneLight* l);
    bool OnAddToRender(Component* pSC, SceneObject* pSO) override;
  protected:
    float CutOffDistance = 25.0f * 25.0f;
};
```

Here, we override the `OnAddToRender()` member function:

```
bool LoDDepthRenderPass::OnAddToRender(Component* pSC, SceneObject* pSO) {
    float dist2 = 0;

    //If this Component does not cast a shadow to other objects in the
scene, no need to render in depth render pass
    if (pSC->castShadow == Component::eShadowCastingType::NoShadow)
        return false;

    //Check if the object is within a certain distance to the view camera
    SceneActor* pActor = dynamic_cast<SceneActor*>(pSO);
    if (pActor != nullptr) {
        //Only render shadow for a certain distance
        SceneCamera* pCam = pScene->GetMainCameraActor();

        //use bounding box distance if available, otherwise fallback to
actor position distance
```

```
        if (IsBoundingBoxValid(pActor->WorldBoundingBox)) {
            dist2 = PointToBoxDistanceSqr(pCam->GetPosition(), pActor-
>WorldBoundingBox);
        } else {
            //fallback to use actor position if bounding box is not valid
            dist2 = Vector3DistanceSqr(pActor->GetWorldPosition(), pCam-
>GetPosition());
        }

        if (dist2 > CutOffDistance)
            return false;
    }

    //Rest of the code
    //…
}
```

In the preceding code snippet, it's important to note that when we refer to the camera used for distance calculations, we mean the scene's main camera.

During the depth render pass, the `pActiveCamera` in `LoDDepthRenderPass` represents the camera derived from the light's position and direction. However, when calculating the distance from the camera, we use the scene's main camera, retrieved via `GetMainCameraActor()`. If the above function `OnAddToRender()` returns false, the passed-in `Component` will not be used to render into the shadow map texture.

If the `SceneActor` has a valid `WorldBoundingBox`, we will calculate the distance between the camera's view position to this bounding box. If the `SceneActor` doesn't have a valid `WorldBoundingBox`, we then fall back to using the calculated world position of the `SceneActor` to calculate the distance.

Similarly, we need to extend `ShadowMapRenderPass` into a new class: `LoDShadowMapRenderPass`:

```
#include "ShadowMapRenderPass.h"

class LoDShadowMapRenderPass : public ShadowMapRenderPass {
public:
    LoDShadowMapRenderPass(float cutoff, ShadowSceneLight* l, int id);
    void Render() override;
```

```
protected:
    float CutOffDistance = 25.0f * 25.0f;
};
```

We add a new `ShouldRenderShadow()` function to determine if this `Component` in the `RenderContext` should render a shadow:

```
int LoDShadowMapRenderPass::ShouldRenderShadow(const RenderContext& rc) {
    //No shadow receiving if the component is set to not receive shadow
    int receiveShadow = rc.pComponent->receiveShadow ? 1 : 0;

    //disable shadow receiving for far-away background objects to save
performance
    if (rc.distance2 > CutOffDistance)
        receiveShadow = 0;

    return receiveShadow;
}
```

Unlike `LoDDepthRenderPass` class, this time we override the `Render()` function:

```
void LoDShadowMapRenderPass::Render() {
    //render background objects …
    //render opaque geometry from nearest to farthest
    multiset<RenderContext, CompareDistanceAscending>::iterator opaque =
pScene->_RenderQueue.Geometry.begin();
    while (opaque != pScene->_RenderQueue.Geometry.end()) {
        int receiveShadow = ShouldRenderShadow(*bk);
        SetShaderValue(shadowShader, receiveShadowLoc, &receiveShadow,
SHADER_UNIFORM_INT);
        opaque->pComponent->Draw(&Hints);
        ++opaque;
    }

    //rest of the function
    //…
}
```

This function is long, but we only need to focus on the part that renders opaque objects. Since the world position of each `Component` and its distance from the main camera have already been calculated when creating its `RenderContext`, we don't need to repeat the calculation. Instead, we can directly compare the existing `distance2` value against the `CutOffDistance`.

The `SetShaderValue()` call tells our shadow map rendering fragment shader whether this object should draw a soft shadow.

In the actual shadow rendering process of the `LoDShadowMapRenderPass` class, we already check whether each `Component` is set to receive shadows to decide if a soft shadow should be rendered. With this optimization, we simply add another condition: objects that would normally receive shadows but are beyond a distance greater than the `CutOffDistance` will be flagged as not requiring shadow rendering.

After implementing these optimizations, let's push the scene further—by increasing the number of decorative objects to 2,000—and observe the impact on rendering performance:

Figure 11.6 – A scene with 2,000 decorative objects

Even though we increased the number of decorative objects by more than three times, performance did drop by nearly 50%, but the cost was not in the depth rendering pass. If we take a closer look and measure the execution times of `Update()`, `DrawOffscreen()`, and `Draw()` functions in `BonusGameWorld02` project, we can see that the depth rendering pass (the time spent in `DrawOffscreen()`) did not increase much. This indicates that our distance-based optimization for controlling which objects are rendered into the shadow map texture was effective.

Another benefit of limiting the range of rendering real-time shadow is that we can use a smaller orthogonal view size of the light camera. This also results in better quality of shadow map rendering.

In this section, we used the `BonusGameWorld02` project to demonstrate both the thought process and the implementation steps involved in optimizing graphics performance. Of course, this project still has plenty of room for further optimization; for example, avoiding repeated calculations of world coordinates and `WorldBoundingBox` values for static objects that don't move. Or, how about trying to minimize raylib's `SetShaderValue()` call to reduce unnecessary rendering status change? You might find an unexpected performance boost as well!

Exploring such improvements would make an excellent self-practice exercise.

Looking forward

Now that you have a solid foundation, what do you envision for yourself in the next step of your journey? In this section, we'll discuss resources that you can use to sharpen your expertise in what you've learned so far. We'll also delve into strategies to bolster continuous learning in your game development journey.

Expanding your knowledge

Expertise is built on continuous learning and practical experience. Consider revisiting key topics with a deeper focus—experiment with optimizing data structures further, and explore advanced algorithms that can push the boundaries of performance in your games. Here are a few suggestions for how to further your expertise:

- **Deep dive into advanced algorithms**: While you have learned all sorts of building blocks of video game programming, challenge yourself with more complex algorithms, such as advanced search techniques, optimization methods, and real-time procedural generation. Engage with academic papers, open source projects, and community forums to see how these concepts are evolving in the industry. The following resources offer solid starting points for deepening your knowledge of advanced data structures and algorithms in C++:
    - **W3 Schools** (`https://www.w3schools.com/cpp/cpp_data_structures.asp`): This site provides a quick tutorial of frequently used data structures supported by the C++ standard template library.

    - **GeeksforGeeks** (`https://www.geeksforgeeks.org/learn-dsa-in-cpp/`): This site covers many advanced algorithms for future learning and serves as a good reference.
- **Gain proficiency in modern GPU programming**: As graphics continue to advance, becoming proficient in modern GPU programming and shader development is invaluable. Experiment with advanced lighting models, post-processing effects, and even real-time ray tracing. Consider learning additional graphics APIs or frameworks to complement your knowledge of raylib. Here are some useful resources:
    - **Khronos** (`https://www.khronos.org/opengl/wiki/Core_Language_(GLSL)`): This site provides complete references to the GLSL shader language
    - **GPU Shader Tutorial** (`https://shader-tutorial.dev/`): This site has comprehensive graphics shader programming tutorials
- **Explore machine learning in gaming**: With the introduction to neural networks, you have seen just the tip of the iceberg. Consider taking courses or participating in workshops focused on deep learning and reinforcement learning. Experiment with training models on more complex game scenarios, such as adaptive AI opponents or dynamic content generation. The *Machine learning in video games* Wikipedia page (`https://en.wikipedia.org/wiki/Machine_learning_in_video_games`) is a good starting point to explore how various machine learning algorithms are used in game development.
- **Extend your animation skills**: As character animation becomes more central to immersive game experiences, learning advanced techniques such as motion capture integration, procedural animation, and physics-based character movement can set your games apart. To enhance realism and interactivity in your games, check out the following links:
    - **Animation Programming** (`https://animationprogramming.com/`): This is another good Packt book that focuses on game animation with C++ and OpenGL. Here are the details: Gabor Szauer. *Hands-on C++ Game Animation Programming*. Packt Publishing Ltd, 12 June 2020.
    - **AI4Animation by Sebastian Starke** (`https://github.com/sebastianstarke/AI4Animation`): This repository explores how to apply deep learning for character animation. Even though it's developed with Unity 3D/PyTorch, the concept can also be applied to your C++ game project.

- **Engage with the community**: The game development community is rich in resources, tutorials, and collaborative projects. Join online forums, attend game development conferences, or contribute to open source projects. Engaging with other developers will expose you to new ideas and practices that can refine your skills further. However, each community has its own rules; make sure you check them out first. The following platforms offer opportunities to connect with fellow developers, seek guidance, and stay updated on the latest news in game development practices:
    - **Gamedev.net** (`https://gamedev.net/`): One of the oldest yet most vibrant developer-focused portals, offering active forums and a wealth of learning resources.
    - **raylib's Discord channel** (`https://discord.com/channels/426912293134270465`): This is the official raylib Discord channel. This is the place to hang out with other developers using raylib, or for asking raylib-related technical questions.

Future learning suggestions

The world of game development is ever-changing, with new tools, techniques, and paradigms emerging constantly. To stay ahead of the curve, consider the following strategies for continuous learning:

- **Stay up to date with industry trends**: Follow industry news, subscribe to newsletters, and participate in webinars hosted by experts in game development and AI. Staying current with trends will ensure you are aware of emerging technologies and methodologies. The following websites provide insights into current trends, technologies, and discussions shaping the game development landscape:
    - **Game Developer** (`https://www.gamedeveloper.com/`): This portal features not only general game industry news but also many game development learning resources
    - **Gamedev.net** (`https://gamedev.net/`): One of the oldest yet most vibrant developer-focused portals, offering active forums and a wealth of learning resources
- **Pursue advanced courses and certifications**: Consider enrolling in specialized courses in advanced C++ programming, real-time graphics, or AI applications in gaming. Many online platforms and universities offer courses that can help you deepen your understanding and gain certifications that bolster your resume. **MIT OpenCourseWare** (`https://ocw.mit.edu/`) offers several undergraduate and graduate-level courses on a wide range of topics, from game design and animations to AI.

- **Build personal projects**: The best way to learn is by doing. Create personal projects that challenge you to apply what you have learned in new and creative ways. Whether it's a small indie game, a sophisticated simulation, or an experimental project, practical application is key to mastery.
- **Collaborate with peers**: Collaborate with fellow developers to work on projects or participate in game jams. The exchange of ideas and teamwork often leads to innovative solutions and provides new perspectives that you might not discover on your own.

  Game Jams and hackathons, which are held in many regions, offer exactly these kinds of opportunities. **DevPost** (`https://devpost.com/`) is a useful resource for finding information about upcoming hackathons. If there aren't any hackathons happening near you, a local user group or dev club can also be a good place to start or the online community we introduced in the previous section.

- **Read widely and diversely**: Expand your learning by reading books, research papers, and case studies on game development, computer graphics, and AI. Each new perspective can offer insights that enrich your understanding and inspire creative problem-solving. These sources offer in-depth reading on graphics, game design, and academic perspectives:
  - **Real-Time Rendering** (`https://www.realtimerendering.com/`): This site has curated many free e-books about graphics rendering available to read
  - **Game Studies** (`https://gamestudies.org/2501`): Game Studies is a non-profit, open-access, cross-disciplinary journal dedicated to games research

Summary

Before you close this book, take a moment to appreciate the journey you have taken. Your journey began with the fundamentals of the sample game project, using the lightweight Knight engine and raylib graphics library as the foundation for every example in this book. Then, you progressed through intricate data structures and rendering techniques, and tackled the challenging domains of character animation and AI. With every chapter, you have built a robust foundation that not only makes you a better developer but also positions you to explore and innovate within the gaming industry.

Cheers to your success!

Although this book marks the final chapter of our journey together, it is by no means the end of your path in game development. In fact, as you turn the last page, your adventure is just beginning—one filled with boundless possibilities.

Fortunately, you're not sailing into uncharted waters alone. Beyond the additional resources we've included here, Packt Publishing offers a wide range of books on game development to support your growth, too.

We hope that someday soon, our paths will cross again on the road to learning how to create great games!

packtpub.com

Subscribe to our online digital library for full access to over 7,000 books and videos, as well as industry leading tools to help you plan your personal development and advance your career. For more information, please visit our website.

Why subscribe?

- Spend less time learning and more time coding with practical eBooks and Videos from over 4,000 industry professionals
- Improve your learning with Skill Plans built especially for you
- Get a free eBook or video every month
- Fully searchable for easy access to vital information
- Copy and paste, print, and bookmark content

At www.packtpub.com, you can also read a collection of free technical articles, sign up for a range of free newsletters, and receive exclusive discounts and offers on Packt books and eBooks.

Other Books You May Enjoy

If you enjoyed this book, you may be interested in these other books by Packt:

C++ Game Animation Programming, Second Edition

Michael Dunsky, Gabor Szauer

ISBN: 978-1-80324-652-9

- Create simple OpenGL and Vulkan applications and work with shaders
- Explore the glTF file format, including its design and data structures
- Design an animation system with poses, clips, and skinned meshes
- Find out how vectors, matrices, quaternions, and splines are used in game development
- Discover and implement ways to seamlessly blend character animations
- Implement inverse kinematics for your characters using CCD and FABRIK solvers
- Understand how to render large, animated crowds efficiently
- Identify and resolve performance issues

Mastering C++ Game Animation Programming

Michael Dunsky

ISBN: 978-1-83588-192-7

- Master the basics of the Open Asset Import Library
- Animate thousands of game characters
- Extend ImGui with more advanced control types
- Implement simple configuration file handling
- Explore collision detection between 3D models and world objects
- Combine inverse kinematics and collision detection
- Work with state machines, behavior trees, and interactive NPC behaviors
- Implement navigation for NPC movement in unknown terrains

Packt is searching for authors like you

If you're interested in becoming an author for Packt, please visit `authors.packt.com` and apply today. We have worked with thousands of developers and tech professionals, just like you, to help them share their insight with the global tech community. You can make a general application, apply for a specific hot topic that we are recruiting an author for, or submit your own idea..

Share your thoughts

Now you've finished *Data Structures and Algorithms for Game Programming in C++*, we'd love to hear your thoughts! Scan the QR code below to go straight to the Amazon review page for this book and share your feedback or leave a review on the site that you purchased it from.

`https://packt.link/r/1835889875`

Your review is important to us and the tech community and will help us make sure we're delivering excellent quality content.

Index

Symbols

A

B

C

D

H

I

J

K

L

O

P

Q

R

S

T

U

V

W

Made in the USA
Monee, IL
15 September 2026

63035027R20236